Dr Michael's book is a well-researched and well-written contribution to the current focus on stylistics in the literature of the Old Testament. Still, the book avoids a mere 'art for art's sake'; the stylistic devices are seen as fulfilling certain semantic functions that express a message to the world of the author as well as to readers of today. As such, the question of contemporary relevance – which is a major focus of Dr Michael's immediate academic context, that of African Old Testament scholarship – is not absent, rather approached from a new and fascinating perspective.

Professor Knut Holter
Prorector for Research
MHS Misjonshøgskolen, Norway

I found in this work a thoughtful and thought-provoking analysis of stylistic features of the (reported) divine speeches in the narratives about Abraham (and YHWH) in the book of Genesis and their significance for both the communication of central ideological positions and esthetic pleasure to its intended readers.

Professor Ehud Ben Zvi
Department of History and Classics
University of Alberta, Canada

Yahweh's Elegant Speeches of Abrahamic Narratives

A Study of the Stylistics, Characterizations, and Functions of the Divine Speeches in Abrahamic Narratives

Matthew Michael

MONOGRAPHS

© 2014 by Matthew Michael

Published 2014 by Langham Monographs
an imprint of Langham Creative Projects

Langham Partnership
PO Box 296, Carlisle, Cumbria CA3 9WZ, UK
www.langham.org

ISBNs:
978-1-78368-975-0 Print
978-1-78368-973-6 Mobi
978-1-78368-974-3 ePub

Matthew Michael has asserted his right under the Copyright, Designs and Patents Act, 1988 to be identified as the Author of this work.

All rights reserved. No part of this publication may be reproduced, stored in a retrieval system or transmitted, in any form or by any means, electronic, mechanical, photocopying, recording or otherwise, without the prior written permission of the publisher or the Copyright Licensing Agency.

All Scripture quotations, unless otherwise indicated, are from the Holy Bible, New International Version®, NIV®. Copyright © 1973, 1978, 1984, 2011 by Biblica, Inc.™ Used by permission of Zondervan. All rights reserved worldwide. www.zondervan.com The "NIV" and "New International Version" are trademarks registered in the United States Patent and Trademark Office by Biblica, Inc.™

British Library Cataloguing in Publication Data
Michael, Matthew author.
  Yahweh's elegant speeches of the Abrahamic narratives.
  1. Bible. Genesis--Language, Style. 2. Direct discourse in
  the Bible. 3. Rhetoric in the Bible. 4. God (Judaism)
  5. Abraham (Biblical patriarch)
  I. Title
  222.1'1067-dc23

ISBN-13: 9781783689750

Cover & Book Design: projectluz.com

Langham Partnership actively supports theological dialogue and a scholar's right to publish but does not necessarily endorse the views and opinions set forth, and works referenced within this publication or guarantee its technical and grammatical correctness. Langham Partnership does not accept any responsibility or liability to persons or property as a consequence of the reading, use or interpretation of its published content.

Contents

Acknowledgments ix

Chapter One 1
Introduction
    1.1. Introduction 1
    1.2. Methodology 7
    1.3. Conclusion 10

Chapter Two 11
Dominant Studies on the Literary Features of the Divine Speeches
    2.1. Introduction 11
    2.2. General Studies on Biblical Speeches 13
        2.2.1. Charles Conroy 15
        2.2.2. E. J. Revell 19
        2.2.3. Robert Longacre 22
        2.2.4. Alviero Niccacci 27
        2.2.5. George Savran 31
        2.2.6. Cynthia Miller 35
    2.3. Specific Studies on Divine Speeches 42
        2.3.1. Casper Labuschagne 44
        2.3.2. Hugh White 48
        2.3.3. Wilfried Warning 52
        2.3.4. Samuel Meier 55
    2.4. Conclusion 59

Chapter Three 61
Stylistic Aspects of the Divine Speeches
    3.1. Introduction 61
        3.1.1. Genesis 12:1–9 65
            3.1.1.1. Structure 65
            3.1.1.2. Literary Context 71
            3.1.1.2. Grammatical Analysis 75
                3.1.1.2.1. Quotative Frames 75
                3.1.1.2.2. Syntactical Considerations 78
                3.1.1.2.3. Imperative Commands 82
            3.1.1.3. Stylistic Aspects 84
                3.1.1.3.1. Metaphor 85
                3.1.1.3.2. Paronomasia 94

- 3.1.1.3.3. Repetition 98
- 3.1.1.5.4. Allusion 101
- 3.1.1.3.5. Suspense 105
- 3.1.1.3.6. Gradation 107
- 3.1.1.4. Significance 108
- 3.2.1. Genesis 13:1–18 110
  - 3.2.1.1. Structure 110
  - 3.2.1.2. Literary Context 115
  - 3.2.1.3. Grammatical Analysis 117
    - 3.2.1.3.1. Quotative Frames 117
    - 3.2.1.3.2. Syntactical Considerations 119
    - 3.2.1.4.3. Demonstrative Commands 121
  - 3.2.1.4. Stylistic Aspects 122
    - 3.2.1.4.1. Metaphor 122
    - 3.2.1.4.2. Simile 124
    - 3.2.1.4.3. Wordplay 126
    - 3.2.1.4.4. Repetition 127
    - 3.2.1.5.5. Allusion 129
    - 3.2.1.4.6. Hyperbole 129
    - 3.2.1.4.7. Suspense 131
  - 3.2.1.5. Significance 132
- 3.3.1. Genesis 15:1–21 133
  - 3.3.1.1. Structure 133
  - 3.3.1.2. Literary Context 138
  - 3.3.1.3. Grammatical Analysis 140
    - 3.3.1.3.1. Quotative Frames 140
    - 3.3.1.3.2. Syntactical Considerations 142
    - 3.3.1.3.3. Dialogical Speeches 145
  - 3.3.1.4. Stylistic Aspects 147
    - 3.3.1.4.1. Metaphor 148
    - 3.3.1.4.2. Ellipsis 150
    - 3.3.1.4.3. Wordplay 151
    - 3.3.1.4.4. Hyperbole 155
    - 3.3.1.4.5. Alliteration 157
    - 3.3.1.4.6. Euphemism 158
    - 3.3.1.4.7. Allusion 160
  - 3.3.1.5. Significance 162
- 3.4.1. Genesis 17:1–22 163
  - 3.4.1.1. Structure 163
  - 3.4.1.2. Literary Context 167

- 3.4.1.3. Grammatical Analysis 169
  - 3.4.1.3.1. Quotative Frames 169
  - 3.4.1.3.2. Syntactical Considerations 174
  - 3.4.1.3.3. Dialogical Speeches 176
- 3.4.1.4. Stylistic Aspects 177
  - 3.4.1.4.1. Metaphor 177
  - 3.4.1.4.2. Wordplay 180
  - 3.4.1.4.3. Irony 182
  - 3.4.1.5.4. Euphemism 184
  - 3.4.1.4.5. Hyperbole 186
  - 3.4.1.4.6. Repetition 187
  - 3.4.1.4.7. Allusion 189
- 3.4.1.5. Significance 191
- 3.5.1. Genesis 18:1–33 192
  - 3.5.1.1. Structure 192
  - 3.5.1.2. Literary Context 198
  - 3.5.1.3. Grammatical Analysis 200
    - 3.5.1.3.1. Quotative Frames 200
    - 3.5.1.3.2. Syntactical Considerations 204
    - 3.5.1.4.3. Dialogical Speeches 206
    - 3.5.1.3.4. Divine Monologue 208
  - 3.5.1.4. Stylistic Aspects 209
    - 3.5.1.4.1. Metaphor 210
    - 3.5.1.4.2. Rhetorical Questions 215
    - 3.5.1.4.3. Euphemism 217
    - 3.5.1.4.4. Irony 219
    - 3.5.1.4.5. Allusion 222
  - 3.5.1.5. Significance 224
- 3.6.1. Genesis 22:1–19 226
  - 3.6.1.1. Structure 226
  - 3.6.1.2. Literary Context. 228
  - 3.6.1.3. Grammatical Analysis 231
    - 3.6.1.3.1. Quotative Frames 231
    - 3.6.1.3.2. Syntactical Considerations 234
    - 3.6.1.3.3. Dialogical Speeches 236
  - 3.6.1.4. Stylistic Aspects 237
    - 3.6.1.4.1. Metonymy 238
    - 3.6.1.4.2. Simile 239
    - 3.6.1.4.3. Hyperbole 241
    - 3.6.1.4.4. Euphemism 242

              3.6.1.5.5. Repetition 244
              3.6.1.4.6. Suspense 246
              3.6.1.4.7. Irony 247
              3.6.1.4.8. Allusion 248
           3.6.1.5. Significance 251
        3.7.1. Conclusion 252

Chapter Four 255
   The Functions of the Divine Speeches
      4.1. Introduction 255
      4.2. General Characteristics 262
      4.3. The Ideological Functions 272
      4.4. Conclusion 283

Chapter Five 287
   Conclusion

Bibliography 295

Acknowledgments

This book is a part of a long journey in the arena of academics and it is only right to acknowledge individuals and institutions who have made this journey possible. My gratitude goes to my supervisor, Prof. Wolfgang Bluedorn, and his family who greatly supported me during and after the course of my PhD program. During my doctoral research, they opened their door to me both at Cologne and Niewed in Germany and made my stay in Germany truly exciting. I want to also give my appreciation to the faculty, staff and students of *Bengelhaus* at *Eberhard Karls Universität Tübingen* in Germany under the leadership of Prof. Rolf Hille who welcomed and offered me warm Christian fellowship which made my stay at *Tübingen* indeed memorable. I am also indebted to the fellowship of the members and elders of *Evangelische Freie Gemeinde* at Reutlingen in Germany who, during the course of my doctoral research, offered me a home away from home. In particular, the love of Elder Reinhard Schultze and his family has continually been a blessing to my life.

I am also thankful to the PhD committee of Jos ECWA Theological Seminary (JETS) who provided me academic guidance during the course of my PhD work. I am forever indebted to Prof. Yusufu Turaki, Prof. Randy Ijatuyi-Morphe, Prof. George Janvier, Prof. Bulus Galadima and his wife Dr. Rose Galadima. I would also like to thank Prof. Zamani Kafang and his family, and the various encouragements offered to me by Prof. Dogara J. Gwamna of Nasarrawa State University, Nigeria; Dr. David H. Kajom of Kaduna State University; Dr. Nathan Ciroma, Stellenbosch University, South Africa; Prof. Hendricks Bosman of Stellenbosch University, South Africa; Dr. Dickson Dyaji of Kaduna State University, and Prof. John Kwasua of Alhamdu Bello University, Zaria, Nigeria; Rev. Dr. Joel K. T. Biwul, JETS, Nigeria; Rev. Michael I. Ijah, Gordon-Cornwell Theological

Seminary, South Hamilton, Massachusetts, United States; Rev. Zachs Toro-Gaiya, Trinity International University, Chicago, United States.

I am also grateful to Langham Partnership International who provided me with the grant and the needed encouragement during my PhD studies. In particular, I am grateful to Diane Moon, Elaine Vaden and Jack Swanson for their devotion, encouragement and support.

In the same vein, I want to thank the provost of ECWA Theological Seminary Kagoro (ETSK), Rev. Dr. Sunday B. Agang, for his encouragement and support in finishing this book. I am also indebted to Dr. Rick Creighton of ETSK's Research Centre for his friendship, critique and support. In addition, I would like to thank the entire faculty, staff and students of ETSK for their love, support and encouragement during the difficult period of turning this dissertation into this present book.

I cannot appreciate enough the significant role played by my wife Juliana and our children (Kolel, Keli and Yadael) during the course of revising and turning my dissertation into this book. I am really grateful to all your contributions in order to see that this book is now finished. I only hope that the future will give to us more opportunities to love and care for one another.

CHAPTER ONE

Introduction

1.1. Introduction

Memorable speeches, whether in public or private conversations, are often elegant, electrifying and persuasive. Intentionally crafted, great speeches are also the product of artistic creation and find their permanent elegance in this literary wrapping. Looking closely at human history, defining speeches have often been characterized by their persuasive eloquence and literary beauty. For example, one is enthralled by the elevated speeches of Demosthenes, the highly rhetoric speeches of Cicero, the Gettysburg speech of Abraham Lincoln, the speeches of Winston Churchill during World war II, and the highly elegant speeches of Martin Luther King Jr in the 1960s.[1]

In more recent times, one is also fascinated by the defining speeches of Nelson Mandela in South Africa, and the high-sounding rhetoric of change in the campaign speeches of Barak Obama before and after the

---

1. In contemporary times, there have been various independent studies on the political and oratory attainments of these individuals. For the study of these personalities see Rahul Sagar, Martin Guther, *Divine Talk: Religious Argumentation in Demosthenes*. Oxford Monographs (Oxford: Oxford University Press, 2009); "Presaging the Moderns: Demosthenes' Critique of Popular Government," *Journal of Politics* 71, no. 4 (2009): 1394–1405; James M. May, ed. *Brill's Companion to Cicero* (Leiden: Brill, 2002), 1–21; A. E. Elmore, *Lincoln's Gettysburg Address: Echoes of the Bible and Book of Common Prayer* (Carbondale: Southern University Press, 2009); Richard Toye, "Winston Churchill's 'Crazy Broadcast': Party, Nation, and the 1945 Gestapo," *Journal of British Studies* 49, no. 3 (2010): 655–680; Eric J. Sundquist, *King's Dreams: The Legacy of Martin Luther King's 'I have A Dream' Speech* (New York, CT: Yale University Press, 2009);George Henderson, "Lift Every Voice and Let Freedom Ring," *Phi Kappa Phi* (2013): 8–10.

US presidential elections.[2] These few instances in history point to the importance of speech-making, its literary effects and the persuasive use of speeches by individuals to shape the course of human events.

In the same way, one finds also the presence of influential attributed speeches in fictional literature. For example, the same defining nature of speeches can be seen in literature whether in the Shakespearean portrayal of Mark Antony in his play *Julius Caesar* or in the proverb-coated speeches of Okonkwo in Chinua Achebe's, *Things Fall Apart*. In the former, the speeches of Mark Antony, particularly at the burial of Caesar, were clearly laced with repetition, emotive language, innuendos, sarcasm and even satire. In the latter, to show and characterize Okonkwo, as the true embodiment of the African culture, Achebe often colors the speeches of Okonkwo with African proverbs and wise sayings in order to achieve this literary aim.[3]

Similarly too, biblical narrative is often characterized by the high frequency of attributed speeches. As part of its literary technique, the attributed speeches in biblical narrative help in characterization, intensification of the plot, and the direct enhancement of the mimetic quality of the story. While one finds quoted speeches, public addresses, and private conversations decorated with the presence of attributed speeches in the Hebrew Bible, the elegance of these speeches had not been primarily researched or investigated in a systematic manner. Unfortunately, apart from the uncoordinated recognition of wordplay, alliteration or other stylistic devices in these speeches, there is no collective effort to read and study an entire pericope in terms of the elegance and persuasion of its attributed speeches.

---

2. David M. Marx *et al*, "The 'Obama Effect': How a Salient Role Model Reduces Race-Based Performances," *Journal of Experimental Social Psychology* 45 (2009): 953–956; Alessandro Capone, "Barack Obama's South Caroline Speech," *Journal of Pragmatics* 42 (2010): 2964–2977; Charles Wolf Jr. and Brian Rosen, "Public Diplomacy: Lessons from King and Mandela," *Policy Review* 133 (2005): 63–80; Nelson Mandela, *Conversation with Myself* (2010).

3. Concerning the characterization of Okonkwo in *Things Fall Apart*, Achebe placed memorable proverbs on the lips of his leading character. For example, on the unmanliness of Nwoye his son, Okonkwo said, "Where are the young suckers that will grow when the old banana tree dies?" He also said, "A chick that will grow into a cock can be spotted the very day it hatches." He also said, "A child's fingers are not scalded by a piece of hot yam which its mother puts into its palm." See Chinua Achebe, *Things Fall Apart* (London: Heinemann Educational Books, 1985), 46, 47.

The reason for this neglect primarily comes from the diachronic treatment of biblical narrative. Recognizing the divergence of sources, the elegance of these attributed speeches had often eluded modern scholarship. Within this sentiment, for example, David Damrosch described biblical narratives generally as a "purposeful patchwork" which despite its highly literary disposition is largely "a *poor* literature."[4] This same ambivalence towards biblical narratives has also characterized the study of Genesis in particular. Thus for example, in the late seventies, B. Vawter observed that the narrative of "Genesis is a scissors-and-paste composition" which falls apart because it lacks literary artistry.[5] Similarly, S. E. McEvenue talks of the unpolished tales of the patriarch narratives, which despite their stylistic features are a work in the category of children's literature.[6] In more recent times, D. M. Carr spoke of these same narratives as "fractures," "multi-voiced" and "conflation."[7] In addition, Frank Polak speaks of a "crisp 'plain' style" of the Genesis narratives, which primarily fulfils the longing of an orate speech community.[8] On the other hand, J. S. Baden has put a methodological wedge between its "literary artistry" and its "literary unity."[9]

However, even though H. Gunkel was schooled in the source and form of critical traditions, he nonetheless conceded that the Genesis stories "are perhaps the most beautiful and most profound" stories "ever known on earth."[10] In particular, R. L. Cohn had noted the "theological sophistication" of the Abrahamic narratives,[11] and similarly describing the general

---

4. David Damrosch, *The Narrative Covenant: Transformations of Genre in the Growth of Biblical Literature* (San Francisco: Harper & Row, 1987), 325, 32.
5. B. Vawter, *On Genesis: A New Reading* (London: Geoffrey Chapman, 1977), 16.
6. S. E. McEvenue, *The Narrative Style of the Priestly Writer*. Analecta biblica (Rome: Biblical Institute Press, 1971), 12–21.
7. Furthermore, using the chorale imagery, Carr also talks about their "discordant" and "cacophonous character." See D. M. Carr, *Reading the Fractures of Genesis: Historical and Literary Approaches* (Louisville, Kentucky: Westminster Press, 1996), 3, 13, 20.
8. See Frank Polak, "Sociolinguistics: A Key to the Typology and the Background of Biblical Hebrew," *Hebrew Studies* 47(2006), 149–152.
9. Joel S. Baden, "The Tower of Babel: A Case Study in the Competing Methods of Historical and Modern Criticism," *JBL* 128, no. 2 (2009), 222.
10. H. Gunkel, *The Stories of Genesis*, trans. John Scullion, ed. William Scott (Vallejo, California: Bibal Press, 1994), 6.
11. R. L. Cohn, "Narrative Structure and Canonical Perspective in Genesis," *JSOT* 25 (1983), 6.

artistry of Genesis, G. Rendsburg observed, "all of Genesis is brilliantly constructed, the accomplishment of an ancient Israelite genius who formed the book into a literary whole."[12] In addition, Joseph Blenkinsopp suggested that the narrators of the Abrahamic narrative "have skillfully combined available written sources into a compelling narrative . . ."[13]

Despite these two common approaches towards Genesis in general, and the Abrahamic cycle in particular, which are expressed often either in praise of its genius or criticisms of its unskillful design, yet the Abrahamic cycle, according to the biblical accounts, cradles the origin of Israel's religion and history, and thus, as should be expected, both ancient and modern interpreters have continually wrestled with the significance of these stories.[14] Within the traditions of Jewish, Christian and Islamic faiths, the significance of these stories has become increasingly defined. Interestingly, even though the Abrahamic cycle has provided the fundamental framework for the ideological mapping of the world's leading religions, yet it has done so, not by the complication of philosophies, rhetoric or sermons, but by the mere medium of persuasive stories, which a huge block of the world has now believed and continues to believe.[15] In this sense, the dictum of Harold Goddard is right that "[t]he destiny of the world is determined less

---

12. G. A. Rendsburg, *The Redaction of Genesis* (Winona Lake, Indiana: Eisenbraus, 1989), 4.

13. Joseph Blenkinsopp, "Abraham as Paradigm in the Priestly History of Genesis," *JBL* 128, no. 2 (2009), 228.

14. On the philosophical questions arising from the claims by biblical narrators that God has spoken to them, see Nicholas Wolterstorff, *Divine Discourse: Philosophical Reflections on the Claim that God Speaks* (Cambridge: Cambridge University Press, 1995).

15. The religious message of the Hebrew Bible was placed in a literary piece. Hence, it is needful to recognize the intricate relationship between the message and the literary form. Underscoring this thesis, R. Alter affirmed the "remarkable literary qualities" of the biblical narratives which are not merely "accidental by products" or "felicitous embellishment" of the "imperative religious concerns that are the heart of Scripture," but whose use of aesthetics in literary composition has clearly defined significance for the transmission of its religious message because the form as well as the content of revelation are equally important. See Robert Alter, "Biblical Imperatives and Literary Play," *"Not in Heaven": Coherence and Complexity in Biblical Narrative*, eds. Jason P. Rosenblatt & Joseph C. Sitterson, Jr. (Bloomington: Indiana University Press, 1991), 13.

by the battles that are lost and won than by the stories it loves and believes in."¹⁶

Significantly, the popularity of the stories of the Abrahamic cycle among these leading religions shows the power of these stories and points to their artistry because they have become engraved not only in the paintings and sculptures of arts, but in the minds of the millions of the followers of these religions in every generation.¹⁷ This consideration partly points to the success of the narrator of the Abrahamic cycle as a "great storyteller" and despite the quest of the critical scholarship to discredit his existence or even the genius of his writings, yet his writings have become the masterpiece and favorites of these leading religions. It is from this perspective that R. N. Whybray had rightly observed, "[t]he fact that Abraham" has "become such [an] outstanding" figure "in both Judaism and Christianity may be due more to the skill of the narrator than to any ancient long traditions that preceded him."¹⁸ Consequently, the quest to fragment or tear his works into literary pieces and endless sources seems to have failed because his stories have continued to persuade or even to define the religious worldview of more than half of the world's population. The failure of such a quest is because it has treated with levity the credentials of the narrator of the Abrahamic cycle as a great storyteller who has crafted a great story which influences and transcends his lifetime and has continued to our time.¹⁹ Even though the continuous appeal of these stories lie in their

---

16. Harold Goddard, *The Meaning of Shakespeare*, vol. 2 (Chicago: Chicago University Press, 1965), 208.
17. To this end, T. R. Wright conceded that though the stories in Genesis lack "the sophistication and complexity of the modern novel" because "they are certainly much shorter" however, "these stories remain powerful and provocative . . . " even in modern times. See T. R. Wright, *The Genesis of Fiction: Modern Novelists as Biblical Interpreters* (Aldershot: Ashgate, 2007), x.
18. R. N. Whybray, *Introduction to the Pentateuch* (Grand Rapids, Michigan: William B. Eerdmans Publishing Co., 1995), 50.
19. At the heart of the success of the Abrahamic narratives lies the literary representation of the character of Abraham within these narratives. Concerning the literary representation of Abraham in Genesis, Adele Berlin said, "Abraham in Genesis is not a real person any more than a painting of an apple is a real fruit. This is not a judgment on the existence of apples. It is just that we should not confuse a historical individual with his narrative representation" [Adele Berlin, *Poetics and Interpretation of Biblical Narrative* (Sheffield: Almond Press, 1983), 13]. In patriarchal narratives, the narrative representation

powerful claims about Israel's origin, particularly the elective purposes of God in history, however, these concerns were woven into story which literary appeals lie in the way the narrator told his story and the artistry by which he crafted the plot, speech, and character of these stories. Ignoring the narrative power of these stories, past research has taken merely historical, archaeological, traditional, structural and theological interest in these stories, and have failed to appreciate their literary artistry as story, hence losing the primary framework by which these stories have been framed and the basis for their continuous appeal throughout the course of their transmission. Admittedly, these preceding researches have shed light on our understanding of the Abrahamic cycle especially in providing ample archaeological, historical and ancient near-eastern parallels or backgrounds to these stories, yet they often fail to provide clues to the artistry of these stories particularly in their final forms.[20] To this end, the present work seeks to study the distinctive and stylistic character[21] of the speeches of God in Abrahamic cycle.[22] One controlling hypothesis of this present study is

---

and the historicity of Abraham converge because the narrator has successfully bridged these two horizons by the power of his skilful narration.

20. For example see John van Seters, *Abraham in History and Tradition* (New Haven: Yale University Press, 1975), 123–131; *idem, Prologue to History: The Yahwist as Historian in Genesis* (Louisville, Kentucky: Westminster Press, 1992); T. L. Thompson, *The Origin of Ancient Israel: The Literary Formation of Genesis and Exodus 1–23*. JSOTSup 55 (Sheffield: Sheffield Academic Press, 1987).

21. Style is a "slippery and elusive" term because it is difficult to define. Moreover, what one author considers a style might not be taken as style by another. Similarly, cultural factors could also affect the concept of style since one cultural concept of style might be different from another. Furthermore, even within a given culture, different time spans may affect the conception of style or even lead to conflicting understanding of style. In the course of its history, some have primarily considered "style" or "stylistic" as a "deviation from the normal use of language," while others have understood the term to mean "recurrence or convergence of textual pattern." In different texts, these two conceptions may have equal validity; however, within the present study we will use the former nuance rather than the latter. For the history and different understandings of the term see Tova Meltzer, "Stylistics for the Study of Ancient Texts: Wanderings in the Borderlands," *Discourse Analysis of Biblical Literature: What it is and What it offers*. Semeia Studies. SBL (Atlanta, Georgia: Scholars Press, 1995), 131–141.

22. The stories in the Abrahamic cycle began with divine speeches (12:1–3). Significantly, the divine speeches define the main plot of the stories and also provide the integrating nucleus of the entire cycle. Past scholarship has invested much interest in the historical and theological concerns of these speeches; even though these concerns are necessary and complementary to this present study, this present study primarily explores the stylistic features of these divine speeches.

that the concentration of metaphor/figurative image, alliteration, allusion, wordplay and other literary devices in the speeches of God which are deliberately denied other characters of Abrahamic narratives, points to the distinctiveness of the divine character and also underscores the ideological importance of these divine speeches.[23] Consequently, the study primarily engages the six dominant divine speeches of the Abrahamic cycle (Gen 12:1–9, 13:1–18, 15:1–21, 17:1–27, 18:1–33, and 22:1–19) and treats them as a unified piece.[24] While adopting such a synchronic approach, however, one is not naïve about the long history of traditions that culminate in the final form of the present text. All the same, we engage the Abrahamic cycle in the final form rather than following after the elusive contours of the pre-literary traditions behind the text.

1.2. Methodology

The present work employs a literary/synchronic methodology in the study of Yahweh's speeches within the Abrahamic narratives. This method explores the distinctive literary artistry of the speeches of the dominant character of the Abrahamic narratives, namely Yahweh, and demonstrates how understanding the artistry of the divine speeches will help us in the quest to find the functions of the Abrahamic narratives to the world of the author or redactor. Even though the study duly recognizes the complexity of the

---

23. For the gravity of speech in biblical narratives see Yael Ziegler, *Promise to Keep: The Oath in Biblical Narrative* (Leiden: Brill, 2008), 25–49.
24. The ground for the treatment of the Abrahamic narratives in this definition comes from the contemporary unifying reading of the Pentateuch in critical scholarship. For example, Whybray opined that, "the Pentateuch bears the marks of a single distinctive purpose" which points to the possibility or existence of a singular authorship [see R. N. Whybray, *The Making of the Pentateuch: A Methodological Study*. JSOTSup Series 53 (Sheffield: Sheffield Academic Press, 1987), 17–131, 221–242]. In a different direction, this line of reasoning has also found expression in the work of D. J. A. Clines particularly in his assumption that there is a particular theme running through the entire Pentateuch. Interestingly, he located this theme in the partial fulfilment of the patriarchal promise. Even though he did not deny the possibility of sources, he largely affirmed the coherence of the Pentateuch around a given theme [See D. J. A. Clines, *The Theme of Pentateuch*. JSOTSup 10 (Sheffield: JSOT, 1978)].

source traditions behind the collection, redaction and adaptation of these narratives, it persistently seeks to read these narratives in their final form.

From this methodological template, the present chapter describes the problem, significance and hypothesis of the study. The second chapter presents the dominant works already undertaken in the general studies of the mechanics of biblical speeches, and the specific works which are tailored particularly to the study of the artistry of the divine speeches. Concerning the former, the present study evaluates the works of Charles Conroy, E. J. Revell, Robert Longacre, Alviero Niccacci, George Savran, and Cynthia Miller. While acknowledging the contributions of the preceding works in their recognition of the stylistic nature of biblical speech's attribution techniques, however, the present study also differs from the preceding works by its distinctive engagement of the divine speeches and its concentration on the elevated divine style in the literary categories of metaphor, simile, wordplay, irony, alliteration, euphemism, hyperbole, repetition, allusion and other literary devices within the divine speeches of the Abrahamic narratives. In addition, the second half of the chapter presents specific studies on the divine speeches and the recognition of its possible stylistic character. In this direction, the works of Casper Labuschagne, Hugh White, Wilfried Warning and Samuel Meier are investigated. Underscoring the contribution of these works, the study also reveals the distinct direction of the present study which differs from the mathematical interest of Labuschagne, who generally treated the divine speeches as a numerical device which will help the reader of the Pentateuch to unravel its compositional mysteries; the philosophical interest of White who underscored the "otherworldliness" of the divine speeches in the narrative world of Genesis; the structural interest of Warning who emphasized the use of divine speeches as a compositional device that marks the structure of Leviticus; and the historical interest of Meier who largely provided the possible historical contexts for the discourse markers that introduce the divine speeches in the prophetic and narrative literature.

The third chapter undertakes a detailed study of the highlighted divine speeches in the Abrahamic narratives (12:1–9, 13:1–18, 15:1–21, 17:1–27, 18:1–33, and 22:1–19). In particular, it describes each text within the framework of its structure, literary context, textual variants, grammar and syntax. Following these considerations, the study highlights and points to the presence of stylistic features within the divine speeches in each pericope. In addition, it emphasizes the specific significance of the highlighted stylistic elements of the divine speech in the reading of the text especially within the narrative world of the Abrahamic stories.

Beyond the world of the narrative, however, the fourth chapter describes the possible functions of these rhetorically-styled divine speeches in the world of the author. The chapter begins by noting the general characteristics of the divine speeches as gathered from the studies in chapter 3. These characteristics include its excessive optimism, defining particularity, universal vision, elevated language, futuristic orientation, and covenantal concerns. Noting the importance of these highlighted characteristics of the divine speeches, the study emphasizes the ideological character and the functions of the divine speeches to the world of the final author or redactors. In particular, it notes the polemic goal, the legitimizing agenda, the consolatory function, the identity-creating role, and the prophetic task of the divine speeches to the world of the author, redactors and original audience.

In chapter five, the present study describes the basic conclusions of the preceding chapters, and highlights the significance of the study for the contemporary world particularly in the quest to create hope, identity and optimism by the Christian religious communities. Even though the conclusion acknowledges the worth of the stylistic features of the text, it notes that the stylistic features point beyond themselves to the world outside the text. In this understanding the stylistic elements within the text receive, ultimately, a secondary status because they become ideological tools of the author in his quest to address the ills of his own world. Consequently, while stylistic techniques of the divine speeches in Abrahamic narratives are significant, they are not there only for their mere aesthetic value, but they look forward towards addressing the problems in the author's world, and by the canonical or Christian extension to address, even though distant, the ills of our modern world.

1.3. Conclusion

The chapter begins by noting the general ambivalence in the study of the Genesis narratives in the rejection or acceptance of its stylistic character. In the direction of the latter, the chapter states the basic hypothesis of the present work in its persistent claims that there are stylistic features in the speeches of Yahweh which are largely absent in the speeches of the other characters of the Abrahamic narratives. Consequently, the chapter provides the foundation for the present work by describing the problem, the scope, the hypothesis and the significance of the present study. In addition, it shows methodologically how the different chapters of the dissertation relate to each other. In this regard, the chapter highlights the distinctive direction of the present work and hence its contribution to the works already generated in the study of biblical speeches.

CHAPTER TWO

Dominant Studies on the Literary Features of the Divine Speeches

2.1. Introduction

It is now largely established that direct discourse or direct speech is fundamental in the description of biblical narratives.[1] This comes from the recognition in literary studies that most of the biblical narration is carried out by means of direct discourses. In fact, as readily observed by Robert Alter, there is a "predilection" for direct discourse in the Bible that even the inner thoughts, soliloquies or monologues are also framed by the medium of direct discourse.[2] Similarly, speeches were so pronounced that in rare cases even animals or trees are endowed with the capacity for speech.[3]

One of the powers of direct discourse among human characters is that it adds dramatic presence to the biblical story and creates a verisimilitude which gives biblical narrative a sense of real life because the characters are forcefully brought alive on the pages of the Bible.[4] The direct discourse

---

1. The works reviewed below underscored the fundamental importance of speeches in biblical narratives.
2. Robert Alter, *The Art of Biblical Narrative* (New York: Basic Books, 1981), 63–87; 182–85.
3. See George Savran, "Beastly Speech: Intertextuality, Balaam's Ass and the Garden of Eden," *JSOT* 64 (1994):33–55. cf. Judges 9:7–15; 2 Kings 14:9.
4. In fictional novels, verisimilitude is created by the life-like exchange or conversation between the characters because the narrative "becomes fresher, livelier, and clearer when natural conversation is introduced." See R. M. Dorson, "Oral Styles of American Folk

helps us to see or even judge the characters of biblical narratives since the speeches of the characters are presented directly to the readers, thus helping the characterization agenda of the biblical narrator.[5] In divulging the speeches of the biblical characters, the biblical narrator breaks from his reticence to tell us a lot about his characters by his selection, arrangement and presentation of their speeches.[6] In this understanding, the presence and placement of the speeches of biblical characters are not accidental, but they are strategically employed in order to underscore a particular point of view or ideological persuasions by the biblical narrator.[7] To this end, Herbert C. Brichto observed, "[t]he artistic control of the biblical narrator is, I believe, revealed by the observation that his deployment of direct discourse is never accidental or capricious."[8] Despite the recognition of the significance of this literary phenomenon in biblical narratives, it is also true, as observed by Normand Bonneau, that "[s]cholars tend to pay little attention to direct discourse in the Bible because of the perplexity surrounding the topic in narrative theory."[9] Even though some of the studies on this phenomenon have underscored the presence, nature and significance, generally speaking a lot of these works have paid little attention to the inner working of the

---

Narrators," *Style in Language* (Cambridge, Massachusetts: Cambridge University Press, 1960), 27.

5. Michael V. Fox, *Character and Ideology in the Book of Esther* (Columbia, South Carolina: University of South Carolina Press, 1991), 6–9; Kenneth M. Craig, Jr., *A Poetic of Jonah: Art in the Service of Ideology* (Columbia, South Carolina: University of South Carolina Press, 1991), 66–72; Hugh S. Pyper, *David as Reader: 2 Samuel 12:1–15 and the Poetics of Fatherhood*. Biblical Interpretation Series, vol. 23 (Leiden: Brill, 1996), 59–62.

6. The vividness of the narrative is further enhanced by situating the biblical speeches in an appropriate real life social setting. For example, Asnat Bartor had categorized a group of "juridical dialogues" in biblical narrative and showed their possible court-like settings. See Asnat Bartor, "The 'Juridical Dialogue': A Literary-Judicial Pattern," *VT* 53, no. 4 (2003): 445–464.

7. For example, Mark A. Throntveit has underscored the significance of the royal speeches within Chronicles particularly in determining the structure, theology or even ideology of the chronicler. See Mark A. Throntveit, *The Significance of the Royal Speeches and Prayers for the Structure and Theology of the Chronicler* (Ann Arbor, Michigan: University Microfilms International, 1988), 14–63.

8. Herbert C. Brichto, *Toward a Grammar of Biblical Poetics: Tales of the Prophets* (New York: Oxford University Press, 1992), 11.

9. Normand Bonneau, "The Illusion of Immediacy: A Narrative-Critical Exploration of the Bible's Predilection for Direct Discourse," *Theoforum* 31 (2000), 133.

biblical speeches.¹⁰ In particular, as subsequent discussion would seek to show, the various works already generated in the study of this biblical phenomenon appear to have paid little or no attention to the stylistic features of the divine speeches.¹¹

Consequently, this chapter presents the dominant studies on this phenomenon. Firstly, it describes the general works already carried out on the biblical speeches, particularly the recognition of the importance of direct discourse in biblical narratives by past studies. Secondly, it pays close attention to specific studies on the stylistic features of the divine speeches especially works that appear to recognize the apparent or implicit stylistic features of the divine speeches in biblical narratives. Even though some of these studies are not entirely devoted to this phenomenon, they, no doubt, provide a springboard on which to begin our studies on the stylistic features of the divine speeches within Abrahamic narratives.

2.2. General Studies on Biblical Speeches

The description of "general studies" in this work will cover the few works that have played a dominant role in the studies of direct discourse. In this direction, we must make reference to the work of Alter, Meir Sternberg, and Adele Berlin who have in various ways drawn attention to the importance of direct speeches in biblical narratives. For example, Alter has

---

10. The inner working of biblical speeches in this particular understanding will be studies on the presence and use of stylistic devices within speeches. The stylistic features will include metaphor, simile, irony, euphemism, alliteration, paronomasia and a host of other literary devices, which often enrich the speeches of biblical characters.
11. In biblical narrative, speeches were given preeminent position over visuals because of the auditory nature of the biblical world and its anti-iconic orientation. In relationship to the divine being, it appears the speeches of God are given priority over his visual representations [For a different view see George Savran, "Seeing is Believing: On the Relative Priority of Visual and Verbal Perception of the Divine," *Bib Int* 17 (2009): 320–361), *idem, Encountering the Divine,* 49–89]. This audio-oriented nature of divine character within the text put a lot of pressure on biblical narration to verbally make up for the absence of an iconic representation. Consequently, it is not surprising to find distinctive stylistic features in some cases within the divine speeches.

emphasized the domineering nature of discourse in comparison to narration.[12] Similarly, Sternberg has also drawn attention to the various features of biblical discourses such as the place of ambiguity, level of awareness, and rhetoric.[13] Also, Sternberg has observed the intriguing relationship between the narrator and the characters who are his creations, voices or even spokesmen because through them he speaks to his readers.[14] In addition, Berlin has brought to the fore, the place of point of view in the interchange of biblical dialogues.[15] The common trait of these three works is that they form an introduction to the study of biblical speeches because the main emphasis of their works is to show or underscore the importance of biblical dialogue. In this same perspective are the works of Efrat and J.P. Fokkelmann who also differently emphasized the significance of dialogues in biblical

---

12. In particular, he has underscored the dominance of character's speech, hence Alter noted, "[t]he biblical writers, in other words, are often less concerned with actions in themselves than with how individual character responds to actions or produces them; and direct speech is made the chief instrument for revealing the varied and at times nuanced relations of the personages to the actions in which they are implicated." [Alter, *The Art of Biblical Narrative*, 66].

13. Meir Sternberg, *The Poetics of Biblical Narrative: Ideological Literature and the Drama of Reading* (Bloomington: Indiana University Press, 1987), 203–9; 287–94; 297–99; 300–8. See also Sternberg, "Proteus in Quotation Land: Mimesis and the Forms of Reported Discourse," *Poetic Today* 4 (1982): 107–56.

14. Hence he noted, "[l]iterary dialogue entails indirection by its very form, because in staging it the artist communicates with the audience *through* the communication held among his speaking characters, the dialogists. Itself silent or silenced, the frame then quotes a vocal inset. This is even more perceptible in narrative than in drama, because the narrator could always do otherwise. Free to speak in his own voice and to his own addressee, he could tell us everything straight: what happens, why it happens, where the sense and the point of the happening lie. Instead, in the role of dialogue-maker he withdraws behind the scenes to leave the floor to the dialogists themselves–but without surrendering for a moment his privileged viewpoint on what they say and do. After all, he brings them on purpose. As scriptwriter and stage manager rolled into one, even if he speaks in voices other than his own, he still speaks through voices and words and obliquities of his own devising. Hence every piece of dialogue enacts no less than a double message: two levels of communication, two pairs of communicators, each having its peculiar sphere, norms, horizons, intentions, rhetoric, but with the artistic one always overlaid or *mediated* by the lifelike." [Sternberg, "Double Cave, Double Talk: The Indirection of Biblical Dialogue," *"Not in Heaven": Coherence and Complexity in Biblical Narrative*, eds. Jason P. Rosenblatt and Joseph C. Sitterson, Jr., 28–57 (Bloomington: Indiana: University Press, 1991), 28].

15. Berlin, *Poetics and Interpretation of Biblical Narrative*, 38–9; 43–110.

narratives.¹⁶ Similarly, G. Goldenberg has shown distinctive grammatical differences in the framing of indirect and direct speeches within biblical narratives.¹⁷ From the introductory nature of these works, we will now turn our attention to works that continued the emphases of these works, but also adding other important slants in the studies of the biblical speeches. We will study the works of Charles Conroy, E. J. Revell, Robert Longacre, Alviero Niccacci, George Savran and Cynthia Miller in this direction.

2.2.1. Charles Conroy

In 1978, Charles Conroy's monograph, *Absalom Absalom!: Narrative and Language in 2 Sam 13–20,* explores the different literary features in second Samuel 13–20.¹⁸ Even though his work is not generally given due recognition, the work of Conroy was seminal in its understanding of the literary features of biblical narratives. He explores the different features such as the transitional formula, point of view, contrast and reversal, control of sympathy and antipathy, sound stratum in the consonant and vowel patterning, rhythm, uncommon words, phrases and usages, repetition and variations, word-play and paronomasia, parallelism and figurative language. To this repertoire of literary features of the biblical text, Conroy also adds the techniques of organization on the level of the whole text and within varying

---

16. For example, Bar-Efrat observed that the speeches of biblical characters could reflect an individual's wisdom, social standing, royalty, or sign of respect. Underscoring the place of speeches in biblical narrative as a means of characterization, Bar-Efrat noted, "[t]he correspondence between the style and content of speech reinforces the impact of what is said. In addition, the combination of form and content in deviations from accepted court style carries considerable weight in characterizing the speakers . . ." [See Bar-Efrat, *Narrative Art in the Bible*, 68]. On the other hand, even though primarily concerned with the subject of structure in biblical narrative, J. P. Fokkelman notes in a few instances the subtlety in the speeches of biblical character. For example, he has noted the "corroding irony" and "subtle humor" in the presence of הָבָה (translated, "come, on") in the speeches of God and the builders of the tower [Fokkelman, *Narrative Art in Genesis: Specimens of Stylistic and Structural Analysis* (Eugene, Oregon: Wipf & Stock, 1991), 14]. See also Fokkelman, *Narrative Art and Poetry in the Books of Samuel: A Full Interpretation Based on Stylistic and Structural Analyses*, vol. 1–4 (Assen, The Netherlands: Van Gorcum, 1993).

17. See Gideon Goldenberg, "On Direct Speech and the Hebrew Bible," *Studies in Hebrew and Aramaic Syntax Presented to Professor J. Hoftijzer on the Occasion of his Sixty-fifth Birthday*, eds. K. Jongeling, H. L. Murre-Van Den Berg and I. Van Rompay (Leiden: Brill, 1991), 79–96.

18. Charles Conroy, *Absalom Absalom!: Narrative and Language in 2 Sam 13–20* (Rome: Biblical Institute Press, 1978).

pericopes. In particular relationship to our present review, he underscores the different uses of direct speech in biblical narratives particularly in his study of second Samuel 13–20. In this definition, he noted the frequency and centrality of direct speeches in biblical narrative, the use of quotation formulas, the use of inner direct speech and monologue, number of speakers and exchanges, structural elements in the speeches, vocatives, questions and emotions reflected in language, and lastly the use of courtly style in speeches.

Taking the items one after another, concerning the centrality and frequency of direct speeches in second Samuel 13–20, Conroy observed that out of the 259 verses of this text, 171 contain direct speech. This occurrence of direct speech makes direct speech "almost two-thirds of the total" verses. He noted that the entire story in this pericope is framed in the structure of "narrative/dialogue/narrative" with the "crucial part of the sub-unit in direct speech." Similarly, Conroy observed,

> There is a second sense too in which it can be said that dialogue has a central part in the story, for two of the scenes that have the most decisive bearing on the action are largely in direct speech, namely, the Tekoite woman's plea in ch.14 which brings about the recall of Absalom and thus leads on to the rebellion, and the duel of words between Ahithophel and Hushai in ch. 17 which decides the outcome of the rebellion before ever a blow is struck on the field of battle.[19]

Concerning the quotation-formulas in this passage, Conroy identified them and suggested their possible "stylistic effects of variation in the wording of quotation-formulas." He also went ahead to talk about the use of inner direct speech and monologue. He mentioned nine different uses of the inner direct speech or interior quotation. These nine uses of the inner quotation include the communication of message or item of news; command or instructions; reference in conditional sense to what another person may have said or may say; a speaker telling another character what

---

19. Ibid., 128.

to say; when a speaker tells another character what not to say or think; description of intention or thought; when the speaker quotes his own words in the past; when a speaker apostrophizes himself and lastly when a speaker quotes a common saying or proverb. Conroy concluded his observation on the inner direct speech by noting that "[t]he many functions performed by this usage shows that it is an important part of a Hebrew narrator's stock of technique."[20] Following this, Conroy further observed the number of speakers in the biblical dialogues, and showed that the dialogues or conversations are often between two persons and a third character and only appear after the exchange between these two persons. Conroy also discussed some of the structural elements in speeches such as הנה and ראה which he described as "attention-callers."[21] Similarly, Conroy noted the use of vocatives, for example, the thirteen vocatives present in the grief-ridden speeches of David in order to show the "outburst" of his grief. According to Conroy, some of the terms used in vocatives include the divine name, name of a people, personal name, patronymic labels, titles, and relationship terms.[22] In addition, Conroy identified the presence of ordinary and rhetorical questions in the passage and their possible functions. Concerning the use of questions in the speeches of biblical characters, Conroy noted,

> Questions both genuine and rhetorical add to the dramatic force of the story by presenting the interaction of the personages in a more striking way. A question involves the hearer more actively than an affirmation; one can listen passively to affirmations but not to questions. The person addressed is summoned to take up a position, either by giving a genuine answer or by having the expressive and emotional force of the speaker's words impressed more vividly upon him. Thus the dramatic quality of the narrative is heightened when the

---

20. Ibid., 131.
21. Ibid., 133.
22. Ibid.

already dramatic dialogue form is supplemented by frequent questions.[23]

On emotional language as reflected in the speeches of a biblical character, Conroy noted that even though ordinarily the context could suggest to the reader that the character of a biblical passage is "in a heightened emotional state," often there are literary indicators which point to this heightened state of emotion in the speeches of biblical characters. For Conroy, these literary indicators include rhetorical questions, massive concentration of vocatives in the speeches of biblical characters, *waw*-sentences to show the "speaker's breathless agitation," the broken rhythm of sentence, awkward syntax, inner direct speech and rhetorical exaggerations."[24] Conroy also observed the use of courtly language style in the speeches of the characters. This is the "use of polite forms of address."[25] In particular, Conroy noted various occurrences of these polite addresses in the speeches of biblical character and ends with the conclusion that "texts seem to suggest that there was a tendency to avoid [courtly language] in military contexts."[26]

In retrospect, Conroy's work was a trailblazer in the form of literary appreciation that is now closely associated with the names of Alter and Sternberg. There is an overwhelming understanding of the literary characteristics of the Bible as readily seen in his ability to identify these literary features and also to categorize them. The sheer force of his many examples and his meticulous analysis of even the minute details of the text make his work exceptional in many ways. Most importantly, his work is a departure from a diachronic reading of the biblical text and the excessive quest to place the biblical text in the ambit of historical inquiry. Thus Conroy acknowledged the unity of the biblical text and his literary appreciation comes from this underlying presupposition.

In our present research's interest, the work of Conroy is exceptional in its detailed description of the biblical direct speeches and the possibility of

---

23. Ibid., 139.
24. Ibid., 140.
25. Ibid.
26. Ibid.

artistic representation of these speeches by the narrator. In this sense, the direct speeches are conceived as a very important point in biblical narratives which could provide us with very important insights in the artistry of the biblical narrator. His work underscores not merely the importance of these speeches, but the possibility of understanding the entire biblical pericope by a proper understanding of the mechanism and artistic nature of the speeches of the characters in such biblical pericope. Even though his work excludes the treatment of the divine speeches because they are not present in the pericope he studied, his work provides light into the general workings of the biblical speeches, and underscores the complex and insightful use of language in the speeches of biblical characters. To this end, his work becomes a prototype of the subsequent quest to stress the importance of biblical speeches and the light these speeches could throw in our understanding of the general workings of biblical narratives.

2.2.2. E. J. Revell

In the study of biblical narratives, little or no attention has been paid to the different ways in which the biblical narrator designated or labeled his characters particularly as found in the speeches of the characters to one another.[27] To remedy this need, E. J. Revell pioneered a detailed study on the various designations employed by the biblical narrator to describe the characters. In his major work, *The Designation of the Individual: Expressive Usage in Biblical Narrative*, Revell sought to describe and analyze "the way individual characters are referred to or addressed in the biblical narratives"[28] with the hope of providing a better understanding of the relationship between these designations and the primary thrust of the narratives where these speeches or designations are found.

In this study, Revell went through the various designations for rulers such as David, Saul, Solomon, the kings of Judah, the kings of the northern

---

27. See L. de Regt, "Devices of Participant Reference in Some Biblical Hebrew Texts: Their Importance in Translation," *Jaarbericht "Ex Oriente Lux,"* 32 (1991–92): 150–71; Christo H. J. van der Merwe, "Discourse Linguistics and Biblical Hebrew Grammar," *Biblical Hebrew and Discourse Linguistics*, ed. Robert D. Bergen, 13–49 (np: Summer Institute of Linguistics, 1994), 34–37.
28. E. J. Revell, *The Designation of the Individual: Expressive Usage in Biblical Narrative* (Kampen, The Netherlands: Kok Pharos Publishing House, 1996), 10.

kingdom and the various designations for foreign kings. For example, in his study of the speeches addressed to king David, he observed that the speeches of subjects who regard David as their king addressed David as "the king." However, those who are not subjects such as the Jebusites and Abner use the "name" David rather than the title of king in their speeches (2 Sam 3:12, 21; 5:6). Similarly, God himself is said to address the king using his name rather than his title as king. The same also is true of the speeches of prophet Nathan to David (2 Sam 7:17; 12:7, 13).[29] Concerning these nuances, Revell observed,

> Where King David addresses others, the choice of designation is determined by the relevance of his royal status to the speech. God is addressed only by 'David.' Where humans are addressed, the choice of designation correlates generally with the status of the person addressed, and the nature of the speech.[30]

According to Revell, "the compound designation 'my lord the king' is used as the first designation of the king in a speech, including a unit of speech within a dialogue."[31] Similarly, Revell paid close attention to designation in the speeches or addresses to priests and prophets. Concerning the use of designation of priests in the speeches of biblical character, Revell observed that the "designation of priests" shows "clear patterns" since it is "typically used in spoken reference" however, "failure to use" the title "suggests lack of the respect due to the holder of the office."[32] On the designation of the prophet, Revell noted that there is a "different possible designation for prophets" which is "less consistent than the use of those for priests and kings." However, the "use of designations in speech appears to be uniform, and generally consistent with expectations derived from the designations of kings."[33] Similarly, Revell investigated the other forms of designations of named individuals especially as patronymics, gentilics, rela-

---

29. Ibid., 94.
30. Ibid., 96.
31. Ibid., 104.
32. Ibid., 162.
33. Ibid., 172.

tionships to unnamed characters, and the different designations employed in the description of God.

Significantly, Revell also described the use of "deferential speech" in the dialogue of biblical characters. Concerning this phenomenon, Revell observed, "[w]here an addressee is superior in status to the speaker, the difference in status is often recognized by the use of 'deferential forms' in the speech."[34] According to Revell, these "deferential speeches" in the dialogue of biblical characters often reflect the social context of the different characters. Similarly, the speeches could also reflect the genre of the speeches because genre such as "request or contradiction, require particular care in presentation, as they may adversely affect the relationship between the speaker and addressee."[35] Hence, often such differences of genre require "polite forms" in the speeches of the speakers. He also observed the occurrences of modal clauses, interrogative clauses, and declarative clauses in these deferential speeches. Furthermore, he observed the unique nature of speeches addressed to God especially in requests, criticism and opposition, thanks and praise and even confessions. Concerning these biblical speeches to God, Revell noted,

> Speech addressed to God, then, shows much the same characteristics as speech addressed to humans, with the exception of the fact that a third person subject is not used to represent the addressee, and not often to represent the speaker. This is an interesting point, as it suggests that the master-servant relationship, and so the language addressed to kings, did not provide the model for speech addressed to God.[36]

Lastly, Revell also shows how interlocutors such as vocatives and the free first person singular pronoun are used in the speeches of biblical characters in order to designate these speeches. He also describes the designation of speaker or addressee by name or title in human speeches or within speeches

---

34. Ibid., 267.
35. Ibid., 269.
36. Ibid., 321.

ascribed to God. The possible implications of this study are quite obvious especially as it relates to the interest of the present study. For example, the thrust of his study already presumed that the speeches of biblical characters are not haphazardly done but reveal a certain degree of consistency that is suggestive of style. To this end, Revell had earlier observed:

> ...it became apparent that the use of designations often follows consistent patterns. This is something of a surprise in material frequently seen as put together from sources which can be recognized by their contrasting features, and as characterized by numerous errors in transmission. Nevertheless, further analysis does not refute the suggestion that the use of different designations for the same character is a matter of choice, not of chance.[37]

Within the understanding of the preceding review, Revell's work underscores the uniqueness of the biblical speeches by his studying of the various designations which introduce the speeches of biblical characters. Similarly, his work also presupposes the uniqueness of the speeches of the biblical characters particularly as seen in the distinctive usage of designation in the speeches of biblical characters in their speeches to each other. In this last point, Revell's study shows that the presence of various designations in the speeches of biblical characters point to their stylistic features because through these designations the narrator reflects social contexts, gender, genre and possibly cultural, religious or even political categories which are necessary to the understanding of biblical narratives. In this understanding, despite the common familiarity with the speeches of biblical characters, they offer important stylistic clues that ultimately point to the purposeful manner in which the speeches are employed by the biblical narrator.

2.2.3. Robert Longacre

The depth and technical nature of his work in *textlinguistic* or biblical discourse has made his work a defining work in the field of *textlinguistics*.

---

37. Ibid., 11.

Dominant Studies on the Literary Features of the Divine Speeches

To this end, it becomes appropriate to consider his perception or understanding of biblical speeches. Longacre observed that like Greek, Slavic and Romanian languages, biblical speeches have a "peak."[38] Concerning this peak, Longacre observed,

> the term discourse peak must be defined relative to other types of prominence in discourse. The very idea of discourse as a structured entity demands that some parts of discourse be more prominent than others. Otherwise, expression would be impossible. Discourse without prominence would be like pointing to a piece of black cardboard and insisting that it was a picture of black camels crossing black sands at midnight.[39]

For Longacre, biblical discourse peaks are what he calls "zones of turbulence" because in this place of discourse there is heightened activity.[40] According to Longacre, there are three general markers of such heightened activity. The first marker of such heightened activity is the use of a "given tense-aspect (or other feature of the verb)" in order "to mark the verbs of some clauses as more crucial to the structure of the discourse than the verbs of other clauses." Through this device, it "is understood that clauses marked by such verbs are of greater prominence."[41] Secondly, the "zone of turbulence" is also indicated "not necessarily" by its connection directly to a verb, but when such particle is attached "at one or more places in the clause to tag the clause as main line."[42] Lastly, a "zone of turbulence" is also marked by "a characteristic word order" whereby the main-line clauses of a discourse are differentiated from the rest of the clauses in a discourse. However, in a distinctive usage by Longacre, the understanding of a discourse peak is synonymous to the climax in a particular narrative by fol-

---

38. Robert E. Longacre, "Discourse Peak As Zone of Turbulence," *Beyond the Sentence: Discourse and Sentential Form*, ed. Jessica R. Wirth (Ann Arbor: Karoma Publishers, 1985), 83.
39. Ibid.
40. Ibid., 83–105.
41. Ibid., 83.
42. Ibid.

lowing the general development of a story. He also identified a possible *thematic* or didactic peak in a narrative.[43]

From the general description of the peak of narrative, Longacre makes a close study of the Hebrew language in comparison to Ga'dang, Totonac, and Greek languages. Longacre draws ten markers of peaks in discourse. These ten markers include the rhetoric of repetition and paraphrase, heightened vividness by a tense shift or person shift, use of quasi-dialogue or dialogue devices such as rhetorical question, dialogue, or drama, change of pace by varying the length of clauses, sentence and paragraph, use of onomatopoeia, increased ratio of verbs to non-verbs, emphasizing categories not on event line, removing usual markers of event line and replacing them with markers found in peak, removing "sequence signals and conjunctions" that give cohesion to a story, and framing the peak of a discourse of one type with the "features of another" or by the placement of one form of literary feature in another one.[44]

In particular relationship to the present review, Longacre's work, *Joseph: A Story of Divine Providence—A Text Theoretical and Textlinguistic Analysis of Genesis 37 and 39–48* shows the application of tagmemic theory to the study of Genesis 37 and 39–48.[45] Here, Longacre explored the several relationships between the characters and their speeches in the immediate pericope of his study. First, he noted that "every language has a system of discourse types" and that "each discourse type has its own characteristic constellation of verb forms" especially in terms of a given tense, aspect, mood which featured chiefly in that discourse type.[46] He divided biblical discourses into narrative, predictive, expository, and hortatory discourses. For example, concerning hortatory speeches, Longacre observed that hortatory discourses or speeches occurred when a character in the biblical text "tries to influence the conduct of another" character.[47] These speech-

---

43. On the use of *weqatal* forms to mark the peak, climatic or pivotal events in biblical narrative see Longacre, *Biblical Hebrew and Discourse Linguistics*, ed. Robert D. Bergen, 50–98 (np: Summer Institute of Linguistics, 1994), 66–91.
44. Ibid., 96.
45. Longacre, *Joseph: A Story of Divine Providence-A Text Theoretical and Textlinguistic Analysis of Genesis 37 and 39–48* (Winona Lake, Indiana: Eisenbraus, 1989), 1–56.
46. Ibid., 59.
47. Ibid., 119.

es include the speeches between a father talking to his son, brothers to brothers, an imprisoned slave-boy to an imprisoned courtier, a commoner to a reigning monarch, a monarch to a commoner, and other dialogue situations. He further noted that such hortatory discourses or speeches "contain variety of linguistic formespecially of mainline verbs, thus not only are imperatives, cohortatives, and jussives found, but also types of mitigated commands." In this purported peculiarity of linguistic forms in hortatory discourses, Longacre described the distinctiveness of hortatory speeches especially when compared to narrative, predictive, and expository discourse types. Significantly, Longacre observed that such hortatory discourses or speeches could be placed in a particular social situation. Hence he earmarked the particulars of such social setting by noting whether the speakers and hearers are peers or the speaker socially speaking is to another character of unequaled status. Even though the quest to frame a distinction between the biblical characters of the Joseph cycle is largely unconvincing, Longacre's thesis that different biblical speech types have distinctive linguistic forms have certain justification since, as subsequent study of the stylistic features of the divine speeches would seek to show, the speeches of biblical characters could be framed stylistically different in order to assert a distinctive point of view. Similarly, Longacre also observed that there are different variations in the framing of the quotative formulas, which introduce biblical speeches. Significantly, Longacre proposed that the discourse markers performed four basic functions in biblical narratives namely for dialogue initiation, continuance, redirection and mid-dialogue dynamics.[48] This distinction in the functions of the discourse markers points ultimately to the use of discourse markers in biblical narrative as a structural device. In addition, Longacre also describes the presence of simple, complex, and compound dialogues in the Joseph cycle. Concerning the simple dialogue, for example, he observed the initiating speech or utterance comes in the form of a question, proposal, or remark. This question, proposal, or remark could either be resolved or unresolved if the resolving utterance by the second speaker is either an answer when the initiating utterance is a question, a response when it is a proposal and statement of evaluation when the

---

48. Ibid., 184.

initiating speech is a remark.[49] In a complex dialogue, however, the fairly simple structure of question-answer, proposal-response, remark-evaluation in the simple dialogue is complicated in complex dialogue by the presence of counter-question if the initiating utterance is a question, a counter-proposal if it is a proposal, and a counter-remark if the initiating speech is a remark. In this process, the speeches of the two speakers reveal alternating, different, and possibly opposing perceptions.[50] Lastly, concerning the compound dialogue, Longacre observed:

> Compound dialogue paragraphs are dialogue that, although one unit, articulate into clear subdivisions, which can be called Exchanges. Each Exchange consists of a single or a complex dialogue, whether resolved or unresolved. At the seam between Exchanges, exclusion of a former or inclusion of a new speaker can occur.[51]

Longacre also discusses other forms of dialogues such as execution and stimulus-response. However, these divisions of dialogues into several types bring not only clarity to the biblical narratives, but also reveal the striking thesis that it is the dialogues in biblical narrative that "carried forward" the plot of the biblical narrative,[52] and most importantly, the dialogue part of the biblical narrative formed the "more dramatic part of the story."[53] In the long run, the significance of the works of Longacre could be underscored in three aspects.[54] Firstly, his works show that biblical speeches are not haphazard, but they are a product of carefully crafted story telling. Indirectly, this thesis further points to the stylistic nature of the biblical speeches particularly in the perception that biblical speeches or discourse have distinc-

---

49. Ibid., 186.
50. Ibid., 190.
51. Ibid., 197.
52. Ibid., 185.
53. Ibid., 205.
54. For Longacre's earlier works see Longacre, *An Anatomy of Speech Notions* (Lisse: Peter de Ridder, 1976); *idem*, "Discourse," *Tagmemics*, vol. 1, Aspects of the Field, eds. R. M. Brend and K. L. Pike (The Hague: Mouton, 1976), 1 – 44; *idem*, *The Grammar of Discourse*. TLL (New York: Plenium, 1983).

tive linguistic forms. Secondly, Longacre's study shows the importance of discourse markers in the initiation, continuance, and redirection of the speeches of biblical characters.[55] Thus, the presence of these discourse markers in biblical narrative ought to alert the readers to the dynamics of biblical discourse markers despite the offhand translations or reading of these discourse markers. Lastly, by categorizing the different dialogues into mainly simple, complex and compound dialogues, Longacre noted the "sophistication" of biblical dialogue especially as seen in the exchange between biblical characters since it points to the possibility of counter-questions, counter-remarks, and counter-proposals between two characters in biblical narratives. Consequently, the presentation of alternating, conflicting and counter-perceptions between biblical characters already suggests the complication of the biblical art of story telling despite its seeming familiarity.[56]

2.2.4. Alviero Niccacci

Alviero Niccacci's work is mainly in the area of Hebrew grammar and the relationship of the grammar to the subject of biblical speeches. In his particular study of the Hebrew verbal system, Niccacci made a distinction between the verbal constructions found in narration and biblical speeches. Niccacci opined that the main development in narration is achieved by the use of a chain of initiating *wayyiqtol* forms while in biblical speeches the mainline of communication is carried out by the use of continuative forms of *wayyiqtol* which have no tense value of their own. Concerning the distinction between biblical narration and speeches in terms of verbal system, Niccacci noted:

> a basic distinction is necessary in order to understand the different verb forms, namely the distinction between historical narrative and direct speech. This distinction is not *a priori*, but rather it is based on the fact that practically every language

---

55. On the subject of redirection of direct speech particularly in reference to specific pattern of character's introduction in biblical narrative see L.J. de Regt, *Participants in Old Testament Texts and the Translator*, 20–22.

56. On a critique of Longacre see David Allan Dawson, *Textlinguistics and Biblical Hebrew*. JSOTSup 177 (Sheffield: Sheffield Academic Press, 1994), 52–69.

uses separate sets of verb forms for these two genres. Historical narrative . . . and direct are, then, meaningful in reference to the verbal system of various languages.[57]

This distinction between biblical narration and speeches has found an earlier expression in the writings of Mark S. Smith and Leslie McFall who had argued differently on certain distinctions between biblical narration and speeches.[58] Smith opined for this distinction along the lines of the imperfect consecutive employed in biblical narration and speeches, while McFall has also noted that the first and second person singular perfect consecutive forms within biblical direct speeches show a change in the stress of the accent to the final syllable, which he claimed is different in biblical narration.[59] Unfortunately, Niccacci observed, "discourse linguists do not make the distinction that is really basic from the point of view of the verb forms used, that is, narrative versus direct speech or comment."[60] For Niccacci, the distinction between narration and direct speech on the basis of the verbal system used is not only true in languages such as French, Spanish, Italian, but also myriad other such languages, hence the need to investigate this phenomenon within the biblical narratives.

Concerning the distinctive verbal system found in biblical narration and speeches, some defining conclusions of Niccacci could be highlighted here.[61] First, on the verbal system employed in biblical narration, Niccacci

---

57. Alviero Niccacci, "On the Hebrew Verbal System," *Biblical Hebrew and Discourse Linguistics*, ed. Robert D. Bergen, 117–137 (np: Summer Institute of Linguistics, 1994), 119.

58. Mark S. Smith, *The Origins and Development of the Waw-Consecutive: Northwest Semitic Evidence from Ugarit to Qumran*. HSS39 (Atlanta: Scholars Press, 1991); Leslie McFall, *The Enigma of the Hebrew Verbal System: Solutions from Ewald to the Present Day*. Historic Texts and Interpreters in Biblical Scholarship (Sheffield: Almond, 1982), 193–97; Robert S. Kawashima, *Biblical Narrative and the Death of the Rhapsode* (Bloomington: Indiana University Press, 2004), 35–76.

59. Different from the views of Niccacci, Dawson had observed that the clause types in narrative and direct speech are the same with the exception that in case of direct speech the first verbal clause is never consecutive. See Dawson, *Textlinguistics and Biblical Hebrew*, 174–75, 187–208, 214–15.

60. Niccacci, "On the Hebrew Verbal System," 119.

61. Similarly, Mats Eskhult has noted the distinction between dialogue and narrative in terms of freer word order in dialogue in contrast to narrative. See Eskhult, *Studies in*

observed, a "narrative text is produced by alternating mainline verb forms (*wayyiqtol*) and secondary-line verb forms (nominal constructions with a finite verb in the second position, or without any finite verb)."[62] In this syntactic relationship, the "first set constitutes a chain of sequential events of pieces of information" or foreground while the "second set signals a break in the chain for a special purpose."[63] This special purpose may include the need to provide "a detail of the main information, or to express the writer's comment on his story, or to restage the story and introduce a new character or some other background."[64] In this relationship, "[a]lternation from one set to another provides relief and displays the writer's strategy of communication."[65] On the other hand, "[d]irect speech is richer than narrative in that it uses more diverse verb forms and constructions" which embraces freely the three temporal domains of past, present and future whereby the narrative is grammatically bound to the past.[66] By nature, "direct speech prefers foreground and straight relationship to the addressee." In its relationship to the past axis, direct speech often begins with "*qatal* or X-*qatal*, continues with *wayyiqtol*, and then behaves exactly with as historical narrative, with *waw-X-qatal* indicating the background."[67] On its description of present tense, direct speech shows a grammatical relationship whereby "both the mainline and the subsidiary line are represented by simple nominal clauses." However, in the description of the future, "the mainline begins with a simple nominal clause (frequently with a participle) or an indicative X-*yiqtol*, and continues with *weqatal*, which constitutes the foreground, while *waw-X-yiqtol* indicates the background."[68] Similarly, the volitive verb namely cohortative, imperative and jussive also feature

---

Verbal and Narrative Technique in Biblical Hebrew Prose. Acta Universitatis Upsaliensis, SSU 12 (Uppsala: Almqvist, 1990), 37–41.
62. Ibid., 131.
63. Ibid.
64. Ibid.
65. Ibid.
66. Ibid.
67. Ibid.
68. Ibid.

prominently in direct speech by their use as the mainline, however, at other times, the secondary line could feature the jussive X-*yiqtol*.

In this perspective, by the positioning of the verbal elements in a sentence or paragraph, the biblical narrator distinguished between his narration and the introduction of direct speech. According to Niccacci, this distinction based on the Hebrew verbal system suggests that within the verbal construction, the biblical narrations are distinctive, and hence point to the general working of the biblical narrative on the basis of its verbal system. This observation that, based on the verbal system, biblical narrations are different from biblical speeches has several implications as conceived by Niccacci. Firstly, it shows on the grounds of the verbal system that there are distinctions in the mind of the biblical writers and readers on the presence and relationships between biblical narrations and speeches.[69] Secondly, it reveals that biblical narration and speeches are possibly framed by means of difference in verbal system as argued by Niccacci in order to create a certain literary effect in the deeper domain of its verbal system. Even though this latter thesis is not pursued by Niccacci, the possibility of the use of language stylistically in the domain of its verbal system may not be farfetched. Lastly, the proposition by Niccacci that through the syntax of the verbal system there is a distinction between narration and speeches placed in biblical narration and speeches in antithetical relationship, thus underscoring the independence and interdependence of this relationship.

Despite the general problem of Niccacci's propositions especially in his insistence that there is a clear-cut distinction between biblical narration and speeches, our present work takes as a point of departure his basic thesis on the distinctiveness of biblical speeches in comparison to biblical narration. As subsequent studies will seek to show, we note that such "distinctiveness" is not primarily on the lines of the verbal system as argued by Niccacci, but on the literary devices employed by the narrator to shape the biblical speeches particularly the divine speeches in the Abrahamic cycle.

---

69. On how the biblical narrative works, Niccacci observed that "[c]hain of *wayyiqtol* in narrative and of *weqatal* in direct speech enhance the 'textuality' of a text; that is, they confer its coherence and consistency . . . They also signal a more-or-less open intervention of the author intended to capture the attention of the reader." See Niccacci, "Analysis of Biblical Narrative," *Biblical Hebrew and Discourse Linguistics*, ed. Robert D. Bergen, 175–197 (np: Summer Institute of Linguistics, 1994), 178.

2.2.5. George Savran

The literary phenomenon of quotations or reported speeches[70] by biblical characters is fairly a common occurrence in biblical narratives, hence George Savran's interest on this "poetics of dialogue."[71] Savran identifies the nature, use and purpose of reported speeches in biblical narrative, especially the retelling or rephrasing of a previous speech by a biblical character. He recognizes that often in repetition of previous reported speech by a biblical character the language and syntax of the original speech are replaced or reworded slightly in order to assert a particular point of interest in the new context. Accordingly, Savran observed, biblical characters quoted each other not "primarily to tell of the past for its own sake, but to recollect" the past "in service of a present argument."[72] Savran underscored the presence and significance of these repetitions in biblical narrative and its relationship to quoted direct speeches. Defining quoted direct speech, Savran observed:

> quoted direct speech has a narrower and more specific meaning: a character actually or purportedly speaks certain words in the course of a story; at a later point in the narrative those words are quoted aloud by the same character or by another, with specific reference to the original locution and the original speaker. The quotation may occur within the same pericope as the original speech, in a later chapter, or even in a later book.[73]

Thus he differentiates this literary phenomenon from the general quotation which embraces broadly "allusions, summaries, and oblique references to other words and phrases" in an earlier pericope.[74] Savran went further to

---

70. On the use of "constructed dialogue" as a replacement for "reported speech" see Deborah Tannen, "Introducing Constructed Dialogue in Greek and American Conversational and Literary Activity," *Direct Speech and Indirect Speech*, ed. Florian Coulmas (Berlin: Walter de Gruyter, 1986), 311–32.
71. George W. Savran, *Telling and Retelling: Quotation in Biblical Narrative* (Bloomington: Indiana University Press, 1988), ix.
72. Ibid., 21.
73. Ibid., 7.
74. Ibid.

differentiate between "verifiable" and "unverifiable" quotations of reported speeches. Savran observed that "verifiable" quotation of reported speeches occurred "where both the original locution and the quotation are presented," on the other hand, "unverifiable" quotation takes place "[w]hen the original speech is not specifically attested in the text."[75] Savran placed more emphasis on the verifiable quoted reported speeches rather than the unverifiable because of the interest of his study to find out the relationship between style and meaning as they occur in these repeated reported speeches of the biblical text.

Similarly, Savran also noted that through the medium of direct speech the biblical narrator shows "attitudes, motivations, and personalities of the characters through their own words."[76] This propensity of the biblical narrator to describe his characters by the means of their own speeches became significant because of the reticent nature of the biblical narrator who tells us little about his character. In these speeches, the reticent narrator dropped the curtain he cast over the characters, and most importantly give them the freedom to express themselves, thus giving the reader the intrigue and complication of the plot of the story. This further adds "dramatic presence" to the story and also serves as a means of confrontation or engagement between the characters of the story since in these speeches the characters come face to face with each other, and their point of interests, concerns, motivations and flaws are verbalized rather than described in narration by the biblical narrator.

Secondly, Savran also observed some formal literary features of these quoted direct speeches. He began first by noting the two basic functions of these quoted reported speeches namely they help to provide information and they also are employed to describe or show confrontational scenes among biblical characters. In addition, Savran described the four basic patterns in which the quoted reported speeches are framed. Firstly, in almost half of all quotations, it describes a situation when "X quotes Y to Z (XYZ), X being the present speaker, or 'quoter,' Y the quoted, original speaker and

---

75. Ibid.
76. Ibid., 12.

Z the listener."⁷⁷ Secondly, the quoted reported speeches are also patterned differently whereby X quotes X to Y (XXY). In this pattern, X represents the speaker quoting himself "from an earlier point in the narrative, and Y is the present listener."⁷⁸ Thirdly, there is also another "heightened" scenario which is primarily confrontation. This heightened scenario is patterned with X quoting Y to Y. In this confrontational scene, X stands for the speaker, and Y is both the original speaker and the one who is also now listening to his own original speech quoted by X. Lastly, there is a few occurrences whereby the narrator intrudes the story and repeats an earlier speech of a character (cf. Jude 21:18; 1 Kgs 12:12).⁷⁹

Savran also briefly referred to divine speech in passing. He recognizes a "noticeable number of quotations" which involve divine speech. These divine speeches include "God's quotations both of himself and human's speeches." However, since the delimitation of his study ruled out quotations of Yahweh's promise to the patriarchs,⁸⁰ it is no wonder that Savran did not pay close attention to literary features of these divine speeches, he merely noted their occurrences and the fidelity and freedom of God in quoting himself or other human speeches, and whether biblical human characters exercises enough freedom in their quotations of divine speeches.

Furthermore, Savran also noted that quotations of previously reported speeches are either shortened, lengthened or paraphrased versions of earlier original speeches. In addition, Savran also stressed the function of quotations in the levels of story and discourse. He differentiated the two terms by observing that story "indicates the world inhabited by the characters, the events of the plot, the behavior and motivations of the actors, the words spoken by them as heard by their fellow characters."⁸¹ On the other hand, he noted that discourse "refers to the means by which the narrator conveys that story and its meaning to the reader. The characters in the text remain unaware of the discourse level, for the biblical narrator always stands

---

77. Ibid., 24.
78. Ibid.
79. Ibid., 25.
80. Ibid., 20.
81. Ibid., 15.

outside the story he narrates."[82] However, the reader "has access to both levels of understanding because like the narrator, he is not confined by the limits of the story-world."[83]

Significantly, Savran observed that there are more direct speeches in the book of Genesis, then anywhere in biblical narratives. To this end, he noted:

> In considering the distribution of quoted direct speech among the narrative books, we find that Genesis contains both the highest number of speeches with verifiable quotations . . . as well as the most individual quotations . . . This particular predilection for the use of quoted direct speech may reflect the exceptional amount of dialogue in the patriarchal narratives.[84]

The observation that Genesis has more quoted reported speeches than any part of biblical narratives, justifies, even though indirectly, our quest to study the divine speeches within this book since it is only appropriate to study the stylistic features of the divine speeches especially in a book already noted for its dominant use of speeches. Thus this "predilection" for speeches or dialogues in Genesis provides the immediate justification for our study of the divine speeches in this book.

Concerning the contribution of Savran to the study of biblical speeches, a few quick remarks must be made. Firstly, Savran shows the intriguing phenomenon of quoted speeches as reported by the biblical characters. He notes the common stylistic changes that do often occur in the process of such exchange. Secondly, Savran also underscores the presence of "formal aspects" that could be seen in the general patterning of these reported speeches. Lastly, Savran stresses the fact that on the discourse level, quotations of speeches by biblical characters are positioned in order to fulfill certain literary functions. For example, there are elements of characterization involved in the framing of these quoted speeches. Thus Savran observed,

---

82. Ibid.
83. Ibid.
84. Ibid., 23.

"[c]haracterization is most often accomplished by having the quoter change the language of his original in a significant and revealing way."[85] In this perspective, the speeches of biblical characters are not haphazardly framed but they are purposely positioned in the storyline in order to underscore literary functions which go beyond their obvious and immediate "dramatic effect." Using this line of thought, the biblical narrator throws away his reticence, and for the moment, by the means of the characters themselves, allowed the reader into their thoughts and speeches. Even though he rarely comments on his characters, through their own speeches, he allowed his readers to become the final judge of these characters.[86] In the long run, the biblical speeches become tools of characterization. Similarly, they also play a role in the development of the plot, shifting of point of view, and to also create ambiguity. In the final analysis, the speeches of biblical characters become a powerful literary device by which the narrator skillfully knits his story.

2.2.6. Cynthia Miller

The writings of Cynthia Miller have primarily explored the syntactical mechanisms in the introduction of direct speeches and their possible discourse-pragmatic functions within biblical narratives. For example, in her work, "Introducing Direct Discourse in Biblical Hebrew Narrative," following this particular work closely, Miller observed that "reported speech permeates the Biblical Hebrew Bible" and "[a]lmost half of narrative is reported speech."[87] She divided the reported speech into two parts namely the *quotation*, which represents the original locution, and the *quotative frame*, the indicator or the report which introduces the quotation. She largely focused on the relationship between the *quotative frame* and the semantics of the *quotation*. Miller began by observing that "reported speech is essentially reflexive" since "it is language describing language" and thus it

---

85. Ibid., 80.
86. Clines noted that the biblical narrative "avoids the didactic and dogmatic" modes of communication and rather "insisting its readers judge for themselves the persons and the acts they encounter in its pages." See Clines, *Interested Parties: The Ideology of Writers and Readers of the Hebrew Bible*. JSOTSupp. Series 205 (Sheffield: Sheffield Academic Press, 1995), 189.
87. Savran, *Telling and Retelling*, 199.

is a kind of *metalanguage*. This term is generally used to describe language used to talk about language.[88]

Furthermore, Miller identifies on the basis of the syntactical forms of the quotative frames,[89] (that is, the discourse markers which introduce biblical speeches), the following consistencies in the introduction of direct speeches in biblical narratives. Firstly, Miller realizes that single-verb frames with one finite speech are commonly used to introduce biblical speeches. Secondly, she also discovers that multiple-verb frames with two or more speech verbs which refer to the same locutionary act are also employed in the introduction of the biblical speeches. Lastly, she also shows that one finite verb and an infinitival form of the verb אמר, that is, לאמר are also used in the introduction of biblical speeches. For Miller, she invested a lot of interest in the use of לאמר in the introduction of biblical speeches because she realizes that this discourse marker is not a gerundive infinitive, but a complementizer (that is, introducing the complement of a direct speech), and also exhibits unusual patterns of pronominal reference, and could be used to introduce a reported speech even where the matrix verb or main verb is not a speech verb. She discovers that the discourse-pragmatic function of לאמר as discourse markers in a given pericope is largely dependent on certain linguistic considerations such as syntactic, semantic, and pragmatic factors. These factors include the semantic use of the matrix verb, the distribution of matrix verbs within three frames, identification of central and marginal configurations, identification of marked and unmarked constructions and the possible inferences drawn from the larger context in which this discourse marker is situated. Noting the specifics of Miller's work, especially on the use of לאמר as a quotative frame in the introduction of biblical speeches, she observed that they should not be treated as gerundive infinitives because of three reasons. Firstly, it does not exhibit ordinary features closely associated with the internal syntax of infinitives. Secondly, "the semantics of the matrix verb" do not provide "circumstantial information" to the main verb as commonly conceived to be the function

---

88. Ibid., 200.
89. Cynthia L. Miller, "Introducing Direct Discourse in Biblical Hebrew Narrative," *Biblical Hebrew and Discourse Linguistics*, ed. Robert D. Bergen, 199–241 (np: Summer Institute of Linguistics, 1994), 199–241.

of gerundive infinitives. Lastly, the external syntax of לֵאמֹר reveals that it is not a verbal complement; hence it is not reinforcing the idea of the main verb.[90]

Consequently, Miller noted, "[a] better approach is to see לֵאמֹר as an infinitive that has become grammaticalized as a complementizer introducing the complement of direct speech."[91] This understanding inevitably "explains two important syntactic features of לֵאמֹר: its appearance always at the end of the quotative frame immediately preceding the quotation and its failure to govern subjects, objects, prepositional phrases, or adverbial phrases" which are partly the functions of infinitives. In the argument for the treatment of לֵאמֹר as a "complementizer" Miller draws on the distinctive discourse-pragmatic functions of לֵאמֹר especially when compared to the quotative frames with single verb or multiple verbs. For example, she noted the obligatory configurations of לֵאמֹר in connection with the "greatest number of metapragmatic verbs and expressions."[92] She highlighted fourteen metapragmatic verbs that are obligatory tied to לֵאמֹר. These metapragmatic verbs include אלה (Hiphil) "to take an oath," באר "to give news," דין (Niphal) "to argue with," דרש "to seek," חנן "to implore favor," חרש "to be silent," ידע (Hiphil) "to cause to know," כחש "to lie," נבא (Hithpael) "to prophesy," סות "to incite," עוד (Hiphil) "to testify," פאר (Piel) "to boast," צחק "to laugh," and רמה "to deceive." Similarly, she also emphasized ten biblical expressions which are syntactically tied to לֵאמֹר. These ten expressions include גלה אזן "to uncover ears," הנה דבר יהוה "behold the word of Yahweh was to," הציא דבה "to cause an evil report to go out," מצות "commandment," ספר "letter," נתן מופת "to give a sign," העביר קול "to cause the sound to cross over/through," הרנה עביר "a shout crossed over/through," and שׂים עלילת דברים "to put wantonness of words."[93]

In addition, using the parameters of centrality and marginality of the three quotative frames to matrix verbs, Miller also underscored the centrality of לֵאמֹר to matrix verbs such as דבר "to speak" זעק and צעק "to cry

---

90. Ibid., 207.
91. Ibid., 209.
92. Ibid., 213.
93. Ibid.

out," נגד "to tell," (both Hiphil and Hofal stems), צוה "to command," שאל "to ask," שבע "to swear," (both Niphal and Hiphil), שלח "to send," בכה "to weep," כתב "to write," שמע "to hear," and with the communication expression השיב דבר "to cause word to return." Differentiating between central and obligatory configurations, Miller noted, "[a]n obligatory configuration must occur with a particular matrix verb (or verb phrase) and carries *no* discourse-pragmatic function" whereas "[a] central configuration occurs most commonly with a particular matrix verb (or verb phrase) and *does* carry a discourse-pragmatic function."[94] In the same way, Miller employed the criteria of frequency, complexity and prototypicality in order to describe the markedness of לֵאמֹר. For example, on prototypicality, that is, the degree by which a speech-act reflects an experiential speech event, she recognizes that לֵאמֹר captured even a non-dialogue situation especially where the two dialogue participants are not immediately together. This is clearly seen in the use of כתב "to write" as an index "written communication which takes across distance and in a nonverbal medium."[95] However, this verb is only found in the quotative frame of לֵאמֹר rather than the other two. In the same way, שמע "'to hear' does not index communication but rather the reception of communication."[96]

Building on the insights of the above work, her major work, *The Representation of Speech in Biblical Hebrew Narrative*, explored broadly the highlighted categories, but also extended the horizon in the study of biblical speeches by additional emphases.[97] For example, Miller shows the narrator's use of reported speech even when no speech event is being reported and the possibility of a seemingly reportage of dialogue even though no interaction between speech participants is being represented. She also shows the intriguing relationship between biblical conversation and narration. In particular, she notes the use of *waw* ('and') as a discourse marker. Concerning this conjunction, Miller observed,

---

94. Ibid., 214.
95. Ibid., 230.
96. Ibid., 231.
97. Miller, *The Representation of Speech in Biblical Hebrew Narrative: A Linguistic Approach.* HSM 55 (Winona Lake, Indiana: Eisenbrauns, 2003).

The conjunction *waw*, which regularly conjoins nominal phrases, verbal phrases, clauses, and sentences, occasionally occurs at the beginning of a direct quotation. In this context, the conjunction serves as a discourse marker to connect (often contrastively) the speech it introduces to a previous speech of the same speaker or a different speaker.[98]

She presented three possible contexts whereby *waw* serves as a discourse marker. The first context is when the "quotation beginning with *waw* bears a connection to a previous speech by the same speaker."[99] In this context, "*waw* signals to the hearer that a connection should be made between the speech event at hand and a previous speech event of the same type by the same speaker."[100] However, in the second context, "a speaker's quotation begins with *waw* when the conjunction serves to provide a logical connection or link with the other speaker's previous pair-part, often as a way of refuting or rejecting it."[101] In the third context, where *waw* is used as a discourse marker, "two or more successive pair-parts are attributed to a single speaker in a decidedly one-sided conversation." For example, this use of *waw* as a discourse marker to describe the speeches of a single speaker occurred in Genesis 17:1–16. In this example, four consecutive quotations are attributed to Yahweh. This "interposition of additional quotative frames within the deity's lengthy speech" breaks the speeches into clearly defined parts.[102] As we are going to also see in our study of this pericope, Miller observed that the first discourse marker introduces the topic of God's covenant with Abram, the second discourse marker describes God's responsibilities in the covenant and it is introduced by אני or "I." The third discourse marker indicates Abraham's responsibilities and the quotation opens with a "speech-initial *waw*" which is attached to a second person pronoun, ואתה, "and you." The last discourse marker describes the responsibilities of Saraiʾ in

---

98. Ibid., 262.
99. Ibid., 263.
100. Ibid.
101. Ibid., 264.
102. Ibid., 267.

the covenant and it is introduced by the name שׂרי (Sarai).¹⁰³ This illustration shows the use of a discourse marker as a segmenting device in a single speech of a character.

Miller also notes there are some linguistic or literary indicators in the speeches of biblical characters that point to their social status. The speakers of the biblical narratives often use deferential terms in their addresses in order to indicate the "social distance" or "social intimacy" between them and the person they are addressing. According to Miller, some of the terms used to show "social distance" in the speeches of biblical characters include, אדני "my lord," המלך "the king," אדני המלך "my lord the king," השׂר "the officer," איש אלהים "man of God," and ברוך יהוה "blessed of YHWH." On the other hand, some of the terms in the speeches of biblical characters that are indicators of "social intimacy" include אבי "my father," אמי "my mother," אחי "my brother," אחותי "my sister," בני "my son," and בתי "my daughter." Miller also describes the presence of semi-direct speeches within biblical narratives. These are a "quotation in which specific details of the original discourse are replaced by more general terms such as כה 'thus,' זה 'this' (m.), זאת 'this' (f.), or פלני אלמני 'such and such.'"¹⁰⁴ She observes that semi-direct speech "does not purport to be a verbatim account of the speech event, or even a paraphrase of it; it is a literary construct used to condense information in the narrative."¹⁰⁵ Examples of semi-direct speeches could be in Genesis 24:30; 1 Samuel 17:27, 21:3–4; 2 Samuel 17:21; 1 Kings 1:6, 2:30, 14:5; Judges 18:4; Joshua 7:20–21; 2 Kings 5:4, 9:12, 6:8; and Ruth 4:1.

Similarly, Miller also notes the presence of "internal speech" within biblical narrative. This occurrence of internal speech, also known as "monologue", is a "process of thinking-speaking" whereby a biblical character conducts "internal dialogue with oneself."¹⁰⁶ In the internal speech, things very intimate are shared and the motivation for a character's course of action are presented, explained, or even interpreted. Furthermore, Miller observed:

---

103. Ibid.
104. Ibid., 281.
105. Ibid.
106. Ibid., 291.

Although Hebrew has a number of verbs for the representation of mental processes (e.g., חשׁב "to think," זכר "to remember," הגה "to meditate"), these verbs are almost never found in quotative frames introducing the content of thought. Most often the content of thought is represented as an internal quotation introduced with a matrix speech verb. The narrative representation of thought as speech contributes to the development of characterization as the character's internal point of view is presented.[107]

In addition, Miller notes the presence of other non-conversational reported speeches in biblical narratives. Some examples of these non-conversational reported speeches include the Levitical regulations in Leviticus 11:1–47 and the priestly creation account in Genesis 1:3–30 where the entire narrative is cast in a "reported speech." In a sense, the presence of these narratives in the Bible which are framed as a kind of "reported speech" clearly shows the dominance of "dialogues or speeches" in the thought of the minds that wrote the Bible stories.

From the following reviews, the significance of Miller's work is no doubt obvious. However, two important aspects of her work to the present study in passing must be hereby underscored. Firstly, Miller's work reiterated the presupposition that biblical speeches themselves in relationship to their discourse markers revealed a certain consistency that warrants study, hence the quest to categorize or to label these perceived linguistic patterns. Secondly, she emphasized the stylistic relationship between the quotative frame and the direct speeches, thus pointing to the intriguing relationship between the direct speeches and the narrative where these speeches are found. To this end, Miller rightly observed, reported speech in biblical narratives "involves unique and intriguing complexities."[108]

Despite the many benefits of her work as a springboard for our present study, this study differs from hers. Firstly, our present interest lies in the presence and use of literary devices such as metaphor, simile, euphemism,

---

107. Ibid.
108. Ibid., 3.

hyperbole, paronomasia, repetition, irony, and suspense in the divine speeches rather than merely on the quotative frames which introduce the divine speeches. Moreover, this study is a departure from Miller's work in its quest to find an overall purpose in the use of the "elevated language" in the divine speeches particularly within the context of the Abrahamic cycle. Lastly, the central interest of Miller's work is built around the metapragmatic use of the discourse marker לֵאמֹר and other such related concerns, thus justifying her use of linguistic methodology. The interest, however, of the present study is primary within the literary studies, hence our focus on some concentration of stylistic devices in the divine speeches.

Similarly, we must pause here briefly in order to note the converging importance of these previous works that have generally been done on biblical speeches. Despite their various methods, concerns and persuasions, they show four basic trends. Firstly, they establish the importance of speeches in biblical narratives. Secondly, they show that there are stylistic devices which are often built in and around biblical speeches. Thirdly, they present the dominant place of the speeches of the characters in charting the main focus of a particular pericope or book especially as it relates to the subject of characterization, since the biblical narrator is reticent about his characters or even the purpose of his entire narratives. Lastly, these previous studies have shown that biblical speeches are not randomly placed or positioned but located, arranged or organized purposefully by the biblical narrator.

2.3. Specific Studies on Divine Speeches

Unfortunately, there are few works that concentrate mainly on a literary study of the divine speeches. This negligence is ironic because the entire biblical narrative is understood or conceived as the "word of God." However, the occurrence, nature and stylistic features of the divine speeches, whether in prose or poetry, have received little or no attention. The reasons for this neglect are many; however, two reasons could be mainly responsible for this neglect.

Firstly, the overriding traditional Christian and Jewish assumptions of the Scriptures as the "word of God," hence it presupposes that treatment of any part of the biblical narrative is generally conceived as a study of "God's word." Ironically, this canonical tendency in the traditional reading of the entire Bible as God's word normally does not allow a careful study of the speeches of God who is represented as a character in the text. Even though it is true that the Bible is "God's word" to the community of faith, since God is also represented as a "character" in the story which makes up the Bible with his distinctive personality, and sometimes even speeches, there is no justifiable reason to ignore or discourage the treatment of God as a character in the text of the Bible. In fact, it is actually a disservice to God, especially in places where the biblical narrator distinguished God in his speeches, not to pay careful attention to the stylistic features by which God is literarily represented.

Secondly, the modern and postmodern idea of God often imposes its agenda on biblical studies. Last century saw the thriving of the "death of God" movement, which basically described the "non-existence of God." However, the present century has rediscovered "God" but it is an "impersonal" deity "which" or "who" looks totally different from the biblical representation of God. This postmodern depiction of God has its influence directly or indirectly on the general study of God within the Bible since often it is the ideological agenda of a particular age that normally colors its treatment or interpretation of the Scriptures. Unfortunately, this trend did not allow any serious engagement of God as a literary representation within the biblical text; rather energy was largely exhausted in the theological defense of his existence, attributes and personality in reaction to this postmodern agenda.

Despite these trends, a few individuals have undertaken to underscore the literary representation of God as a character in biblical stories, and most importantly, the presence of stylistic features in the speeches attributed to God. Even though these attributed speeches to the divine being are conceived to be framed primarily in order to underscore or assert a particular theology, some studies in this area have shown that the narrator did not describe or transcribe these attributed speeches indifferently rather he employed stylistic features or elevated language to further underscore the importance of these speeches. Even though not every divine speech is placed or framed in such literary style, and it would be exaggeration to talk of "divine language" in the biblical narrative, there are some narratives that show some stylistic features which we could not readily ignore.[109] It is such stylistic features that preoccupied the works of Casper Labuschagne, Samuel Meier, Hugh White and Wilfried Warning.[110]

2.3.1. Casper Labuschagne

Labuschagne's work has been described as "an arithmetical exercise" in the study of the divine speeches.[111] To understand the works of Labuschagne, one must first understand the overriding presupposition of his work. One particular presupposition that formed the premises for his work is his assumption of the presence and use of a numerological framework in the composition of the Pentateuch. For Labuschagne, this numerological framework is unlocked by paying adequate attention to the "divine speeches." In his work, *The Pattern of the Divine Speech Formulas in the Pentateuch*, Labuschagne opined that a "consistent" pattern of the divine speeches in the Pentateuch "might prove to be the key to the solution of the problem of the literary structure of the Pentateuch."[112] According to Labuschagne, the divine formula occurred in cases when Yahweh "is the subject of the verbs *'āmar, dibbèr, qārā'* and *ṣiwwāh*, and where the noun *dābār* is used in connection with YHWH."[113] He observed such divine speeches as a compositional formula which guides the composition of the Pentateuch, that could be traced in Genesis-Numbers and even within the

---

109. Agreed, as observed by Savran, "[o]n a purely literary level, the narrator treats God like any other figure" and that "[t]here is no particular vocabulary or syntactic features" which indicate that a "divine speech" [Savran, *Telling and Retelling*, 88] is different from other biblical characters; however, there are times when stylistic features of the divine speeches set it apart from other speeches of biblical characters.

110. Yehuda Radday and Haim Shore using computer-based methodology which they defined as "statistical linguistic approach" also engaged in showing the division of the biblical narration in Genesis along the line of the narrator, human speech and divine speech, their work is not reflected here because it is not literary but focuses more on statistical information. See Yehuda Radday and Haim Shore, *Genesis: An Authorship Study in Computer-Assisted Statistical Linguistic* (Rome: Biblical Institute, 1985).

111. Philips R. Davies and David M. Gunn, "Pentateuchal Patterns: An Examination of C.J. Labuschagne's Theory," *VT* 34, no. 4 (1984), 406.

112. Casper J. Labuschagne, "The Pattern of the Divine Speech Formulas in the Pentateuch," *VT* 3 (1982), 268.

113. Ibid.

book of Deuteronomy.[114] Beginning from the book of Genesis, he recognized that "there were clusters of divine speech formulas in the book of Genesis."[115] He observed that in addition to the ten divine formulas found in the story of creation in Genesis 1 and the flood story in Genesis 6–9, "clusters of *seven*" occur in Genesis 3, 15, 17, 31 and 35 "which seem to be deliberately so constructed."[116] There are also a "smaller clusters of *three*" in Genesis 12 and 46:1–4, and "*four*" in Genesis 4, 16, 18:1–5 and 32:23–33. Numerically, these divine speeches form the cluster of 7 + 4 or 3 + 1.[117] According to Labuschagne, this pattern of the divine speeches in clusters of seven, three or four is employed as a numerological compositional device in the composition of Genesis. In this perspective, "the clusters of seven divine speech formulas occur right through Exodus and Leviticus till the end of Numbers, totalling four series of seven clusters of seven formulas."[118]

Similarly, Labuschagne also underscored the "crucial part played by the verb *qārā'* in the overall structure of the Tetrateuch."[119] He noted that this verb occurred 23 times with Yahweh as subject with the two instances in Genesis 35:10b and Numbers 12:5 where the verb is integrated in a cluster of seven formulas. The remaining 21 occurrences of the verb are found first in one series of seven instances in the Primeval story, and a series of three instances in Genesis 21–22, thus forming a 7 + 3 pattern of this verb in Genesis. This pattern is continued in Exodus with a second series of seven at 24:16 and the third series of seven beginning in Exodus 31:2 and ending in Numbers 11:3. Further reiterating this pattern of 7 + 4 or 3 + 1 in the framing of the divine speeches, Labuschagne observed:

---

114. See Labuschagne, "Some Significant Composition Techniques in Deuteronomy," *Scripta Signa Vocis: Studies about Scripts, Scriptures, Scribes and Languages in the Near East Presented to J. H. Hospers*, ed. H. L. J. Vanstiphout *et al* (Groningen: Egbert Forsten, 1986), 121–31.
115. Ibid., 268.
116. Ibid.
117. See also Labuschagne, "Additional Remarks on the Pattern of the Divine Speech Formulas in the Pentateuch," *VT* 34, no. 1 (1984): 91–95.
118. Labuschagne, "The Pattern of the Divine Speech Formulas in the Pentateuch," 269.
119. Ibid.

It is obvious that *qārā'* is a major structural element in the Tetrateuch. It functions as a key-word in a long-range bracketing system which not only unites and gives structure to the four series of seven clusters of seven formulas in the books of Exodus, Leviticus and Numbers, but also brackets together the entire body of material in the Tetrateuch by its three series of seven occurrences from Genesis to Numbers.[120]

Labuschagne also further noted that the pattern of 7 + 4 or 3 + 1 in the divine speeches as seen in the framing of *qārā'* is also consistent with the presence and use of the word *dabar*.[121] In addition, Labuschagne also observed that phrases such as "this is the word which Yahweh commanded" or זֶה הַדָּבָר אֲשֶׁר צִוָּה יְהוָה with *ṣiwwāh* or צִוָּה forming almost the same pattern of 7 + 3 + 1 as *qārā'*. The same is also true of the phrase "as the Lord spoke to Moses" or כַּאֲשֶׁר צִוָּה יְהוָה אֶת־מֹשֶׁה, and its variant phrase "as the Lord spoke to Moses and Aaron."[122] Labuschagne also reiterated the use of the phrase "according to the mouth of Yahweh" or עַל־פִּי יְהוָה within this numerological scheme of seven in the book of Numbers. The same observation is also true of *wayyōʾmer* ("and he said") with Yahweh as the subject in Genesis. This discourse marker also forms a numerological scheme of 7 + 3 + 1.[123] In many cases, this numerological scheme as reflected by the use of the divine speech functioned, according to the Labuschagne, as an introductory device which served as a "reliable criterion for delimitating coherent pericopes."[124] For example, the use of the divine speeches as an introductory device for the opening of new sections could be seen in the book of Exodus especially in the Red Sea episode (13:20–17:7), Sinai (19:1–3a), and the building of the Tabernacle (34:29–40:38). On the other hand, Labuschagne recognizes the absence of the pattern of 7 + 4 or 3 + 1 in the book of Deuteronomy. Instead, the book has a preference for the framing of the divine speeches in the series of ten and eight. For Labuschagne, it

---

120. Ibid., 270.
121. Ibid., 272.
122. Ibid., 271.
123. Ibid., 274.
124. Ibid., 276.

"cannot be a matter of coincidence" that the divine speeches in the book of Deuteronomy are patterned in the numbers of ten and eight. The pattern of the divine speech in the series of ten, Labuschagne noted, might be in imitation of the ten in the Decalogue.[125]

In conclusion, it is necessary to underscore the problems of numerological composition of the Pentateuch as promoted by Labuschagne on the basis of divine speeches.[126] Davies and Gunn had shown a series of flaws in his works particularly in its miscalculation of the divine speech formulas and most importantly its subjective imposition of a numerological structure on the biblical narrative along the lines of the divine speeches.[127] In particular, Davies and Gunn have questioned the optional or subjective nature by which phrases are included or excluded from the label of the divine speech formula. For them, Labuschagne's result comes from his "interpretative framework" which tends to manipulate data.[128] They have also questioned his subjective and inconsistent use of the terms such as "cluster," "series," and "bracket" in his definition of the divine speeches, and thus rendering his conclusions as "invalid."[129]

Though Labuschagne himself responded to these criticisms, some of the basic observations of these criticisms have generally remained.[130] To be fair to Labuschagne, some merits of his works could also be highlighted. Three of these merits are closely related to the study of the divine speeches by this present study. Firstly, even if the basic hypothesis of Labuschagne appears to be largely problematic, the evidence marshalled by him on the centrality of the divine speeches in the composition of the Pentateuch cannot be jettisoned or easily ignored since the biblical narratives themselves assume the importance of these divine speeches. Secondly, his observation on the im-

---

125. Ibid., 279.
126. Labuschagne has also undertaken the study of the Psalms based on numerological framework. See Labuschagne, "Significant Compositional Techniques in the Psalms: Evidence for the Use of Number as an Organizing Principle," *VT* 59 (2009): 583–605.
127. Davies and Gunn, "Pentateuchal Patterns: An Examination of C.J. Labuschagne's Theory," 399–406.
128. Ibid., 402.
129. Ibid., 406.
130. C. J. Labuschagne, "Pentateuchal Patterns: A Reply to P. R. Davies and D. M. Gunn," *VT* 34, no. 4 (1984): 407–413.

portance of the divine speeches particularly in Genesis and the possibility of its use as a "consistent" literary device bears on the present quest to show the artistic features of the divine speeches in Abrahamic narratives. Lastly, the overriding literary unity framed around the divine speeches as argued by Labuschagne already justified the synchronic treatment of the stories in the Abrahamic cycle despite the diversity of its sources.

2.3.2. Hugh White

If the work of Labuschagne is "arithmetical" or even a mathematical exercise in divine speeches as labeled by Davies and Gunn, the work of White should be labeled a "philosophical one" on the divine speeches since it seeks to find the "logic" of the divine voice or speech in biblical narratives especially as reflected in the narratives of Genesis.[131] Thus he employed philosophical-semiotic reflections in order to underscore the intriguing relationship between divine speeches, the speeches of other characters, and effacing of the narrator. Concerning the philosophical nature of his work, White himself modestly said:

> The philosophical enigma here is how to speak of the divine voice in the inner dialogue of a human being . . . Our primary concern, however, is not the philosophical issue but rather the way in which this issue arises and is treated within Biblical literature, and particularly the 'logic' of narrative literature.[132]

In particular, White noted that the narratives of Genesis are the best part of the Bible where the intriguing presence of the divine voice should be studied since the first occurrence of the "divine speech" occurred here.[133] White questioned the function of the divine voice or speech in biblical narratives, and hence he asked, "[i]s the divine Voice a personage in this narrative, unequivocally, or does it rather perform some of the function of the

---

131. Hugh C. White, *Narration and Discourse in the Book of Genesis* (New York: Cambridge University Press, 1991).
132. Ibid., 96.
133. Ibid., 99.

narrator?"[134] Since according to White, the "chief function of the character" in a narrative is to serve as a "voice" for the narrator, thus the divine voice acts as an external consciousness which is situated outside of the enclosed world of the narrative through whom the narrator speaks to the reader.[135] The divine voice is the only voice in biblical narrative not from this world. It is from the world outside the world of biblical characters, that is, a world which is celestial, thus it comes to the reader of biblical narratives, especially in Genesis, like a second "consciousness" or "otherness" within the story. Similarly, White placed the narrator on the same plane namely outside the world of the story. The narrator, in a sense, is outside the story by his effacement or reticence, and the divine character is placed outside the locus of human context; that is, he is not like other characters that are from a clearly defined social, political, cultural or economic context. In fact, the narrator "confined" his characters to "the internal world of the narratives."[136] Concerning the place of the divine speech within this narrative scheme, White observed, "[i]t is obvious that the divine voice does not belong to the closed, relativistic world of the expressive narrative."[137] In particular, White noted:

> It is here, then, that we can discern the general location of the divine Voice in the discursive structure of the Genesis narrative. The divine Voice is presented as the voice of a personage by the narrator, since the narrator speaks of 'he' when referring to the instance of the divine speech. But unlike a personage, the Voice does not speak from a recognizable position within the social structure or spatial/temporal register within which the characters exist. Neither the narrator's discourse nor the direct discourse of the characters usually provide any clues as to the outer form, or the social and physical position of the divine Voice in relation to the human spatio-temporal sphere.[138]

---

134. Ibid.
135. Ibid.
136. Ibid., 100.
137. Ibid.
138. Ibid., 101.

This unique feature of the divine voice or character made him the same as the narrator, but also different from him and even the author. In this scheme, is the divine Voice a constructed "ideological character" by which the narrator sanctions, critiques or interprets cultural, political and social categories of his world? For White, the divine speech is fundamental in Genesis because the characters of Genesis become only characters in any sense from their direct interaction or relationship to the divine Voice or speech. This observation is true of biblical characters such as Adam as well as Abram.[139] According to White, the divine speech "provides a perspective from beyond the closed world of the personages" and hence become important in this role.[140] Importantly, the narrator often maintains a "passive stance towards the divine Voice" despite the apparent significance of the divine speech, hence pointing more to the ideological functions of these divine speeches. Underscoring the place of the divine speeches as interpretative framework, White further revealed:

> But by representing the third subject-of-consciousness as a fully independent personal divine Voice who is clearly separated from the narrator, and speaks to the characters in direct speech, the narrator provides a specific interpretative framework for understanding the characters and the events.[141]

White opined that the otherness of the divine Voice or speech presents itself as an "ideology" and in this "ideology" the "self-contained narrative world" and "the world beyond the story", that is the world of the "actual author", actually converged.[142] The convergence is found in "intersubjective" category, which linked these two worlds together. This "intersubjective" category, White understood to be found in the term "promise" and it is not surprising that the divine speech could be categorized as "promises." Noting the "intersubjective" nature of "promise" White further observed:

---

139. Ibid., 102.
140. Ibid.
141. Ibid., 103.
142. Ibid.

> For the Biblical narrative, it is clear that the presence of the human character is found upon a promissory world which establishes her/his consciousness as intersubjective, and that the source of this promise is a Voice which speaks from the boundary into the narrative world which both the character and the author share . . .[143]

In the category of promise within the divine speeches, the world of the author and the narrative is linked, thus making the divine speeches a very important segment of the biblical narratives since within them we see possible clues of the motifs or motivations for the telling of the biblical narratives. Even though it is a sweeping claim to make, the divine speeches as studied by White provide us a window into the interests or ideology of the author of Genesis. In a particular sense, "[t]he recovery of the past" by the narrator "is a recovery of her/his own subjective past, and the projection of the future by the promisor", so the divine speeches "open[s] up a future also for the promisee as it is accepted in faith."[144] In the divine speeches, the past, the present and the future converge, and so also the interests of the author, and possibly the original readers.

We must pause to stress the significance of White's semiotic conclusions on the present study. In this particular sense, two influences of his work on the present study could be highlighted. Firstly, we shall use his treatment of the divine speeches as "otherness" or what he understood as a "third subject-of-consciousness" in order to stress the uniqueness and importance of the divine speeches in chapter 4 of the dissertation. Secondly, in the same chapter, we will also use his treatment of divine speeches as specimens of the author's ideology in our study of the functions of the divine speeches. Thus, we shall treat the bulk of the divine speeches in White's category of an "intersubjective" frame which connects the worlds of the author and his original audience.

---

143. Ibid., 105.
144. Ibid., 104.

2.3.3. Wilfried Warning

The work of Wilfried Warning on divine speeches is clearly within the field of structuralism. Working from the book of Leviticus, he shows that the divine speeches were not haphazardly placed within the book, but their positioning in the book is a product of stylistic arrangement. Warning persuasively argued that the structure of the book of Leviticus is primarily built around the divine speeches, particularly in the "repetition of the formulaic phrase, 'and the Lord spoke to Moses'" or Aaron. Hence he observed:

> It has never been proposed that the possibly deliberate distribution of this introductory formula may be the key for deciphering the overall structural outline of Leviticus. It is my contention that if taken seriously as a structural device, the formulaic introductory addresses bring to light a significant structure encompassing the whole book of Leviticus.[145]

Warning proposed that there are thirty-seven occurrences of the formulaic address in the book which are distributed throughout the book of Leviticus. Using the framing of the divine speeches as a structural literary device, Warning largely shows how the narrator employed numerological devices such as seven, chiastic structures, open-envelopes, wordplay, identical verbal and nominal forms in order to craft skillfully the entire book of Leviticus. In this sense, the divine speeches are not accidental but they are framed as a structural device for the entire book. In this perspective, Warning treated the use of the divine speeches as a structural device on two levels namely on the microstructural and macrostructural dimensions. Concerning the use of the divine speeches on the microstructural level, Warning shows, for example, the employment of the verb דבר as a structuring device. On the use of דבר, he noted, "[i]n contradiction to the general notion that common words are of minimal value in indicating structure, the common verb 'speak' . . . seems to function as a structural device in several" divine speeches.[146]

---

145. Wilfried Warning, *Literary Artistry in Leviticus* (Leiden: Brill, 1999), 37.
146. Ibid., 65.

Dominant Studies on the Literary Features of the Divine Speeches

Similarly, he underscores the use of particle כל, and nouns such as דם, אש, קדש, ארץ in structures of the divine speeches which are framed or based on the number seven.[147] He also shows the chiastic structures around the nouns נפש, בגד, מלאכה, and the phrase יהיה לכם and ארץ מצרים on the microstructural level of the divine speeches.[148] Noting the importance of these chiastic structures, Warning observed, "chiastic structures impart literary integrity and, at times, enhance the theological message."[149] In addition, Warning notes how divine אני, the verb מות, the noun ברית, and the verb פרר are framed in an open-envelope structures in these speeches.[150] Similarly, on this same microstructural level, Warning also observes the place of the verb יצא, the phrase פתח אהל מועד, the noun חקה, and the wordplay on אשה as a stylistic form of a closely-enveloped structure in the divine speeches.[151] In the conclusion to his study at the microstructural level of the artistic nature of the divine speeches in Leviticus, Warning further observed, "Leviticus has been artistically arranged according to thirty-seven distinct" Divine speeches.[152] In particular, each divine speech appears "to exhibit definite literary designs, such as seven part, chiastic, numerological, open-envelope, envelope, and 'identical verbal/nominal' structures."[153]

On the other hand, he also presented the macrostructural framing of Leviticus on divine speeches. On the macrostructural level, he also notes the seven-part structures around the nouns גוי, פרכת, and the verb שבר.[154] Similarly, Warning also observes that on this high-level structure there are chiastic structures around the verbs יצק, טבל, and the phrase ארץ מצרים. In addition, there are numerological structures around the verbs מצא, שלח, ירא, שקן, דשׁף, נשׂא; nouns כליות, קרן, בקר, שעיר; and phrases על המזבח סביב, אל יסוד המזבח. In addition, Warning also underscores the open-envelope structures by the use of the noun איל and the

---

147. Ibid., 66.
148. Ibid., 82.
149. Ibid.
150. Ibid., 115.
151. Ibid., 120.
152. Ibid., 129.
153. Ibid.
154. Ibid., 133.

closed envelope on the noun תֹּועֵן. Lastly, Warning also sees style in the identical verbal and nominal forms of the noun רצן. Concerning the relationship between the microstructural and macrostructural structures which are framed by the means of the divine speeches, Warning noted:

> The investigation of the microstructure of the different Divine Speeches has revealed numerous literary devices, most of which were based on numerical notions. By means of these complex, creatively employed techniques not only has textual cohesiveness been created but at the same time significant theological statements were made. Repeatedly proof of the inextricable interrelation of form and content was given. Therefore we should not wonder that even on the macrostructural level the same literary devices have been used by the ancient author in order to create long-range connective links on the structural and theological levels.[155]

On these two levels of structures, Warning underscored a conscious literary artistry in the mind of the ancient narrator who knits his work skillfully by the help of the divine speeches. In this perspective, according to Warning, the divine speeches are not accidentally placed or haphazardly positioned but are a product of a conscious artistic design which employed the divine speeches as an organizing device for the proper arrangement of the materials in Leviticus. For example, the "predilection to interlink diverse materials by means of seven-part patterns"[156] which are also framed neatly in a clearly marked frame of divine speeches, show a conscious quest by the author of Leviticus to provide a cohesive artistic framework for his work. In the conclusion of his work, Warning entertained the possibility of the divine speeches playing a dominant role in the structure of the entire Pentateuch, hence he noted, "[i]f these 'hidden' structures, structural outlines which come to light only after careful checking and weighing of almost every word of Leviticus, are present in the heart of the Pentateuch,"

---

155. Ibid., 133.
156. Ibid., 174.

then argued Warning, "a similar scrutiny of Genesis, Exodus, Numbers, and Deuteronomy may result in detection of similar terminological patterns and structures."[157]

Despite the shared interest between the present work and the one by Warning in the framework of divine speeches, our study of the divine speeches is a departure from the mere structural emphasis of Warning. In particular, the present study moves away from issues of structure of the divine speeches but it seeks to underscore the stylistic content of the divine speeches in terms of literary devices such as metaphor or metaphoric language, simile, wordplay, irony, alliteration, euphemism, paronomasia, repetition and other stylistic features which are found in the divine speeches. While the quest for the microstructural and macrostructural importance of the divine speeches is needful, our present interest lies largely in the highlighted concerns. Moreover, Warning's work merely marshaled the evidences for the significance of the divine speeches in the structuring of the book of Leviticus on both inward and outward framing of the divine speeches. On the contrary, our present work seeks to provide a plausible reason for the elevated nature of the divine speeches, and hence moves beyond the mere observation on the significance of the divine speeches and the emphasis on the possible functions of these speeches in the context of the Abrahamic narratives.

2.3.4. Samuel Meier

The work of Samuel Meier is generally on biblical speeches, hence the title of his work, *Speaking of Speaking: Marking Direct Discourse in the Hebrew Bible*.[158] However, a particular chapter of this work, "Problems in the Marking of the Divine Speech," is primary devoted to the subject of biblical divine speeches. Significantly, his conclusions have further very important implications for dating the marked divine speeches of biblical literature.

To come to this important point in his work, which ironically is placed at the last chapter, we must first underscore the importance of the preceding

---

157. Ibid., 180.
158. Samuel A. Meier, *Speaking of Speaking: Marking Direct Discourse in the Hebrew Bible* (Leiden: Brill, 1992), 21–57.

part of the work. Meier began his study by noting the diversity in the usage of the various discourse markers. For example he notes the various use of אמר in biblical narratives. He also explores the various uses of the infinitive לאמר as a discourse marker. In addition, he reveals the different usage of the verbs such as דבר, שאל, ענה,נגד, צעק /זעק, נבא, צוה, שבע, התפלל, and the different use of the discourse markers in the prophetic literatures.[159] Concerning the use of the discourse markers in the Bible, Meier observed, "different books and even discrete sections or chapters within a single book" in the Bible "display widely varying usage in the employment of specific words used to mark direct discourse."[160] For Meier, the factor responsible for this diversity could be traced to the "pluralistic literary environment" that gave rise to the literary traditions of the Bible. This factor is also compounded by the distinct geography, dialect, tradition and innovation.

Related to this interest of the present study, Meier also presented some general problems associated with the marking of the divine speeches in the Hebrew Bible. He presented several phraseologies employed in the Hebrew Bible to introduce the divine speeches. For example, he noted the problem inherent in the conception of the phrase such as כה אמר יהוה or "thus said Yahweh" as a discourse marker in the introduction of the divine speeches. He described particularly the difficulty in the treatment of כה אמר יהוה as a messenger formula or a marker of royal proclamation in modern scholarship. Meier observed that כה אמר יהוה is frequently found in prophetic literature particularly that of exilic period (e.g. frequently in Ezekiel, Haggai, and Zechariah).[161] He also argued that biblical and extra-biblical evidences do not support the conception that כה אמר יהוה was used to interrupt the speeches of the messenger. In the same way, "If the use of כה אמר יהוה re-

---

159. See Regt, *Participants in Old Testament Texts and the Translator*, 88–94.
160. Meier, *Speaking of Speaking*, 323.
161. For some pioneering studies on speeches in the prophetic literature see Hans Walter Wolff, "Das Zitat im Prophetenspruch," *Gesammelte Studien zum Alten Testament* (Munich: Chr. Kaiser Verlag, 1964), 36–129; A. S. van der Woude, "Micah in Dispute with the False Prophets," *Vetus Testamentum* 19 (1969): 244–60; W. J. Horwitz, "Audience Reaction to Jeremiah," *CBQ* 32 (1970): 555–64; James Crenshaw, *Prophet Conflict*, *BZAW* 123 (New York: Walter de Gruyter, 1971), 23–38; G. V. Smith, "The Use of Quotations in Jeremiah XV 11–14," *VT* 29 (1979): 229–31. On a recent study see A. R. Pete Diamond, "Interlocutions: The Poetics of Voice in the Figuration of YHWH and His Oracular Agent, Jeremiah," *Int* (2008): 48–65.

Dominant Studies on the Literary Features of the Divine Speeches

flects a royal proclamation style, it is one whose evidence is confined to the Persian period" because in this period it "is attested as a literary phenomenon in royal inscription of the Persian period."[162] However, even here, "its structuring value is variable, unpredictable, and often dispensable."[163] Similarly, Meier also observed the general problem associated with the use of the phrase, נאם יהוה or "word of Yahweh" as a discourse marker of divine speeches. In particular, he notes the problem in the translation of this phrase, which comes from its problematic etymology, vocalization and usage. Concerning the use of these divine discourse markers and their sensitivity to the historical context, Meier noted:

> In sum, one may observe at least three distinct ways of treating the voice of God in biblical literature. In pre-exilic poetic texts, God's words easily merge and are submerged in the words of others with little care taken to disentangle who says what. This feature corresponds with the customs of poetry in general. A second technique surfaces in narrative prose where God's voice is marked, but the markingand even the voice itself as in the preceding categoryis undistinguished from that of other voices which participate. The third technique is that of the exilic and post-exilic prophetshere one finds an obsessive interest in the divine voice and the conveyance of its articulations. The use of the phrases נאם יהוה and כה אמר יהוה belongs primarily in the context of the latter.[164]

In addition to these divine discourse markers, he also considered the phrase, היה דבר יהוה אל PN לאמר where "PN" stands for "personal name." Meier observed that the distribution of this discourse marker is concentrated "with highest intensity" in the works of Deuteronomistic history, Jeremiah, Ezekiel, and Haggai.[165] Together with the preceding two divine

---

162. Meier, *Speaking of Speaking*, 298
163. Ibid.
164. Ibid., 314.
165. Ibid., 319.

discourse markers, they reflect a literary practice of a particular era namely the exilic or post-exilic period. In this period, Meier noted that the biblical literature is characterized with work that shows the convoluting presence of "quotation within quotations, and even these within further quotations."[166] This literary phenomenon of multiple embedding of direct discourse is also characterized by a dangling divine discourse marker, which points to the divine speaker.[167] In this historical perspective, even though "[m]uch narrative, poetry, and prophetic material marksand even fails to markdivine speech in a fashion no different than the words of other characters" however, "a persistent concern to highlight God's words becomes evident in certain narrative, poetic and prophetic texts after the seventh century B.C."[168] In this same period, "[a] persistent and sometimes over-zealous employment of a specialized vocabulary is drawn from both archaic and contemporary rhetorical style in order to achieve this highlighting."[169] For Meier, the "conclusion is inescapable" that the sixth century is the formative period for the "standardization" of the divine discourse markers. Thus Meier presupposed that the marking of the divine discourse markers are mostly found in the books dated in this period. If this hypothesis of Meier is right, one could take this thought a little further, since the marking of the divine speeches could also be made to embrace the decorative or elevated divine speeches, which could also be assigned to this same period. However, this observation fails because it presumes that literary artistry of the text is a product of a later period and hence the earlier period is associated with primitiveness or less artistic phase in the evolution of the text. In this regard, sophistication of the text is arbitrarily associated with the ingenuity of exilic or post-exilic environment while the less artistic text is assigned to pre-exilic or earlier period. This distinction is often unfair since artistic creation can be the product of any period in history depending on the artistic inclinations of the authors or the times.

---

166. Ibid., 320.
167. Ibid.
168. Ibid., 323.
169. Ibid.

Against this consideration, Meier, through the device of distinctive marking of the divine speeches, reasoned that a "poetic tolerance of ambiguity in early" prophetic literature or narratives "gives way to a later insistence that God's words be discretely identified and delimited."[170] This distinction could easily be overstretched to a breaking point, however, it rightly observes that later redactors or narrators paid careful attention to the divine speeches, and hence pointing to the significance attached to these speeches by the evolving community. On the other hand, even though the presence of highly decorative languages or clear identification of the divine speeches might be possible indicators of lateness, these considerations in themselves are not conclusive parameters in determining the presence of a later hand.

2.4. Conclusion

As we close this chapter, it is needful to once more underscore the emerging significance of the biblical speeches. The significance of these biblical speeches is not merely for their dramatic effect or their possible importance in the structuring of the text, but their fundamental role in helping us to better understand the intriguing elements of characterization by the narrator through the speeches of these biblical characters. To this end, Alter rightly observed:

> The biblical scene, in other words, is conceived almost entirely as verbal intercourse, with the assumption that what is significant about a character, at least for a particular narrative juncture, can be manifested almost entirely in the character's speech.[171]

On the other hand, the speeches of biblical characters in a sense are not only concerned about the characters, but they are also framed in harmony to the overall purpose of the entire discourse by the narrator. This is true

---

170. Ibid., 326.
171. Alter, *The Art of Biblical Narrative*, 70.

because each of the assigned or featured speeches of a character are clearly arranged by the narrator for certain theological reason. In this particular understanding, each speech or dialogue by the characters, especially the major characters of the narrative, help on the long run to build a story in a particular point of view. Significantly, this point of view ultimately fits to the general frame of thought or unexpressed reasons for telling the stories. Consequently, the speeches of the characters not only characterize the characters themselves but also characterize the reticent narrator because through the speeches of his leading characters we see his unexpressed thought or reasons by way of their speeches.

For the moment, we must suspend these observations until chapter 4 where we hope to show the possible functions of the divine speeches within the pericopes under study. To summarize the preceding reviews, we will briefly make reference to three defining trends in the studies of biblical speeches and their relationship to the present study. Firstly, the preceding studies reveal the significance of biblical speeches and established the justification for the present study. Secondly, the preceding studies underscore the artistic nature of biblical speeches. In particular, the immediate studies on the divine speeches show that the divine speeches were products of conscious artistic framing and skill. And finally, these previous studies have shown that biblical speeches are not haphazardly positioned but they are arranged or organized purposefully by the biblical narrator. In a particular instance, Meier's study seeks to stress an organizing principle around the marked divine speeches in a given historical context. He demonstrates the possible historical location of these marked divine speeches in an exilic or post-exilic context. Even though the present study takes over the contribution of preceding studies, our point of departure lies in its quest to identify the presence of literary devices in divine speeches of the Abrahamic narratives, thus our next chapter is centered on finding these stylistic features in the divine speeches.

CHAPTER THREE

Stylistic Aspects of the Divine Speeches

3.1. Introduction

The qualifier "stylistic" in the phrase "stylistic aspects" modifies and limits the noun "aspects."[1] By the phrase, "stylistic aspects" we mean the "distinctive use" of language or the "special expressive" way by which the divine speeches are framed.[2] For most readers of the Abrahamic cycle, the divine

---

1. There is a popular idiom that "style is everything." In everyday life, we normally talk about styles in our descriptions of things such as the "elegant style of a house," "the new style of music," "the style of dress" and even the "style of teaching." This use of the term "style" is often a way of saying that something is unique, distinctive and different. To this end, Peter Verdonk defined style in literary study as "a distinctive linguistic" way of "expression" [See Peter Verdonk, *Stylistics* (London: Oxford University Press, 2003), 3]. Accordingly, since "style" forms the primary concern of stylistics, Verdonk further defined "stylistics" as "the analysis of distinctive expression in language and the description of its purpose and effect" [Ibid., 4]. Naturally, our present study of "stylistic aspects" of speeches falls within this domain of stylistics. On the other hand, there is a sense in which every piece of writing is somehow characterized by a certain degree of style or "distinctiveness" whether it is prose or poetry. Since every work maintains somehow a distinctive literary identity, it thus should merit the label of "style." In the history of stylistics, these two different views of "style" have often dominated discussion in stylistics. However, the present work's use of "style" or "stylistic" in describing the "literary devices" such as "metaphors," "simile," "paronomasia," "euphemism," "hyperbole," "irony" "repetition," "suspense" and "allusion" which are found in the divine speeches, approaches "style" in the perspective of "deviation" from the normal use of language. In prose, such elements of style also include characterization, plotting, structure, narrative voice, speech representation and other literary features of the narrative.
2. Graham G. Hough uses the phrase, "special expressive devices" to describe a certain stylistic interest in the text that is primarily concerned with "special kinds of imagery, special choices of vocabulary, special syntactical usages," "wit and irony," "word-order," "repetition," "rhythmical and musical patterns," "metaphor," "symbol and imagery," "local color," "synesthetic effects" and other literary features of a given piece of literature

speeches are merely treasures of theological truths, but we see very little by way of "stylistic" features or aesthetics in these speeches. There is no doubt that within these speeches there are profound theological truths, however, we must also recognize the presence of "stylistic features" and their defining role in the communication of these truths[3]. Even though the words in the divine speeches were not strange, rare or technical words *per se* but simple words which could be found in other parts of the Scriptures, they are framed in such a way that gave "Yahweh" a distinctive style of speech particularly with the presence and highest concentration of metaphoric expressions, similes, paronomasia, euphemism, hyperbole, repetition, suspense, and allusion in the divine speeches which appear to be absent in the speeches of other characters such as Abraham, Sarah and Lot.[4]

To his credit, the narrator of the Abrahamic cycle generally told his stories with great simplicity. However, on closer look, the divine speeches are highly elegant and colorful discourses, which immediately emboss their significance on the entire Abrahamic narratives by careful reading. Unfortunately, the "illusion" of simplicity as seen in the larger stories of the Abrahamic cycle has often prevented readers from seeing the artistry as well as rhetoric of these divine speeches which seem to be deliberately framed to support some particular ideological position.[5] Before undertaking such a quest for ideological factors or functions of these divine speeches, we must first establish, based on grammatical and literary studies, the presence of

---

[Graham G. Hough, *Style and Stylistics* (London: Routledge, 1969), 33–38]. Our present approach explores the "stylistic features" of the divine speeches in this definition of "special expressive devices."

3. In the present study, the stylistic features of the divine speeches are identified as literary categories, which are not only verifiable, but also retrievable, by other readers. For further information on why this criteria is important in the study of stylistic features of a text, see Paul Simpson, *Stylistics: A Resource for Students* (London: Routledge, 2006), 4.

4. Shlomith Rimon-Kenan rightly observed that "[a] character's speech, whether in conversation or as a silent activity of the mind, can be indicative of a trait or traits both through its content and through its form." In fact, "it is almost impossible to speak without betraying some personal 'point of view,' if only through the very language used." See Rimon-Kenan, *Narrative Fiction: Contemporary Poetics* (London: Methuen, 1983), 63, 72.

5. On the debates whether authors have conscious control over their works see Louis T. Millic, "Rhetorical Choice and Stylistic Option: The Conscious and Unconscious Poles," *Literary Style: A Symposium*, ed. Seymour Chatman, 77–94 (London: Oxford University Press, 1971), 87.

such stylistic features in the divine speeches.⁶ The burden of this chapter is to identify stylistic features in divine speeches and to show how such stylistic features are not only peculiar to one particular divine speech but cut across them all.⁷ Since these divine speeches are placed by the narrator within the narratives of the Abrahamic cycle it is important to make brief references to issues of structure, literary, textual and grammatical aspects because these considerations will provide a clear perspective to the stylistic aspects within these divine speeches.⁸ Consequently, the following work undertakes the studies of Genesis 12:1–9, 13:1–18, 15:1–21, 17:1–27, 18:1–33, and 22: 1–19.⁹ In this present study, we take interest in the entire

---

6. The main dangers of studying stylistic features of a given text as noted by Pierre Guiraud are many. In particular, he noted the possibility of the interpreter or reader deciphering "the text by means of his own code and takes from it meanings and stylistic effects which are independent and sometimes very far from those the author might have put there, consciously or unconsciously. Each text 'has the meaning which one attributes to it,' and we know how much this meaning can vary among individuals and, still more, among milieus and eras." However, despite this danger, Guiraud observed, "[e]ach author has a personal language [or style] which his readers must learn," in order to understand such a piece of work [Guiraud, "Immanence and Transitivity of Stylistic Criteria," *Literary Style" A Symposium*, ed. Seymour Chatman, 16–23 (London: Oxford University Press, 1971), 19]. This last reason validates the contemporary quest for the stylistic features in literary works.

7. According to Roland Barthes, "what would have to control the stylistic work is the search for models, of patterns: sentence structures, syntagmatic clichés, divisions and *clausulae* of sentences; and what would inspire such work is the conviction that style is essentially a citational process, a body of formulae, a memory (almost in the cybernetic sense of the word), a cultural and not an expressive inheritance"[Barthes, "Style and Its Image," *Literary Style" A Symposium*, ed. Seymour Chatman, 3–15 (London: Oxford University Press, 1971), 9]. It is such literary "patterns" or "devices" that are within the divine speeches that the present chapter seeks to show.

8. See Mark Allan Powell, "What is 'Literary' about Literary Aspect?" *Seminar Papers SBL Annual Meeting* (1992): 40–48.

9. There are three divine speeches which are omitted in this present study. These divine speeches include Yahweh's speeches to Hagar in Genesis 16: 8–12, his speeches to Abraham in Genesis 21:12–13 sanctioning the sending of Hagar away and the divine speeches to Abimelech in a dream to give Sarah back to Abram in Genesis 20:3–7. There are stylistic devices found in these three texts. For example, there is the use of metaphor, which is clearly seen in the divine speeches particularly in Yahweh's calling of Ishmael as a "donkey of a man" (פֶּרֶא אָדָם). This metaphor is to describe Ishmael's "usualness" which is possibly defined in terms of his character and way of life. It can also describe the "freedom" or "unaccountable" nature of Ishmael's life to anyone. This understanding is particularly significant in light of the slavery of his mother, thus Yahweh is saying that "Ishmael is going to be a free being like the wild donkey" rather than a slave like his mother. However, he has to fight his way in order to make this freedom possible. The first reading of this metaphor is negative while the second reading is positive since it

narrative unit where these divine speeches occurred. This is because it is only within the context of its pericope that the stylistic character of these divine speeches becomes obvious to the reader.[10] To this end, Bar-Efrat had rightly noted that,

> [t]he best approach to a discussion of style is by undertaking a stylistic analysis of an entire narrative unit. Only in this way can the stylistic phenomena be seen within their contexts . . . and their special significances discerned.[11]

Thus the following work is defined within this sensitive approach to the pericope of each of the divine speeches.

---

emphasizes the liberating character of Ishmael's future life. Similarly, the divine speech also employed another metaphoric phrase "his hand against all and the hands of all against him" in order to describe the life of hostility, which will become the trademark of Ishmael and his descendants. In addition, he is also called the "son of the bondwoman" and there are references to "seeds," "breaking of faces" to describe the demeanor of Abraham in the divine speeches when Sarah told him to send off Hagar and her son. Furthermore, there is wordplay on the name Ishmael in verse 11 of the first text. There is also the use of the term "touch" as a sexual euphemism for Yahweh's protection of Sarah in Abimelech's harem. This same text made allusion to Genesis 2:7 and 3:4 in the speech by Yahweh to Abimelech when he said, מוֹת תָּמוּת which is translated, "you should surely die." Thus the choice of the present six texts is not because stylistic features are absent in these three passages; on the contrary, the selection of the six divine speeches is merely to serve as a representative framework or a kind of research template for the study of these stylistic features, which are clearly found in all the divine speeches.

10. Josephine Miles had rightly observed that "[o]bviousness can arise not only from the nature of the text but from the nature of the reader; it could, for example be the result of a strong sensitivity to a trait lacking or present in his own style or culture." See Miles, "Style as Style," *Literary Style: A Symposium*, ed. Seymour Chatman, 24–28 (London: Oxford University Press, 1971), 24.

11. Bar-Efrat, *Narrative Art in the Bible*, 200.

3.1.1. Genesis 12:1–9

3.1.1.1. Structure[12]

This pericope is situated within the תוֹלְדֹת of Terah which began in Genesis 11:27.[13] From this verse, the תוֹלְדֹת of Terah ran through the entire Abrahamic cycle and ends in Genesis 25:11 with the death of Abraham and the narrator's comments of divine blessing on his son Isaac.[14] This is followed by the תוֹלְדֹת of Ishmael. Consequently, the story of Abraham stands in between the תוֹלְדֹת of Shem and the תוֹלְדֹת of Ishmael. As a structuring device, the תוֹלְדֹת divided the book of Genesis into ten blocks of narratives, thus according to Wenham, these ten parts are the following:[15]

---

12. On the general relationship between structure and style particularly in terms of verbal, syntactic, and semantic aspects see Tzvetan Todorov, "The Place of Style in the Structure of the Text," *Literary Style" A Symposium*, ed. Seymour Chatman (London: Oxford University Press, 1971), 32–35; Simpson, *Stylistics*, 18–21.

13. Brichto observed that the "term *pericope*" is used "for a passage of text isolated by one criterion or another from what precedes and what follows it; these pericopes may defy editorial demarcations of verse and chapter. Just as verse and chapter are late editorial demarcations and themselves open to question, so is the matter of where a pericope begins and ends." [Brichto, *Toward a Grammar of Biblical Poetics*, 14]. In this present work, we follow the chapter demarcation or division of the Hebrew Bible since they appear to preserve the text-boundaries of the various episodes in the Abrahamic cycle.

14. On the use of biblical genealogies particularly in Genesis as a literary device such as foreshadowing see Nicholas A. Bailey, "Some Literary and Grammatical Aspects of Genealogies in Genesis," *Biblical Hebrew and Discourse Linguistics*, ed. Robert D. Bergen, 267–282 (np: Summer Institute of Linguistics, 1994), 273.

15. G. J. Wenham, *Genesis 1–15*. Word Biblical Commentary (Dallas: Word, 1987),xxi.

	Prologue	1:1—2:3
1	History of Heaven and Earth	2:4—4:26
2	Family History of Adam	5:1—6:8
3	Family History of Noah	6:9—9:29
4	Family History of Noah's sons	10:1—11:9
5	Family History of Shem	11:10—26
6	Family History of Terah	11:27—25:11
7	Family History of Ishmael	25:12—18
8	Family History of Isaac	25:19—35:29
9	Family History of Esau	36:1—37:1
10	Family History of Jacob	37:2—50:26

However, primarily concerned with the Abrahamic cycle, we take as our point of departure the introductory verses of the תּוֹלְדֹת of Terah in Genesis 11:27–32. Following the תּוֹלְדֹת of Terah closely, we see a structure within the verses.[16] This introduction forms a microstructure and a kind of inclusio around the major concern of the Abrahamic cycle, namely the condition of Sarai.[17] Ironically, Sarai is the first barren woman in the Bible. This is significant in the light of the mandate at the creation to be "fruitful and multiply."[18] This microstructure around the condition of Sarai is rightly seen in Genesis 11:26–32. The text is structured thus:

---

16. This microstructure is glaring as seen from verses 26 to 32 while verse 27 forms an introduction to the entire תּוֹלְדֹת of Terah.

17. Concerning the mentioning of Sarah in the genealogy, Susan Bradford observed, "Sarai, therefore, would not be considered a good wife and her status as a woman would be minimal. This unflattering and unexpected statement in the context of a genealogy, however, sets up narrative tension for what follows. Furthermore, her continued barrenness will drive the plot of several stories. Here, however, it disrupts the genealogy" [See Susan Bradford, *Genesis*. Septuagint Commentary Series (Leiden: Brill, 2007), 289]. Contrary to this submission, as the following chiasm structure will show, information on Sarah did not "disrupt" the genealogy but the genealogy itself is built around it.

18. See Genesis 1:28, cf. 8:17; 9:1, 2,7.

Death of Haran	11:28
Taking of Wives by Abraham and Nahor	11:29
Sarai's Barrenness	11:30
Taking of Abraham, Lot, and Sarah by Terah	11:31
Death of Terah	11:32

This microstructure opens and closes with the similar theme of death.[19] The taking of wives by Abraham and Nahor and the taking of Abraham, Lot and Sarah are both described by the use of the verb לקח. The chiastic structure is seen in the way the theme of death, the taking of wives by Abraham and Nahor and the journey of the family of Terah to Haran enveloped the condition of Sarah.[20] In this understanding, the narrator makes the condition of Sarah the central issue in the story of the Abrahamic cycle by the structuring of the introductory section of the תּוֹלְדֹת of Terah.[21] This structure is clearly seen when depicted thus:

---

19. For the structuring of the entire Abrahamic narratives in a palistrophic macrostructure see John E. Hartley, *Genesis: New International Biblical Commentary*. OTS (Peabody, Massachusetts: Hendrickson Publishers, 2000), 3–9.

20. Noting the pessimistic tune by which the present pericope opened, Laurence Turner observed, "the ancestral history commences with a pessimistic reminder of the human condition. This gloomy scenario is embodied in the deprivation experienced by two characters. Lot has no father while Abram has no child" [Turner, *Genesis* (Sheffield: Sheffield Academic Press, 2000), 62]. It is this latter condition that the divine speeches seek to address; hence it is not surprising that the bulk of the divine speeches are filled with optimism in contrast to the pessimistic opening of the Abraham narratives.

21. As in the Hebrew text, the Septuagint also preserved the "very different style" of narration from this section of Genesis throughout the entire Abraham narrative. In particular, Bradford noted that "the genealogy departs from a typical format and reports the names of [the] wives" of the leading characters. Bradford further observed that, "the inclusion of Micha's family makes Sarai's lack of family more noticeable. She is the only person in this part of the genealogy whose paternity is unreported. What follows contrasts even more with the implied theme of a genealogy, i.e, the continuity family line. Not only does she have no prior family, she has no potential for bearing offspring [Bradford, *Genesis*, 288]. This noticeable detail in Sarah agrees with the chiasm below which appears to be around her.

   A   Death of Haran
      B   Taking of Wives by Abraham and Nahor
         C   Sarai's Barrenness
     B'   Taking of Abraham, Lot, and Sarah by Terah
   A'   Death of Terah

Structurally, this chiasm is followed by the first divine speech which is marked by the discourse marker וַיֹּאמֶר in Genesis 12:1. The second divine speech is introduced by וַיֵּרָא and וַיֹּאמֶר respectively in verse 7a. The obedience of Abraham is captured by the verb וַיֵּלֶךְ and acts of worship within the speeches by the verb וַיִּבֶן.

It is from the opening of the תּוֹלְדֹת of Terah that the story of Abraham begins. However, our concern is not only with the introductory verse of Genesis 11:27–32, but the structure of the present text, namely Genesis 12:1–9.[22] The present text stood at the beginning of the Abrahamic cycle and introduced the subsequent stories in the life of the patriarch,[23] thus we presume it has certain structure that shows its relationship to the selected pericope, and also to the larger cycle of the Abrahamic narratives.[24] As gen-

---

22. On the centrality of these divine speeches at the beginning of the Abrahamic cycle see Gunkel, *Genesis: übersetzt und erklärt*. 6th ed. (Göttingen: Vandenhoeck, 1964), 167; von Rad, *Genesis*, trans. J.H. Marks (Philadelphia: Westminster, 1972), 165–67; Muilenburg, "Abraham and the Nations: Blessing and World History," *Int* 19 (1965), 398; Ronald Clements, *Abraham and David: Genesis XV and its Meaning for Israelite Tradition* (London: SCM, 1967), 15; Gerhard Wehmeier, "The Theme 'Blessing for the Nations' in the Promises to the Patriarchs and in Prophetical Literature," *BTF* 6 (1974), 2; Westermann, *The Promises to the Fathers: Studies on the Patriarchal Narratives*, trans. D.E. Green (Philadelphia: Fortress, 1980), 156; *idem*, *Genesis 12–36: A Commentary*, trans. J.J. Scullion (Minneapolis: Augsburg, 1985), 146; Martens, *Plot and Purpose in the Old Testament* (Leicester, InterVarsity Press, 1981), 26; Laurence A. Turner, *Announcements of Plots in Genesis*. JSOT 96 (Sheffield: Sheffield Academic Press, 1990), 51.

23. In verse 1, the *vav* consecutive and the imperfect introduce a new narrative. When this occurs as it does here, Christo H. J. Merwe, Jacke A. Naudé and Jan H. Kroeze observed that, "it is usually accompanied by an *introduction of the characters of the new story and a change* of location." However, "a change in time is hardly ever involved." See Merwe *et al*, *A Biblical Hebrew Reference Grammar*. Biblical Language: Hebrew 3 (Sheffield: Sheffield Academic Press, 1999), 166.

24. A little remark about the connection between the תּוֹלְדֹת of Shem to Terah is in place here. The תּוֹלְדֹת of Shem preceded the one of Terah in Genesis 11:10–26. The תּוֹלְדֹת of Shem traced the genealogy from Shem down to Terah. It takes a particular individual to describe his age and his heir and then concluded by saying that he has other "sons and daughters" (וַיּוֹלֶד בָּנִים וּבָנוֹת). This phrase וַיּוֹלֶד בָּנִים וּבָנוֹת continued through the genealogy

erally argued by Westermann and Coats, the structure of this pericope does not stand alone, but relates to the preceding materials particularly Genesis 11: 27–32.[25] From this relationship, we could readily outline the structure of our present text as follows:

Introduction	11:27–32
Divine Speech	12:1–3
Abraham's Obedience	12:4–6
Divine Speech	12:7a
Abraham's Worship	12:7b–8
Conclusion	12:9

The structure of the present text readily shows introduction and conclusion to the pericope. It also shows that for each divine speech, Abraham, though silent, responded first in obedience and second in worship. Hence, without speech, Abraham obeyed and worshiped Yahweh. Within this structure itself, we see a quest to characterize Abraham namely that Abraham is a faithful worshipper of Yahweh.[26] Even though the subsequent stories of Abraham show the patriarch involved in some questionable ethical practices, such as lying about his wife in Genesis 12:10–20 and 20:1–18, the entire Abrahamic cycle validates this earlier description that Abraham was an obedient and faithful worshipper of Yahweh. Thus at the beginning of the Abrahamic cycle, the narrator by the use of structure, already tells his readers that Abraham was a faithful servant of Yahweh. To this end, it is not surprising that the last picture of Abraham and God that we have

---

of Shem but significantly is absent after reaching the family of Terah. The three sons of Terah Abram, Nahor and Haran were mentioned. Significantly, the name of Abraham is twice placed at the beginning of the list of the sons of Terah in Genesis 11:26b and 27b, which presupposes his importance. It is possible that Abraham was the firstborn of Terah's family, however, since the Bible is silent we could only guess or speculate. He is also mentioned at the front of the list in verses 29 and 31.

25. George W. Coats, *Genesis: With an Introduction to Narrative Literature* (Grand Rapids, MI: William B. Eerdmans Publishing Co, 1983), 97–102.

26. On the characterization of Abraham and Sarah within the story world of the Abrahamic narratives see D. M. Gunn and D. N. Fewell, *Narrative in the Hebrew Bible*. OBS (London: Oxford University Press, 1993), 90–100.

in Genesis 22 was also within this dominant thought since this text, as subsequent discussion would show, is basically a trial of the faithfulness of Abraham particularly to show his quest to please Yahweh against all the odds.[27] Following this reading, Thomas L. Brodie observed, "Abram was tested thoroughly. In particular, he was tested first and last – here, and when asked to offer Isaac."[28] In this sense, there are elements of characterization by the narrator, in the opening of the story of Abraham, by the way he structured the divine speeches and the responses of Abraham to them.[29]

Significantly, Abraham's obedience is sandwiched between the two divine speeches and also his acts of worship are framed at the end of the pericope which moves smoothly towards conclusion. In this understanding, the structure of the text could be framed in the following way:

    A   Introduction
        B   Divine Speech
            C   Abraham's Obedience
        B'   Divine Speech
            C'   Abraham's Worship
                D   Conclusion[30]

---

27. For the ten trials of Abraham see Umberto Cassuto, *A Commentary on the Book of Genesis: From Noah to Abraham*, vo. 2 (Jerusalem: Magnes, 1964), 294–295.

28. Thomas L. Brodie, *Genesis as Dialogue: A Literary, Historical and Theological Commentary* (London: Oxford University, 2001), 209.

29. Stressing the importance of characterization in Genesis, Turner observed, "[m]ore than anything else it is the depth of *characterization* that adds interest and verisimilitude to the narratives" [Turner, *Genesis*, 14]. This characterization is particularly obvious in the Abrahamic narratives because by means of explicit divine speeches, the narrator's comments (see his rare comments in Genesis 15:6), structure, comparison, use of theological loaded words, (see for example, the significance of the Lord appearing to Abram in Genesis 12:7) and contrast (see the contrast between Abraham and Lot in Genesis 18–19), the narrator presents an imposing narrative picture of Abraham.

30. This structure did not form a complete symmetry. For a discussion of partial symmetry see Jerome T. Walsh, *Style and Structure in Biblical Hebrew Narrative* (Collegeville, Minnesota: The Liturgical Press, 2001), 57–79.

Along this line, it seems the activities in the life of Abraham are motivated by divine speech.[31] This is in contrast to his father Terah whose intended journey to Canaan is not backed by these divine speeches. No wonder he was unable to reach his intended destination. Interestingly, the narrator opened the Abrahamic cycle not by the speeches of Abraham, but by divine speeches. However, while Abraham did not speak, his deeds of obedience and worship were fundamental and hence exemplary to the community of the narrator whether in pre-exile, exilic or post-exilic contexts. Similarly, the second divine speech which talks specifically of the promise of land and descendants is also sandwiched by Abraham's obedience and worship, hence pointing to the timeless need of obedience and worship in Israel's quest to posses or repossess the Promised Land.

3.1.1.2. *Literary Context*

Even though our immediate concern is the literary context of the pericope, as already highlighted, the pericope is situated within the תּוֹלְדֹת of Terah and hence it has the entirety of the book of Genesis as its literary context particularly the other תּוֹלְדֹת.[32] However, we could delimit such literary context to encompass the few key chapters preceding our pericope. Since

---

31. This is evidently seen in the use of the same of verb "go" which ties together the divine commands in Genesis 12:1 and the obedience of Abraham in verse 4. It also formed a kind of "inclusio" between Genesis 12 and 22. See B. K. Waltke and Cathi J. Fredricks, *Genesis* (Grand Rapids, Michigan: Zondervan, 2001), 195–196; Hartley, *Genesis*, 130.

32. To this end, Wenham had readily observed, "[v]ery properly, 12:1–3 has been the subject of close scrutiny because these verses are so central to the understanding of the whole of Genesis. The genealogy and the promises link the primeval history with the patriarchal stories. Verbal and ideological connections with the primeval history are numerous. Land (ארץ and אדמה), descendants, nation, name, greatness, curse and blessing, Canaan and the Canaanites have all already been broached in chapters 1–11 and are here reintroduced with pregnant brevity" [See Wenham, *Genesis 1–15*, 267]. Similarly, Thomas W. Mann has also noted, "While this passage represents a radical shift from the Primeval cycle, it is also a bridge joining the Primeval stories with the Ancestral Saga that follows. In fact, unless we see how the story of Abram and Sarai is also a *continuation* of the Primeval cycle, we shall fail to understand the full significance of their story as a new departure. In other words, the whole [divine] speech to Abram produces a critical turn in the Pentateuchal narrative, it is only a turn, not a new plot. The pivotal function of the speech is evident in its content, forged out of the thematic elements that run throughout the Primeval cycle: a journey from an old land to a new land, a movement from curse to blessing, and a new divine charge that both empowers and commands" [See Thomas W. Mann, *The Book of the Torah: The Narrative Integrity of the Pentateuch* (Louisville, Kentucky: John Knox Press, 1988), 28]. See also Brodie, *Genesis as Dialogue*, 210–11.

we hope to discuss the subsequent divine speeches in their literary contexts we would only pay attention to the few verses following after our present text.[33]

The point to begin is the story of creation in the beginning of Genesis which opens with divine speeches that have its climax in the dominant theme of blessing first to the entire creation and then to the first couple (Gen 1:26–31).[34] In the traditions behind the creation stories, there lies a strong emphasis on the subject of man designated by God to be the means of blessing to the entire cosmos. Here, at the opening of Genesis, we come across God's expressive speeches which proclaim blessing to the entire creation through the first human couple Adam and Eve. This motif of blessing mediated through a particular man assumed a primary importance in the Abrahamic narratives because this subject is reiterated in the first divine speeches to Abraham (Gen 12:1–3). It might also lie behind the Jacob and Joseph traditions where we see these patriarchs becoming dominantly a blessing to Arameans and Egyptian peoples.[35] This subject of blessing has its climax in the future descendant of Abraham, namely Joseph, who becomes a source of divine blessing to the Egyptian people at the most critical moment of famine. The theme of divine blessing to the nations has also a connection to the divine blessing in the Noahic traditions whereby God verbalized his blessings on the family of Noah after the flood (Gen 8:15–22; 9:1–17). He also made a covenant with him which was symbolized by the rainbow (Gen 9:8–17), and also gave some moral guidelines (Gen 9:1–7). These four motifs of blessing, moral perquisite, covenant and covenant sign are also reflected in the Abrahamic narratives. In the same way, the Abrahamic narratives emphasize blessing, covenant, covenant sign

---

33. For a comprehensive treatment of the literary context of the present text see K. N. Grüneberg, *Abraham, Blessing and the Nations: A Philological and Exegetical Study of Genesis 12:3 in its Narrative Context* (Berlin: Walter de Gruyter, 2003),136–142.
34. Clines, ed. *The Dictionary of Classical Hebrew*, vol. II (Sheffield: Sheffield Academic Press, 1995), 272-3.
35. Concerning the ideological importance of Egypt and Arameans see these two works: F. V. Greifenhagen, *Egypt on the Pentateuch's Ideological Map: Constructing Biblical Israel's Identity*. JSOTSUp 361 (Sheffield: Sheffield Academic Press, 2003) and Carl-Johan Axskjöld, *Aram as the Enemy Friend: The Ideological Role of Aram in the Composition of Genesis–2 Kings*. ConBOT 45(Stockholm: Almqvist & Wiksell, 1998).

and a partial moral demand particularly in Genesis 17.[36] In addition, the table of nations in Genesis 10 also formed a literary connection to the present pericope since the nation that would receive the divine blessings promised to Abraham are members of the international community already established in this chapter. The chapter gave a genealogy of nations and their intricate relationship to each other. However, the blessing of these nations will only come from the Abrahamic family or descendants (Gen 12:3). The narrator made such explicit connection by his use of מִשְׁפְּחֹת in Genesis 12:3 which has already appeared in various forms within the table of nations (Gen 10:5, 18, 20, 31, 32. cf. 8:19).[37]

Similarly important to the present pericope is the story of the tower of Babel in Genesis 11:1–9. This text could be contrasted with the pericope in several ways. For example, the characters of the tower of Babel spoke arrogantly about their intended project, but the character of Abraham is depicted as silent in the opening of this pericope. The speeches of these persons opened the episode of the tower, however, in contrast, it is the divine speech that opened this present pericope.[38] Similarly, while these individuals sought a name for themselves, it was God himself that promised Abraham a name, and subsequently a change of name for Abraham. In addition, the people of the tower of Babel wanted to station themselves in a particular geographical location for security's sake, while the character Abraham was ready to risk the comfort of family ties in order to obey God. In the preceding text, God came down from the heavens to see the city which these people were building; in this pericope, God directed Abraham to the land which he would show him without the indication of his heavenly abode. The two texts employ different variations of the same Hebrew

---

36. On the relationship between the literary contexts of Genesis 12:1–3, and chapters 15, 17, 22:15–18 see P. R. Williamson, *Abraham, Israel and the Nations: The Patriarchal Promise and Its Covenantal Development in Genesis*. JSOT 315 (Sheffield: Sheffield Academic Press, 2000), 217–259.

37. See David J. A. Clines, ed. *The Dictionary of Classical Hebrew*, vol. V (Sheffield: Sheffield Academic Press, 2001), 554–556.

38. For the critique of this dominant "pride and punishment" interpretation of the tower of Babel see Theodore Hiebert, "The Tower of Babel and the Origin of World's Cultures," *JBL* 126, no. 1 (2007): 29–58. See also John T. Strong, "Shattering the Image of God: A Response to Theodore Hiebert's Interpretation of the Story of the Tower of Babel," *JBL* 127, no. 4 (2008):625–634.

verb for "seeing." The tower of Babel uses the *qal* infinitive construct of ראה and our pericope uses the *hifil* imperative common singular of the same verb with God as the subject in each of these occurrences.

Furthermore, our present pericope has relationship with the subsequent story of Abraham in Egypt. Geographically, this pericope stands in between Babylon and Egypt. Many commentators, such as Wenham and M. Z. Brettler, have already pointed to the likely symbolic nature of the episode of Abraham going down to Egypt in Genesis 12:10–20.[39] This observation comes from the nuances of the enslavement of Sarai in Pharaoh's harem, the striking of Pharaoh's family with a great plague and the returning of Abraham to Palestine with material possessions as gifts from the Egyptians.[40] In the same way, Abraham also left Babylon or the land of the Chaldeans to Palestine. This event has a lot of significance for the exilic community in Babylon if they are the intended or original audiences of the narrator.[41] By such a portrayal, the narrator wanted to persuade the exiles to also seek to return to Palestine like Abraham did earlier. Even though the narrator employed a timeless context since he denied us the knowledge of his geographical location or intended audience, we presume that the pericope is sandwiched between Babylon and Egypt not by accident since these two geographical locations played a key role in the subsequent lives of the descendants of Abraham. It appears that the pericope is sandwiched between these geographical locations with the thoughts of the Babylonian captivity and exodus in the mind of the narrator. In both ways, the character of Abraham becomes a persuasive model for the quest to return to

---

39. Wenham, *Genesis 1–15*, 291; Marc Zvi Brettler, *The Creation of History in Ancient Israel* (London: Routledge, 1995), 51–55.

40. Jeffrey M. Leonard suggests the narrator fashioned Abraham's story here in light of the exodus. See 260. See Leonard, "Identifying Inner Biblical Allusions: Psalm 78 as a Test Case," *JBL* 127, no. 2 (2008), 260.

41. To this end, Gerhard von Rad rightly observed, "Even though . . . this tells actual fact about Israel's beginning, yet it is doubtful that the narrator's interest here and in what follows is solely the representation of past events. In this call and this road which was taken [by Abram], Israel saw not only an event in her earliest history, but also a basic characteristic of her whole existence before God. Taken from the community of nations (cf. Num 23.9) and never truly rooted in Canaan, but even there a stranger (cf. Lev 25.23; Ps 39.12), Israel saw herself being led on a special road whose plan and goal lay completely in Yahweh's hand." See von Rad, *Genesis: A Commentary*, rev. ed. (London: SCM, 1972), 159.

Palestine.⁴² Consequently, the life of Abraham appears to be symbolically modeled after these two events.⁴³

3.1.1.2. Grammatical Analysis

We now pay attention to issue of grammar particularly in terms of imperative commands, the quotative frame and the verbal syntax of the pericope.⁴⁴ The choice of these elements of grammatical analysis comes from the assumption that these grammatical constituents are important in understanding the context or the pericope where the divine speeches are found.

3.1.1.2.1. Quotative Frames

In the present pericope, there are two quotative frames which both introduce the divine speeches. These discourse markers are located in verses 1 and 7. The significance of discourse markers has been illustrated already in the writings of Meier and Miller. In particular, Miller has drawn attention to the fact that the use of quotative frames as discourse markers in biblical Hebrew often creates the illusion that the narrator has no interference with the speech of the original speaker, and hence normally vies for our immediate trust rather than indirect speech. However, she pointed out that "[w]hile the direct representation of speech adds a sense of vividness and immediacy to biblical narrative, direct speech, no less than indirect speech, remains ultimately within the control of the biblical narrator."⁴⁵ The biblical narrator alone has access to this original speaker and he alone saw the

---

42. To this end, John Sailhamer opined that the narrator of "Genesis already puts Abraham's call in the context of 'Ur of the Chaldeans,' drawing a line connecting the call of Abraham (12:1–3) with the dispersion of Babylon (11:1–9) and thus making Abraham prefigure all those future exiles who, in faith, wait for the return to the Promised Land." See Sailhamer, *The Pentateuch as Narrative: A Biblical-Theological Commentary*. LBI (Grand Rapids, Michigan: Zondervan Publishing House, 1992), 138.

43. This treatment of Abraham as a model for subsequent generations is glaringly seen in the Targum of Isaiah. In the study of these Targumim, Alberdina Houtman noted, "[i]n the course of the tradition, Abraham was developed as a corporate personality. What was said about Abraham, implicitly also concerned Israel." See Alberdina Houtman, "The Role of Abraham in Targum Isaiah," *Aramaic Studies* 3, no. 1 (2005), 7.

44. On the relationship between grammar and the study of stylistic aspects of a text see Simpson, *Stylistics*, 10–18.

45. Miller, *The Representation of Speech*, 144.

need of beginning the story of Abraham by making direct reference to these divine speeches.[46]

The discourse marker employed by the narrator is the quotative frame וַיֹּאמֶר.[47] This is the common speech marker found in biblical narratives. Even though it is normally translated "and he said," it could also have temporal nuances such as "Now, he said," or "When he said." The former temporal sense should be employed in the translation of the quotative frame in verse 1 since it generally marked a temporal as well as subject change from the events of Genesis 11:32. Semantically, even though this quotative frame is common in the preceding chapters of Genesis, it introduces here a different episode, that is, a speech directed to a character known as Abram. The character Abram has a direct speech from Yahweh which in itself is significant because God has often in the preceding stories of Genesis spoken in anger or displeasure. We would expect that Abram had many speeches from family and friends, but the narrator did not tell us about these speeches, on the contrary, he is only interested in what God told Abram. It is here he began his story. We are not told who is the mother of Abram or something about the marriage arrangement to Sarai as we see done for Isaac. The narrator denied us access to the childhood of Abram.[48] He also refused to tell us about his youth. In fact, we meet Abram in the text already a mature and married man who is here commanded by God to an unknown destination. In this portrayal of Abram, there is a characterization particularly in the refusal of the narrator to tell us about the childhood

---

46. It seems the narrator of the patriarchal narratives builds his stories around the divine speeches within Genesis 12–50. Mann rightly observed the significance of these divine speeches when he noted, "[t]he repetition of this thematic charge formal divine speeches throughout chapters 12–50 serves as a structural pillar undergirding the entire narrative edifice." See Mann, *The Book of the Torah*, 30.

47. The divine speech lacks what in linguistics is known as "adjacency pairs." This term is used to describe the "alternating turns" of a speech between two or more parties [Miller, *The Representation of Speech*, 235]. Even though the divine speech lacks verbal "adjacency pairs," we saw Abram's affirmative response to the divine proposal or speech by his acceptance to embark on the journey in verse 4.

48. On the traditions concerning the childhood of Abraham particularly as seen in the book of *Jubilees* and other pseudepigraphies see Andrei A. Orlov, "'The Gods of My Father Terah': Abraham and the Iconoclast and the Polemics with the Divine Body Traditions in the *Apocalyse of Abraham*," *Journal for the Study of the Pseudepigrapha* 18, no. 1 (2008): 33–53; James L. Kugel, *Traditions of the Bible: A Guide to the Bible As it was at the Start of the Common Era* (Cambridge, Massachusetts: Harvard University Press, 1998), 244–274.

or youth as seen in the subsequent characters of Isaac, Jacob and Joseph. The patriarch Abram has no childhood or youthful life because the narrator not only understood this as a digression but most importantly because by refusing to tell us of his childhood or youthfulness he presents us with a mature person, thus removing from the character of Abram the childishness or exuberance which is normally associated with the youthful age as clearly seen in the stories of Jacob and Joseph.[49] He dignified Abraham and also mystified him. This characterization is further sustained by the divine speeches to him and not to Terah, Haran, Lot, or Nahor. Consequently, the first quotative marker beyond its structural function assists in the characterization of the character Abram. He received the words of God, which are deliberately denied the prominent members of his genealogical trees such as Shem, Eber and Terah. Significantly, the personal interest of these first divine speeches in Abram are absent in divine speeches to Noah or even Adam. Thus the quotative frame with God as the subject here introduced a personality which the narrator gives prominence, not only by the silence of the character himself and the absence of his childhood, but by the eloquent and personal words of God to him which are absent in the earlier stories of Genesis.

While the first quotative frame introduced us to the character Abram, the second quotative frame extends this quest to characterize Abram. This is particularly seen in the use of וַיֵּרָא יְהוָה ("and the Lord appeared") which immediately comes before the quotative frame in verse 7. Most interpreters often miss the significance of this phrase. In the preceding stories of Genesis, nobody has been described as honored to witness the appearance of Yahweh. However, the character Abram witnessed thrice the appearance of Yahweh—namely here, but also in Genesis 17:1, and 18:1. The significance is that God honored Abram by appearing to him. Hence, the phrase, וַיֵּרָא יְהוָה following the quotative frame is used by the narrator to characterize Abram, that is, Abram has experienced the divine appearance which

---

49. Technically speaking, this denial of information is known as "holes or gaps" within a story. Concerning this phenomenon, Rimon-Kenan noted, "[h]oles or gaps are so central in narrative fiction because the materials the text provides for the reconstruction of a world (or a story) are insufficient for saturation. No matter how detailed the presentation is, further questions can always be asked; gap always remain open" [Rimon-Kenan, *Narrative Fiction*, 128].

God has denied the characters preceding him. This theophany becomes like a "welcome" theophany of the patriarch to the Promised Land. One may ask why it is that the narrator refused to tell us the nature of divine speeches in verse 1 and reserved such for the present in verse 7? It seems the narrator shows that God honored Abram's obedience by appearing to him. Even though this is speculative, the text provides grounds for this speculation because the divine appearance to Abram comes only here when he was in the Promised Land. On the other hand, the phrase וַיֵּרָא יְהוָה also characterizes God since it suggests that God has something important to say to Abram hence his self-disclosure to Abram. In both ways, the phrase וַיֵּרָא יְהוָה following after the quotative frame is used to characterize the two characters of this pericope namely Abram and Yahweh.

In this understanding, through the quotative frame of וַיֹּאמֶר, even though commonly found within the biblical narratives, its strategic positioning and related context reveal its use as an instrument of characterization in the hands of the narrator who primarily gives prominence to Abram by means of two divine speeches to him in the space of one episode. These divine speeches strategically place Abram above the characters preceding him and hence introduce another different era of divine relationship to human society. Hence, the quotative frames, beyond their normal functions of structure, are strategically located here to characterize Abram. Similarly, such occurrences of divine speeches and particular appearance to Abram also characterize God since it shows that God has something important to say to Abram.

3.1.1.2.2. Syntactical Considerations

Concerning the syntax of these divine speeches, David W. Cotter noted, "[t]he first words spoken to Abraham are mysterious, or at least grammatically unusual."[50] In particular, we will concentrate for the moment at the verbal syntax of the two divine speeches within this pericope.[51] The first divine speech has seven verbs which are subordinated to the governing

---

50. David W. Cotter, *Berit Olam: Studies in Hebrew Narrative and Poetry-Genesis* (Collegeville, Minnesota: The Liturgical Press, 2003), 89.
51. For a detailed study of the syntax of this pericope see Grüneberg, *Abraham, Blessing and the Nations*, 142–152.

verb, לְךָ.⁵² Even though this imperative verb has its immediate object in the relative clause אֶל־הָאָרֶץ אֲשֶׁר אַרְאֶךָּ it syntactically controls the understanding of the seven subsequent verbs.⁵³ The seven verbs are וְאֶעֶשְׂךָ, וַאֲבָרֶכְךָ, וַאֲגַדְּלָה, וֶהְיֵה, וַאֲבָרְכָה, אָאֹר, and וְנִבְרְכוּ.⁵⁴ There is an alternative parallelism in terms of *a-b-a-b* structure in the verbal arrangement of verse 2.⁵⁵ This shows two different ideas in two different clauses in alternating relationship to each other. The alternative parallelism is thus seen in the syntax relationship of the verbs of verse 2 as follows:

    A   And I will make you a great nation
        B   And I will bless you
    A'   And I will make your name great
        B'   And you will be a blessing

In the first line, the first verbal clause (וְאֶעֶשְׂךָ לְגוֹי גָּדוֹל) is repeated in the third clause which employed the verbal form (וַאֲגַדְּלָה) of the adjective גָּדוֹל used in the first clause. Similarly, the idea of blessing in the second verbal clause is repeated in the fourth by the use of בְּרָכָה first as a verb (וַאֲבָרֶכְךָ) and then latter repeated as a noun (בְּרָכָה). In particular, this alternating style by the narrator creates a heightening of the two concepts of greatness and blessing, thus pointing the reader to the special interest Yahweh has taken in Abram. Significantly, the syntax as seen in the alternating structure

---

52. For these seven clauses see Waltke and Fredricks, *Genesis*, 203.
53. In this verse, there is the combination of the verb of motion and communication. On the possibility of this grammatical arrangement, Merwe *et al* observed, "verbs of motion and communication occur regularly." See Merwe *et al, A Biblical Hebrew Reference Grammar*, 166.
54. These seven verbs had occasioned the assumption of the sevenfold blessing of Abram among some interpreters. See Victor P. Hamilton, *The Book of Genesis: Chapters 1–17*(Grand Rapids, MI: William B. Eerdmans Publishing Co, 1990), 371.
55. There is synonymous parallelism whereby the same idea is repeated in the first and second lines in term of *a-a*. Similarly, there is an antithetical parallelism whereby the second line introduces a different idea that is contrasted with the idea of the first line in the form of *a-b*. Then there is also an introverted or chiastic parallelism, whereby two ideas are in *a-b* relationship are also repeated in *b-a*, thus forming an *a-b-b-a* sequence. Lastly, there is also an alternating parallelism, whereby the first and second ideas are repeated in an *a-b-a-b* relationship.

of these verbs is employed as a means of characterization since there is no character preceeding Abram who has the opportunity of these alternating divine blessings.

This alternating parallelism in verse 2 is followed by a chiasmus in the first clauses of verse 3, which breaks the chain of preceding cohortatives (וַאֲבָרְכָה, וַאֲגַדְּלָה, וְאֶעֱשְׂךָ). This chiasmus is seen in the word order of "verb-object" which is paralleled by "object-verb" of the later half of the sentence. Concerning this chiastic arrangement, Wenham observed, "[t]he chiasmus and parallelism make this a poetic couplet."[56] William D. Barrick also noted, "[t]he word order of the first half of the verse is a chiasm in which each word or phrase is mirrored by an equivalent word or phrase in reverse order"[57] This chiastic syntax and poetic couplet is seen thus:

    A   I will bless
        B   those blessing you
        B'   the one disdaining you
    A'   I will curse[58]

According to Barrick, "[t]he purpose of such a structure is to emphasize the central members. In this particular case the people blessing or cursing Abraham and his descendants are highlighted. That leads naturally into the last part of the verse whose emphasis is again on people: 'all the families/clans of the earth.'"[59] Even though the people of the world are emphasized in the arrangement of this syntax, Abram is the center of attraction because it is the relationship of the people to him that determines whether they will receive divine blessing or his curse.

On the other hand, the purpose of this verbal syntax, particularly as seen in imperatives, imperfects and cohortatives which are often prefixed by *vav*, is to show divine purpose or intention that culminates in the last

---

56. Wenham, *Genesis 1–15*, 276.
57. Barrick, "The Integration of OT Theology with Bible Translation," 19.
58. Ibid.
59. Ibid.

clause וְנִבְרְכוּ בְךָ כֹּל מִשְׁפְּחֹת הָאֲדָמָה. This seems to be the purpose of divine blessing in Abram, that is, through Abram "the families of the earth will be blessed."[60] This divine speech characterizes Abram because it suggested that the fate of the world lies on the shoulder of Abram, hence pointing to the importance of the character of Abram in Genesis and the entire Pentateuch.

The syntax of the second divine speech in verse 7 is fairly simple since only one verb is found. This verb however is placed in the middle of the divine speech (לְזַרְעֲךָ אֶתֵּן אֶת־הָאָרֶץ הַזֹּאת) because the divine speech wanted to emphasize the noun לְזַרְעֲךָ, thus it is placed in the beginning.[61] The importance of this arrangement is obvious because for the first time, the divine speech now addresses concretely the two basic concerns of the Abram narrative, namely land and a child. In fact, the verb אֶתֵּן stands between these two concerns and divides the sentence into two equal halves with the noun לְזַרְעֲךָ at the beginning and the noun הָאָרֶץ at the end. In this way, the main concerns of the patriarch are clearly seen in the placement of the verb in the middle rather than the beginning. Similarly, the verb אֶתֵּן appears to suggest that the land is a gift from God to Abram and his descendants.

Consequently, these two divine speeches characterize Abram, and without the verbal responses of Abram or an explicit comment from the narrator such as the ones in Genesis 13:13 or 15:6, the narrator through the divine speeches shows the importance of the character of Abram since it appears that none of the preceding divine speeches to the character before Abram have the luxury of this syntactical arrangement of the verbs. The verbs are arranged in simple but alternating parallelism and chiasmus, which point to the significance of the divine speeches of this pericope and within the patriarchal narratives.

---

60. There are endless debates on the right translation of this clause, וְנִבְרְכוּ בְךָ כֹּל מִשְׁפְּחֹת הָאֲדָמָה. Some have opined that the verb (וְנִבְרְכוּ) be translated passive in light of its niphal stem, however, some had argued for a reflexive, reciprocal or even middle voice. For the different debates see Michael A. Grisanti, "The Missing Mandate: Missions in the Old Testament," *Missions in a New Millennium: Change and Challenges in World Missions*, ed. by W. Edward Glenny and William H. Smallman (Grand Rapids: Kregel, 2000), 60–62; Grüneberg, *Abraham, Blessing and the Nations*, 191–246.

61. In this case, the preposition לְ marks the indirect object possibly for emphasis on זֶרַע. See Merwe *et al*, *A Biblical Hebrew Reference Grammar*, 240.

3.1.1.2.3. Imperative Commands

As already seen, the divine speech in verse 1 opened with an imperative which controls other verbs within the divine speeches.[62] There is also the occurrence of another imperative in the last clause of verse 2 which brings to an end the three preceding cohortatives.[63] In the first, the imperative *qal* second masculine לְךָ is followed by לְ preposition. This attachment of the לְ preposition with the imperative has been called *dativus ethicus* or ethical dative.[64] Noting this grammatical form, Gesenius noted that ethical dative always gives "emphasis to the significance of the occurrence in question *for* a particular subject. In this construction the person of the pronoun must always agree with that of the verbal form. By far the most frequent use of this לְ is with the pronoun of the 2nd person after imperatives."[65] Similarly, explaining the significance of this dative construction, Muraoka noted that a Hebrew verb of motion followed by the לְ preposition with a pronominal suffix creates a "centripetal force."[66] Grammatically, according to him, "this construction creates "a self-contained little cosmos around the subject, detached from the surrounding world, an effect of focusing on the subject . . ."[67] Similarly, it gives

---

62. See William Yarchin, "Imperative and Promise in Genesis 12:1–3," *Studia Biblica et Theologica* 10 (1980): 164–78.

63. The narrator places importance to these imperative speeches of Yahweh hence he sandwiched the Abrahamic cycle within these imperatives since the same לֶךְ־לְךָ occurred in Genesis 22:1. Concerning this bracketing of the Abrahamic cycle around these imperative commands, Hamilton observed, "Yahweh's first and last words to Abram (12:1; 22:1) begin with an imperative ('Go . . . Take . . .'). Both times the imperative is followed by a triple object: 'Go forth from (1) your country, (2) your homeland, (3) your father's house'; 'Take (1) your son, (2) your only son whom you love, (3) Isaac.' The objects in 12: 1 are arranged in a sequence of less intimate to more intimate. Each succeeding phrase narrows the base as far as Abram is concerned. In both chapters 12 and 22 God's directive to Abram falls short of supplying explicit directions; Abram is simply pointed in the right direction. About the terminal point of the pilgrimage he is unclear. Here is told to go to a land 'which I will show you.' In chapter 22 he is told to take Isaac to a mountain 'of which I shall tell you.'" See Hamilton, *The Book of Genesis*, 370.

64. See J. A. Naudé, "The Syntactical Status of the Ethical Dative in Biblical Hebrew," *JSem* 9 (1997): 129–65.

65. Gesenius, *Gesenius' Hebrew Grammar*, §119s.

66. T. Muraoka, *Emphatic Words and Structures in Biblical Hebrew* (Jerusalem: The Magnes Press, 1985), 122. cf. *idem*, "On the So-called Dativus Ethicus in Hebrew," *JTS* 29 (1978): 495–98.

67. Ibid.

the impression on the part of the speaker or author that the subject establishes his own identity, recovering or finding his own place by determinedly dissociating himself from his familiar surrounding. Notions of isolation, loneliness, parting, seclusion, or withdrawal are often recognizable.[68]

In its particular usage in verse 1, it seems the idea of dissociation or distancing of Abram from the familiar homeland is in view. However, even though this command is to part with familiar environment or family in terms of one's father's house (מֵאַרְצְךָ וּמִמּוֹלַדְתְּךָ וּמִבֵּית אָבִיךָ), we saw Abram taking along with him Lot (Gen 12:4–5), thus suggesting that divine command even though a quest for radical separation also take into cognizance the responsibility of Abram to his nephew Lot.

Significantly, the narrator employed twice the imperfect forms of הלך and once its infinitive form to describe the obedience of Abram in verses 4 and 5.[69] The use of the same word in the divine command and the narration appears to be a deliberate quest to point the reader to Abram's obedience of Yahweh. This is especially plausible in the light of the immediate comment by the narrator that, "so Abram went forth as the Yahweh had spoken to him."[70]

On the other hand, the second imperative is within a subordinate clause, which brings the preceding cohortatives to a rest in verse 2. In the alternating parallelism that has already been described above, this imperative וְהְיֵה functions as a clause which points back to the second clause of that same verse. In this location, this imperative verb functions along with the preceding cohortatives and thus together describes the divine intention to bless and make Abram a blessing.[71] However, while the first divine

---

68. Ibid.
69. See Clines, ed. *The Dictionary of Classical Hebrew*, 545–559.
70. There is also repetition of the verbs that characterized the journey of his father Terah particularly לקח, יצא, בוא, and הלך. See Genesis 11:28–31.
71. Abraham is commanded to be a blessing. As agued by Francis Andersen, the force of the two imperatives set the command tone of the entire divine speeches. Thus even though the imperatives are separated by the promises, yet according to Andersen, they still assert their grammatical force here. See Francis Andersen, *The Sentence in Biblical Hebrew* (The Hague: Mouton, 1974), 108.

speech is built around the imperative, the second divine speech has no such imperative but merely shows Yahweh's statement declaring the land as a gift for the descendants of Abram.

3.1.1.3. Stylistic Aspects

Concerning the stylistic aspects of Genesis 12:1–3, K. A. Matthews rightly observed, "[t]he language of the call in 12:1–3 possesses many poetic characteristics, such as parallelisms, rhyme, and chiasmus."[72] However, the divine speeches are often treated as plain or unadorned by many modern readers. This is because after many years of reading and rereading, the readers normally become too familiar with the tempo, literary features and even the significance of the passages so that its stylistic features are often missed. However, stepping out of this familiarity to the text, one can readily see the unusualness of this passage that has come to have a significant place in the traditions of both the Jewish and the Christian faiths. The significance of this passage not only comes from the content or theology within the wording of this divine speech but also comes from the stylistic ways by which the narrator framed this theology that has become the trademark of the monotheistic or Abrahamic faiths. It is the concern of this study to show the stylistic features of this passage and to also, in the long run, account in the next chapters its possible functions for the original readers.

For the moment, we must realize that in a given text there are several possible stylistic features and we can only highlight the few that have potential in helping to understand the divine speeches. To this end, in his discourse on speech, Todorov observed:

> Every utterance will thus have a multitude of stylistic characteristics. But only a part of them will normally be 'actualized.' In other words, the structural descriptions of a particular text will not consider a property stylistic if it cannot show that this

---

72. Kenneth A. Matthews, *Genesis 11:27–50:26*. NAC, vol. 1B (Nashville, Tennessee: Broadman & Holman Publishers, 2005), 109.

property is found in relationship with others, at other levels, or, to put in other terms, that is meaningful.[73]

This consideration informed the selection and treatment of the following stylistic features. The stylistic features in this pericope include metaphor, paronomasia, repetition, suspense, allusion and gradation. It is assumed that these literary features found in the divine speeches illuminate the underlying rhetoric of the divine speeches as well as the theological importance.

3.1.1.3.1. Metaphor[74]

Figurative expressions or metaphors are fundamental to the biblical thought.[75] To this end, Alter rightly observes that "[o]ne of the most salient characteristics of biblical Hebrew is its extraordinary concreteness, manifested especially in a fondness of images."[76] However, most often we talk of metaphor in close relationship to poetry rather than prose.[77] This is because

---

73. Todorov, "The Place of Style in the Structure of the Text," 36.

74. The use of metaphor in the entire work is primarily within the cognitive school pioneered by George Lakoff. Acording to this description, "the locus of metaphor is not in language at all, but in the way we conceptualize one mental domain in terms of another." Consequently, metaphor "is not any particular word or expression. It is the ontological mapping across conceptual domains" [See George Lakoff, "The Contemporary Theory of Metaphor," *Metaphor and Thought*, ed. Andrew Ortony, 2nd ed. (Cambridge: Cambridge University Press, 1993), 203, 208; see also George Lakoff and Mark Johnson, *Metaphors We Live By* (Chicago: The University of Chicago Press, 1980)]. For a practical introduction into this understanding of metaphor see Zoltán Kövecses, *Metaphor: A Practical Introduction* (Oxford: Oxford University Press, 2002), vii–77].

75. In fact, G. B. Caird had noted, "[a]ll, or almost all, of the language used by the Bible to refer to God is metaphor" because it uses human terms to describe or even to understand the unknown divine being. See G. B. Caird, *The Language and Imagery of the Bible* (Philadelphia: The Westminster Press, 1980), 19.

76. Alter, *Genesis: Translation and Commentary* (New York: W. W. Norton & Company, 1996), xii.

77. In the study of metaphor, there is disagreement of the definition of a metaphor or what constitutes a metaphor. However the consensus emerging from these past debates on metaphors is that words in themselves do not constitute metaphor, rather it is the particular way in which a word is used in a given context. For the different works which describe these different studies on metaphors see Marten Michiel Leenzenberg, *Context of Metaphor: Semantic and Conceptual Aspects of Figurative Language Interpretation* (Plantage Muidergracht: Universiteit van Amsterdam, 1995), especially part two on the twentieth century view on metaphor; Andrea L. Weiss, *Figurative Language in Biblical Prose Narrative: Metaphor in the Book of Samuel* (Leiden: Brill, 2006),1–47, 85–92; Roger White,

by the nature of poetry it is fairly common to find metaphor or other figures of speech within it;[78] however, prose is often expected to be plain and straightforward in reading.[79] Thus there is often the possibility of missing figurative expressions or metaphors in prose when they do occur since we do not normally associate prose with them. However, there are a few occurrences of metaphors or figurative expressions in biblical prose, which studies could deepen our understanding of biblical narratives.[80] On the other hand, whether in prose or poetry, biblical metaphors are not merely fanciful literary wrappings which the narrator embeds with his message; on the contrary, metaphors are essential in understanding or reaching the true concerns of the narrator.[81] In the modern world, with its own slang or colloquial dictions, we may easily miss the metaphors or figurative expressions of a pre-modern society. It is in this perspective that David H. Aaron talks about the need to rediscover the *"foreignness"* which characterized biblical thinking.[82] Alter also talks of the "price for the avoidance of the metaphorical" in biblical narratives.[83] For most ancient societies, metaphors, symbolic thinking or proverbs are fundamental in their understanding of realities and often these features characterized their writings.[84] The use of

---

The Structure of Metaphor (Cambridge, MA: Blackwell Publishers Inc., 1996); Eva Kittay, *Metaphor: Its Cognitive Force and Linguistic Structure* (Oxford: Clarendon Press, 1987).

78. Concerning the centrality of metaphor in poetry, Alonso Schökel noted metaphor or "[i]mages are the glory, perhaps the essence of poetry, the enchanted planet of the imagination, a limitless galaxy, ever alive and ever changing." See Schökel, *A Manual of Hebrew Poetics*, trans. Adrian Graffy. SB 11 (Rome: Editrice Pontificio Istituto Biblico, 1988), 95.

79. This assumption appears to be the overriding criteria for the selections of works in a recent study on metaphor because the contributors to this work generally ignored the narratives of the Old Testament and concentrated mainly on the poetic sections of the Old Testament particularly the Psalms and the prophetic literature. See Pierre van Hecke, ed. *Metaphor in the Hebrew Bible* (Belgium: Leuven University Press, 2005).

80. For a recent example of the study on metaphors in biblical narrative see Weiss, *Figurative Language in Biblical Prose Narrative*, 47–84.

81. See Mordechai Z. Cohen, *Three Approaches to Biblical Metaphor: from Abraham Ibn Ezra and Maimonides to David Kimhi* (Leiden, The Netherlands: Koninklijke Brill, 2003), 1–32.

82. David H. Aaron, *Biblical Ambiguity: Metaphor, Semantics, and Divine Imagery* (Leiden: Brill, 2001), 31.

83. Alter, *Genesis*, xiii.

84. It is from this perspective that C. B. Caird in his work, *The Language and Imagery of the Bible,* noted that the "frequent" use of these forms of expression in ancient societies

this medium is not merely to decorate plain ideas, but they use such forms to frame great ideas in just a few words or phrases. Consequently, since the biblical narrator is reticent or economical in his description or telling of his stories, we must thus pay close attention to his use of metaphor in word, words or phrase because they may have profound importance to the understanding of his message.[85] Unfortunately, it appears that narrative criticisms as spearheaded by Alter and Sternberg have generally ignored the presence and significance of metaphors in biblical narratives since little space is given to it in their writings.[86] On the contrary, Conroy has rightly observed that the use of "metaphor is one of the clearest signs of a heightened use of language in a text."[87]

In the present pericope, though often overlooked, are seven such figurative images or metaphoric expressions which are embedded in the present

---

"arises out of a habitual cast of mind" [See Caird, *The Language and Imagery of the Bible* (London: Duckworth, 1980), 109–121]. In the same way, Thorkild Jacobsen following Rudolf Otto's conception of religion in terms of the "numinous" has noted the centrality of metaphor in religion in order to describe this conceived "numinous" nature of the divine or spiritual experience in religious circles. Due to the centrality of metaphor in his studies of the Mesopotamian religions, Jacobsen defined their religious conceptions in terms of metaphors such as "fourth millennium metaphors" which conceived gods as providers, and the "third millennium metaphors" which conceived gods as rulers in cosmos polity and "second millennium metaphors" which conceived gods as parents. See Jacobsen, *The Treasure of Darkness: A History of Mesopotamian Religion* (New Haven: Yale University Press, 1976), 3–4, 23–74, 93–164, and 165–220.

85. To understand the biblical narrative, we must pay careful attention to the metaphors or figurative expressions employed. This is because according to Janet M. Soskice, "[t]he purpose of metaphor is both to cast up and organize a network of associations. A good metaphor . . . [is] a new vision, the birth of a new understanding, a new referential access. A strong metaphor compels new possibilities of vision." See Soskice, *Metaphor and Religious Language* (Oxford: Clarendon Press, 1985), 57.

86. The exception is the work of Shimon Bar-Efrat [see Bar-Efrat, *Narrative Art in the Bible*, 109]. On the criticism of this trend in narrative criticism see Weiss, *Figurative Language in Biblical Prose Narrative*, 20–34. On the other hand, to his credit, Alter has rightly noted the place of metaphor as "the determinative force of style" in fiction [Alter, *The Pleasures of Reading in an Ideological Age* (New York: A Touchstone Book, 1989), 92]. Concerning its significance, Alter further observed, "[g]iven the interest in metaphor evinced by most stylists, and the positive addiction to it shown by some, it is remarkable how many different kinds of style, how many different novelistic worlds, can be shaped through the central agency of metaphor" [ibid]. However, despite acknowledging the centrality of metaphor, Alter fails to engage biblical metaphors and to underscore their true importance.

87. Conroy, *Absalom Absalom!*, 124.

divine speeches.⁸⁸ The first metaphor is the use of בֵּית אָבִיךָ or the "house of your father" to describe Terah.⁸⁹ In a strict sense, the use of the "house" here is actually a metonymy because in metonymy one word or phrase is substituted for another with which it is closely associated. It is a rhetorical strategy when a speaker or writer refers indirectly to things around the persons or things described without the direct mentioning of the object or thing. For example, in today news, "the White House" is used as a metonymy for the "American government." In this sense, the house occupied by the American president becomes the label for the "American government." In the same sense here, בֵּית אָבִיךָ is not merely referring to the "physical shelter" or house by Terah, but the family of Terah who now are described by the metonymy of a "house."⁹⁰

---

88. Differentiation between a metaphor and non-metaphor could be a difficult exercise. But following the lead of Aaron, he uses the term, "gradience" to help in this quest at differentiating metaphor from non-metaphors. Aaron rightly observed, "[t]hus, instead of focusing exclusively on the question, Is that statement metaphorical or not? We can consider whether one comment is *more* metaphorical than another comment; put differently, we can discuss the *degree* to which a statement is metaphorical and what causes the metaphoricalness. Our assessment of the variables causes us to place a given statement at one point rather than another point on the continuum. Certain variableswhat we will eventually *conditions*cause us to read one metaphor as more intense than another. Thus, we speak of the continuum as gradient because we are constantly adjusting our assessment of meaning based on fluctuating variables" [See Aaron, *Biblical Ambiguity*, 29]. For Aaron and the present studies, it is the "fluctuating variables" or "conditions" in the context of the text which ultimately define the metaphoricness of a given phrase or statement as metaphor or not. It is not merely the phrase or statement itself, even though there are statements that are metaphoric without the helping power of the context. For example, "God is a lion"however, other metaphors need the helping relationship of their context in order to understand the nature of their metaphoricness. To this end, Weiss observed, "[t]he study of figurative language in biblical narrative confirms that understanding a metaphor requires one to consider more than just an isolated lexeme; one must examine the relationship between words and their surrounding context." See Weiss, *Figurative Language in Biblical Prose Narrative*, 3.

89. One may consider this particular metaphor as a "dead metaphor" since it is possible to reason that the metaphor has lost its metaphoricness, however, Alter cautioned against this form of thinking when he noted, "[d]ead metaphors, however, are the one persuasive instance of the resurrection of the deadfor at least the ghosts of the old concrete meanings float over the supposedly abstract acceptations of the terms, and this is something the philologically driven translators do not appear to understand." See Alter, *Genesis*, xiii.cf. Caird, *The Language and Imagery of the Bible*, 66; Kövecses, *Metaphor*, ix.

90. On the idiomatic or metaphoric nuances of the related term "doing a house" or עשה בתים in Exodus 1:21 see Shalom M. Paul, "Exodus 1:21: 'To Found a Family'—A Biblical and Akkadian Idiom," *Maarav* 8. Let Your Colleagues Praise You: Studies in Memory of Stanley Gevirtz (1992): 139–42.

In the preceding section, we are already introduced to the family of Terah (Gen 11:27–32). God would have literally said to Abram to go from the house of Terah his father to another land.[91] However, he refuses to call Terah by name instead he uses descriptive labels such as "your land," "your relatives" and "your father's house."[92] In the subsequent narratives, Yahweh has clearly identified himself with the characters of covenants such as "Abraham, Isaac and Jacob" particularly in the introduction of himself. However, here God used "your father's house" as an epithet for Terah, who in many Jewish traditions had been depicted as an idol worshipper.

Consequently, "your father's house" in particular metaphorically stands for the family of Terah who is not here mentioned by name. The divine speeches in this sense seem to have an apparent verbiage or circumlocution because the label "from the house of Terah, your father" would have taken care of these three extra words employed by Yahweh to describe the movement of Abram from his family to a foreign land. In this circumlocution, however, lie elements of characterization firstly of Terah because he is not mentioned by name as traditionally done for individuals having covenant relationship with Yahweh, and secondly of Abram because he is going to be the focus of the entire narrative. To this end, the narrator moves the attention of the reader from Terah to his son Abram, thus even though it is the תּוֹלְדֹת of Terah, yet the subsequent stories are not about Terah, but are going to be about Abram and his descendants.[93]

Based on this metaphor of house, one could also see the importance of Abram's movement from the "house of his father" to בֵּית־אֵל "the house of God" in verse 8 and subsequently of Sarai in the house of Pharaoh (בֵּית פַּרְעֹה) in verse 15. In the immediate pericope, it seems Abram moves from the house of his father Terah to the "house of God" in a metaphoric

---

91. See Clines, ed. *The Dictionary of Classical Hebrew*, 151–164.

92. God also used בֵּיתוֹ or "his house" as a metaphor for the descendants of Abraham in Genesis 18:19.

93. In psychological terms, the "father's house" also has much symbolic meaning. Hence, Gustav Dreifuss and Judith Reimer have observed, "The 'father's house' symbolizes the collective masculine principle of security and honor, family continuity, and tradition passed on from father to son . . . The personality that is driven toward change and development toward individuation and psychic wholeness must break free of this setting." See Gustav Dreifuss and Judith Reimer, *Abraham: The Man and the Symbol. A Jungian Interpretation of the Biblical Story* (Wilmette, Illinois: Chiron, 1995), 9.

sense because "Bethel" was mentioned twice in verse 8 as a place for worship. It is at this particular location that Abram called on the "name" of the Lord which clearly is a metaphor for worship. Consequently, in the metaphor of a house we see the movement of Abram from the obscurity of Terah's house to the worship of the house of faith.

The second figurative expression lies in the relative clause, "the land which I will show you." This relative clause has been described as "an enigmatic statement" because of its initial vagueness.[94] There is no doubt that the reference here to the "land" is an indirect reference to Canaan since the patriarch's final destination was there. However within the divine speeches this is not clearly spelled out. In the previous section the land of Canaan was mentioned several times. In fact, the genealogy of Canaan is given in Genesis 10, and Terah himself initially has Canaan as his final destination (Gen 11:31). However, the divine speeches in Genesis 12:1–3 and even 7 did not mention Canaan by name. Yahweh either called Canaan "the land which I will show you" or "this land." One would have expected that Yahweh would have told Abram that he is going to Canaan instead of the vague statement "the land which I will show you."[95] However, Yahweh refused to call Canaan by name and only referred to Canaan indirectly. One would further wonder how Abram was able to discern that Canaan was actually the land intended by God since it is not explicitly stated in the first divine speech. However, in the second speech, we now know it is Canaan because Yahweh confirmed by saying, "To your descendants I will give this land" in verse 7. The use of "land" in this divine speeches is a metaphor for Canaan, thus Yahweh used "land" to describe the future home of the patriarch, even though his speeches have no hint it is going to be Canaan. Significantly, in verse 5, the narrator made two references to Canaan in order to point to the reader that the final destination intended by Yahweh was indeed Canaan.

---

94. Turner, *Announcements of Plot in Genesis*, 52.
95. Isaac Kalimi has noted "a certain lack of precision in divine speech" particularly in the Abrahamic cycles. See Isaac Kalimi, "The Land of Moraih, Mount Moriah, and the Site of Solomon's Temple in Biblical Historiography," *HTR* 83, no. 4 (1990), 346.

The third figurative expression lies in the description of Abram as the origin of a "great nation" in Genesis 12:2a.[96] The author, the original readers and ourselves already know that this is a hidden reference to Israel because through hindsight we trace the origin of ancient Israel to the person of Abram. The narrator, telling the story after many years, also did not call Israel by name but merely revealed the divine promise that Abram will be the source of a "great nation." To this end Westermann observed, "[w]hat is promised to Abraham points to the *future* Israel. It is the blessing that sheltered and accompanied Abraham, the effects of which are to extend to the Israel of the monarchy and beyond that to all the families of the earth."[97] Consequently, the representation of Israel as a "great nation" has no doubt clear optimism in the mind of the narrator or editor who as many assumed is writing from the context of exile. As we are going to see, the metaphor of a "great nation" as a symbol for Israel has a consolatory function since the narrator points Israel backs to Yahweh's speeches who promised their forefather Abram the potential to be a great nation. It does not matter where you place the narrator or editor, his task remained unchanged whether exilic or pre-exiliche carefully told the stories of the past that are filled with promises of greatness which could be realized in each generation by the children of Abraham.

The fourth metaphor is seen in the divine promise to make the "name" of Abram great. Modern versions such as the New American Bible, Revised Standard Version, New King James Version and even the New International Version have maintained the traditional translation of Genesis 12:2c in the idiomatic rendering of "making the name of Abram great." However, as rightly captured by the New Living Translation and the New Jerusalem Bible, the divine promise is a metaphor that aims at making Abram famous. In essence, Yahweh is promising Abram the fame that was possibly attained by the hybrid of Genesis 6:1–4 and the ambition of the arrogant builders of the tower of Babel in Genesis 11:1–9. The giant hybrid of Genesis 6 were known as "men of name," "legendary figure" or "men of renown." Similarly, the builders of the tower wanted a "name" for themselves, that is,

---

96. See Clines, ed. *The Dictionary of Classical Hebrew*, 322–324; 329–334.
97. Westermann, *Genesis 12–36*, 147.

they wanted to attain the fame possibly of the giants.[98] However, Yahweh promised Abram this fame without the aggressiveness of the tower of Babel or the immorality of the hybrids of giants. In a sense, within the context of the genealogy of Shem, which means "name" or "fame", Abram is promised "fame" thus suggesting or showing that Abram is the truest son of "Shem" ("name"). Ironically, "fame" is promised to the "son of fame."

The fifth figurative expression speaks of "those who will bless you" and "one who will belittle you." These participles are figures of speech describing the "friends and enemies" of Abraham. However, instead of just merely saying "friends" or "enemies" of Abram, the divine speeches working with the motif of blessing employed a different way to describe friends or enemies of Abram. Put simply, Yahweh's speech presupposes that friendship to Abram will bring about divine blessing and becoming Abram's enemy will bring about a divine curse.

The sixth figurative or metaphoric expression is found in verse 3c when God said that the "families of the earth" will find blessing in Abram. The phrase "families of the earth" represents the nations of the earth. In the preceding genealogy of the table of nations in Genesis 10, the word translated "families" that is, מִשְׁפָּחָה features prominently in verses 5, 18, 20, 31, and 32. While in the above verses it was used for the different branches of the sons of Noah, in Genesis 12:3, it is employed as a metaphor for the entirety of the human race. In this perspective, מִשְׁפְּחֹת הָאֲדָמָה stands for the "people of the earth" who according to the divine speeches are going to find blessing in Abram and his descendants. In the usage of הָאֲדָמָה in the creation narratives, which literally could mean "dust, land or earth," the phrase itself might be literally translated as "the families of dust", particularly in light of the creation narratives where God is said to have created man from the earth. Even if this rendering is contested, however, the combination of the "families of the earth" is another way of speaking of the entire humanity, thus the phrase is used in place of the people of the

---

98. Ronald Hendel treated שם as a *leitwort* which connects Genesis 6:4, 11:4 and 12:2. See Ronald Hendel, "Leitwort Style and Literary Structure in the J Primeval Narrative," *Sacred History, Sacred Literature: Essays on Ancient Israel, the Bible, and Religion in Honor of R.E. Friedman on His Sixtieth Birthday*, ed. Shawna Dolansky (Winona Lake, Indiana: Eisenbrauns, 2008), 107.

world. In fact, with the exception of its occurrence in another divine speech of Genesis 28:24 and Amos 3:2, this combination of words even though looking simple is never again found in the entirety of the Hebrew Bible. In the context of Genesis, the "families of the earth" is a metaphor for the different nations of the world.

The last metaphor is found in the second divine speech in verse 7. The metaphor is the word זֶרַע or "seed" which is used to describe the descendant of Abram.[99] Concerning this term, Alter noted:

> The Hebrew noun *zeraʿ* has the general meaning of 'seed,' which can be applied either in the agricultural sense or to human beings, as the term for semen. By metaphorical extension, semen becomes the established designation for what it produces, progeny. Modern translators, evidently unwilling to trust the ability of adult readers to understand that 'seed' as regularly in the King James Version may mean progeny, repeatedly render it as offspring, descendants, heirs, progeny, posterity. But I think there is convincing evidence in the texts themselves that the biblical writers never entirely forgot that their term for offspring also meant semen and had a precise equivalent in the vegetable world.[100]

Thus, in translations, the metaphoric nature of the term "seed" is often lost in the quest for a dynamic equivalent since the English terms such as "descendants," "posterity" or "offspring" do not have the double nuances for "progeny" and the intended agricultural imagery of a physical crop. Significantly, up till this time in the narration of Genesis, with the exception of the use of the term for Seth by Eve in Genesis 4:25 and the divine curse in Genesis 3:15, the word was mainly used to describe fruit trees or the flora. However, here we see God applying this term to the descendant of Abram. Like the seed or crop, he expected descendants from Abram. The

---

99. Clines, ed. *The Dictionary of Classical Hebrew*, vol. III (Sheffield: Sheffield Academic Press, 1996), 141–144.
100. Alter, *Genesis*, xiii.

agricultural imagery here is indeed strong, look at the way the divine speech juxtaposed land and seed in verse 7. The "seeds" of Abram are promised the "land." In a physical agricultural understanding, the "seeds" need "land" to grow, thus validating the need of Abram's "seeds" to have a "land."[101] From the context of creation, the seeds grew out of the earth or land in an almost metaphoric sense, Yahweh gives the "seed" of Abram a land in order to grow and multiply.[102] Consequently, the "seeds" become unproductive or even useless if they are not planted on a "land" or in the earth. In almost the same way, Yahweh promised the "seeds" of Abram a "land" in order to grow or multiply.[103] It is not surprising that the next divine speeches in Genesis 13:14–18 and even Genesis 15:5 focused on the theme of divine blessing particularly the multiplication of the "seeds of Abram."

3.1.1.3.2. Paronomasia

The literary device of paronomasia is defined by Isaac Kalimi as a "collection of words which resemble one another in their roots or consonantal sounds," but which "differ in meaning."[104] The purpose of paronomasia in text is primarily "to shape an utterance in an aesthetic fashion, rendering it pleasant to the ear of the listener or the reader; to arouse the

---

101. In this particular instance, the metaphor of "seeds" in close proximity with the theme of a "land" already provoked a vivid agricultural image. This connection is the powerful role of metaphor as a "coping mechanism" which seeks to define or understand reality. Thus Ekkehart Malotki observed, "Man, in confronting reality, faces a kaleidoscope of phenomena ranging from the natural to the man-made, to the imaginary, to the totally abstract. Comprehension of such a broad inventory of reality and non-reality requires language, the tool that permits man to take verbal stock of objective and subjective experiences alike. In man's ongoing endeavor to conceptualize and verbalize a world that can never be fully known, language is the vital intermediary. Language provides a repertoire of coping mechanism, of which metaphor is one of the most powerful and useful." see Malotki, *Hopi Time* (Berlin: Mouton, 1983), 13.

102. Baruch A. Levine observed that "land" in the Bible is often compared to the womb, and thus the fertilization of a male sperm, which is represented by seed in a womb, is derived from an agrarian metaphor which associates human sexual intercourse with the physical fertilization of "seed" in a "land" or soil. See Baruch A. Levine, " 'Seed' Versus 'Womb': Expressions of Male Dominance in Biblical Israel," *Sex and Gender in the Ancient Near East*, eds. Simo Parpola and R.M. Whiting, Part II. Proceedings of the XLVII Roncontre Assyriologique Internationale, Helsinki, 337–343 (Helsinki: The Neo-Assyrian Text Corpus Project, 2002), 341.

103. Hartley, *Genesis*, 134.

104. Isaac Kalimi, "Paronomasia in the Book of Chronicles," *JSOT* 67 (1995), 27.

reader's or listener's interest and to render the significance of the utterance profound."[105] Following R. Weiss, Kalimi further noted that this literary aesthetic is achieved in paronomasia because "the repetitive sounds link separate entities, draw distant ones nearer to one another, bestow shape upon allusions, and reveal hidden truthsthey emphasize and explain."[106] As a literary device, paronomasia has been fairly common in both modern and ancient literature. This literary device has been found within the ancient Near Eastern literature particularly those of Mesopotamia, Egypt, and Arabic sources. It has also been found in the writings of the New Testament and even in post-biblical religious literature. Despite its presence in these writings, paronomasia is somehow difficult to fully categorize because there are different tropes which are considered under the rubric of paronomasia.[107] For example, B. J. Beitzel in his treatment of paronomasia in Exodus 3:14 gave at least fourteen different categories under the rubrics of paronomasia.[108] These different tropes include gematria, atbash, acrostic, notrikon, acronymy, anastrophe, epanastrophe, equivocal, parasonance, farrago, assonance, onomatopoeia, and antanclasis.[109] The different categories he further placed under two divisions, namely visual and oral paronomasia. Despite the complex nature of the term and the association of the term with these different categories, Beitzel, defined paronomasia as the placement of one word alongside "another which appeared or sounded similar or identicalthus producing an aura of literary ambiguitybut which was actually quite different in origin and meaning."[110] In its common usage, paronomasia is conceived as the association or placement of words

---

105. Ibid.
106. R. Weiss, "Paronomasia in the Bible," *Mishut Ba-Mikra* (Jerusalem: A. Rubinstein, 1976), 163; Kalimi, "Paronomasia in the Book of Chronicles," 27.
107. For a classification of wordplay see Wilfred G. E. Watson, *Classical Hebrew Poetry: A Guide to Its Techniques*. JSOTSup Series 26 (Sheffield: JSOT Press, 1984).
108. B. J. Beitzel, "Exodus 3:14 and the Divine Name: A Case of Biblical Paronomasia," *TJ* 1 (1980): 5–20.
109. For the definition and example of these categories see Ibid., 5.
110. Ibid.

together, which even though different in etymology, have similarity of sound.[111]

Naturally, these definitions by Beitzel and the earlier one by Kalimi bring paronomasia in close relationship to alliteration and rhyme. Though this category appears absent in the categories of Beitzel, in the classical treatment of paronomasia, Immanuel Casanowicz placed alliteration, assonance and rhyme under "sound paronomasia" while he placed the combination of words of similar sounds to produce or show wit, jest or pun under "sense-paronomasia."[112] In these categories for paronomasia, the divine speeches also reveal the presence of alliteration, rhyme, and wordplay, hence justifying our present use of the term paronomasia as a broad literal label for these combined devices.

Beginning with alliteration, Casanowicz observed that "[a]lliteration is the simplest, most frequent, and probably the oldest form of paronomasia."[113] He defined alliteration as "the recurrence of the same initial letter or its phonetic equivalent in two or more words in close or immediate succession."[114] Unfortunately, recent decades in the study of biblical narratives have not adequately paid attention to the presence of alliteration in the biblical text. Noting this neglect, Rendsburg observed:

> The recent decades have seen a flowering of literary study of the Bible. Scholar after scholar has uncovered technique after technique in his or her reading and interpretation of biblical literature, both prose and poetry. In my reading of this vast amount of secondary literature, from which I and many others have learned a great deal, I am struck by how relatively little attention has been paid to the use of alliteration. Obviously, various examples of alliteration have been pointed out in certain instances . . . But on a relative scale, I believe

---

111. See Robert B. Chisholm, Jr., "Wordplay in the Eighth-Century Prophets," *BSac* 144, no. 573 (1987): 44–52.
112. Immanuel M. Casanowicz, *Paronomasia in the Old Testament* (Boston: Norwood Press, 1894), 3–4, 8, 12.
113. Ibid., 8.
114. Ibid.

Stylistic Aspects of the Divine Speeches

that my observation above is accurate—that in general, scholars have not paid sufficient attention to the role of alliteration in biblical literature, especially prose texts.[115]

Even though, generally as observed by Rendsburg, alliteration has been neglected, due to the strategic nature of our present pericope, scholars have rightly identified the alliteration surrounding the framing of these divine speeches. In particular, we see alliteration in וַאֲבָרְכָה מְבָרְכֶיךָ . . . וְנִבְרְכוּ . . . וֶאֱעֶשְׂךָ . . . וַאֲבָרֶכְךָ וַאֲגַדְּלָה . . . וֶהְיֵה בְּרָכָה . . . Repeatedly within this alliteration are the dominant verbs and nouns of blessing, which appeared here about five times.[116] Taking note of the importance of this alliteration in relationship to the name of Abram, Wenham observed, "Every mention of the term 'bless,' [or] 'blessing,' ברך, evokes the name "Abram," אברם . . ."[117] This wordplay in alliteration also possibly binds the name of Abram, blessing and "he passed through," עבר in verse 6 which occurred in its nominal form as title for Abram (אברם עברי "Abram the Hebrew,") in Genesis 14:13.[118] Similarly, there is also an apparent alliteration in the opening of the divine speeches in verse 1 especially in the nouns מֵאַרְצְךָ וּמִמּוֹלַדְתְּךָ וּמִבֵּית אָבִיךָ with their "alliterative 'from' [min]" heading "each phrase . . . reinforcing the command of separation required of Abram by God."[119] In addition, there is an alliteration in the framing of the first divine command in the Abrahamic cycle namely, לֶךְ־לְךָ.[120] Thus, through alliteration and wordplay, the narrator distinctively presented the divine speeches.

Lastly, the narrator also employed some form of rhyme in his presentation of the divine speeches within this pericope. The use of rhyme is

---

115. Rendsburg, "Alliteration in the Exodus Narrative," *Birkat Shalom: Studies Presented to Shalom M. Paul on the Occasion of His Seventieth Birthday* (Winona Lake, Indiana: Eisenbraus, 2008), 83.
116. According to Wenham, "The root ברך occurs more frequently in Genesis than in any other part of the OT: 88 times in Genesis as against 310 times elsewhere." See Wenham, *Genesis 1–15*, 274.
117. Ibid., 269.
118. Ibid., 274.
119. Matthews, *Genesis 11:27–50:26*, 109.
120. Ibid.

visible in the second pronominal suffixes which are attached to the key nouns and verbs of the divine speeches. The narrator employed a total of eleven second-person pronominal suffixes, thus grammatically directing the attention of the divine speeches on the character Abram, who formerly was just a name in a genealogical tree. Consequently, this second-person pronominal suffix produces a "kâ . . .kâ . . . kâ" sound which breathes continually throughout the divine speeches, and hence gives the divine speeches a kind of rhythm and rhyme. To this, Matthews observed that the "most prominent" stylistic "feature is the repetition of the pronoun 'you/your' *(kā)*, referring to Abram, and the first-person verbs, 'I will . . .,' referring to God."[121] Similarly, the "kā" rhyme at the end of the nouns and verbs are also blended artistically with alliteration of various forms of ברך within the divine speeches. In this way, the divine speeches are given a kind of rhythm which is not found within the sounding words that frame them. This rhyme and rhythm within the divine speeches are no doubt significant literary devices because they successfully project the divine speeches above the surrounding narrations so that the attention of the reader is captured by the repeated rhyme at the endings of the nouns and verbs and by also the inherent alliteration of the verbs and nouns themselves.[122]

3.1.1.3.3. Repetition

Revell defined repetition as the "avoidable re-statement of the same ideas using (at least in part) the same words."[123] According to him, repetition "is a common feature of Biblical Hebrew which is treated with a "sort of aversion" by speakers of English or other European languages.[124] On the importance of repetition in Genesis, Turner observed that repetition, "among other things," seeks "to reinforce the important, remind the hearer

---

121. Ibid.

122. There are stylistic studies on the use of paronomasia in other parts of the Bible. For example see Nachman Levine, "Twice As Much of Your Spirit: Pattern, Parallel and Paronomasia in the Miracle of Elijah and Elisha," *JSOT* 85 (1999): 25–46; Duane L. Christensen, "Anticipatory Paronomasia in Jonah 3:7–8 and Genesis 37: 2," *RB* 90, no. 1 (1983): 261–263.

123. Revell, "The Repetition of Introductions to Speech as Feature of Biblical Hebrew," *VT* 47 (1997), 92.

124. Ibid.

of antecedent steps in the plot, or sometimes merely to delight in the aesthetics of hearing the cadences of familiar phrases."[125] Even though formerly misunderstood, through the works of Alter and Sternberg, repetition has now become increasingly recognized as an artistic feature of biblical narrative, rather than a form of unskillful assembling of sources by the biblical narrator or redactor.[126] Unfortunately despite this new understanding, we still cannot discern fully the significance of repetition to an ancient Jewish narrator or even its significance in the thought of the Semitic people.[127] For example, this is true especially in reference to the repeated episode of the "wife-sister" in the patriarchal narratives, which misunderstanding has engendered various hermeneutical proposals. In particular, the problem with repetition is that it runs contrary to the economical and reticent character of the biblical narrator who often gives merely a few comments and, as a general rule, does not divulge information. However, in repetition, the biblical narrator breaks away from the usual reticent persona by which he is known in order to assert what from his point of view demands repetition.

Particularly important in our study of the present pericope is the repetition of *leitwort* or motif, which had already been mentioned in the preceding section of Genesis.[128] One of such motif or *leitwort* is the theme of divine blessing which is clearly seen in the creation story and the flood, but which is now given to Abram. By the repetition of blessing which appeared five times in a space of two verses (Gen 12:2–3), the narrator wanted the reader to go back in time to the preceding stories. Significantly, two characters come to mind, whom the narrator told they were blessed by God, namely Adam and Noah. Consequently, the *leitwort* here seems to be ברך

---

125. Turner, *Genesis*, 15.
126. Alter, *The Art of Biblical Narrative*, 88–113; Sternberg, *The Poetics of Biblical Narrative*, 365–440.
127. For example, Barbara Johnstone in her study of the Arabic language talks about the "morphological repetition" inherent in Arabic which also appears to be true in other Semitic language, thus the nature of the Semitic language itself made "repetition" a necessary aspect of their language use or expression. See Barbara Johnstone, *Repetition in Arabic Discourse: Paradigms, Syntagms, and the Ecology of the Language* (Amsterdam: Benjamin Publishers, 1991), 53–75, 109–13.
128. On the binding power of leitwort in Genesis stories see Hendel, "Leitwort Style and Literary Structure in the J Primeval Narrative," 93–109.

which appeared in the creation story and at the end of the flood narrative.[129] This repetition of ברך in the two verses of the divine speeches no doubt has a significant place in our reading of the entire Abrahamic stories in the light of Genesis. One overriding significance will be that in the mind of the narrator he draws a comparison between Adam and Noah.[130] In this understanding, he might have seen Abram as a new Adam or even a new Noah.[131] As a new Adam, Abram is free from the disobedience of the first couple, who refused to follow totally the divine command not to eat from the tree.[132] In this perspective, Abram exemplified the virtue of obedience which is absent in the story of Adam. In his obedience, he attracted lasting divine blessing rather than the curse of Adam. It is this way of thinking especially in the association of Abram with Adam that reasoned that the framing of the blessing using five clauses in the present pericope is not without its significance. To this end, Wenham had reasoned that the mentioning of the five blessings in the present pericope might possibly be to counteract the five curses found in the preceding section of Genesis namely from 3:1 to 11:26,[133] thus he noted:

> [b]ut the promises first made to Abraham in 12:1–3 begin to repair that hopeless situation. The fivefold blessing here

---

129. See for example Genesis 1:22, 28; 2:3; 5:2. cf. 9:1, 26.

130. Structurally, this comparison is seen by giving the space of ten generations from Adam to Noah and from Noah to Abraham. See Gary V. Smith, "The Structure of Genesis 1–11," *JETS* 20, no. 4 (1977), 321.

131. On the indirect characterization of Abram as a new Adam, Sailhamer observed, "Abraham is represented here as a new Adam and the 'seed of Abraham' as a second Adam, a new humanity." Similarly, concerning the depiction of Abram as a new Noah, Sailhamer also noted, "[t]he similarities between the two narratives are striking and show that Abraham, like Noah, marks a new beginning as a return to God's original plan of blessing 'all humankind' (1:28)." See Sailhamer, *The Pentateuch as Narrative*, 140, 139.

132. Comparing Abram with Adam, Wenham noted, "In the beginning man had been told to be fruitful and multiply: the Abrahamic promises mean that at least one nation is going to achieve that goal. Man had been told to subdue the earth. From Abraham are to come kings and princes (17:6, 20). The Lord God created Adam a garden in which he enjoyed the intimate presence of God: Abraham is likewise Promised Land and an intimate covenant relationship in which the Lord would be their God, and they would be his people. Finally, the Abrahamic covenant will not just benefit Abraham and his descendants, but in him all the nations of the earth shall find blessing." See Wenham, *Genesis 1–15*, li.

133. These curses are recorded in Genesis 3:14, 17; 4:11; 5:29 and 9:25.

counteracts the five curses that have been pronounced earlier. What is more, the promise of land, nationhood, the presence of God, and blessing to the nations restores what has been lost by man through his misbehavior recorded in Gen 3–11.[134]

Consequently, through the repetition of the *leitwörter*, the narrator directed the reader to the significance of the Abrahamic cycle yet he told the story in relationship to the preceding stories of creation and the flood.

3.1.1.5.4. Allusion

Gordon H. Johnston defines allusion as "a subtle reference by an author or speaker to a statement, theme, or motif from another source."[135] Differentiating allusion from quotation, Johnston further observed, "[b]oth allusions and quotations draw on a source text, but allusions do so in a manner different from quotations."[136] In addition, "quotations are signaled by introductory quotation formulas, whereas allusions are signaled by more subtle means."[137] Understood in this way, allusions involve a subtle relationship between the source materials and the said allusion.[138] In particular, Biblical allusions or inner-biblical exegesis as they are now called, is a new label for a previous Jewish and Christian recognition of the mechanics or dynamism of intertextuality, especially the dependence of the

---

134. Wenham, *Genesis 1–15*, li.
135. Gordon H. Johnston, "Nahum's Rhetorical Allusions to the Neo-Assyrian Lion Motif," *BSac* 158, no. 631 (2001), 287.
136. Ibid.
137. Ibid., 288.
138. For several interesting studies on allusions see Ziva Ben-Porat, "The Poetics of Literary Allusion," *Journal for Descriptive Poetics and Theory of Literature* 1 (1976): 105–28; idem, "The Poetics of Allusion: A Text-Linking Device," in *A Semiotic Landscape: Proceedings of the First Congress of the International Association for Semiotic Studies*, ed. S. Chatman (The Hague: Mouton, 1979), 588–93; Carmela Perri, "On Alluding," *Poetics* 7 (1978): 289–307; idem, "Knowing and Playing: The Literary Text and the Trope Allusion," *American Imago* 41 (1984): 117–28; idem, "Allusion Studies: An International Annotated Bibliography, 1921–1977," *Style* 13 (1979): 178–225; James H. Coombs, "Allusion Defined and Explained," *Poetics* 13 (1984): 475–88; Earl Miner, "Allusion," in *Princeton Encyclopedia of Poetry and Poetics*, ed. Alex Preminger *et al.* (Princeton, NJ: Princeton University Press, 1974), 17–18; Udo J. Habel, *Intertextuality, Allusion, and Quotation: An International Bibliography of Critical Studies* (Westport, CT: Greenwood, 1989).

biblical materials on each other.¹³⁹ Christians as well as Jews have through the course of their respective histories seen a forged literary and even typological connection between the different parts of the Old Testament. For the Christian this allusion is furthermore stretched in order to encompass the relationship, use, or quotation of the Old Testament by the New. Within both of these traditions, the allusion to the present pericope is fairly common. For example, allusion to the divine statement is presented as a reason for the establishment of the Israelite ancient or even modern state. Similarly, within the Christian tradition, especially the distinctive Pauline usage or allusion to this pericope, it is assumed that divine statement here looked for its future fulfillment in Jesus Christ.

Our present interest is not the allusion made to this highlighted reference, but to underscore the thesis that this pericope as a "janus-like" strategic unit looked both ways to the past and the future of the Israelites.¹⁴⁰ Within the divine statements the past and the future are presented even though in vague or allusive forms. In the preceding work, we have shown how the divine speeches looked backward to the episodes of creation and the flood by repetition of the theme of blessing, hence forming a kind of allusion to creation and the flood. In the present treatment, we could also

---

139. Yair Zakovitch describes this presence of "literary allusions" which is particularly seen in the way the chapters in the Abrahamic cycle placed against or complementing one another in what he called, "juxtaposition." Speaking of this phenomenon in the Abrahamic cycle, Zakovitch observed, "much material that is embedded in the biblical text is itself exegetical material, consisting 'inner-biblical interpretation.' One verse or story intended to influence our reading of another, either to solve a problem in that text, or to adopt it to the interpreter's beliefs and ideas. One type of inner-biblical interpretation is achieved through juxtaposition of two units: the placement of two texts one after the other, one or both of which is meant to affect our reading of the other" [Zakovitch, "Juxtaposition in the Abraham Cycle," *Pomegranates and Gold Bells: Studies in Biblical, Jewish, and Near Eastern Ritual, Law, and Literature in Honor of Jacob Milgrom*, eds. David P. Wright, David Noel Freedman and Avi Hurvitz (Winona Lake, Indiana: Eisenbraus, 1995), 509–24]. Zakovitch showed the presence of such allusions or juxtaposition of materials from Genesis 12–24. If chapters are framed as allusion to one another as described by Zakovitch, it thence follows that the presence of allusion in divine statement itself might be derived from this dominant motif of allusions or juxtapositioning of the chapters.

140. "Allusion" as Alter rightly observed, "is not merely a device, like irony, understatement, ellipsis, or repetition, but an essential modality of the language of literature." See Alter, *The Pleasures of Reading in an Ideological Age*, 111.

see how the future of Israel is in embryonic form buried or expected in allusive form within the boundary of the divine speeches here.

Firstly, the entire episode of the "land" and in particular the land of "Canaan" already is an explicit allusion to the cardinal place "the issue of land" played in subsequent biblical narratives particularly the post-exodus narratives. The philosophy of conquest between Israelites and the Canaanites, even though not clearly reflected on the pages of Genesis, mentioning by the narrator in that the "Canaanites" were already in the land at critical points in the narration which looked forward to the possibility of conflict in the future since God promised to Abram a land which is already inhabited. One may ask why did God not give Israel an empty land rather than giving to them a land which already had owners? Thus the divine statement of the gift of land to the descendants of Israel already anticipated the question of ownership or the modality by which the land would become successfully Abram's.

Secondly, the allusion to the greatness of Israel and the giving of a famous name to Abram who is going to vouchsafe divine blessing to the nations of the earth is likely an allusion to the glory days of David and even Solomon when ancient Israel reached the apex of its glory. Similarly, like Abram, God promised David a "great name" and "future royal descendants."[141] Thus buried within these divine speeches are the expectations of the founding of a nation and the greatness of that nation among the community of nations. Using the biblical plot, such a lofty vision of ancient Israel became a reality in the reigns of David and Solomon.

Lastly, there is an allusion to those that blessed Abram and his descendants and those that would curse them. In the immediate context of the Pentateuch, this reference for the blessing of Abram might be an allusion to Melchizedek who ironically comes from Salem or Jerusalem, which will be

---

141. According to Matthews, the promise "is proleptic of the divine oath to David, which shares in the language of 12:2 (2 Sam 7:9). The seed promised to Abram finds its future reality in the monarchic ideal through David's house." See Matthews, *Genesis 11:27–50:26*, 114. Similarly, John Goldingay has observed that "Abraham influences the portrayal of David, his testing on a mount in Moriah is now part of the justification for building a temple there, and his acknowledging of Melchizedek is part of the justification for acknowledging David, who has inherited Melchizedek's position" [See John Goldingay, *Theological Diversity and the Authority of the Old Testament* (Grand Rapids, Michigan: Eerdmans, 1987), 8].

the future seat of King David. For those that will curse Abram and his descendants, the immediate persons that come to mind are Balak and Balaam who sought to curse Israel (Num 22–24). There in the book of Numbers, we see the futility of seeking to curse the descendants of Abram. Finally, the allusion to Abram becoming a blessing to other nations could also be seen in its embryonic form within the book of Genesis and the subsequent climax in the lofty universal vision of the "second" part of Isaiah. In the pages of Genesis, we see Abram becoming a blessing to the nations of Sodom and Gomorrah particularly in his militant war against the nations of the east in Genesis 14.[142] We also see him interceding for this same people in Genesis 18. The descendants of Abram are also depicted as continuing the blessing motif that lies within the divine speeches. In particular, we see God blessing Laban the Aramean because of Jacob, and Joseph becoming a blessing to the house of Potiphar, Pharaoh and subsequent the entire land of Egypt and the neighboring communities. Due to the strategic importance of Egypt in the affairs of the international community of the ancient society, the last picture of a descendant of Abram in the person of Joseph holding a political position which becomes a blessing to the land of Egypt at the critical moment of famine (like the same famine in Genesis 12:10 that pushed his forefather Abram to Egypt) in Egypt, no doubt for the moment is a fulfilment of the key element of the divine speeches that nations of the world will find blessing in Abram and his descendants.[143]

---

142. On the difficulty of this chapter see J. A. Soggin, "Abraham and the Eastern Kings: On Genesis 14," *Solving Riddles and Untying Knots: Biblical Epigraphic, and Semitic Studies in Honor of Jones C. Greenfield*, ed. Ziony Zevit, Seymour and Michael Sokoloff (Winona Lake, Indiana: Einsenbraus, 1995), 283–291.

143. In addition, the motif of blessing many people and cursing a few is also maintained in the divine speech of Exodus 32:6–7 where the Bible says, "The Lord, the Lord, the compassionate and gracious God, slow to anger, abounding in love and faithfulness, maintaining love to thousands, and forgiving wickedness, rebellion and sin. Yet he does not leave the guilty unpunished; he punishes the children and their children for the sin of the fathers to the third and fourth generation."

3.1.1.3.5. Suspense

Suspense is a common stylistic feature of modern fictions.[144] Through this literary device a narrator holds the continuous interest of his reader, feeding this suspense until the resolution of the plot. This literary and cinematic device is not, however, a modern creation or invention, since storytellers in almost all generations have used the same technique of suspense in order to hold their listeners or readers bound to their tale.[145] In particular the biblical narrative and its reticent character already introduces elements of suspense within the telling of biblical stories. This characteristic of suspense is clearly seen within these opening divine speeches, which leave many things unsaid, and seem vague about the things that are said. For example, we are not told the final destination of Abram. We are not told the reason for the choice of Canaan. We are not told how Abram will have future descendants when he and his wife Sarai are barren. We are not told how such a barren couple would become a blessing to the nations of the earth. We are not told who are going to be the one to bless or curse Abram. We are not told whether Abram will occupy the land immediately or it would take him many generations to do so. We are not told what part Lot would play in this journey particularly in the light of frequent mentioning of his name.[146]

However, it is within this reticent character of the divine speeches that lies the suspense which becomes inevitable in any good story. The problem with these divine speeches is not necessarily that they are vague, even though they are, but that they are economical or reticent on the ways or means by which Abram will become a blessing to other nations or telling the readers the means by which Abram will possess the land or even the means by which Abram will become a father of a son. On the contrary, the divine speeches do not major on these cardinal thoughts or means,

---

144. Delay or suspense "consists in not imparting information where it is 'due' in the text, but leaving it for a later stage. Depending on the temporal dimension to which the withheld information belongs, delay can create suspense of two different types: future-oriented and past-oriented (i.e. oriented toward the future or the past of the story)" [Rimon-Kenan, *Narrative Fiction*, 125].

145. See Rachelle Gilmour, "Suspense and Anticipation in 1 Samuel 9:1–14," *JJSC* 9, no. 10 (2009): 2–16.

146. See G. W. Coats, "Lot: A Foil in the Abraham Saga," *Understanding the Word: FS B. W. Anderson*, ed. J. T. Butler, E. W. Conrad, and B. C. Ollenburger. JSOTSup 37 (Sheffield: JSOT Press, 1985), 113–32.

but concentrate mainly on the end. In particular, the divine speeches are in plurality rather than singularity. For example, Abram needs only a son, but the divine speech in verse 7 in particular talks about descendants or "seeds." He needs only a family after him, but the divine speech is promising a "great nation." Similarly, Abram needs only blessing to meet the need of his immediate family but God is promising a blessing that would reach the "families of the earth." Thus in the bogus nature, plurality or universal nature of these divine speeches, the narrator put before us the element of suspense particularly in the question how a person like Abram who was a moment ago an inconsequential branch of his family tree, can become a blessing to the whole family of nations? The suspense is built in the reticence of the narrator who refused to tell us everything from the beginning and gradually, step-by-step, introduces us to the realization of these divine speeches. He could have begun from the realized point of these divine speeches and then traced it backward to how it all began, but instead he chooses to tell us from the beginning how these divine speeches formed the origin of ancient Israel.

Adopting the usual plot line of biblical stories, which moves from creation to the chaos of the exile, the narrator employed suspense as a means to hold the reader or listener on the edge as they seek to find out in the life of Abram how these divine speeches actually become true. From the hindsight of exile, or wherever the narrator is historically situated, he sees the past backward to his time. He introduces different kinds of dangers to the Abram stories that could jeopardize these divine speeches, but over and over again the character Abram comes out of each danger and thus shows that Yahweh is committed to making his speeches true in the life of the patriarch. As subsequent studies will show, some of the dangers are the temporary enslavement of Sarah in Pharaoh's harem in Genesis 12:10–20, the attack on the heir apparent in Genesis 14, the aging of the couples in Genesis 15 and 17, the introduction of the character Hagar in Genesis 16, the second endangering of Sarah in Genesis 20:1–18, and even the divine request to slaughter Isaac in Genesis 22. These episodes of dangers also extend the story of Abram and put the reader on edge, whether these divine speeches and many of these divine speeches within the cycle will at the end become true for Abram.

Thus the suspense and plot of the Abrahamic cycle is built on nothing but the divine speeches. The divine speeches with their "bogus" promises are placed constantly in danger, hence building the stories to their final resolution. The divine speeches move the selection and arrangement, as well as the plotting, of the Abrahamic narratives, thus underscoring partly the reason for their stylistic features.

3.1.1.3.6. Gradation

Gradation is a literary and stylistic device whereby the narrator describes items, persons or categories of his narrative by means of progression, that is, from tallest to the lowest, richest to the poorest, general to the specific, or the other way round. For example, we see gradation in the creation story which starts with light, firmament, land, solar system, bird and sea creatures, and then on the sixth day the creation of man. Thus by this arrangement, the narrator already points to the direction of his story, that is, it is not going to be stories about birds, sea creatures or the solar system, but about man. In this way, the narrator makes man the center of God's creation. In the same way, the curses in Genesis 3:14–19 are also placed in gradation first beginning with the curse on the Serpent, the woman, and then the man. Yairah Amit has significantly brought to the attention of biblical studies, the present and overwhelming nature of this literary device within the Bible.[147] In particular, she has shown how the narrator of biblical narratives often employed this technique in the framing and presenting of his narrative materials.

We also see the technique of gradation at work within the divine speeches in four areas. Firstly, the divine speech in Genesis 12:1, as shown by Amit, begins with the broadness of מֵאַרְצְךָ or "from your land," and followed by וּמִמּוֹלַדְתְּךָ or "from your clan" and then lastly to וּמִבֵּית אָבִיךָ or "and your father's house."[148] The divine speech shows here a progressive

---

147. See Yairah Amit, "Progression as a Rhetorical Device in Biblical Literature," *JSOT* 28, no. 1 (2003): 3–32.

148. In this verse, the preposition מִן governs more than one complement, hence it is repeated before each of the complement. There are however cases where a preposition is written only before the first complement (cf. 1 Sam 15:22). See Merwe *et al*, *A Biblical Hebrew Reference Grammar*, 240.

logic from the land, to smaller family unit and then the father's house. Here, there is a stylistic progression in the arrangement of these nouns at the opening of the divine speeches. It also moves from the broadness of the "your land" to the specificity of "your father's house." Similarly, the divine speeches move from the emphases on Abram as evidenced by the second pronominal suffixes of the divine speeches in verses 1–3 and climaxes at the end with the "families of the earth." It seems that the divine speeches here move between the polarities of particularity to universality as seen in the speeches directed to the person of Abram and then having at the end significance for the "families of the earth." In the same way, the divine speeches move from the broadness or generality of the statement "to the land that I will show you" in verse 1 and then to the specificity of the land in verse 7 as seen in the divine statement, "this land." Lastly, there is also gradation in the description of the divine speech to Abram. In the context of the silent genealogy of Genesis 11:27–32, there is a progression in the divine speech to Abram in Genesis 12:1, which culminates in this pericope with not merely a divine speech, but a divine appearance in verse 7. Thus it seems to suggest that from the ignominy and obscurity of the genealogical tree God selected Abram and spoke to him, and then appeared to him again with reassuring words of promises. This progression is evident as already seen in the close relationship between verses 1–3 and 7 because God merely spoke to Abram in verse 1 and moves now to a more closer relationship as seen in God now appearing and speaking to Abram in verse 7. Thus, through the stylistic device of gradation, the narrator helps us to progressively see the ensuring relationship between Abram and Yahweh.

3.1.1.4. Significance

From the foregoing investigations in the stylistic features of the divine speeches, the significance of the divine speeches in Genesis 12:1–9 becomes obvious to the reader of the Abrahamic cycle. Looking at these literary-styled divine speeches, six significances emerge as one reads the stories of the Abrahamic cycle. Firstly, the divine speeches in Genesis 12:1–9 initiate the plot of the entire Abrahamic narratives. It sets the Abrahamic stories in motion. The plot of the entire Abrahamic stories lies in the thesis that Yahweh called Abraham to be a blessing to the nations. The divine speeches in this present pericope provide the fulcrum on which the entire Abrahamic narratives swing. Consequently, the presence of stylistic features in these divine speeches points to their importance in understanding the main concern of the Abrahamic narratives. Secondly, the literary-styled divine speeches in this pericope function as tool of characterization. In particular, the divine speeches help to characterize Abram by bringing Abram out of the genealogical list of the preceding chapter and asserting his importance on the world scene. Through the divine speeches, Abram moves from being a name dotting the ancestry tree of Shem towards becoming a character in the truest sense of the word. Thirdly, the divine speeches introduce or awake the feeling of suspense, anticipation and anxiety in the heart of the reader as he or she reads through the Abrahamic narratives because the divine speeches present a different reality that conflicts directly with the experiences of Abram. For example, the divine speeches promised Abram that he would become a "great nation" while Abram is reported earlier as being childless (11:30). Fourthly, these divine speeches present the divine point of view, which duly helps as a guide to the reader as he or she reads through the present pericope. In narrative, the character's speeches are important pointers toward the point of view of narrative characters. To this end, these first divine speeches in the Abrahamic narratives provide a fundamental piece in understanding the subsequent succession of events in the Abrahamic narratives especially as closely related to the subject of the divine point of view. In particular, the divine speech in the present pericope shows a distinctive divine perception and interest on Abram and his descendants. Everything in the world is defined around Abram and his descendants. Fifthly, the divine speech serves as a structuring device which stands at the head of the Abrahamic cycle. The reader of Genesis is hereby presented with new materials which differ in many ways from the preceding primeval materials (Gen 1–11). One could readily discern the newness of this section because it is the first time in Genesis that Yahweh has to command a biblical character to move from a particular geographical location to another and with the mind-blowing promises to make this fellow a blessing to the nations of the earth. Lastly, the styled divine speeches in this pericope even though new, explore motifs that look backward to the preceding stories in Genesis, and also forward to other divine speeches and events in Genesis and the entire Pentateuch, thus these divine speeches serve as a "literary and theological" bridge which links the preceding stories in Genesis to the immediate Abrahamic narratives and to the larger concerns of the book of Genesis. Specifically through allusions and repetitions, the divine speeches look forward to the subsequent events in Genesis, but also backward to the preceding events.

3.2.1. Genesis 13:1–18

3.2.1.1. Structure

The structure of Genesis 13:1–18 seems to be clearly defined. Firstly, there is a reminder in verse 1 that Abram returned from his journey to Egypt. The narrator took his time to tell us about the return by a repetition of the phrase in the immediately preceding verse in Genesis 12:20 which says "his wife and all that belongs to him" (וְאִשְׁתּוֹ וְכָל־אֲשֶׁר־לוֹ). This same phrase is repeated in Genesis 13:1, thus our new passage looked backward to the events in the preceding passage. This part of the passage introduced key issues that are fundamental to the plot of the present pericope namely the return of Abram, his growing wealth, and his worship of Yahweh in the vicinity of Bethel. The information given was not merely given for the sake of giving information but vital to the understanding of the plot of the story. Primarily, this introduction helps to further reveal the character of Abram despite his blunders at Egypt. In particular, the narrative noted that "Abram called on the name of Yahweh" in verse 4b. This in itself is a repairing work by the narrator to show the commitment of Abram towards Yahweh despite his immediate failure to trust Yahweh in the account of his journey to Egypt. This introduction covers from verses 1–4 and presents the basic narrative elements which are needed in order to understand the following story.

The next section of the present pericope is seen in verses 5–7. There the narrator made use of וְגַם that is, "and also" to introduce the reader to the conflict of the story. Even though the waw conjunction when attached to a non-verb signalizes a disjunctive clause, in this context the conjunction should be understood not as disjunctive because it gives the reader additional information rather than making contrast. The additional information here is that the nephew Lot has also acquired great wealth, thereby making it impossible for the two of them to stay together.[149] In addition, the new subsection in the pericope is introduced by the paragraph-like break carried out in his use of וַיְהִי. Even though this paragraph-marker is often translated as "and it was" or in the archaic King James "and it came to pass" the idea is to introduce sequence or a break from the preceding narration. Here, this break is not a break into another story but a break that shows development in the events which made up the present story.

Following this section is verses 8–13, which describe the speeches of Abram to quell the conflict between himself and his nephew. This section of the pericope is introduced by the discourse marker וַיֹּאמֶר which is translated "and he said." This וַיֹּאמֶר is a break from the flat narration of the context. The narrator wanted through this discourse to create a vivid picture of the events already described. This is the second speech by Abram in the Abrahamic cycle and helps us to see the character of Abram vividly. If the first speech of Abram in Genesis 12:11–13 shows his selfishness, this second speech remedies that because it shows his selflessness. However, both speeches have one basic attribute—they were speeches made to the member of one's family and were not directed at the outsider. They seem to have taken place in the privacy of communion firstly between a husband and his wife and secondly between an uncle and his nephew. On the other hand, the speech of Abram talks about spatial categories in terms of "left" or "right." However, as we are going to see in our treatment of the following divine speech in verse 14–17, the divine speeches also used "spatial categories" though not in terms of "left or right" but "north, south, east and west" and also "length and breadth" of the land.[150] This speech of Abram is

---

149. See L. A. Turner, "Lot as Jekyll and Hyde," *The Bible in Three Dimensions*, ed. D. J. A. Clines, S. E. Fowl, and S. E. Porter. JSOTSup 87 (Sheffield: Sheffield Academic Press, 1990), 85–101.

150. The presence of the cardinal points is a case of literary device known as *merism*. This literary device is described as an expression employed "for a totality consisting of two opposites joined by a conjunction." In fact, "many instances of merism in English correspond to biblical Hebrew equivalents: up and down, near and far, heaven and earth" [Brichto, *Toward a Grammar of Biblical Poetics*, 42]. In our text, north is the opposite of south (צָפֹנָה וָנֶגְבָּה), and east is also the opposite of west (וָקֵדְמָה וָיָמָּה). Both of these opposite geographical points are joined together by the conjuction וְ. Possibly, the merism here in the divine speech is employed as a literary device in order to counter another

followed by narration and comment by the narrator in verse 10–13, thus this subsection covers from the discourse marker of verse 8 to the winding narrator's comment about Lot's selfish choice and relocation to Sodom and the wickedness of this place in verse 13. In contrast to Lot's selfishness, Abram remained true to staying in the land. This section shows the resolution of the conflict by the selflessness of Abram.

The next section begins by a break from the preceding section. This break is introduced by the phrase, "and Yahweh said" in verse 14. One of the significances of the divine speech here is that it gives the true resolution to the conflict in the narratives. "After Lot departed from him" provided the immediate context for the divine speeches and shows that Yahweh spoke from the atmosphere of the selfish choice of the Jordan valley by Lot. As subsequent studies will show, the speech, through vivid imagery, metaphor and other techniques, created a vivid picture of Yahweh's quest to tell Abram that he had made the right choice in remaining in the land. This divine speech runs from verses 14–17.

The last section in verse 18 closes the pericope and tells of the settlement of Abram in Moreh within the region of Horeb, and there he built an altar to the Lord in appreciation of this divine speech which might have served here as a means of comfort to Abram. Thus we see once more a subtle characterization of Abram whereby in both beginning and end of this pericope, the narrator makes a reference to his commitment to the worship of Yahweh. Theologically speaking, "Abram called upon the name of the Lord" in verse 4 and Abram "built an altar to the Lord" at the last verse in 18 formed a kind of theological inclusio pointing ultimately to the piety of the patriarch.

Following this already highlighted structure, we could vividly outline the structure of the entire pericope of Genesis 13:1–18 thus:

---

merism in the speech of Abraham namely the juxtaposing of "left" and "right" in verse 9 (וְאַסְהִימִין וְאַשְׂמָאִילָה אִם־הַשְּׂמֹאל וְאֵימִנָה). For a classic treatement of merism see A. M. Honeyman, "Merismus in Biblical Hebrew," *JBL* 17, no. 1 (1952): 11–18.

Stylistic Aspects of the Divine Speeches

Introduction	13:1–4
Conflict	13:5–7
Semi-Resolution	13:8–13
Final Resolution	13:14–17[151]
Conclusion	13:18

The transitional markers of this structure are built around the opening imperfect prefixed with *vav* וַיַּעַל, the conjunction *vav* which is prefixed *vav*, the discourse marker וַיֹּאמֶר, similar discourse marker אָמַר which introduces the divine speeches and a final imperfect prefixed (וַיֶּאֱהַל) with *vav* which serves as a break from the divine speech, thus bringing the passage to an end.

For our present interest, the divine speeches show some kind of concentric patterning. In this direction, Wenham had recognized the concentric structure of the divine speeches in the following framing:

v. 15   I shall give it to you
                 your descendants
v. 16   dust of the earth
                 dust of the earth
                 your descendants
v. 17   I shall give it you[152]

However, a more stylistic structure based on the patterning of the ideas in the divine speeches could be seen by the following structure:

---

151. Interestingly, the divine speeches formed the resolution to the conflict of the present pericope. Thus the divine speeches like the speeches of Abram in the preceding section helped to resolve the conflict because from the divine perspective Abram had made the best decision to stay in the land of Canaan and Yahweh in his speeches underscored this decision of Abram.
152. Wenham, *Genesis 1–15*, 294.

    A   Command to look v. 14a
        B   Spatial reference v. 14b
            C   Divine gift of the Land v. 15
                D   Promise of descendants v. 16

    A'   Command to walk v. 17a
        B'   Spatial References v. 17b
            C'   Divine gift of the Land v. 17c

It seems the narrator patterned the divine speeches into two equal frames that close verse 16—the promise of descendants with its dense imagery—into a kind of bracket. This bracket forms like a type of Janus with each side of the divine speech concentrated on the idea of land, while the central part, verse 16, primarily centers on the promise of descendants. Thus the idea of descendant is bracketed by two similar emphases on the land. Through the structuring of the divine speeches, the narrator already has given a hint to his readers that the concern of descendants will play a great role in the subsequent narrative. This is in line with the subsequent picture we see of Abram and his wife Sarai, whose main concern is not the land, but the quest to have an heir. From the point of view of the patriarch and the narrator, the promise of an heir is the primary motif which is complemented by the secondary necessity of a land. Even though the first half of the divine speech—that is from verses 14–15—is a little bit longer, all the main ideas expressed there have similar counterparts in verse 17.

From this structure, the central verse is 16. It also seems that the central verse is built around a kind of chiasm. This chiasm could be seen in the following frame:

    A   I will make your Seed
        B   Like Dust of the earth
            C   If any man is able to count
        B'   The Dust of the earth
    A'   He will count your seed

The framing of the divine speeches along "C" shows an interesting motif. This motif is clearly seen in the impossibility of any man to be able to count the "dust" of the earth, and since no man is able to count the "dust" of the earth, hence the possibility that Abram will have future heirs in overwhelming number as the "dust" of the earth.[153] The divine logic is that the impossibility of man to count dust is a sure assurance that Yahweh will give Abram future descendants. Consequently, through the patterning of parallel thoughts in each half of the divine speeches, the narrator draws the reader's attention to the major concern of the Abrahamic cycle. Significantly, by means of a chiasm in verse 16, the narrator through metaphoric logic presupposes the certainty of heirs for Abram.

3.2.1.2. Literary Context

The literary context of the present pericope is situated primarily around the events in the preceding verses, particularly in the journey to Egypt.[154] There is an explicit assumption that the patriarch got his wealth from his stay in Egypt in Genesis 12:10–20. There is tacit wordplay in the common Hebrew word used to describe the famine in Genesis 12:10 and the wealth of Abram in verse 2.[155] In both cases, the adjective כָּבֵד was used to describe the famine as well as Abram's wealth. The return of Abram to Canaan in the opening verses and his acts of worship are no doubt significant for the exilic and post-exilic audience of the narrator, who could see in the "pre-exodus" of Abram from Egypt and his return to worship in the Promised Land a typological relevance with their own condition in diaspora, and their quest to return to the purity of worship in the Promised Land.[156] The picture of Abram in a "pre-exodus" kind of portrayal offers hope to the contemporary

---

153. See Clines, ed. *The Dictionary of Classical Hebrew*, vol. VI (Sheffield: Sheffield Academic Press, 2007), 184–189.

154. Zakovitch tied interestingly the events in the present chapter with chapter 14 see Zakovitch, "Juxtaposition in the Abraham Cycle," 512–13.

155. There is an inclusion in Genesis 12:3b with Genesis 12:8 since it appears the narrator repeated the earlier itinerary of Abram verbatim.

156. Thus Joseph Blenkinsopp observed, "Abraham is presented as an example for those in the Babylonian diaspora who answered the call to return to the homeland and rebuild the nation." See J. Blenkinsopp, *The Pentateuch: An Introduction to the First Five Books of the Bible*. ABRL (New York: Doubleday, 1999), 125.

situation of the writers.[157] Significantly, beyond such associations with the exodus, there is the possibility that the "quarrel" or "struggle" over the land by Abram and the father of the Moabites and the Ammonites[158] in the person of Lot is also a typological frame of mind that is at work in the knitting of this biblical passage. Thus, from the point of view of the narrator, the struggle after the exodus had already been prophetically laid down in the struggle over the land by the patriarch and his nephew, who possibly are eponyms of their future descendants. The narrator understood his materials not merely as stories but as works of prophecies since the lives of the patriarch in the past mirrored the lives of his future descendants. By this possible reading of the narrative, it solves the problem in two places within the Abrahamic cycle whereby Abram is called a prophet. The first is the calling of Abram a prophet in Genesis 20:7 and the prophetic caption in Genesis 15:1 which reads, "After these things, the word of the Lord came to Abram in a vision." These two explicit incidents point to the prophetic nature by which the narrator understood his materials.[159]

Within the interplay of these literary, historical and prophetical interests, the narrator tells his present story, thus depicting Abram "after the temporary" enslavement in Egypt coming to the Promised Land and becoming embroiled in a quarrel with his nephew. However, the problem was peacefully resolved rather than the subsequent ideology of conquest. The reticent narrator categorically characterized Lot by an explicit comment on Lot, the father of the future enemies of Israel. He pictures Lot as self-seeking and greedy in his choice. In this and many contrasts between Abram and Lot, the narrator also explores temporally the motif of ethnic

---

157. Different traditions configured the stories of Abraham to serve different needs. For example, Abraham was conceived strangely enough as a "physician" in Syria. See Tryggve Kronholm, "Abraham, the Physician: The Image of the Abraham the Patriarch in the Genuine Hymns of Ephraem Syrus," *Solving Riddles and Untying Knots: Biblical Epigraphic, and Semitic Studies in Honor of Jones C. Greenfield*, ed. Ziony Zevit, Seymour and Michael Sokoloff (Winona Lake, Indiana: Einsenbraus, 1995), 107–115.

158. In Genesis 15:16, interestingly, the Ammonites are symbolically used as a representation for the entire inhabitants of the Promised Land.

159. Psalm 105:12–15 describes the patriarchs as prophets. Abraham is seen as a prophet in his prayer for Abimelech's family, Yahweh causing a deep sleep to fall upon and through this sleep revealing to him the destiny of his descendants (Gen 15:13–16) and his call also in Genesis 12 is likely framed with this thought in mind by the narrator. See Hartley, *Genesis*, 9.

tensions between Israel and her neighbors. Thus Genesis 13:1–18 in microcosm serves as a prototype of the ethnic tensions. This reading of Genesis 13:1–18 as a prototype or forerunner of the event of the future is built on the obvious quest by the narrator to show that "Abram" is a type of the blessed future Israelites who are going to possess the land of Canaan and Lot the type of "Ammonites and Moabites" or even enemies of Israel who also laid claim to the Promised Land.

This reading shows that the narrator selected, framed, and engaged his materials from a certain ideological prism, which, in the context of the present text, seeks to see in Abram and his nephew a miniature history of the people of Israel. It is also significant that this form of reading could also be stretched to include the subsequent chapter in Genesis 14 whereby we see a militant picture of Abram who went to redeem Lot. The kings of Canaan subsequently recognize Abram as a political figure. The portrayal of Abram as a conqueror who went to fight the kings from the east is a continuation of the thought already begun in this present pericope which described the "exodus" of Abram, the quarrel with the father of the Moabites and Ammonites, and the reception granted to him by the kings, particularly the enigmatic figure the king of Salem. Thus framed in this way, the events in the life of Abram mirror the future challenges of his descendants. Even though this reading may not be evidenced in certain points of the narratives, the narrator dominantly sees his materials as prophetic and hence has a cyclical understanding of history whereby events in the past mirror in some mysterious ways the events of the future.

3.2.1.3. Grammatical Analysis

Even though references to some grammatical issues have been made in passing already, we now turn our attention to the analysis of grammatical issues from our discussion of the quotative frame, verbal syntax and the demonstrative commands of the divine speeches.

3.2.1.3.1. Quotative Frames

There are two quotative frames found in the present pericope. The first quotative frame וַיֹּאמֶר introduces the selfless speeches of Abram to Lot in verse 8, and the second quotative frame אָמַר is employed in verse 14 when describing the speeches of God. Grammatically, both as discourse markers break the pericope into manageable units and become key in determining the sub-units of the pericope. From the literary point of view, the first quotative frame characterized Abram against Lot since it introduces "high sounding" speeches of Abram against the silent character of Lot. The narrator put words into the mouth of Abram, but denied words to Lot. The only response of Lot we see through the eyes of the narrator who describes for us what the greedy eyes of Lot saw in verses 10–14, thus the narrator, by giving Abram and Yahweh discourse markers which point to their respective speeches, clearly embossed their presence in the text against the mute Lot. Ironically, by the use of these discourse markers, we only see Lot's roving eyes rather than his "mouth." In fact, the narrator directed the reader to the eyes of Lot while redirecting our attention to the mouth of Abram and God. In this direction, redirection or even "misdirection" by the narrator we see the inward character of Lot and not his speeches, while we see the speeches of Abram, but not the hidden dynamism of his thought.

From the preceding thoughts, several functions of these quotation frames become significant. Firstly, the narrator used the quotation frame to give structure to this pericope since each of the speeches by Abram and God divide the episode into scenes or sub-units. Secondly, the quotative frame was used to characterize the characters of this episodeAbram and Yahweh are described positively and the silent Lot painted negatively. Through his roving eyes we see what is going on in his heart, thus the narrator considers it unnecessary to give him the luxury of speech. Lastly, the quotative frame introduced at the crucial moment of the episode, the resolution of the conflict through the speeches of Abram, and the final climax in the divine speeches, bring the episode to a close. In both of these speeches, the narrator brings to the attention of his reader how the speeches were keys to the resolution of the conflict and the winding down of the episode. After the speech by Abram, Lot chose the plain of Jordan and departed and after the speech by Yahweh, Abram moved and pitched his tent at Hebron, offering a sacrifice there, thus bringing the story to a temporary close. In both cases, the speeches of these individuals were crucial to the turn the story took, and thus significant from the point of view of the narrator. Thus grammatically and literarily, these quotative frames, while acting as discourse markers in the division of the episode into units, also characterized both the speakers and the silent Lot. In addition, they introduced the crucial moments or turning points in the plot of the story.

3.2.1.3.2. Syntactical Considerations

The verbal syntax began with the dominance of the two verbs commonly associated with sight and ends with two verbs of motion. The first two verbs שָׂא ("lift up") and וּרְאֵה ("and see") of the divine speech governs the subsequent verbs in verses 15 and even 16. Interestingly, these two verbs on the lips of Yahweh are a direct imitation of the narrator's description of the perception of Lot in verse 10. The narrator observed that Lot "lifted up" (וַיִּשָּׂא) his eyes and "saw" (וַיַּרְא). In this particular instance, the divine speech took over the wordings of the narrator in his description of Lot thus using the same verbal root to describe the actions of Lot and the intended desired course of action by Yahweh from Abram. Following these two verbs is a כִּי clause in verse 15 which acts as a purpose clause. It states the purpose for the divine command that Abram should lift up his eyes and see.[160] The purpose of the two imperatives is not merely to see the land but because God has given this vast land to Abram forever. There is a contrast here, while the choice of Lot is temporal as evidenced by the narrator's foreshadowing comment[161] on the destruction of Sodom in verse 10c, Yahweh's gift of the land to Abram is to be forever (v. 15).[162] Significantly, to make prominent the subject of the land in verse 15, the normal Hebrew verbal syntax or word order was not followed, thus instead of beginning with verb, the clause begins with a noun (אֶת־כָּל־הָאָרֶץ) and places the main verb (אֶתְּנֶנָּה) in the middle of the sentence, thus breaking the natural symmetry of the two objects of the verb. Literally, it reads in English, "For all the land which you are now

---

160. For the comparison of the syntax of the כִּי clause in biblical narratives and Ben Sira see Menaḥem Zevi Kaddari, "The Syntax of כִּי clause in the Language of Ben Sira," *The Hebrew of the Dead Sea Scrolls and Ben Sira: Proceedings of a Symposium Held at Leiden University 11–14 December 1995*, eds. T. Muraoka and J. F. Elwolde (Leiden: Brill, 1997), 87–91, especially 89ff.

161. On the technique of foreshadowing in Genesis see Sarna, "The Anticipatory Use of Information as a Literary Feature of the Genesis Narratives," *The Creation of Sacred Literature*, ed. R. E. Friedman (Berkeley: University of California Press, 1981).

162. See Clines, *The Dictionary of Classical Hebrew*, 300–307.

seeing (*qal* participle masculine singular commonly translated present), to you, I will give, and to you descendants forever." This literal translation shows how the Hebrew breaks the normal syntactical connection between the two objects (לְךָ and וּלְזַרְעֲךָ) of the verb (נָתַן). The purpose of breaking this symmetry is to emphasis the land, but possibly to also emphasize the two objects of the main verbthat is Abram and his descendants. Even though continuing the motif of the verb נָתַן, the verb וְשַׂמְתִּי adds the dimension of increased descendants which, though assumed in the preceding clauses, is now however vividly pictured. As we are going to subsequently see, Yahweh gives the hypothetical and funny picture of a man counting the tiny pieces of dust. The embedded irony here is obvious even though often missed. Lot lifted up his eyes and saw the plain of Jordan "like the garden of Yahweh" (that is "garden of Eden") and "the land of Egypt"[163], however, God wanted Abram to imagine the impossible picture of a man counting the tiny pieces of dust. In this sense, the vivid imagery of verse 16 points to the quest by the narrator to underscore graphically the certainty of the divine promise to Abram. Like the preceding discussion on the structure of verse 16 has readily shown, the syntax of this verse is straightforward. The nouns זַרְעֲךָ are repeated twice, the verb מָנָה, "to count" is repeated twice, the construct עֲפַר הָאָרֶץ is also repeated twice and the verbs יָכֹל and שִׂים occur once. Grammatically, there is a conditional construction in verse 16. The protasis reads "אִם־יוּכַל אִישׁ לִמְנוֹת אֶת־עֲפַר הָאָרֶץ" and then followed by the apodosis, "גַּם־זַרְעֲךָ יִמָּנֶה." The logic of this condition clause is that if the protasis is true, inevitably the apodosis will also be true. In reference to Abram, God is saying that his future descendants could only be numbered if only there is a man who is able to count the tiny pieces of the dust of the earth. Since this is impossible, it shows that Abram's descendants cannot equally be numbered.

Following this verse, the second part of the divine speech in verse 17 also forms a parallel to the first half. The two imperatives, "arise" and "walk" (קוּם and הִתְהַלֵּךְ), are also followed by a כִּי clause which has נתן as its main

---

163. This mentioning of Egypt is significant considering that the two of the characters just came out of Egypt in the immediately preceding passage. The grandeur of Egypt might be in the mind of the narrator particularly when one recognizes that the wealth of Abram was closely associated with his going down to Egypt.

and only verb. The significance of the syntax is that the narrator paralleled the divine speeches into two halves with each of the halves concentrated on land while the central idea employs vivid imagery to describe the future descendants of Abram. In this parallel scheme by the narrator, he stylistically focused on the two concerns of the Abrahamic stories.

3.2.1.4.3. Demonstrative Commands

As already shown, there are four imperative commands in the divine speeches, which are equally positioned in the two halves of the divine speeches. The first two are placed in the first half of the divine speeches in verse 14 and the last two imperatives in the last half of the divine speeches in verse 17. The first imperatives which are primarily concerned with sense of sight remind us of the divine speech in Genesis 12:1 where God told Abram to "go" to the land which he will show him. As in the divine speech of Genesis 12:1–3, the narrator framed the divine speeches using the verb of sight and motion. The difference here, however, is that he added נשׂא and קום. The significance of these divine imperatives is far reaching. The first two divine imperatives placed the geography of the Promised Land no longer on a divinely stipulated boundary but on the sight of Abram. Similarly, the divine imperatives also gave the "occupation right" to Abram by his command that Abram should walk throughout the "length and breadth" of the land. After these divine speeches, even though silent, Abram went ahead to make his camp at Hebron in verse 18. Since the early Davidic kingship began here (2 Sam 5:3–5), the narrator has already given us a clue that Abram prophetically located himself in a place that one day would become associated with the dynasty of David.[164]

Consequently, the narrator employing the imperative verb of sight and motion artistically framed the divine speeches to show Yahweh's quest to provide Abram with land and descendants. At the end, Abram's obedience is captured by his silent movement to a very strategic site in the history of ancient Israel. In this heeding of the divine speeches as seen in Abram's

---

164. See T. Rudin-O'Brasky, *The Patriarchs in Hebron and Sodom (Gen 18–19): A Study of the Structure and Composition of a Biblical Story* (Jerusalem: Simor, 1982).

movement, Abram prophetically began the process of possessing the land that saw its climax in the days of David and Solomon.

3.2.1.4. Stylistic Aspects

From the following analysis, it is increasingly becoming clear that the divine speeches in the pericope have some simple stylistic features which often had partly accounted for the continuous influence of these passages of Scriptures to the modern times. We are making reference to the simple but profound stylistic features which indirectly point us to the importance that the narrator places on these divine speeches. The origin of Israel is attributed to these divine speeches, and it is only necessary to look at the literary features of these speeches which have come to occupy the forefront of our theological discussions. We are making reference to such stylistic features such as metaphor, simile, wordplay, repetition, allusion, hyperbole and suspense.

3.2.1.4.1. Metaphor

The metaphor in this pericope is readily seen in verse 16 with its extensive use of imagery. There is first a comparison between the "dust of earth" and the "seed" of Abram then the divine speech switches to the metaphor of a man "counting" dust.[165] In Hebrew, the metaphor is described using a conditional clause, that is, אֲשֶׁר ׀ אִם־יוּכַל אִישׁ לִמְנוֹת אֶת־עֲפַר הָאָרֶץ גַּם־זַרְעֲךָ יִמָּנֶה. This conditional clause is framed within a sentence, which compares the "seed" of Abram to the "dust of the earth."[166] The imagery of this conditional clause is that it creates the mental picture of a man counting the tiny pieces of dust. Such a vivid imagery has great significance particularly in the context of the verb for sight already used by God in his command

---

165. See Clines, ed. *The Dictionary of Classical Hebrew*, 345–6.
166. According to Scott Noegel, the "'*im yukl*" or אִם־יוּכַל "is rather rare in the Bible, occurring elsewhere only four (or five) times: Gen 13:16; 1 Sam 17:8–9; 2 Kgs 18:23–24 (=Isa 36:8); and Job 33:5." In his studies of these verses, he observed three characteristics that are common to these texts. Firstly, each of the passages has an implied answer to the indirect question that is primarily "no." Secondly, the אִם־יוּכַל construction occurs in context of taunting and tests of faith. Lastly, the construction signals an "unexpected twist of events." See Scott Noegel, "A Crux and a Taunt: Night-Time Then Sunset in Genesis 15," *The World of Genesis: Persons, Places, Perspectives*, eds. Philip R. Davies and David J.A. Clines. JSOTSup Series 257 (Sheffield: Sheffield Academic Press, 1998), 128–135.

for Abram to "lift up" (שָׂא) his eyes and "to see" (וּרְאֵה). These verbs are employed for sight even though they primarily have the direct objects of cardinal points of north, south, east and west (צָפֹנָה וָנֶגְבָּה וָקֵדְמָה וָיָמָּה), however, their function extends to the pictorial imagery of verse 16.[167] In this regard, Yahweh wanted

Abram to graphically see the possibility of having future descendants by the impossible picture of the hypothetical man counting tiny particles of dust. The picture of the hypothetical man counting grains of dust has further importance. First, it shows that the increase of future descendants for Abram is an impossible task that only Yahweh alone could bring about. Thus there is a tacit comparison between the power of God and the limitation of man. Similarly, the metaphor itself invokes other images since it seems humans count money, people, and days, but not dust. Thus the same word was used for counting money in 2 Kings 12:10 and flocks in Jeremiah 33:3. The Psalmist prayed, "teach us to count our days" in Psalm 90:12, and the same root word was used to describe David's counting of people in 2 Chronicles 21:17. Thus the special use by God here draws the normal use of the term counting. The picture takes the normal counting of money, people and days and applied such to the counting of the tiny particle of dust. The imagery draws its vividness by the close association of this term to the normal usage in the daily world of the Bible. Even though we cannot describe vividly the daily life of the biblical world with certainty, we could at least say that the imagery of a "man counting" dust is the extension of the common practice of counting whether of days, money or people which are now metaphorically employed to describe the populous nature of the future descendants of Abram. The structure of the pericope, as we have earlier seen, makes the "hypothetical man" counting the dust the center of the structure for verse 16. In this carefully styled structure, the narrator juxtaposed the force of the verb וְשַׂמְתִּי against the verb יוּכַל which describes semantically the limitation of human possibilities. In this

---

167. There is element of gradation even here. The divine speeches describe the cardinal points orderly, that is the north following the south, and the east following the west. Without gradation, it will have been something like north, west, south, east or the placement of the cardinal points not following any necessary order. The description of these cardinal points shows an orderly description of these geographical points.

way, divine certainty is contrasted with the possible human action. This contrast puts force on the verb וְשַׂמְתִּי and points to the implied conclusion that no human ingenuity or mathematics of the "dust" could stop divine determination to increase the seeds of Abram.

Talking of the "seed," this metaphor has already been noted in the preceding pericope and hence we will not dwell on it but pass only here a quick remark. The image of a man counting the "dust of the earth" and the image of "seed" to describe the future descendants are two new metaphors never used together before in the description of the speeches of any character in Genesis. It puts a new vision on the lips of God but also the mental image in the mind of the reader. The combined force of the graphic speeches of Yahweh here and within the preceding pericope alert the reader that in Abram, God had not only his game plan, but God has chosen to do something different than seen earlier in the primeval stories. Thus in the simple stylistic features of these divine speeches the reader already knows that Yahweh seemed different in his speeches here than in the earlier part of Genesis. This points to the narrator's desire to show in graphic terms how Yahweh becomes the God of Israel.

3.2.1.4.2. Simile

The simile is seen in the comparison made between the "seed" of Abram and the "dust" of the earth.[168] The simile is described in the phrase וְשַׂמְתִּי אֶת־זַרְעֲךָ כַּעֲפַר הָאָרֶץ which is translated, "and I will make your seed like the dust of the earth." In the pericope, the force is laid on this comparison by the repetition of the two terms under comparison twice namely "the dust of the earth" and "your seed." The simile draws similarity between the "dust of the earth" and "your seed." Here the idea of counting is an imagery left to the next clause, but only a comparison between the two terms is made obvious.[169] The future seeds of Abram are compared to the

---

168. For the study of simile in relationship to issues of gender within biblical narratives see Tarja Philip, "Woman in Travail as a Simile to Men in Distress in the Hebrew Bible," *Sex and Gender in the Ancient Near East*, eds. Simo Parpola and R. M. Whiting, Part II. Proceedings of the XLVII Rencontre Assyriologique Internationale, Helsinki, 499–505 (Helsinki: The Neo-Assyrian Text Corpus Project, 2002), 499–505.

169. On the difference between metaphors and similes see William P. Brown, *Seeing the Psalms: A Theology of Metaphor* (Louisville, Kentucky: Westminster John Knox Press,

"dust of earth" in numbers. In this pericope, the divine speech explored the overwhelming nature of the particle of dust, thus promising Abram such future descendants.[170] The divine speech as in the metaphor of counting explores the uncountable nature of the tiny dust of the earth in order to make comparison to the future descendants of Abram. The infiniteness of the tiny pieces of dust is made equivalent to the numbers of Abram's descendants. For a people who are familiar with the dust of Palestine, the idea of having children as many as the dust of the land is gripping and indeed vivid, thus immortalizing these divine speeches in the hearts of future generations after the narrator. Significantly, this comparison is also between a vivid metaphor "seed" which either as "seed" for crop or "semen" has also the idea of numbers hence drawing this comparison together in a simile puts the reader at edge and literally forces the reader to paint this comparison vividly. The power of this simile is also seen in a similar simile made in this pericope in verse 10 whereby the narrator employed two similes to describe the sight of Lot on his perception of the plains of Jordan. The two similes are כְּגַן־יְהוָה כְּאֶרֶץ מִצְרַיִם which are translated "like the garden of the Lord, like the land of Egypt," thus like these two similes, the divine speech in verse 16 even though having one simile, repeated the "dust of the earth" and "your seeds" each twice. The narrator brings to focus these two similes since they are found within the same pericope. However, the difference between the two similes is that while the two similes in verse 10 are about the land, that of the divine speech in verse 16 is concerned with the promise of innumerable heirs for Abram. The implication that the quest for the descendants and land is far more important in the divine speeches is seen in the simile and metaphor employed to underscore these central themes. Similarly, it implies that Lot lost the land ultimately but as subsequent stories show, the descendants of Abram continued to increase and did actually inherit the land of Canaan.[171]

2002), 7–8.

170. On a figurative treatment of simile against the common literal reading see Louise Shabat Bethlehem, "Simile and Figurative Language," *Poetics Today*, vol. 17, no. 2 (1996): 203–240.

171. For extended use of simile see J. Cheryl Exum, "Of Broken Pots, Fluttering Birds and Visions in the Night: Extended Simile and Poetic Technique in Isaiah," *CBQ* 43 (1981): 331–352.

3.2.1.4.3. Wordplay

In his study of the poetics of Genesis, Turner observed that "*[w]ordplay* abounds as part of the narrative's strategy to underline the truly significant, or to encourage a reader to read one passage in the light of another. Sometimes this forms the basis for a motif."[172] However, "[m]ore often it is the narrative's way of emphasizing details in individual episode."[173] As subsequent studies will seek to show, wordplays frequently occur in the divine speeches particularly in the Abrahamic cycle.[174] The wordplay in the present pericope is in the word נשׂא. This verb נשׂא is a polysemy. The literary term polysemy is used to describe a word which has more than one meaning. In the pericope two of its double meanings are used. The first time this verb was used in the present pericope is in verse 6. It was used to describe the problem in the statement, "the land could not sustain them." Here, the verb נשׂא was translated "sustain or support." Interestingly, after the use of this verb here, an inclusio in term of twice similar phrases occurred in verse 6b and 6d. Repeatedly, "to stay together" that is, לָשֶׁבֶת יַחְדָּו was repeated after this verb and again at the end of this verse, thus forming a kind of inclusio. These repeated phrases, however, point back to the main verb נשׂא. In this way, the double repetition of לָשֶׁבֶת יַחְדָּו, which is found in כִּי clause, points back to the activity of the main verb. The reason for this double repetition around נשׂא likely has its importance in the subsequent twice repetition of נשׂא in the comment of the narrator and the speech of Yahweh at critical points in the narrative. The narrator by such inclusio possibly points the reader to the subsequent usage of this verb.

In the description of Lot's perception in verse 10, the narrator employed the verb נשׂא in its second meaning to describe the wrong perception of Lot.[175] The translation in this context is "and Lot lifted up" his eyes. The narrator employed this term not in the earlier meaning of "to sustain" in

---

172. Turner, *Genesis*, 15.
173. Ibid.
174. For some interesting studies on biblical wordplay see Raymond C. Van Leeuwen, "What Comes Out of God's Mouth: Theological Wordplay in Deuteronomy 8," *CBQ* 47, no. 1 (1985): 55–57; Rendsburg, "Bilingual Wordplay in the Bible," *VT* 38, no. 3 (1988): 354–357; Knut Holter, "The Wordplay on ('God') in Isaiah 45:20–21," *SJOT* 7, no. 1 (1993): 88–98.
175. Clines, ed. *The Dictionary of Classical Hebrew*, 758–770.

verse 5 but in its other meaning of "lifted up." Lastly, the word was used in the divine speech to describe the command of Yahweh to Abram to "lift up" his eyes and to see the land in verse 14. The divine speech takes this term and employs its meaning as a verb of sight. In these three occurrences of the verb נשׂא, the polyseminous character of the verb is explored. Firstly, the narrator employed the verb to describe the conflict between Abram and Lot. Secondly, the narrator used the term to describe the roving eyes of Lot which lead to his choice of the plains of Jordan. Lastly, the narrator used the term in its imperative form in order to describe the command of Yahweh to Abram.

In particular, the wordplay is that while the "land" could not "sustain" them, each one of them sustained himself somehow by his sight. For Lot, it is the personal greed in his roving eyes that landed him into trouble, but for Abram, it was God who told him to lift up his eyes to see. Similarly, there is also an irony here because while Lot "lifted up" his eyes and saw a beautiful place, the narrator specifically told us that in that same place God saw wickedness and destruction. On the other hand, in the unenviable place left for Abram, God told Abram to "lift up" his eyes to see his beautiful future in terms of the possession of the land and his many children.

3.2.1.4.4. Repetition

As already highlighted in our discussion of the last pericope, the literary device of repetition is increasingly recognized as a reoccurring device in biblical narrative. In the present pericope, Wenham has shown the different repetitions between the verses 9–13 and verses 15–17.[176] This repetition is worth noting. In particular, the verb פרד or "to separate" which occurs in verses 9 and 11 is also repeated in the context of the divine speech in verse 14. Similarly, as already shown, the combination of verbs that is "lift up" and "to see" occurred in verse 10 and also reappeared in verse 14 of the divine speech. Also, "all the plain" in verses 10–11 match "all the land" of the divine speech in verse 15. In this repetition of motifs in the divine speeches, the narrator tied the divine speeches to the context of narration.

---

176. Wenham, *Genesis 1–15*, 294.

However beyond this repetition in its immediate context, we see repetition of the idea of "seed" which also featured in Genesis 12:7. Thus the idea of "descendants" which was generally begun there now finds graphic and vivid representation in the divine speeches here. Similarly, the idea of land possession which began in Genesis 12:7 also finds repetition in the divine speeches of the present pericope. Similarly, the motif of sight that was first begun in Yahweh's declaration that Abram should go to the land that "I will show you" finds repeated emphasis in the usage of the verb of sight to command Abram to see the Promised Land in verses 15–17. It seems Yahweh is saying, "here is the land that I told you that I will show you, lift up your eyes and see the length and breadth of it." This motif of Yahweh pointing Abram to the land is already present in Genesis 12:7 but receives here a vividness that is absent in the preceding divine speeches. Similarly, the verb ראה already used once in the divine speech of Genesis 12:1 also appears twice in verses 14 and 15 of the present pericope. Similarly, as in the divine speech in Genesis 12:1, הלך is in its imperative form although Genesis 12:1 it is in *qal* form and the one here in verse 17 is in *hitpael* stem. In addition, there is also a repetition of Abram's piety in response to these divine speeches. After the divine speeches, Abram often builds an altar to Yahweh. This practice occurred in Genesis 12:7c–9 and also in Genesis 13:18.

The narrator also repeated עוֹלָם or "forever" in verse 15. This noun appeared four times in the entire story of Noah.[177] Specifically, it appears twice in the context of God's covenant with Noah in Genesis 9:12, 16. The single repetition of עוֹלָם here suggests that the narrator wanted to relate the covenant of Yahweh with Noah to the relationship that is now developing between Yahweh and Abram. The narrator seems to be working with an assumption, even though unstated, that Abram enjoyed a higher relationship with Yahweh than Noah.

The significance of this repetition is obvious. The narrator gives literary clues on the continuity between his present story and the earlier stories. It shows also continuity in the issues reflected within the divine speeches. Despite this continuity, he also shows the difference between the divine speeches in the present pericope and the earlier ones in Genesis 12:1–3 and

---

177. See Genesis 6:3, 4 and also in Genesis 3:22.

7. From a literary and theological point of view, the divine speech is getting more graphic and more clearly defined rather than general concerns. For example, the divine speeches in Genesis 12:1–3 and 7 only hinted at "descendants" but here we see vividly the innumerable descendants of Abram.

3.2.1.5.5. Allusion

Even though identification of implicit allusion is a controversial endeavor, one could sense such implicit allusions within the divine speeches. The first implicit allusion is in the phrase כַּעֲפַר הָאָרֶץ or the "dust of the earth." This phrase becomes a common phrase to describe something uncountable or grinding of dust in post-Abrahamic narratives,[178] however, within the confinement of the preceding narratives of Genesis, it echoes the narratives of creation where the terms "dust" and "earth" appeared repeatedly, though independently and not as simile here.[179] Since God in the creation accounts commanded man to be "fruitful and fill" the earth, the divine command in verse 14–17 with its promise of innumerable descendants for Abram like "the dust of the earth" points to this allusion. It seemed the narrator wanted to indirectly see in Abram a new fulfillment of this divine command to fill the earth or multiply. God at creation wanted the world to be peopled, and in the same way, God within these divine speeches wanted Canaan to be filled with the descendants of Abram.[180]

3.2.1.4.6. Hyperbole

There are common exaggerations found in the speeches of the characters of biblical narratives.[181] For example, the twelve spies said, "we went in to the land where you sent us; and it certainly does flow with milk and honey,

---

178. See 2 Sam 22:43, 2 Kings 13:7; 2 Chron 1:19; Psalms 18:43; 78:27 and Zech 9:3.
179. See Genesis 2–3.
180. Similarly, this pericope is framed with the stories of Genesis 18–19 in mind. It explicitly made mention of the destruction of Sodom and Gomorrah in verses 10–13. There is a literary device of prolepsis or fast-forwarding which anticipates the story of Sodom and Gomorrah.
181. E. W. Bullinger defines hyperbole as "an overstatement or a conscious exaggeration by the writer to gain effect" that is, "when more is said than is literally meant" [See E. W. Bullinger, *Figures of Speech Used in the Bible* (Grand Rapids, MI: Baker, 1968), 423]. In fact, J. C. L. Gibson describes hyperbole as a "distinctive mark of Semitic speech" and that the "Old Testament in its oriental fashion habitually lets its hair down and exaggerates and

and this is its fruit."[182] They also added, "the people are bigger and taller than we; the cities are large and fortified to heaven. And besides, we saw the sons of the Anakim there."'[183] Furthermore, they said, "we became like grasshoppers in our own sight, and so we were in their sight."[184] Similarly, as a sign of his repentance, the King of Nineveh said, "do not let man, beast, herd, or flock taste a thing. Do not let them eat or drink water."[185] Similarly, David lamenting about Saul and Jonathan said, "in life they were loved and gracious, and in death they were not parted. They were swifter than eagles, they were stronger than lions."[186] Similarly, the women in the book of Samuel sang, "Saul has slain his thousands, and David his ten thousands."[187]

Beyond these examples from characters of biblical narratives, there are instances when the narrator himself exaggerates his points, for example, "among all these soldiers there were seven hundred chosen men who were left-handed, each of whom could sling a stone at a hair and not miss."[188] The narrator of Judges said, "Now the Midianites and the Amalekites and all the sons of the east were lying in the valley as numerous as locusts; and their camels were without number, as numerous as the sand on the seashore."[189] In the same way, describing the coronation of Solomon he said, "and all the people went up after him, playing flutes and rejoicing greatly, so that the ground shook with the sound."[190] These are examples of a few hyperboles from the lips of biblical characters and also in the description of events by the biblical narrator. As this biblical character, God also in this pericope stylistically "exaggerates" firstly in his description and comparison of the future "seed" of Abram to the "dust of the earth and sec-

---

overstates with considerable aplomb" [See J. C. L. Gibson, *Language and Imagery in the Old Testament* (Peabody, MA: Hendrickson Publishers, nd), 14].
182. Numbers 13:27.
183. Deuteronomy 1:28.
184. Numbers 14:19.
185. Jonah 4:10.
186. 2 Samuel 1:23.
187. 1 Samuel 18:7.
188. Judges 20:16.
189. Judges 7:12.
190. 1 Kings 1:40.

ondly, in his ridiculous image of a "hypothetical" man counting the "dust of the earth."¹⁹¹ This last image has a dint of humor and could be treated as a literary device in its own right, but it is discussed here because of the exaggerating nature of the imagery. What is the point of this divine exaggeration? The point is that God has through exaggerated speeches sought to graphically describe his commitment in providing Abram with future descendants. These hyperbolic divine speeches might resonate with the oriental people whose speeches have in many ways characteristics of such hyperbolic or idiomatic language. It is not surprising within this context of "oriental hyperbole" that Yahweh also spoke using this literary medium.¹⁹²

3.2.1.4.7. Suspense

This divine speech vibrates with suspense.¹⁹³ This suspense is largely built in the usage of hyperbolic expressions and imagery that increase the questions in the mind of the reader and hence draw the reader more and more into reading the entire Abrahamic cycle. One paramount question in the mind of a first-time reader will be how Yahweh will bring about the realization of these many descendants as the "dust of the earth." In the subsequent stories of the Pentateuch, the giving of a census and the listing of the names of the tribes of Israel with inflated or exaggerated numbers are in many ways the quest by the narrator to tell the reader that the promises of future descendants to Abram has largely been redeemed in these censuses and genealogical listings. Thus for example, the book of Exodus began by saying, "These

---

191. Grammatically, this is achieved by the use of an indefinite pronoun אִישׁ. See Merwe et al, *A Biblical Hebrew Reference Grammar*, 262.

192. For the use of hyperbole in Greek and New Testament context see Paul Trebilco, *The Early Christians in Ephesus from Paul to Ignatius* (Tübingen, Germany: Mohr Siebeck, 2004), 137; Carol J. Schlueter, *Filling up the Measure: Polemical Hyperbole in 1 Thessalonians 2:14–16* (Sheffield: Sheffield Academic Press, 1994); Robert H. Stein, *Difficult Sayings in the Gospel: Jesus' Use of Overstatement and Hyperbole* (Grand Rapids, Michigan: Baker Book House, 1985).

193. On the craft of suspense in literature see William F. Brewer, "The Nature of Narrative Suspense and the Problem of Rereading," *Suspense: Conceptualizations, Theoretical Analyses, and Empirical Explorations*, eds. Peter Vorderer, Hans Jürgen Wulff and Mike Friedrichsen (Mahwah, New Jersey: Erlbaum, 1996), 107–128; Lothar Mikos, "The Experience of Suspense: Between Fear and Pleasure," *Suspense: Conceptualizations, Theoretical Analyses, and Empirical Explorations*, eds. Peter Vorderer, Hans Jürgen Wulff and Mike Friedrichsen (Mahwah, New Jersey: Erlbaum, 1996), 37–49.

are the names of the sons of Israel who went to Egypt with Jacob, each with his family"[194] and concluded that unit by saying, "but the Israelites were fruitful and multiplied greatly and became exceedingly numerous, so that the land was filled with them."[195] Through these scattered references to numbers of Israelites, the narrator wanted to resolve the tension built in the story of Abrahamic narrative particularly the promises of innumerable descendants to the patriarch. For example, at the exodus, the narrator pointed to the numbers of the Israelites and thus noted, "the Israelites journeyed from Rameses to Succoth. There were about six hundred thousand men on foot, besides women and children."[196] Hence, the ideology behind these statistics in the Pentateuch is that the narrator desired to point to the reader through these numbers that Yahweh had directly fulfilled in the life of the Israelites the promises of innumerable descendants that was made to Abram. Consequently, even though inexplicitly carried out, the genealogical tables are ideological tools by the narrator which look backward to the divine promises made to Abram. By such listings of persons, the narrator or narrators of the Pentateuch resolved the suspense, which though beginning in these divine speeches, runs repeatedly throughout the entire patriarchal narratives. However, for the meantime, Yahweh's exaggerated speech in this present pericope is immediately challenged by the unrest of the land of Canaan and the subsequent enslavement of Lot by the kings from the east in Genesis 14.

3.2.1.5. Significance

On the whole, the divine speeches in this present pericope reveal certain significances in the reading of the Abrahamic cycle. Firstly, the divine speeches continue the motif of "seeing" as already emphasized in the initial command of Yahweh to Abram in 12:1–3. In this earlier pericope, Yahweh promised Abram to "go to a land that I will show you" (12:1b). In the present pericope, we see Yahweh showing Abram this land he promised to show him. In particular, Yahweh said, "look north and south, east and

---

194. Exodus 1:1.
195. Exodus 1:7.
196. Exodus 12:37.

west. All the land that you see I will give to you and your offspring forever." (13:14–15). Even though Yahweh initially points Abram to the land in Genesis 12:7, it is in the present pericope we see a full-scale tour or presentation of the land by Yahweh to Abram. Consequently, this pericope serves as continuation or even fulfillment of the initial promise of Yahweh to show Abram the land. Secondly, the literary-styled divine speeches of the present pericope increase and continue the original suspense and anxiety of the reader by the increasing mind-blowing divine promises which now compared Abram's descendants to the dust of earth. Thirdly, these new divine speeches add another new motif of "forever" to the promise of Yahweh to Abram (v. 15), that is, Yahweh has forever given the land of Canaan to Abram and his descendants. In addition, the divine speeches further complicate the plot of the Abrahamic narratives by the elimination of Lot as a possible heir to Abram and the absence of an apparent heir for Abram. In particular, the divine speeches deliberately refuse the mentioning of the name of Lot and focus mainly on the future descendants of Abram which are hereby compared to the dust of the earth because of their numbers. Similarly, the divine speeches directly approved the staying of Abram in the land of Canaan, and indirectly condemned Lot's separation to live in the vicinity of Sodom and Gomorrah. In this understanding, the divine speeches continued the characterization agenda of the preceding divine speeches (12:1–9). Lastly, the divine speeches of the present pericope not only resolve the conflict between Lot and Abram, but also temporarily resolve the tension in the mind of the reader as the divine speeches serve as the final arbiter in showing the reader that Lot is not the divine choice for an heir for Abram.

3.3.1. Genesis 15:1–21

3.3.1.1. Structure

The present pericope reveals a kind of progression in the relationship between the two main characters of the Abrahamic narrativemainly God and Abram. Up to this point, each of the characters has spoken without the beauty of exchange that we see in this present pericope. Often God spoke and Abram quietly obeyed, thus making the divine speech a kind of monologue rather than dialogue.[197] This is the first time Abraham spoke back to God. Underscoring the importance of this dialogue, James McKeown noted, "[d]ialogues often occur at important junctures in narratives and serve to slow down the pace of the narrative and focus the reader's attention on something significant."[198] Significantly, Abram in the preceding narratives only spoke thrice: firstly, at the road to Egypt in Genesis 12:12–13, secondly, in his negotiation with his nephew in Genesis 13:8–9, and thirdly, in his speeches to the king of Sodom in the immediately preceding chapter (14:22–24). However, here within the present pericope, Abram stands tall, not speaking back merely to the king of Sodom as is the case in the preceding chapters, but questioning the reality of the elevated promises of Yahweh to him in the preceding divine speeches.[199] In fact, the questioning of Yahweh by Abram seems so prominently presented that the narrator has to talk about the faith of Abram in Genesis 15:6 attributing to him righteousness in order to disabuse the minds of some readers who might presume that the father of the Hebrew race seemed to have lost his faith in Yahweh here.[200] Thus instead of the usual monologue, these divine speeches juxtapose symmetrically the speeches of Abram and Yahweh in a continuous cycle of speeches, with a kind of one character speaking and then a response given by the other character. We see here the building tension of the former episode rising to a high pitch before resolution. Built around the divine speeches, the structure of the present pericope is outlined as follows:

---

197. See Sailhamer, *The Pentateuch as Narrative*, 149.
198. James McKeown, *Genesis*. The Two Horizons Old Testament Commentary (Grand Rapids, Michigan: William B. Eerdmans Publishing Co., 2008), 89.
199. Ibid.
200. See Joseph A. Fitzmyer, "The Interpretation of Genesis 15:6: Abraham's Faith and Righteousness in a Qumran Text," *Emanuel: Studies in Hebrew Bible Septuagint and Dead Sea Scrolls in Honor of Emanuel Tov*, eds. Shalom M. Paul, Robert A. Kraft, Lawrence H. Schiffman and Weston W. Fields (Leiden: Brill, 2003), 257–268.

Divine Speech	15:1
Abram's Speech	15:2–3
Divine Speech	15:4–5
Narrator's Evaluation	15:6
Divine Speech	15:7
Abram's Speech	15:8
Divine Speech	15:9
Narrator's Description	15:10–12
Divine Speech	15:13–16
Narrator's Description	15:17–18a
Divine Speech	15:18b–21

Closely looking at this structure, the pericope is first introduced by אַחַר הַדְּבָרִים הָאֵלֶּה (translated, "after these things") which normally in biblical narrative signalled a new episode. As a new episode marker, אַחַר הַדְּבָרִים הָאֵלֶּה while looking forward, but also looked backward to the event of Genesis 14. The first divine speech is introduced by the discourse marker, לֵאמֹר which has the added prophetic frame, הָאֵלֶּה הָיָה דְבַר־יְהוָה אֶל־אַבְרָם בַּמַּחֲזֶה (literally, "the word of the Lord came to Abram in a vision").[201] This frame, as we are going to see, already characterized Abram in this pericope, explicitly making Abram a prophet.[202] Thus it seems the narrator wanted to say that Abram is also the father of prophecy and hence the significance of the materials in this pericope as prophecy from Yahweh to Abram. Following the divine speech in verse 1, the first words of Abram to God are hereby recorded, and these are introduced by the discourse marker, וַיֹּאמֶר. It is important to also note that this first statement of Abram to God is a question and not some lofty statement

---

201. On the general treatment of direct discourse and discourse markers particularly לֵאמֹר in biblical narrative see G. Hatav, "(Free) Direct Discourse in Biblical Hebrew," *Hebrew Studies* 41 (2000): 7–30.
202. Sailhamer rightly observed that the narrator "goes to great lengths to cast" Abraham in the role of a prophet. "The central subject of the chapter deals with the announcement of events that lie in the future (vv. 13–16), and thus it is of utmost importance to the author that Abraham's credentials as a prophet be clearly set forth and defended." See Sailhamer, *The Pentateuch as Narrative*, 149.

of inspiration. Continuing his speech in verse 3, וַיֹּאמֶר is still used even though Abram is the only speaker, and there is no speaker in between. Thus two וַיֹּאמֶר are embedded in this first statement by Abram to God, showing the eagerness of Abram to speak on his plight, which though it is the focus of the prior divine speeches, it is actually not yet solved.

After the objection by Abram, the divine speech is introduced again by לֵאמֹר and the prophetic template, "and behold the word of the Lord [came] to him," even though lacking the verb "come." This round of divine speeches ends in verse 5, and then it is followed by the narrator's evaluative comment on the faith of Abram in verse 6. God took over the speech in verse 7, and his speeches are introduced this time by וַיֹּאמֶר rather than the initial quotative frames לֵאמֹר. Even though Abram is credited with "faith" however, he also raises the question in verse 8 how is he going to know if he is going to possess the land. In this question, we see an "Abram" that is quite different from the passive and obedient Abram of the preceding pericopes. This "Abram" is seeking to know how things will work out at the end. The declaration of his faith by the narrator did not rule out his inquisitive quest to know the path of the future. Inherent in this question alone, is the desire to know the future or the outcome of events. This desire matches with the subsequent revelation of the future path by Yahweh, and thus underscoring the prophetic nature of this pericope. The speech by Abram is introduced by the discourse maker וַיֹּאמֶר and it is a straight question at the preceding divine speeches with their elevated and high sounding rhetoric. The importance of this question is clearly seen in the obscure "covenant ceremony" that follows. Even though we cannot tell precisely the importance of this sacrifice, it shows that the character Abram is now ready to "take God to task" about his promises and it also shows the growing desperation of the character Abram.

The question from Abram is followed by another discourse marker וַיֹּאמֶר in verse 9 which now introduces the speeches of Yahweh. In verse 10, the narrator breaks the narrative in order to describe in detail this obscure covenant ceremony between God and Abram. Following this description, the narrator introduces the divine speeches again in verse 13 with the object of the discourse maker וַיֹּאמֶר being Abram. Here, the divine speeches open with the verb יָדֹעַ which was the main verb of Abram's question in verse 8. In the use of this verb, Yahweh is responding now to Abram's question by giving vivid historical details concerning his descendants and their possession of the land. This long divine speech from verses 13–16 came to an end. After these divine speeches, the narrator gives a break by describing the scenario of the ceremony (v. 17–18). Using again לֵאמֹר as the discourse marker at the beginning of the pericope in verse 1, the narrator explicitly talks about the covenant between Yahweh and Abram, and then, by these divine speeches, brings the pericope to a close. Thus the divine speeches bracket the entire pericope by its presence at the beginning and end of the passage. This structure also shows how the divine speeches envelope the "fears" of Abram. This envelope could be seen by the following structure, which is taken from the preceding table.

- **A** Divine Speech
  - **B** Abram's Speech
- **A** Divine Speech
  - **C** Narrator's Evaluation

- **A** Divine Speech
  - **B** Abram's Speech
- **A** Divine Speech
  - **C** Narrator's Description

- **A** Divine Speech
  - **C** Narrator's Description
- **A** Divine Speech

In this structure, both the speeches of Abram and the comments or description by the narrator are sandwiched in between the divine speeches. Thus, the divine speeches form a kind of "literary bracket" by which the fears of Abram in particular are finally addressed. For the narrator, Abram's growing concern is addressed by the divine revelation or prophecies on the certainty of his promises. From the point of view of the narrator, the present pericope provides a window into the future of Abram and his descendants, but most importantly culminated in a covenant of friendship between Yahweh and Abram, thus suggesting the growing and deepening relationship between Yahweh and Abram.

3.3.1.2. Literary Context

The present pericope has its immediate literary context in the preceding chapter. This quest to connect the present pericope with Genesis 14 is clearly seen in the first phrase that introduces the pericope, that is, "[a]fter these things," (אַחַר הַדְּבָרִים הָאֵלֶּה).[203] This phrase looks backward to the invasion of the Promised Land by the kings from the east, the defeat of the Sodom coalition, the captivity of Lot, Abram's military exploits, his return at the kings valley and the meeting with the enigmatic king of Salem, namely, Melchizedek. The highlighted events form the background to the divine speeches and the dialogue of the present pericope.

The narrator did not hide his quest to connect or place this episode within the matrix of this literary context.[204] There are indications of connection between this present pericope and its immediately preceding chapter. A few of these literary connections are worth noting. Firstly, the הָאֱמֹרִי (the Amorite) in Genesis 14:13 is singled out and mentioned in Genesis 15:16, 21. The word for covenant appears in Genesis 14:13b and reappears again in Genesis 15:18a. The three hundred and eighteen men in the house of Abram in Genesis 14:14b is equivalent to the figurative value of the name of Eliezer in Genesis 15:2b.[205] Even though Dan is anachronistically mentioned in Genesis 14:14c, in the divine speech in Genesis 15:14a, a verbal reference is also made to this same name.

---

203. This phrase is employed as a way of indicating temporal positioning. See Merwe et al, *A Biblical Hebrew Reference Grammar*, 277.

204. Zakovitch has shown how this present pericope is juxtaposed with the events in Genesis 14 and 16. See Zakovitch, "Juxtaposition in the Abraham Cycle," 513–14, 516–17.

205. Concerning this observation, Wenham observed, "[t]hough the number 318 equals the numerical value of Eliezer's name (15:2), this appears to be coincidence." See Wenham, *Genesis 1–15*, 314.

Similarly, there is a mentioning of "Damascus" in Genesis 14:15 and Genesis 15:2b.[206] The use of רְכוּשׁ for "possession" or wealth occurs in Genesis 14:16a and it is also found in Genesis 15:14b. The noun צְדָקָה appears in the name of Melchizedek in Genesis 14:18a and also appears in the evaluative comment by the narrator on the righteousness of Abram in Genesis 15:6. In this sense, the narrator connects Abram to the king of Salem, namely, Melchizedek. In addition, הַשָּׁמַיְמָה or "the heavens" occurs in Genesis 14:19b, 22b and reoccurs in Genesis 15:5a. The form of the word בְּשָׁלֵם ("Salem") occurs in Genesis 14:18a and also in the divine speech of Genesis 15:15a. The form of the word מָגֵן which means "delivers" or "shield" occurs in Genesis 14:20a and Genesis 15:1b.[207] Lastly, it is also possible that the word רְכוּשׁ which occurs in Genesis 14:21 for property may be a paronomasia, which is a backward reversal of the alphabets in the word שָׂכָר in Genesis 15:1b since both words become the other when read backwardly (רְכֻשׁ becomes שָׂכָר).

Beyond these literary connections, theologically speaking, the divine command that Abram should not be afraid would only make sense in the light of the events in Genesis 14. Similarly, the promises of becoming a "shield" and "reward" to Abram have their immediate meaning from the battle and the forfeiting of the spoils of war by Abram. In addition, the priesthood of Melchizedek complements the portrayal of Abram as a prophet in the present pericope. In this light, the encounter between Melchizedek and Abram might be a symbolic representation of the relationship between the priesthood and prophetic traditions of ancient Israel. To this end, through the literary and theological connections, the narrator presents his narratives as the continuity of the events and thoughts already

---

206. Some Greek and Latin texts of Hellenistic period have closely associated Abraham with Damascus. Some writers of this period actually believed that Abraham was born there, and even became a king there. For the studies of this association of Abraham and Damascus particularly in the light of divergence between the Masoretic text of Genesis and these Greek and Latin sources see John A. Emerton, "Abraham and Damascus in Some Greek and Latin Texts of the Hellenistic Period," *Sacred History, Sacred Literature: Essays on Ancient Israel, the Bible, and Religion in Honor of R.E. Friedman on His Sixtieth Birthday*, ed. Shawna Dolansky, 179–193 (Winona Lake, Indiana: Eisenbraus, 2008), 179–193.

207. See Othmar Keel, *The Symbolism of the Biblical World: Ancient Near Eastern Iconography and the Book of Psalms*, trans. Timothy J. Hallett (Winona Lake, Indiana: Eisenbraus, 1997), 222.

encountered in the preceding chapter.²⁰⁸ Thus this hermeneutical assumption is significant to the understanding of the present pericope.

3.3.1.3. Grammatical Analysis

We now turn our attention to issues of grammar. In this subsection we will be primarily concerned with the categories in terms of the different uses of the quotative frames, the syntactical considerations and the dialogical nature of the divine speeches.

3.3.1.3.1. Quotative Frames

At the beginning of this pericope, the quotative frames introducing the divine speeches and those of Abram are placed in a highly tense mood. This is true of the three discourse markers introducing the speeches of Abram in verses 2, 3, and 8. These speeches are not merely friendly chat. For example, as the friendship chat between God and Abram in Genesis 18 when God stopped by at Abram's house in order to "eat" and chat with Abram his "friend." This is the first dialogue between God and Abram, and has elements of arguments or debate with God presenting his proposition and Abram questioning them. Unfortunately, many translations miss this element of tense dialogue and have translated the discourse marker וַיֹּאמֶר introducing Abram's speech merely as "Abram said" rather than showing the contrast "but Abram said."²⁰⁹ In particular, the tempo of this tenseness is seen in the two occurrences of וַיֹּאמֶר which introduce the speeches of Abram in verses 2 and 3. In verse 3, the discourse marker וַיֹּאמֶר is used even though it was Abram still talking. Thus, while the divine speech employed only one discourse marker לֵאמֹר in verse 1, Abram's speeches are

---

208. Williamson has also reveals specific points of continuity as well as discontinuity between the covenant in this chapter and the one in chapter 17, thus stretching the literary context of the present pericope further. For this study see Williamson, *Abraham, Israel and the Nations*, 260–67.

209. The NIV rightly captured this contrast between the divine speeches and those of Abram by translating וַיֹּאמֶר as "but he said" rather than the usual rendering "he said." The force of this contrast is brought to bear on the sentence by the presence of בַּמָּה. This interrogative further questioned or enquired "about the *manner* in which something is to be done," that is, the "how." See Merwe *et al*, *A Biblical Hebrew Reference Grammar*, 325. In a semantic-pragmatic sense, the independent personal pronoun in verse 15 also functions in this contrasting function (Ibid., 253).

introduced by two discourse markers in the space of two verses. This appears to show the tenseness by which Abram spoke. The narrator would have merely used one discourse marker for Abram instead of two since there is no speech or speaker in between verse 2 and 3.[210] This tenseness did not resolve even after the comment by the narrator in verse 6 since the discourse marker וַיֹּאמֶר in verse 8 is in response to the speeches of God in verse 7. This discourse marker should also be translated to show the contrast between the divine speeches and those of Abram. Interestingly, both the introductory speech of Abram in verse 2 and his concluding speech in verse 9 are framed in questions rather than just ordinary statements. The framing of his speeches in questions also shows the contrasting nature of these speeches. The speeches of Yahweh are to be seen as answers to the questions of Abram. The importance of the speeches of Abram here cannot be overemphasizedthat the first dialogue between Abram and God is framed in a question and answer format. This alone points to the tenseness in this pericope which is absent in the preceding ones. This dialogue framed in questions and answers introduces a subtle progression in the mood of the divine speeches to the full-fledged argumentative speeches between Yahweh and Abram in Genesis 18:16–33. In that pericope, as

---

210. Describing this literary phenomenon, Miller observed, "[a]n interesting device of Hebrew is for a single speaker to have two speeches attributed to him/her, each introduced with a quotative frame. No narrative comment intervenes between the two pair-parts. The time frame or spatial orientation of the narrative is the same, and the participant framework of speaker and addressee is identical in both pair-parts" [Miller, *The Representation of Speech*, 239]. Formerly, source criticism has opined that different sources could lie behind this occurrence rather than a literary device. Cassuto observed that such device is not the presence of the diverse sources but the subsequent second speech is to explain "the inner meaning" of the first speech [Cassuto, *A Commentary on the Book of Exodus*, trans. Israel Abrahams, reprint (Jerusalem: Magnes and The Hebrew University, 1983), 38]. On the other hand, Conroy opined that it is an indicator by the narrator which signals "a new point of major importance" and hence part of the "narrative rhetoric" [Conroy, *Absalom Absalom!*, 130] Bar-Efrat points that the narrator hints "that there is a break in the character's words." For him, the double use of the discourse marker in a single speech of Abram is to show the break that Abram needed in order to look at the stars in verse 5 (cf. Exod 3:5–6; Judg 11:36–37) [Bar-Efrat, *Narrative Art in the Bible*, 43]. However, Miller observed that such double discourse markers are to show that the character speaking is responding to two points in the speeches of the former speakers [Miller, *The Representation of Speech*, 241]. In the present context, the double use of the discourse marker may have something to do with the tension of Abram's response. Abram is not only responding to the double items of the divine speech in verse 1, but also stressing his frustrations at the divine promise.

we are going to see, the persuasiveness of Abram moves beyond the staple question and answers to asking and making demands, even to the point of "altering the divine plans" for Sodom. The two subsequent divine speeches in the present pericope in verses 13 and 18 moves the pericope to a close but looks backward to the issues raised by Abram in verses 2, 3 and 8.

However, apart from the function of the quotative frame to show the tenseness or mood of the dialogue between Yahweh and Abram, the discourse markers also help to bring about characterization of the characters. The frame introducing the first two divine speeches in verses 1 and 4 is phrased with "the word of the Lord" came to Abram. This phrasing is not without its significance particularly in the light of the prophetic traditions associated with this mode of introduction in divine revelation. The characterizing functions of this phrasing are dual. Firstly, it characterizes Abram as a prophet and secondly it characterizes the divine speeches here as windows into the future.

Thus the quotative frames employed by the narrator reveal the tension or desperation in the interlocution between Yahweh and Abram. In fact, seven quotative frames introduce the divine speeches while the three quotative frames introduce the speeches of Abram, thus suggesting that God spoke twice for every single speech by Abram. In this sense, Yahweh did dominate the dialogue. But it also shows that Abram's questions were very crucial thus necessitating such a lengthy divine response in the ratio of two to one. Lastly, the quotative frames also become a means for characterization whereby through the frames we get to see the "prophetic" Abram that the narrator wanted us to see. But also through such frames we see the pericope as a window into the worlds of tomorrow.

3.3.1.3.2. Syntactical Considerations

We now pay attention to the syntax of the seven divine speeches in this pericope.[211] We are going to look at the verbs and their relationship to the surrounding words. We begin with the first divine speech in verse 1. The main verb of this first divine speech is ירא, then followed by two verbless

---

211. It is possible that there is importance attached to these seven divine speeches to Abram by the narrator since seven often stood for perfection in the numerology of the Hebrew Bible.

clauses namely אָנֹכִי מָגֵן לָךְ and שְׂכָרְךָ הַרְבֵּה מְאֹד. One would have expected a כִּי clause linking these verbless clauses to the main verb ירא. However, even though absent, it is obvious that the main verb ירא is related to these two clauses. There is exegetical importance in the use of ירא here because it is the first and last time God used this construction that is, "do not be afraid" for Abram.[212] Ironically, while Yahweh told Abram not to be afraid, the last speech of Yahweh to Abram in Genesis 22: 12 in particular emphasize the "reverential fear" of Yahweh by Abram.

The second divine speech found in verse 4 has the main verb ירש then followed by a כִּי clause which functions as a subordinate clause and provides reason why the potential heir mentioned by Abram will not be the one to inherit. In contrast, Yahweh told him that a son from his own "body" will be the one to inherit his property. The reply of Yahweh opened with the frame "וְהִנֵּה" or "and behold" which is also used by Abram in the last part of his complaints to God in verse 3b. If "behold" here introduces a different point of view as argued by Berlin,[213] then it follows that there appears to be a stress on the contrast between the point of view of Yahweh in the divine speeches and the point of view of Abram.

The third divine speech is located in verse 5 whereby God took Abram out and commanded him to look at the stars. Like the command of the last pericope, Abram is commanded to see and number the stars. Here, stars replaced "dust of the earth" in the preceding pericope. Similarly, attention is drawn to Abram rather than a "hypothetical man" counting the star. Yahweh is saying "you Abram if you can count" (אִם־תּוּכַל לִסְפֹּר) the stars rather than the hypothetical "if any man is able to count" (אִם־יוּכַל אִישׁ לִמְנוֹת). This shift from "any man" to "you" (Abram) is quite significant particularly in the context of the tense mood of the narrative. Yahweh is no longer talking about a hypothetical situation but he is confronting Abram to count himself. There is also a tenseness now in the divine

---

212. The same form was used only again in Abrahamic narratives in speech of the "Angel of the Lord" to Hagar in Genesis 21:17.
213. See Berlin, *Poetics and Interpretation of Biblical Narrative*, 62, 91–95.cf. S. Kogut, "On the Meaning and Syntactic Status of הִנֵּה Biblical Hebrew," *Studies in Bible*, ed. S. Japhet (Jerusalem: Magnes Press, 1986), 132–54; D. Slager, "The Use of 'Behold' in the Old Testament," *OPTT* 3 (1987): 50–79.

speech to confront Abram, hence it is no surprise that such a confrontation brings about the faith as evidenced in the narrator's comment of verse 6.[214]

From the subject of "seed" for Abram, the last four subsequent divine speeches are centered on the theme of land, though with reference also to Abram's descendants. Framed in view of exodus, the divine speech in verse 7 employed the verb הוֹצֵאתִיךָ to describe Yahweh's act of bringing Abram from the Ur of the Chaldeans to the land which he now promises to give him as a possession.[215] Thus in the mind of the narrator, the same movement of Abram from Ur of the Chaldeans is a kind of a pre-exodus.[216] This reference in the divine speech justifies our preceding interpretation of Genesis 12 particularly the sandwiching of verses 1–9 between the two geographical locations of Mesopotamia, or Babylon in particular, to Egypt. Thus the divine speech associated the journey of Abram with the exodus, and hence this verse already gives a hint of the subsequent revelation by Yahweh on the events of the exodus in verses 13–16. Significantly, for the narrator, it is not only the divine speeches in 13–16 that mirror the exodus, but the life of Abram himself, particularly his movement from his homeland as suggested by the framing of the divine speeches, which are employed by Yahweh to describe his act of bringing the Israelites to the Promised Land.

The fifth divine speech in verse 9 employed the verb לקח in imperative mood, thus summoning Abram to bring lists of items for sacrifice. The verb has five objects which are namely, עֶגְלָה מְשֻׁלֶּשֶׁת וְעֵז מְשֻׁלֶּשֶׁת וְאַיִל מְשֻׁלָּשׁ וְתֹר וְגוֹזָל. Interestingly, the narrator

---

214. There is a discourse marker in verse 5b which did not begin another new divine speech but acts as continuation of the divine speech which is started in verse 5a. I did not categorize this separately because it did not introduce a new divine speech but merely continues the ideas already expressed at the beginning of the verse. It acts as a subordinate clause to the clause in 5a.

215. See Exodus 20:2; Deuteronomy 5:6.

216. There is a legend that grows possibly from the etymology of אוּר. According to this legend, Abraham was sentenced by Nimrod to be killed by fire, but was miraculously saved by God. This legend might have come from the closer association of אוּר with אֵשׁ in the mind of early interpreters. See G. Vermes, *Scripture and Tradition in Judaism*. SPB 4 (Leiden: Brill, 1961), 85–90; J. Gutmann, "Abraham in the Fire of the Chaldeans: A Jewish Legend in Jewish, Christian and Islamic Art," *FrüStü* 7 (1973): 342–52.

employed the same verb in verse 9 to describe the obedience of Abram in verse 10.

The sixth divine speech following this list of items of sacrifice and the description of the scene in verses 11 and 12, now give the words of Yahweh. The divine speeches here in verse 13 begin with the verb תֵּדַע and its cognate in absolute form (יָדֹעַ), thus suggesting the certainty of the present divine speeches. By this emphasis, and from the point of view of Yahweh, the following events in the divine speeches are a certainty. The divine speech takes the main verb of Abram's question in verse 8 and now emphasizes the certainty of the events outlined in this window on the future of Abram's descendants.

The last divine speech from verses 18–21 presents a list of ten objects which are governed by the verb נָתַתִּי. Thus Yahweh's speech closes with a long list of the inhabitants of the Promised Land. The use of a single verb נָתַתִּי to present this catalogue of nations is stylishly done because it makes the verb נָתַתִּי stand out, and hence points the reader to the force of divine speeches which hang clearly here on this verb.

3.3.1.3.3. Dialogical Speeches

Sailhamer has rightly noted the "elevated style" of the present divine discourse with Abram.[217] Even though we have already highlighted the importance of the dialogical speeches here, some passing remarks could still be made. Pertinent to the present analysis is to find out the significance of dialogue speeches in this pericope. Why did the narrator wait until this point before injecting "divine dialogue" into the Abrahamic narratives? He could have equally begun his stories with such waves of speeches between Yahweh and Abraham. In fact, apart from the cycle of divine speeches between Adam and God, and Cain and God, the dialogically framed speech raising pertinent objections or displeasure with the divine appears to be absent in the preceding narratives.[218] Most commonly, God speaks and the

---

217. See Sailhamer, *The Pentateuch as Narrative*, 149.
218. Stressing the significance of this dialogue McKeown also observed, "[t]he chapter commences with a dialogue between God and Abram. Since Cain, no one in the Genesis account has had such interchange with God. Cain's dialogue represented the end of

narrator confirmed whether the participants did what was demanded by God or not, thus the significance of these dialogical speeches.

Similarly, this divine speech shows a remarkable sense of progress because it moves from the divine speech of Genesis 12:1–3 and 7 to the present dialogues by God in a vision, to the appearance in Genesis 17:1 and culminates in the vivid and physical visitation of God to Yahweh in Genesis 18:1. The introduction of dialogue to the Abrahamic narrative at this point rather than the former semi-monologue between Abram and Yahweh also helps to further the plot of the Abrahamic narratives since the diverse viewpoints expressed by Yahweh and Abram reveal the growing complication in the plot of the story and hence create the possibility of various ends for this story. In particular, in the plot around the land and descendants experienced in this pericope, some first doubts as readily seen in Abram's questions, which are directed at the promises made by Yahweh to him. This motif of doubt is also reflected, though tacitly, in the story of Hagar in the next chapter and the subsequent plea by Abram that Ishmael should be adopted as the promised seed in chapter 17. All these occurrences of doubt were not expressed by the narrator, but he used the dialogue or the personal speeches of Abram or Sarai to show the growing desperation in the life of this couple as years went by. Even though this pericope reiterated the faith of Abram in verse 6, we see in the marriage of Abram to Hagar a situation that indicates the wavering faith of Abram and Sarai. It seems the dialogues are introduced in the narrative to show the different turns and complications that the simple story of Abram is now taking.

The לֵאמֹר that introduced the first set of the divine speeches sandwiched also the two speeches of Abram. Even though Abram's speeches are here bracketed by divine speeches thus pointing more to Yahweh's speech than Abram's doubt, it seems Abram's doubt was merely silence for the time being, but will show up in the future. Thus, the silence of Abram and the narrator's evaluation of his faith, does not presume that everything is settled. The dialogue here introduces underlying complications which show up again and again in subsequent stories. Even though the narrator gave

---

his close relationship with God, but Abram's leads to a deepening relationship." See McKeown, *Genesis*, 88.

Abram a pass mark as to his faith, the subsequent story will be a test of this evaluation by the narrator. This pericope through the dialogue opens up a new Abram that is no longer afraid to question the divine, lofty promises of "innumerable numbers of descendants" and it moves the veil from the "silent" and "obedient" Abram to a more "talking" Abram who is ready to question the promises of Yahweh, and to move Yahweh into some kind of concrete binding oath or covenant as attested by the enigmatic "sacrifice of pieces." In all these concerns, it is the introduction of dialogue that brings out this complication showing us, for the first time, an Abram that is desperate and truly overwhelmed by the quest to have an heir.

3.3.1.4. Stylistic Aspects

This present pericope also reveals certain stylistic features in the divine speeches. The occurrence of these stylistic features in the speeches of Yahweh is deliberate, particularly taken the tense nature of the mood of this pericope. The stylistic features are not just ornamented literary features which are there for decoration, but they are there for persuasive ends. Yahweh must convince Abram that he is going to bring about the initial promises he had made to Abram on the possession of the land and the multiplication of his descendants. In this particular instance, the stylistic features of this pericope go beyond literary necessity to fulfill a hidden function of persuasion. This is particularly true because of the assumed prophetic nature of this piece and the anticipation that the future children of Abram will imitate the "faith" of Abram who, in the midst of growing doubt, still was commended for his faith in Yahweh, whom he trusted to bring about the multiplicity of his descendants and the possession of the land. In this sense, readers can position themselves and identify with the growing anxiety and desperation of Abram to possess the land and also the promised descendants. Thus the stylistic features functioning in this "prophetic" passage go beyond the repetition of the events of the past to persuasion of the future generation of readers. We now turn to the simple stylistic features while the discussion of their literary and ideological functions awaits the subsequent chapters of this present work.

3.3.1.4.1. Metaphor

There are four metaphors in the divine speeches within this pericope. The first metaphor is in the declarative statement at the beginning of verse 1a, when Yahweh says, "I am your shield."[219] This metaphor is a militant metaphor for protectioneven though common in the Psalms it appears only twice in the entire Pentateuch, thus signaling its significance in its occurrence here in this divine speech. The other occurrence appears in the song of Moses in Deuteronomy 33:29. Thus it is only here in the Pentateuch that God himself declared that he is a shield. In the preceding military story in chapter 14, the military use of the "shield" is significant because Yahweh appears to promise Abram protection against the possible military threats from these kings. At least in the context of the Abrahamic narrative, the imagery of shield to Abram goes beyond this military significance since "shield," as shown in the study of the biblical text, iconographies and texts of the ancient Near East by Arne Wiig, could also mean protection, prosperity and promise.[220] Hence the retorting question by Abram in verse 2 should be paraphrased something like this: "what have you given me if you are actually my shield since I am living childless and the one who will inherit my wealth is Eliezer from Damascus?" This paraphrased question reveals the tension and presupposes that the reply of Abram to the divine declaration of Yahweh as a shield is a challenge to Yahweh since Abram conceived that as "shield", Yahweh would have provided him an "heir" which, from the view of the oriental people, is in some sense the true "shield." Thus for Abram, Yahweh as a "shield" makes only sense if he has and "heir" that will inherit his property. Without an heir his estate or wealth is left "unshielded" and hence the reference to a foreigner Eliezer who will likely inherit his property in the absence of his own child. For Abram, life at the moment is "unshielded" as long as there is no heir to pass over his wealth to him. In this perspective, Abram's question in verse 2 is

---

219. Yahweh's speech, "I am your "shield" is placed in parallelism to the idea of the second clause namely "I am your exceeding rich reward." Hence there is a kind of parallelism at work in these opening words of Yahweh to Abram which point to the significance of this metaphor.

220. Arne Wiig, *Promise, Protection and Prosperity: Aspects of the "Shield" as a Religious Metaphor in an Ancient Eastern Perspective* (Lund: University of Lund, 1999).

directly questioning the divine declaration of being his shield. Interestingly, a first person common pronoun אָנֹכִי phrased the declaration of Yahweh and Abram. Yahweh said, "I am your shield" (אָנֹכִי מָגֵן לָךְ), Abram retorted back, "I am going childless" (וְאָנֹכִי הוֹלֵךְ עֲרִירִי).

The second metaphor follows this first one. It occurs in verse 1b when Yahweh literally said, "I will be your wage" or in the modern sense, "I will be your salary." The word translated in most modern translation as "reward" is actually the same word that occurred as "wages" in the context of the transaction between Abram's grandson and Laban in Genesis 30:28; 31:8. It also occurred in Exodus when Pharaoh's daughter told Moses' mother to take care of Moses and that she would pay her wages for nursing him.[221] Even though it is often translated here "reward," the metaphor has the idea of wages. It appears that the second reply of Abram, which is prefixed with another discourse marker to introduce continuity of his thought, seemed to be a tacit refusal to concede to the second declaration of Yahweh that he is his "reward" or "wage." For Abram replied, "You have given me no seed; so a servant in my household will be my heir." Put simply, Abram is saying to Yahweh, "what is the point of being my "reward," "wage" or "wealth," when you have not given me a child?" "It is not wage or wealth that is important to me, it is a child." Thus Abram's speeches are counter-points or arguments on the validity of the divine declaration in his own life. What does it means to be a "reward" or "wage" to a childless old man? Abram does not want a wage or rewardhe only wants a child. For him, such child will be his true "reward" or even greater than any "wage." To this end, Rashi translated the response of Abraham thus; if you will deny me a child, "[w]hat use, then, is all else that thou givest me?"[222]

The third metaphor lies in the phrase, "that which will come from your body" in verse 4b. This phrase metaphorically speaks of the anticipated "son" or "seed" as the "one who is going to come out from your body." The phrase conceals the identity of this expected child. Significantly, it matches also the refusal of Yahweh to call the servant by name in the preceding half

---

221. Exodus 2:9.
222. See Rashi, *Bereshith: Chumash With Targum Onkelos, Haphtaroth and Rashi's Commentary*, trans, ed. A. M. Silbermann (Jerusalem: Feldheim Publishers, 1934), 60.

of the sentence (לֹא יִירָשְׁךָ זֶה). The phrase stands for the "child" who in several places was described as the "seed," but who is described here as "one who is to come from your body." The use of this metaphor is done to balance the other half of the sentence since Yahweh refused to call the servant by name. In the same way, he also deliberately employed the metaphoric expression "one who is going to come out from your body" as an appropriate description of the expected heir of Abram.

Lastly, we turn to the metaphor of "counting" the stars. Even though the metaphor is not phrased like the one in Genesis 13:16, it is seen to present the future descendants of Abram, thus stars here in verse 5 are a representation of the future "seeds" of Abram. The stars now replaced the earlier image of "dust of the earth" in Genesis 13:16. Abram is now directed to look heavenward to see his future descendants rather than the initial earthward command. The metaphor explores the apparently infinite numbers of stars to draw a comparison, that is, as the stars are without number so will be the future seeds of Abram. Similarly, as in the last pericope, it is the imagery of the "seeds" that occupy the heart of the divine imagery rather than the land. It shows ultimately that the concern of having "seeds" rises prominently over the desire to secure a land. As already pointed out in passing, Yahweh directed Abram to count, rather than a "hypothetical person" to do the counting. In this shift or change of object for the counting, the narrator focused the divine speech on Abram and thus confronts him with the certainty of his promise to provide him with descendants. Even though different words for looking and counting are used,[223] the narrator implicitly points to the progression taking place in the relationship between Abram and Yahweh.

3.3.1.4.2. Ellipsis

Ellipsis is simply defined as a deliberate omission of a word, phrase or clause in a literary work especially where one expects such a word, phrase or clause to be present. Ellipsis is also known as "gapping" or "lacunae." Even though ellipsis is mostly found in poetry, it is also fairly common in prose. In the present pericope, the ellipsis is seen in the divine speech of verse 4

---

223. The words used here for looking and counting are נבט and ספר respectively.

which partly reads: "לֹא יִירָשְׁךָ זֶה כִּי־אִם אֲשֶׁר יֵצֵא מִמֵּעֶיךָ הוּא יִירָשֶׁךָ". This is translated, "this one shall not inherit you, but one who will come from your own body he shall inherit you." The phrase "this one" in the Hebrew is merely captured by the demonstrative pronoun "זֶה." In the preceding verse, Abram had described the person to inherit him as "the son of my house," "Eliezer" and the "son of Damascus." One could feel the rough syntax of Abram's speech as he stammers and describes this servant before Yahweh in verse 3. However, Yahweh interestingly refused to call this fellow by any of these names or descriptions and merely referred to him as "this one." Consequently, when the speech of Abram in verse 3 is compared to the one by Yahweh in verse 4, one realizes the speeches of Abram were filled with awkward descriptive labels which aim to name this foreign individual that will inherit him. However, contrary to this stance, in a place that one expects to see the name of this servant mentioned, Yahweh deliberately ignored his name and merely called him "this one." The significance of this ellipsis or Yahweh's deliberate refusal to call the name of this servant is that despite his great standing from the perspective of Abram, Yahweh did not consider him appropriate to inherit from Abram. Hence the divine speech ignored the servant by refusing to call or address him by any of the labels employed by Abramrather he is called a mere faceless "this one." Through this elliptical device, Yahweh asserts that the candidacy of Eliezer is not worth considering as the possible heir to inherit Abram's property.

3.3.1.4.3. Wordplay

There are five wordplays within the divine speeches.[224] The first of these wordplays is מָגֵן in verse 1 which draws attention to Genesis 14:20. The divine speech plays on this word found on the lips of Melchizedek. From the same root, Melchizedek employed מִגֵּן to describe deliverance of Abram

---

224. There is an indication in the biblical worldview that speakers of pun or wordplay are "wise persons." In fact, as argued by Edward L. Greenstein, wordplay and pun are an "index of intelligence", and clever speech is an "indication of wisdom" [see Edward L. Greenstein, "Jethro's Wit: An Interpretation of Wordplay in Exodus 18," *On the Way to Nineveh*, eds. Stephen L. Cook and S.C. Winter, 155–171 (Atlanta, Georgia: Scholars Press, 1999),156–60]. The occurrence of wordplay and pun in the divine speeches might bear on this understanding whereby Yahweh is conceived in an underlying narrative portrait of a "sage."

by God from his enemies.²²⁵ Here also such divine deliverance is envisaged because Yahweh wanted to assure Abram of his continuous commitment to protect and even give prosperity. The problem, as we have already seen, is Abram questioned such divine protection as either a "reward" or "shield" in the absence of an heir for the continuity of his family.²²⁶

The second wordplay is in the polysemous nature of שָׁלוֹם which could both mean "peace" but also "complete."²²⁷ In verse 15, the divine speech assured Abram of resting with his "fathers" and dying in "peace" (וְאַתָּה תָּבוֹא אֶל־אֲבֹתֶיךָ בְּשָׁלוֹם). On the other hand, contrary to this destiny for Abram, the following pointed to the "Sins of the Amorites" which after its "completion" will demand their extinction. Thus while Abram is promised peaceful, eternal rest with his ancestors, the fate of the Amorites, on the other hand, is sealed, though it is temporally delayed because their sins had not been "completed" (לֹא־שָׁלֵם עֲוֹן הָאֱמֹרִי עַד־הֵנָּה). Thus different fates await Abram and the Amorites, and the narrator employed polysemous nature of שָׁלוֹם to underscore these perspectives. By such exploration of the nuances of שָׁלוֹם he also tacitly associated Abram with Melchizedek who is tagged the king of Salem (שָׁלֵם). Interestingly, the Amorites are also stylishly used in a kind of metonymy whereby a part of something is taken

---

225. The wordplay is based on the polysemous or Janus nature of the word מָגֵן which could different vocalization means either "shield" or "benefactor." Concerning this wordplay, Rendsburg noted, "the Janus word *māgēn* as vocalized by the Masora means only "shield." But with another vocalization, such as the *nomen agentis* form *maggān*, or perhaps even with the same vocalization, as in the stative *qal* form *māgēn*, the same word means 'benefactor' from the root *m-g-n*. In fact, when one recognizes that this root is used a few verses earlier, in Gen 14:20, the word play is enhanced. Of course, since Hebrew literature possessed an oral/aural quality in antiquity, the reader of Genesis 15:1 needed to supply one reading only (presumably this is the reading that was retained in the Masora), but the second meaning was present in the text that he or she held." See Rendsburg, "Word Play in Biblical Hebrew: An Eclectic Collection," *Puns and Pundits: Word Play in the Hebrew and Ancient Near Eastern Literature*, ed. Scott B. Noegel (Bethesda, Maryland: CDL press, 2000), 139.

226. There appears to be a wordplay between שָׂכָר in verse 1 and יָרֵשׁ in verses 3b, 4b and 4c. The two words have similar consonants namely *shin* and *resh* but only differs in *yodh* and *kaf*. It appears the wordplay wants to connect Yahweh's sufficiency to Abram's need to have somebody to inherit him.

227. Polysemy is a term used to describe a word with several possible meanings. See Walter Herzberg, *Polysemy in the Bible* (University Microfilms International, 1981); Martine Vanhove, ed. *From Polysemy to Semantic Change: Towards a Typology of Lexical Semantic Associations* (Amsterdam: Benjamins, 2008).

to represent the entire thing. They are stylishly placed as the seventh nation in the list in verses 19–21.[228] They are followed immediately by the Canaanites and preceded by the Perizzites. Concerning this stylistic feature of the Amorite placement here, Rendsburg noted, "the placement of the Amorites in Genesis 15:19–21 is due to a specific literary device that the author of this material implemented. Elsewhere in the Bible where rosters of ten occur, special prominence is given to the entries listed in the seventh and tenth positions."[229] This is because, according to Rendsburg, in Genesis 5 "Enoch and Noah, whose special characters are obvious, occupy slots number seven and ten, respectively."[230] The same sequence of seven and ten is also seen in the arrangement of the ten generations in Ruth 4:18–22 where Boaz is placed in the seventh and David occupied the tenth position.[231] Thus by talking about the "sin of the Amorites" the narrator is talking about the sins of the entire occupants of the Promised Land. However, he uses the Amorites, which are the seventh on the list, as representative of these other nations. In this way, instead of talking about each of them, he only talks about the Amorites.[232] Significantly, the Amorites were the few people who rallied after Abram in Genesis 14:13 and assisted him in the defeat of the coalitions of the four eastern kings, thus they represent the inhabitants of the land that supported Abram. Possibly, this friendly tie between Abram and the Amorites is responsible for the delay in the divine judgment here.

Similarly, the tenth nation on this list is also of great interest. Stylishly, the Jebusites are placed in the tenth position of this divine speech. The significance of this positioning is evidently seen in the close association of the Jebusites with Jerusalem in later biblical thought.[233] Thus "[i]n sum,

---

228. Rendsburg observed that what has "gone unnoticed" in the present study of the text "is the fact that the Amorites appear in Gen 15:19–21 in position number seven, whereas in the other rosters they are mentioned at the head or close to the head of the list." See Rendsburg, "Notes on Genesis XV," *VT* 62, no. 2 (1992), 268.
229. Ibid., 269.
230. Ibid.
231. Ibid.
232. On the relationship between allusion, irony and wordplay see Wilfred G. E. Watson, "Allusion, Irony and Wordplay," *Bib* 65, no. 1 (1984): 103–105.
233. See 2 Samuel 24:1–25; 1 Chronicles 11:4–8.

the positioning of Amorites/Jebusites as seven/ten in Genesis 15:19–21 is not coincidental. Rather, it is due to a well-conceived literary plan." This is because "[t]he placement of these ethnonyms in this list parallels that of Enoch/Noah in Genesis 5 and that of Boaz/David in Ruth iv 18–22."[234] Moreover, "the Amorites are given special prominence because of their appearance elsewhere in the narrative, specifically Genesis 15:7, 13, 16."[235] In this divine speech, the placement of the Amorites and the Jebusites on the seventh and tenth positions respectively points here to the stylistic framing of the divine speeches.

In addition, there is wordplay around the root יצא which appeared at least four times in the divine speeches of this pericope. Firstly, it appears in the divine speech of verse 4b where it is translated "the one who is going to come out from your body" (כִּי־אִם אֲשֶׁר יֵצֵא מִמֵּעֶיךָ). Secondly, the root appears in verse 5 where Yahweh "took Abram outside" (וַיּוֹצֵא אֹתוֹ הַחוּצָה) in order to see the stars. Thirdly, the root also appears in verse 7 in the declaration of Yahweh that he is the one who brought Abram out of the land of the Chaldeans (אֲנִי יְהוָה אֲשֶׁר הוֹצֵאתִיךָ מֵאוּר כַּשְׂדִּים). Lastly, it appears in the prophetic description of the exodus in verse 14b. The wordplay becomes obvious since it appears Yahweh is saying "just as I brought you out of Ur of the Chaldeans many years ago, and I brought you also outside now to see the stars and will bring back your descendant to this land, so also I will bring out from your body a son." Thus there is wordplay between Yahweh bringing out Abram outside to see the stars, his journey from his homeland, the exodus from Egypt and the anticipated birth of the promised child. This wordplay throws great light on the significance of Yahweh taking Abram outside in verse 5 because without the correlation of this wordplay together it becomes impossible to know or understand the rationale behind this observation since we are not told the particular place where this event (which begins in verse 1) actually took place. Thus it comes abruptly to the reader when he is now told that "Yahweh took Abraham outside"[236] in verse 5. However, when viewed as a concentrated kind of wordplay,

---

234. See Rendsburg, "Notes on Genesis XV," 270.
235. Ibid.
236. Even though the "seeing of the stars" demands going out in a sense, however the text did not prepare us for this event because it did not tell us the context for this discourse

the awkward mentioning of Yahweh taking Abram outside becomes clear. Significantly, when these several roots of יצא are treated together as wordplay it seems Yahweh wanted to strengthen the faith of Abram because he brought him outside to see the future faces of his children in the shining of the twinkling stars, he also brought him out of the land of Chaldeans, and at the exodus he would bring his future children into the Promised Land; it thence follows that Yahweh is able to bring out a child from Abram's own body, thus the birth of Isaac becomes a type of exodus from Egypt, Ur and possibly also the "going out" from the "tent" by Abram.

The divine speech also employed wordplay on דָּן in verse 14. Abram pursued the kings in the preceding chapter to Dan (14:14). In a sense, he actually judged them by defeating them there at Dan. In the same way, God said that he is going to judge "the nation" that will enslave the future descendants of Abram (אֲשֶׁר יַעֲבֹדוּ דָּן אָנֹכִי). Thus, as Abram went to defeat the kings and brought back Lot, Yahweh will defeat "the Egyptians" and bring back Israel to their land. Stylishly framed as prophecies, the narrator even though knowing that it is Egypt that Yahweh is talking about, refuses to disclose this information and only gives us clues by the mentioning of Egypt as the first boundary marker in his description of the borders of the Promised Land. As recognized by commentators, this boundary is "bogus" since not even at the time of David and Solomon was the national boundary up to these geographical points. However, the boundary here is not the precise borders, but through this "bogus" or exaggerated map, the narrator points to Egypt which is the subject of the preceding prophecy. Thus the rivers of Egypt and the Euphrates in verse 18 might even be "metaphors" or symbolic representation of the nations which will subsequently seek to enslave the descendants of Abram.[237]

3.3.1.4.4. Hyperbole
Talking about hyperbole, the map of the land according to verse 18 extends from Egypt to the river Euphrates. This elaborate map might be hyperbolic

---

between Yahweh and Abram. Thus "going out" in verse 5 and references to "vision" in verse 1 implies that Abram's dialogue with God possibly took place in his tent.

237. There appears to be a wordplay in the speech of Abram in verse 2 especially in the placement of בֶּן־מֶשֶׁק and דַּמֶּשֶׂק together.

rather than a realistic description of the land that Yahweh initially vowed to give Abram since the "borders of the Promised Land [here] coincide with those of the Garden of Eden (cf. 2:10–14)."[238] As the preceding studies have shown, the land given to Abram was primarily the "land of Canaan" but here we see the extension of the border to include the lands of Egypt and Babylon. The hyperbole in the divine speech is obvious since there is no time in the history of Israel when she was solely in control of these regions. As we have pointed out earlier the narrator of the Abrahamic narrative is incurably optimistic in his vision of a better future for ancient Israel. In the same way, the list of verse 19 is also a hyperbolic description of the nationalities occupying the Promised Land. The first three nations (הַקֵּינִי וְאֶת־הַקְּנִזִּי וְאֵת הַקַּדְמֹנִי) are not even found in the other listings of the original occupants of the Promised Land.[239] This exhaustive list of a perfect ten nations occupying the Promised Land should not be taken literally because there is the possibility that the divine speeches are laden with hyperbolic nuances rather than the "actual description" of the occupants of the Promised Land.[240] One might ask what are the purposes of such hyperbole in divine speeches? As our subsequent discussion will show, beyond the literary function, the divine speeches are ideologically framed in order to provide the readers with a past as well as a future that might be contrary to the present experience of the narrator and the reader. In this ideological function, the hyperbolic boundary satisfied as well as fanned the desire to frame or define the present political structures within the mapping of these divine speeches.

Similarly, there is another hyperbolic expression in the counting of stars or the equation of the Abram's descendants to "stars." As our discussion on a similar identification or comparison of the future descendants of Abram

---

238. See Sailhamer, *The Pentateuch as Narrative*, 152.

239. The other lists are found in Exodus 3:8, 17, 13:5, 23:23, 33:2, 34:11; Deuteronomy 20:17, 7:1; Joshua 10:1, 11:3, 12:8, 24:11; Judges 3:5; 2 Chronicles 8:7; 1 Kings 9:20; Nehemiah 9:8.

240. There are three possible reasons why this list could be construed as a hyperbolic statement. Firstly, it is the first and only list in the Bible with ten separate nations listed as occupants of the land. Secondly, it is the only list which left out the Hivites from the list of original occupants of the Promised Land. Lastly, it is the only list that made mention of the Kadmonites. See Rendsburg, "Notes on Genesis XV," 265.

with the "dust of the earth" has readily shown the divine speeches seek to underscore the certainty of his promises to Abram by references to concrete images. For a people who lived their everyday lives on the dusty roads of Palestine and gathered around the fireplace at night to listen to stories with the clear night sky and multitude of stars before their gaze, it is not surprising that the divine being employed the attraction of these daily realities in order to speak to them.[241] It is the closeness and vividness of these imageries in the everyday lives of these people that had kept the fascination of these divine speeches for many generations.

3.3.1.4.5. Alliteration

In this pericope, there are two alliterations which can easily be seen first in the list of the animals in verse 9. The text reads: "לִי עֶגְלָה מְשֻׁלֶּשֶׁת וְעֵז מְשֻׁלֶּשֶׁת אַיִל מְשֻׁלָּשׁ" containing the occurrence of "three" alliterates with each other, thus pointing to the importance of "three." In the same way, just as these three first items for sacrifice, the first three nations on the list in verse 19 also alliterates, thus it reads: "אֶת־הַקֵּינִי וְאֶת־הַקְּנִזִּי וְאֵת הַקַּדְמֹנִי". What is perplexing is whether the three first lists of items on the sacrifice are made to imitate the first three nations on the list of the occupants of the Promised Land. We cannot tell for sure, but since these two lists are the only lists in this pericope, the similarity between them, particularly as seen in the quest to make the first three items to alliterate, might not be coincidental. However, since we are ignorant about the ceremony of verses 9–18, particularly the significance of the "three year" for the first three animals, we could only point out that the narrator makes these three animals prominent by alliterating or repeating the "three" attached to them. Similarly, we are in darkness as to the significance of the three nations at the beginning of the list in verse 19, especially since they do not occur in this exact form anywhere again in the Old Testament; thus we can only presume that the narrator alliterates the first three of these nations in order to match the first three items of the sacrifice. By such relationship, it is possible that the significance of the sacrifice is an

---

241. On the conception of celestial bodies in Jewish cultural thought see Luis I. J. Stadelmann, *The Hebrew Conception of the World: A Philological And Literary Study* (Rome: Pontifical Biblical Institute, 1970), 92–96.

imitative kind of ceremony whereby the nations themselves are represented as dead animals for sacrifice, thus through this ceremony Yahweh assured Abram that the nations are already symbolically conquered.

3.3.1.4.6. Euphemism

Euphemism has been described as a "language of avoidance." It is a language of politeness.[242] It uses courteous expressions or words to speak or describe something that is deemed offensive by a given society or audience.[243] Defining the term, Keith Allan and Kate Burridge observed that euphemism "is characterized by avoidance language and evasive expression, that is, the speaker uses . . . 'expression that seeks to avoid being offensive.'"[244] Bullinger noted that euphemism occurs in the Bible when "a harsh or disagreeable expression is changed for a pleasant and agreeable one; or, where an offensive word or expression is changed for a gentle one; or an indelicate word for a modest word."[245] On the other hand, the antonym of euphemism is dysphemism.[246] Dysphemism occurs when a speaker uses "an expression with connotations that are offensive either about the denotatum or to the audience, or both, and it is substituted for

---

242. On the language of politeness see Richard J. Watts, *Politeness* (Cambridge: Cambridge University Press, 2003); Penelope Brown and Stephen C. Levinson, *Politeness: Some Universals in Language Usage* (Cambridge: Cambridge University Press, 1999) and Shoshana Blum-kulka, ed. *Politeness* (Amsterdam: North-Holland, 1990). In the use of "politeness" in biblical Hebrew see Ahouva Shulman, "The Particle נא in Biblical Prose," *Hebrew Studies* 40 (1999): 57–82; Benjamin Thomas, "The Language of Politeness in Ancient Hebrew Letters," *Hebrew Studies* 50 (2009): 17–39; Donald F. Murray, "An Unremarked Rhetorical Marker in Biblical Hebrew Prose," *Hebrew Studies* 40 (1999): 33–56.
243. For the different treatments of euphemism in relationship to politics, law, medical profession, media, children, sex, history of Greece and Rome, and religion see D. J. Enright, ed. *Fair of Speech: The Uses of Euphemism* (Oxford: Oxford University Press, 1986).
244. Keith Allan and Kate Burridge, *Euphemism and Dysphemism: Language as Shield and Weapon* (New York: Oxford University Press, 1991), 3.
245. Bullinger, *Figures of Speech Used in the Bible*, 684.
246. For some dysphemism in the Bible particularly in the Targum of Samaritan Pentateuch see Abraham Tal, "Euphemisms in the Samaritan Targum of the Pentateuch," *AS1* (2003), 112, 117–19. In a particular study of euphemism and dysphemism in the book of Samuel see Donald W. Parry, "The 'Word' or the 'Enemies' of the Lord?: Revisiting the Euphemism in 2 Sam 12:14," *Emanuel: Studies in Hebrew Bible Septuagint and Dead Sea Scrolls in Honor of Emanuel Tov*, eds. Shalom M. Paul, Robert A. Kraft, Lawrence H. Schiffman and Weston W. Fields (Leiden: Brill, 2003), 367–378.

a neutral or euphemistic expression for just that reason."[247] In the present pericope, euphemism occurs rather than dysphemism. This euphemism occurs in two places namely in verse 4 and in verse 15 of the divine speeches. The first euphemism is sexual in nature.[248] The divine speech reads: "כִּי־אִם אֲשֶׁר יֵצֵא מִמֵּעֶיךָ הוּא יִירָשֶׁךָ". Several translations have rendered מֵעֶה as "body, bowel, inward parts" or even "stomach, and intestine," but not "source of procreation," which should be the direct rendering in this context that has issues of procreation in view.[249] In a sense, these translations also preserved the euphemism within the text, which seeks to remove inappropriate sexual categories on the lips of the divine. To this end, Abraham Tal observed:

> In many societies a feeling exists that the formal names of organs or secretion and reproduction, as well as their products and their activities, are unacceptable in conversation and written expression. Every such society has developed means to avoid the use of 'dirty' words. However, attitudes change in the course of time and what is considered admissible at a certain moment becomes inappropriate at another.[250]

In this present text, Yahweh avoided the term for "sex organ" and instead used a very neutral word. The present portrayal of Yahweh's speech shows it is sensitive to the sexual decorum of ancient Israel.[251] One may ask whether the wordings of the divine speeches are here recast and reframed in light of this cultural sensitivity. The presentation of the divine speech in consciousness to the decorum of the readers itself points to the ideologi-

---

247. Allan and Burridge, *Euphemism and Dysphemism*, 26.
248. There is the growing recognition that issues of sexuality were central to the thought of ancient Israel. For example, David Biale observed, "[s]exuality was a central issue in Israel's self-conception, with adultery and fidelity the dominant metaphors both for Israel's relationship and for national identity." See D. Biale, *Eros and the Jews: From Biblical Israel to Contemporary America* (New York: Basic Books, 1992), 12.
249. On Euphemism and translation see Paul Ellingworth and Aloo Mojola, "Translating Euphemisms in the Bible," *BT* 37, no. 1 (1986): 139–143; Alter, *Genesis*, xxx.
250. Tal, "Euphemisms in the Samaritan Targum of the Pentateuch," 120.
251. On the study of sexual narratives in Genesis see James E. Miller, "Sexual Offences in Genesis," *JSOT* 90 (2000): 41–53.

cal framing of these divine speeches. Yahweh spoke respectfully the way a respected member of the ancient Israel community is expected to speak.[252] The use of euphemism in the divine speeches shows the close ideological and linguistic mappings between Yahweh and the cultural sensibility of the original readers.

In the same way, the divine speech talks about the death of Abram using euphemism. He noted in verse 15 that "Abram will go to his fathers in peace." This is a euphemism for death. Thus instead of talking about the death of Abram, Yahweh used a euphemism of gathering or going to the ancestors. Prior to this point in Genesis, neither Yahweh nor the narrator uses this euphemism to describe the death of anyone. Thus, there is inherent characterization involved here because God appears to be discreet or polite when talking about the death of Abram. Such divine politeness is significant particularly when placed in the context of prior death notices in the genealogical tables from Genesis 1–11. It is only to Abram that God was polite in his description of his death.[253]

3.3.1.4.7. Allusion

Allusion is glaringly seen in the reference within the divine speeches to the exodus in verse 6 and verses 13–16.[254] The reference to an unnamed nation

---

252. The art of euphemism is commonly seen also in rabbinic works. For the studies of this literary phenomenon in rabbinic works see E. Z. Melamed, "Euphemisms and Textual Alterations in the Mishnaic and Midrashic Texts," *Leš* 47 (1983): 3–17; idem, "Euphemisms and Textual Alterations of Expressions in Talmudic Literature," *Benjamin De Vries Volume*, ed., E. Z. Melamed (Jerusalem: Tel Aviv University Research Authority, 1968), 119–48; I. L. Rabinowitz, "Euphemism and Dysphemism: In the Talmud," *EJ* (Jerusalem: Keter, 1996), 6:961–62. For the emendation of the biblical text in light of eupheministic consideration see Christian D. Ginsburg, *Introduction to the Massoretico-Critical Edition of the Hebrew* (New York: Ktav, 1966), 345–404; William Mckane, "Observations on the Tiḳḳûnê Sôpeʿrim," *On Language, Culture, and Religion: In Honour of Eugene A. Nida*, eds. M. Black and W. Smalley. AS 56 (The Hague: Mouton, 1974), 53–77; W. Emery Barnes, "Ancient Corrections in the Text of the Old Testament (*Tiqqun Sopherim*)," *The Canon and Masorah of the Hebrew Bible* (New York: Ktav, 1974), 379–414.

253. There are also occurrences of euphemism among African people. For the treatment of euphemism among the Yoruba people of southwestern Nigeria see Ọlánipèkun Olúránkinṣé, "Euphemism as a Yoruba Folkway," *ALC* 5, no. 2 (1992): 189–202.

254. Before this allusion, there is another very important possible allusion to Adam's sleep (תַּרְדֵּמָה) in Genesis 2:21. According to this creation account, Eve was created out of a "deep sleep" that fell on Adam. This "deep sleep" is a kind of supernatural stupor" whereby

that will oppress the descendants of Abram in the future is a clear reference to Egypt and particularly the exodus. To what purpose was this necessary? Why is divine reference to the exodus an answer to the question of Abram in verse 8? To assure Abram of the certainty of the divine promises about having many descendants, Yahweh looks to the future and picks the single most important event or episode in the history of the Israelites. He went as far as describing the details. The Israelites are going to come out with "wealth" just as Abram had come out of Egypt with wealth in Genesis 13:14. The reference to the exodus here became a future proof that Yahweh will fulfill his promise to make for Abram numerous descendants, but also to give these descendants the possession of the land. By means of hindsight, the events of the exodus provided a memorable occasion showing the fulfillment of Yahweh's promise to the patriarchs.[255] Even though the Israelites would be in Egypt for four hundred years, Yahweh will see to it that they return to the Promised Land. Similarly, even though Abram will be gathered to his "fathers", Yahweh will be around to see that he fulfills his obligation to him as a covenant partner. Thus the lifespan of Abram is not the issue, but the continuous faithfulness of Yahweh to keep his promise to Abram even when Abram has gone. In this particular instance, the mentioning of the death of Abram also points to the faithfulness of Yahweh to keep his promise. Similarly, it shows that Abram will not fully see these descendants; however, Yahweh has everything covered so that the certainty of

---

Adam's rib was taken in order to fashion Eve. The narrator making reference to the "deep sleep" might have similar point in mind. Yahweh is here seen describing or fashioning for Abram a future descendants. Like "Eve" the nation of Israelite will be part of Abram in particular the "seed" though not the "rib." In this sense, the association of תַּרְדֵּמָה with Abram may point to the narrator's quest to portrayal Abram as a "new Adam," who similarly was promised the entirety of creation, and a woman created out of him. In the same way, Abram is promised the entire land and descendants are going to come out of him.

255. There is a possible literary device of innuendo in verse 14a in the phrase "the nation which oppresses them" (הַגּוֹי אֲשֶׁר יַעֲבֹדוּ). This phrase is a concealed reference to "Egypt." Yahweh concealed the identity of this nation, but a reader of the Bible understood the nation which Yahweh speaks about. Consequently, the divine speech employs indirect means to speak of Egypt instead of out-rightly giving away the name of Egypt as the culprit that will in the future oppress the descendants of Abram. The significance of this hidden reference to Egypt is that it silently undermines the greatness of Egypt especially as portrayed in the Joseph stories, since Egypt is seen here as an oppressor rather than the savior of the Joseph stories (Gen 37–50).

descendants for Abram is assured by this reference to the future. At the end, the memory of the exodus is employed to frame the present pericope, thus pointing to the thesis by the narrator that Abram saw the exodus before the event. This makes Abram a prophet, but beyond that it shows that Yahweh knew the paths of the future and hence he could be trusted again and again to redeem the descendants of Abram wherever they are now scattered. In this way, the narrator offers hope and comfort to his audience and thus saw Yahweh as committed to the future of Abram's descendants.

3.3.1.5. Significance

The literary-styled divine speeches in this pericope have importance in the reading and understanding of the Abrahamic narratives. It is not an overstatement that this pericope has been described as "pivotal for the Abraham tradition" and "the most important chapter of this entire collection" of Abrahamic narratives.[256] Firstly, the divine speeches continued the characterization agenda by casting Abram in the role of a prophet; thus as a prophet Abram is giving a prophetic vision into the future of his descendants. In fact, all the divine speeches of this pericope are framed in a prophetic manner with Yahweh telling Abram about the exodus and the restoration of the exodus community back to the Promised Land. Secondly, the divine speeches record the first covenant between Yahweh and Abram. This covenant shows the progression in the friendship between Yahweh and Abram. In the preceding pericopes, the reader merely reads the call and invitation of Abram by Yahweh and the promises of Yahweh to bless him. However, this present pericope moves the plot forward and shows the progress in the relationship between Yahweh and Abram, which now fully culminate in a covenant relationship. In addition, the divine speeches are the first record of dialogue and exchange between Yahweh and Abram. This dialogue shows the growing restlessness and scepticism of Abram towards the preceding divine promises. In a distinctive quest to quell Abram's restlessness and to provide answers to his growing doubt, the divine speeches function as reassuring words from Yahweh which assure Abram of Yahweh's commitment to bless Abram with many descendants and also to give him

---

256. Walter Brueggemann, *Genesis*. Interpretation (Atlanta: John Knox, 1982), 140.

the land. As reassuring speeches, the divine speeches employ graphic illustrations from the stars and defining moment of Exodus to tell Abram the certainty of the divine promises to him. On the other hand, the divine speeches also increase tension and anxiety for the reader of the Abrahamic narrative, particularly in the elimination of Eliezer as a possible heir to Abram (vv. 3–4). Thus the reader of the Abrahamic narratives is confused about the identity of the heir because Abram has no heir yet from his "body" (v. 4b). In this particular instance, the pericope looks forward to the future for the resolution of the tension and anxiety of the reader. Lastly, the divine speeches presented the first exhaustive list in the divine speeches of the inhabitants of the Promised Land (vv. 19–21). Originally, the preceding pericopes have only mentioned the Canaanites and Perizzites (12:6; 13:7), however, in the divine speeches the reader is confronted here with an exhaustive list, showing Yahweh's comprehensive knowledge of the inhabitants of the land which he promised to Abram. Thus Yahweh's omniscient knowledge is not merely of the distant future, but he also has intimate knowledge of the inhabitants of the land. In this understanding, the present divine speeches exalt the omniscient character of Yahweh particularly his intimate knowledge of events in the life of Abram, and hence his ability to bring to pass the desired end for Abram and his posterity.

3.4.1. Genesis 17:1–22

3.4.1.1. Structure

The present pericope is perhaps the climax of the Abrahamic narratives in terms of the divine speeches to Abram. It takes over certain motifs already highlighted in the preceding pericopes, for example the motif of the eternal divine gift of the land to Abram in Genesis 13:15, but it also introduces a new perspective such as the promise that "kings will come out" of the lineage of Abram and Sarah. Even though this may not necessarily be a new concept since it is inherent in the divine promise that Abram will become a "great nation" in Genesis 12:2a, there is already a hint to this new statement which clarifies the vagueness of preceding promise of nationhood. Similarly, even the change of names within this pericope is tacitly implied in the divine statement in Genesis 12:2b that "I will make your name great." From the divine perspective, a great name also needs a changed name, thus Abram is called the "the father of multitude of nations." In the same way, this phrase "the father of multitude of nations," even though specifically concerned with the increase of descendants for Abram, also shows the inclusion of "nations" (or גוים) into the fatherhood of Abram which, by implication, might be directly connected with the divine thought in Genesis 12:3 that Abram will be a blessing to the "families of the earth."

The pericope opens with the age of Abram in verse 1. It also describes the method of revelation, which is primarily the "appearance" of Yahweh to him. The reference to the age of Abram connects with preceding verses in Genesis 16:16 since there it was stated that Abram was 86 years old when Ishmael was born to him. Thus it shows a total of eleven years had elapsed from the calling of Abram in Genesis 12:4. At the opening of the narrative in Genesis 17:1, the narrator significantly points to the age of Abram. Here, Abram is 99 years old, hence a total of 24 years had gone since Abram's initial call to go Canaan, and a total of 13 years had gone by after the birth of Ishmael. In the same way, the narrator closes the present narrative with a reference to the age of Abram and Ishmael by the time of their circumcision (17:24). According to verse 24, the age of Abraham was 99 and the age of Ishmael was 13 years. The reference to the age of Abram at the opening as well as the closing of this pericope is significant since it points to the desperation of the story as seen in the delay of the promised child.

Concerning the subject of structure, the framing of Genesis 17 has a clearly defined structure. McEvenue describes the structure of the present pericope in terms of chiasm.[257] According to McEvenue the central concern with this series of divine speeches by the structure of the chiasm could be located in the third divine speech which centers on the rite of circumcision, hence, according to this chiastic structure, circumcision seems to be the full intention of these divine speeches and thus ultimately to the overall purpose of this present pericope. For McEvenue, this chiasm is seen thus:

---

257. McEvenue, *The Narrative Style of the Priestly Writer*, 147–48.

Stylistic Aspects of the Divine Speeches

       A   Abraham 99 (1a)
     B   The Lord appears (1ba)
    C   God speaks (1bb)
   D   First speech (1bc–2)
  E   Abraham falls on his face (3a)
 F   Second speech (name-change, nations, kings) (4–8)
G   THIRD SPEECH (9–14)
 F¹   Fourth speech (name-change, nations, kings) (15–16)
  E¹   Abraham falls on his face (17)
   D¹   Fifth speech (19–21)
    C¹   God ceases speaking (22a)
     B¹   God goes up from him (22b)
      A¹   Abraham 99 and Ishmael 13 (24–25)[258]

The full implication of this chiastic structure is that every part of the divine speeches looked either forward or backward to the central concern of this pericope, namely circumcision. Following McEvenue, Wenham has shown that the structure of the present pericope could also be captured differently with a kind of alternating parallel panels. This alternating panel, according to Wenham, is framed thus:

---

258. Ibid.

       A   Yahweh's intention to make an oath about progeny (1–2)
     B   Abraham falls on his face (3a)
    C   Abraham father of nations (4b–6)
   D   God will carry out his oath forever (7)
E   The sign of the oath (9–14)

       A¹   Yahweh's intention to bless Sarah with progeny (16)
     B¹   Abraham falls on his face (17–18)
    C¹   Sarah mother of a son, Isaac (19)
   D¹   God will carry out his oath forever (19b, 21a)
E¹   The sign of the oath (23–27)[259]

On the other hand, based on the structuring of the divine speeches, we could also reframe the structure of this pericope. The structures presented above are primarily driven by the analysis of the content of the individual section of the divine speech which is made to fit a kind of defined structure. For example, both McEvenue and Wenham omitted the speech of Abram in verse 18. For them, it shows that the speech of Abram is not important in the overall structure of the pericope, however, the speech of Abram, as we have seen in the study of the preceding pericope, often introduces a different point of view from the divine, and hence is also important in the structuring of the pericope. From this perspective, we could capture the structure of this pericope by the following simple structure:

---

259. Wenham, *Genesis 16–50* (Dallas: Word, 1994), 17.

A   Introduction v. 1a
    B   First Divine Speech vv. 1b–2
        C   Abram's Response v. 3a
            D   Second Divine Speech vv. 3b–8
                E   Third Divine Speech vv. 9–14
            D'   Fourth Divine Speech vv. 15–16
        C'   Abram's Response and Speech vv. 17–18
    B'   Fifth Divine Speech vv. 19–21
A'   Conclusion vv. 22–27

As readily shown by these three structures, the central section of this pericope is in verses 9–14 which is clearly represented by "E" or "G" in the case of McEvenue's structure. Thus the narrator artistically knitted this pericope in order to emphasize circumcision. Significantly, this is the first time circumcision is mentioned in Genesis. The structuring of the divine speech around this theme points to the significance the narrator attaches to this rite and his clue that it similarly preoccupies a central place in the religious understanding of ancient Israel.

3.4.1.2. Literary Context

The present pericope is placed between the dis-election of Ishmael in Genesis 16 and the subsequent dis-election of Lot in Genesis 18–19.[260] Thus the pericope is situated between the polite rejection of the Arabian and Egyptian stock personified by Ishmael and the Moabites and Ammonites as personified by Lot. In the preceding episode in Genesis 16, Ishmael, even though blessed and circumcised, was deemed unfit to be the elected heir that should continue the covenant relationship with Yahweh.[261] Ironically, in the present pericope, circumcision is described as a sign or symbol of the

---

260. Zakovitch had shown the literary connection between the present pericope with events in Genesis 16 and 18 respectively. See Zakovitch, "Juxtaposition in the Abraham Cycle," 520; 522–23.
261. On the general problems associated with the so-called "Ishmael texts" in the Abrahamic cycle see Roger Syrén, *The Forsaken First-born: A Study of a Recurrent Motif in the Patriarchal Narratives*. JSOTSup Series 133 (Sheffield: Sheffield Academic Press, 1993), 15–52. See also R.C. Heard, *Dynamics of Diselection: Ambiguity in* Genesis 12–36

covenant, however, Ishmael's circumcision did not provide him entrance to the covenant relationship between Yahweh and Abram. He was merely blessed because he is a "seed" of Abram. On the other hand, Lot's descendants were also deemed unworthy to be part of the covenant relationship with Yahweh. In particular, Lot's rejection is first seen in the way the narrator associated him with the inhabitants of Sodom and Gomorrah who in later biblical traditions became the epitome of sin and rebellion against God.[262] However, the narrator gave us a positive picture of Abram, particularly, how the pious Abram refused any material wealth from the king of Sodom. Thus while Lot chooses to live in Sodom, on the other hand, Abram refused the offer of friendship by the people of Sodom as represented by their king (Gen 14:21–24).

Moving away from these temporal concerns, the present pericope repeatedly points the reader to the eternity of the covenant between Yahweh and the descendants of Abram. Even though there is a reference to the eternal gift of the land in Genesis 13:17, it is here in the context of covenant relationship that the present eternality of the covenant is stressed. How does the covenant of Genesis 15 relate to the one within this pericope? Has God not already made a covenant with Abram? Why are there two covenants in the Abrahamic cycle? It seems the first is primarily preoccupied with the theme of land—hence the list of the occupants of the Promised Land at the end of this pericope—but the second covenant in Genesis 17 is particularly concerned with the theme of descendants.

This pericope extends the motif of dialogue already begun in Genesis 15, however, little space is devoted to Abram's speech. In fact, while Yahweh spoke five different speeches, Abram is credited with only one in verse 18. We see Abram's action rather than his speech. Twice the narrator told us in verse verses 3 and 17 that he fell "on his face" in reverence and worship to God. However, the only speech of Abram here is significant since it continued the general picture of a "desperate Abram" who is trying to see things from his own perspective. His only words to Yahweh were simply, "oh that

---

and Ethnic Boundaries in Post-Exilic Judah (Atlanta, Georgia: Society of Biblical Literature, 2001).

262. See S. Niditch, "The 'Sodomite' Theme in Judges 19–20: Family, Community, and Social Disintegration," *CBQ* 44 (1982): 365–78.

Ishmael may live before your face." This implies that while Abram was ready to worship at God's promises, he was not comfortable with the divine *modus operandi*. For Abram, Ishmael should be considered the "promised seed" instead of the expected son from an aged Sarah. In fact, Abram laughed at this divine method in accomplishing the stated promises (v. 17).

Connecting also the first divine speech to the context of this present pericope, one will realize that the first divine speech seems to be a rebuke particularly in light of the preceding complication of Genesis 16.[263] Yahweh told Abram, "אֲנִי־אֵל שַׁדַּי הִתְהַלֵּךְ לְפָנַי וֶהְיֵה תָמִים", which is translated, "I am El-Shaddai, walk before me and be perfect." In the context of the story of Hagar, especially the quest to seek an heir different from divine intention, the wording of the divine speech is an indirect rebuke at the "imperfections" of the last chapter. Consequently, this chapter under study now fits closely with the concerns of the past narratives, but also looks forward to the birth of Isaac and temporally to mosaic circumcision and ultimately to the acquisition of the Promised Land, which, no doubt, formed a continuous motif throughout the Old Testament.

3.4.1.3. Grammatical Analysis

We now turn to issues of grammar. Within this heading we will look at the quotative frames, the syntactical consideration of the divine speeches and the dialogical nature of these speeches. The aim of this analysis is to how show the different parts of the divine speeches fit together within the pericope.

3.4.1.3.1. Quotative Frames

Looking at the pericope, there are five quotative frames which introduce each of the divine speeches.[264] With the temporal break of Abraham's reverence in verse 3a, each of the divine speeches follow each other sequentially

---

263. For the common patterning of this pericope with chapters 16 and 18 see McEvenue, *The Narrative Style of the Priestly Writer*, 152–5.
264. McEvenue missed the significance of this structuring of the divine speeches in five parts, when he said, "the impressive structuring of the whole chapter in 5 speeches it is probably evidence of fidelity to source rather than of interest in dialogue." See McEvenue, *The Narrative Style of the Priestly Writer*, 151.

until we see another reverence and question by Abraham in verses 17–18, then immediately we switch back to the last divine speech. This is perhaps the longest and almost continuous speech by Yahweh in the Abrahamic cycle and has only two interruptions by references made to the reverence and concern of Abram in verses 3a and 17–18 respectively.[265] The first quotative frame of the divine speech is in verse 1. In this first speech, וַיֹּאמֶר is used to describe the words of God.[266] There is also reference to the appearance of Yahweh. This is the second time Yahweh is said to have appeared to Abraham. Like we noted in our discussion of the first occurrence in Genesis 12:7, there is an element of characterization evident in the use of this mentioning of the appearance of Yahweh to Abraham since there is no reference prior to the story of Abraham that Yahweh appeared to another person. Even though it is assumed that Yahweh spoke to the individuals in the earlier part of Genesis, there is no mention that Yahweh appeared to them. This is significant because it shows that Yahweh's relationship to Abram is on a level far beyond the religious and spiritual achievements of the past generations. Abraham by such a label is characterized and placed on a pedestal that is far beyond the Yahweh-human relationships of the earlier part of Genesis. The narrator understanding that Yahweh appeared to Abraham is not only significant within the confinement of the patriarchal narratives, but also the entire Pentateuch, or even the Old Testament, since it presumes that the origin of revelation of Yahweh to humans only first took place in Abraham. Thus even though there are great men or saints before him, it was only to Abraham that God decided to reveal himself.

Here, וַיֹּאמֶר is used to introduce the speeches of Yahweh. Yahweh introduces himself as "El-Shaddai" (אֲנִי־אֵל שַׁדַּי). In the future, Yahweh will introduce himself to the children of Abraham as "the God of Abraham, Isaac

---

265. The discourse marker appeared several times in the continuous speeches of a single speaker. This is a literary device whereby the speeches of a character are divided into different parts. See Miller, *The Representation of Speech*, 262–69.

266. For the use of the discourse marker as a "text-structuring" device particularly when there is repetition of the same discourse marker within the continuous speeches of a character as occurred here in verse 3 and 9 of the divine speeches is a common feature of biblical dialogue. On the other hand, the same phenomenon could also occur in a text without the expressed function of text-structuring. In this form, the second discourse marker merely "complements" or "reaffirms" the first speech [see Revell, "The Repetition of Introductions to Speech as a Feature of Biblical Hebrew," 96–110].

and Jacob", but for now he calls himself "El-Shaddai."²⁶⁷ In the present context, the revelation of Yahweh as "El-Shaddai" is significant especially in the light of Abram's preceding doubt, which is classically expressed in the Hagar saga of chapter 16. In this new name, Yahweh appears to say to Abram, "I am the all Sufficient One," hence, "you can trust me to fulfill my promises to you." Interestingly, the new name "El-Shaddai" for God took place in a context that is also characterized with change of names for Abram and Sarai respectively (vv. 5, 15). Thus God's new name here also matches the change of names of the main characters of the Abrahamic cycle. In addition, this new name for God occurs here for the first time and hence suggests the increasing intimate relationship between Abram and Yahweh. On the other hand, the following command, הִתְהַלֵּךְ לְפָנַי וֶהְיֵה תָמִים (which is literally translated "walk before me and be perfect,") also reveals the gulf between Yahweh's will for Abram and the drifting of Abram from such will. This drifting or doubt is reflected in the preceding narrative of chapter 16, hence being "perfect" in this context is not a kind of lofty moral demand or a quest for angelic perfectness by God from Abram, but a command to Abram to believe that Yahweh will provide him with a son through Sarai. In this understanding, Yahweh wanted Abram to stay within the course of his revealed will and to stay clear of distractions.

The second divine speech is introduced by the discourse marker לֵאמֹר (vv. 3b–8).²⁶⁸ The discourse marker describes the speeches of Yahweh par-

---

267. In this new name or title is also a refusal by Yahweh to identify with other holy persons in the early part of Genesis. Yahweh seemed to strike a discontinuity with the religious past of the primeval world. One would expect, in the light of the reoccurring phraseology which often states the names of the patriarchs, in his introduction of himself that Yahweh will by chance say he is the "God of Adam, Abel, Seth," or the "God of Enoch, Noah and Shem." What of the God of Terah? However, Yahweh distanced himself from these primeval religious men and attached himself in introduction to Abraham, Isaac and Jacob. By such subsequent identification of Yahweh with Abraham in particular, the narrator endorses the assumption that true revelation of God came with the calling of Abraham from Ur to Canaan.

268. This second divine speech is often "divided into three sections (vv. 3b–8, 9–14, 15–16), each marked by the reintroduction of the clause 'and God said': (vv. 3b, 9, 15)." Similarly, "[e]ach section deals respectively with one of the parties of the covenant (the Lord, Abraham, and Sarai), each of whom is specifically named or identified at the beginning of each section: the Lord ('as for me,' v. 4a), Abraham ('as for you,' v.9a), and Sarai ('as for Sarai, your wife,' v. 15a)." Similarly, the "specific content of each section of the covenant is memorialized by a specific sign within that section: the change of

ticularly the change of name for Abraham, the promise of descendants, royalty and the eternal possession of the Promised Land.[269] This is actually the first time that Yahweh called Canaan by name (v. 8). At the beginning of the Abrahamic cycle it was a vague land, which Yahweh promised to show Abraham. However, even though reference to "land" or "this land" appeared in the divine speeches several times, it is here at the peak of the divine speech in the Abrahamic narrative that we are given the name of the land in the divine speech.

Concerning the change of name, Abram, the old name for Abraham was never again used for him. In fact, immediately, in verse 9, the narrator switches from the old name to the new name. What is the significance of this name change? Is it a mere change of name or a change of the personality we now meet called Abraham? How is Abram different from Abraham? Are these two Abrams one and the same or is each a conflicting or even different person? Or is each character the conflicting or complementing aspect of a single personality? No doubt, the "new Abraham" has continuity with the "old Abram," but also different since it appears that the "new Abraham" has a kind of deeper relationship with Yahweh than the wavering "old Abram" of the preceding pericopes.[270] This deeper relationship is clearly seen in the vivid divine visitation to "eat" and "chat" with him in Genesis

---

Abraham's name in the first section (v.5), the circumcision of all males of the family in the second section (vv. 10–14), and the change of Sarai's name in the third section (v.15)." However, our present division is based on the discourse markers employed in the introduction of the speeches of the characters. See Sailhamer, *The Pentateuch as Narrative*, 157.

269. These indicators point to the royal ideology of the present text. Speaking of this royal ideology within the Abrahamic narratives, van Seters observed, "What we have throughout the Yahwist's treatment of Abraham and Isaac is the transformation of the patriarch from that of wandering nomadic forefather to royalty, even though he has neither throne nor kingdom" [See van Seters, *Prologue to History*, 270]. He presented two possible reasons for the application of a royal ideology to the patriarch. Firstly, he notes that "the purpose of this use of royal terminology and characteristics" is due to the elements of "democratization of the royal ideology in the exilic period." Lastly, he attributes the reason for such application to the nature of ancient Near Eastern historiography genre whereby historical texts of many kinds have to do primarily with kings and their deeds. Consequently, "[t]o transform antiquarian traditions about ancestors into history may well have influenced the use of such elements of royal ideology by the Yahwist" [Ibid., 271].

270. There is an irony here in this observation since the "old Abram" seems to be the "young Abram" while the "new Abraham" is the "mature and aging" Abraham.

18. However, the old Abram still continues as seen in the repetition of the wife-sister saga in Genesis 20. In the present pericope, the old Abram is also clearly seen in the doubtful statement of verse 18 whereby Abram still presents Ishmael as his only option for the continuation of his line.

The third quotative frame also employed the use of וַיֹּאמֶר as discourse marker (vv. 9–14). This discourse marker presents the divine speech that is primarily centered on the subject of circumcision. The rite is now introduced as a "sign of the covenant" and members of a Jewish household, whether Jewish or not, are commanded to partake in this covenantal rite.[271]

The fourth divine speech in verses 15–16 is introduced by the quotative frame וַיֹּאמֶר. This divine speech is particularly centered on Sarah. She also has a changed name, a promise of descendants, and royalty.[272] It was these divine promises that Abraham objected to in his first and last speech within this pericope. Firstly, Abram talked to himself in a kind of monologue. This monologue is a kind of thinking since the Bible notes that he said, "in his heart" (בְּלִבּוֹ). Interestingly, Abraham is portrayed here in verse 17 and 18 as thinking and speaking differently. His thought was centered on the impossibility of the last divine speech, but his speech to Yahweh has the solution that is the adoption of Ishmael into the covenant instead of a child by Sarah. In his heart, he said, "Shall *a child* be born unto him that is an hundred years old? and shall Sarah, that is ninety years old, bear?" But while speaking to Yahweh he said, "If only Ishmael might live under your blessing." Thus Abraham posed the difficult question to himself and directed the seeming conclusion of his thoughts to God. However, since Yahweh knows the heart of Abraham, it should be expected that Yahweh knew what he was thinking.

---

271. See Blenkinsopp, "Abraham as Paradigm in the Priestly History," 237.

272. In verse 15, the little כִּי clause grammatically "*expresses a counter-statement after a negative statement.*" It is then "translated as "but" that is a "*co-ordinating conjunction*" [Merwe *et al, A Biblical Hebrew Reference Grammar*, 303]. In the same way, the adverb אֲבָל in verse 19 also "[i]ndicates *the denial of an expectation or view* that a speaker thinks a listener holds," and it is similarly translated "but" [Ibid., 309]. In the long run this form of "counter-statement" embedded within the divine speeches which are also coordinated together helps the reader to see the divine perspective on the issues within the divine speeches.

The fifth divine speech is introduced by וַיֹּאמֶר in verse 19–21 in company of אֲבָל which often is employed to show contrast. Yahweh told Abraham, "no way," "to the contrary," and "despite" your objectives, "the promise child" will come from Sarah rather than Hagar. This divine speech is a rebuke against Abraham. With such high expectation of "Isaac" and the acknowledgement of "divine blessing" on "Ishmael" the divine speeches close.

It is obvious that the divine speeches were artistically arranged as shown by the structure of the present pericope. The quotative frames introduce Yahweh's speeches and underscore their importance. However, while the speeches of Yahweh were lengthy, those of Abraham were short with the most part of the speech as a monologue which is directed by Abraham to himself. On the other hand, Abraham's short speeches are clearly objections to the method by which God wanted to carry out his promises. For the audience of the narrator wherever they are situated, the divine speeches breathe a kind of optimism which is seen in the promise of descendants, royalty, nationhood, and the eternality of the Promised Land as heirs to the children of Abraham. In this particular understanding, the quotative frames treat by subject the themes that are at the heart of ancient Jewish identity.

3.4.1.3.2. Syntactical Considerations

We will now attempt to understand the syntax of the five divine speeches within this pericope. The main verb within the first divine speech is הִתְהַלֵּךְ in verse 1. This is the second time we see this word in the divine speeches of the Abrahamic cycle. The first time, God employed the term in Genesis 13:17 as a command that Abraham should walk through the land in order to possess it; hence, as Abram was commanded by Yahweh to walk the Promised Land so also Yahweh wanted him to spiritually walk before him. Similarly, the term also occurred in conjunction with the description of Noah by the narrator in Genesis 6:9. Thus it seems the narrator wanted to emphasize the spiritual nature of this particular episode particularly in Yahweh's quest to build a spiritual bond between Abraham and himself. Noah was "perfect" in his generation; hence, the narrator sees a connection between Noah and Abraham here. In verse 2, the verb which ordinarily means "to give" must be translated "I will make" since when a cohortative

Stylistic Aspects of the Divine Speeches

follows an imperative as is the case here, the cohortative should be translated to show "an intention or intended consequence."[273] This cohortative is followed by another cohortative וְאַרְבֶּה, both of which point to the divine desire as well as his determination to see that Abraham has many descendants (בִּמְאֹד מְאֹד). The second divine speech opens with "for my part" (אֲנִי) in verse 4 which is syntactically contrasted with "for your part" (וְאַתָּה) in verse 9, thus suggesting the obligation of Yahweh and Abraham as covenant partners. Looking back at creation, in verse 6, the verb וְהִפְרֵתִי employed in the creation narrative is also employed here with the same nuance as the use of the cohortative וְאַרְבֶּה in verse 2b, and the phrase, אוֹתְךָ בִּמְאֹד מְאֹד serving as an inclusio between verse 2 and 6. In the third divine speech (vv. 9–14), the key verb is תִשְׁמֹר which directly seeks to stipulate the responsibility of Abraham and his descendants. The rest of the divine speeches in these verses are governed by this verb, which is repeated twice in verses 9 and 10, since the subsequent verbs seek to describe in terms of circumcision how the observance or "keeping" of the covenant should be carried out.[274]

In the fourth divine speech, the dominant verb is וּבֵרַכְתִּי which occurs twice in this divine speech. After the interruption by Abraham in verses 17–18, the divine speech focuses on Isaac, particularly his birth, which syntactically is told by the relationship between the three verbs namely יָלֶדֶת, וְקָרָאתָ, and וַהֲקִמֹתִי. Together, these verbs describe the birth, name and the covenant relationship between Isaac and Yahweh. Temporally, at the middle of this divine speech, attention is switched to Ishmael. This momentary attention is captured by the verbs such as יוֹלִיד, וְהִרְבֵּיתִי, וְהִפְרֵיתִי, and וּנְתַתִּיו. Quickly, the central attention goes back to Isaac, and it is on him that the last speech of this pericope ends. Ishmael seems to be a distraction, but the major concern of the divine speech is centered on Abraham, Sarah and Isaac.

---

273. See Gesenius, *Gesenius' Hebrew Grammar*, 108d; Waltke and M. O'Conner, *An Introduction to Biblical Hebrew Syntax*, 577.

274. The verb וְהָיָה in the second half of verse 11 is just an ordinary verb which functions in the future. However, for it to fulfill such grammatical functions some prerequisites must be reached. Firstly, "the subject of וְהָיָה must agree with it in number and gender" and secondly "the semantic notion 'become' must be involved." See Merwe et al, *A Biblical Hebrew Reference Grammar*, 331.

3.4.1.3.3. Dialogical Speeches

The divine speech adopts a form of dialogue in this pericope with the often-used cliché, "and the Lord said to Abraham." However, this dialogue is primarily concerned with the issues of land, descendants and the covenant relationship between Abraham, his descendants and Yahweh. Yahweh dominates the speech so much that, to call it a dialogue seems problematic, because Abraham only spoke once in the entire pericope. The single response to Yahweh by Abraham raises a lot of issues. For example, why did Abraham internalize his fears as seen in the narrator's comment in verse 17 that Abraham spoke "in his heart?" In his speech to Yahweh in verse 18, Abraham did not mention the complication of his condition rather he merely talked to God on the option of Ishmael. The narrator, by allowing us an entrance into the "heart" of Abraham, shows us directly the struggle and pains of Abraham and his wife.

Interestingly, Abraham fell on his face in worship, but was also laughing in his heart at the divine statement that Sarah and not Hagar would be the mother of the expected heir (v. 17). The laughter is significant here not because it has an etymological relationship with the name Isaac, but because it undermines the seriousness of the present divine speeches. Abraham seems skeptical about Sarah ever conceiving and this in itself continues the tension we have already seen between the divine point of view and the perception of things by Abraham. In this understanding, this inward-searching question, accompanied with laughter and worship shows the complication of the scenario. Abraham is ready to worship God at the preceding utterances, but the promises concerning Sarah seemed fictitious for Abraham. Why should someone look for a miracle, when already there is one? Abraham already has a son in Ishmael, but the divine point of view saw things differently. In fact, Genesis 22:2 refers to Isaac as Abraham's only son. From this divine point of view, Ishmael seems to be a digression or distraction from the divine plan.[275] It was a human solution, but all the

---

[275]. In spite of this attention and centrality of the narrative on Isaac, "Ishmael remains, nevertheless, a pivotal figure, intimating a broader and more inclusive idea of the Abrahamic covenant, one entirely in keeping with the universalism of the" present narrative. See Blenkinsopp, "Abraham as Paradigm in the Priestly History," 238.

same the Lord blesses Ishmael; however, he refuses to endorse his candidacy as the covenant partner and heir to Abraham.

The dialogical speeches of Yahweh and Abraham in this present pericope show tension, which we initially witnessed in Genesis 15, even though Abraham was allotted just barely a voice. This voice of Abraham, while centered on Ishmael, shows his thoughts were confused particularly on the divine ways of accomplishing his purposes. Abraham's inward thoughts mirrored his fears as to the necessity of going the hard way when there was another alternative. Yahweh blessed Abraham's alternative, but readily declared that the continuity of the covenant would be in Isaac rather than in Ishmael, thus the dialogue, even though not fully as we want it to be, sustained and also continued the suspense and plot of the preceding pericopes.

3.4.1.4. Stylistic Aspects

We will now turn our attention to the simple stylistic features which are present within the divine speeches. These literary features are primarily seen in the divine speeches rather than the speeches of Abraham.

3.4.1.4.1. Metaphor

We will give our attention to two metaphors in the divine speeches. The first of these metaphors is found in the first divine speech of verse 1. Yahweh told Abraham to literally "walk before my faces" (הִתְהַלֵּךְ לְפָנַי).[276] This metaphor has been translated by many modern versions simply as "walk before me", thus the "faces of Yahweh" become a metaphor for "his presence."[277] In the context of the preceding episode with Hagar, Yahweh demands in this pericope that Abraham should "stay or remain" in his presence, which appears to be a metaphor for staying or remaining true to the plans of Yahweh for Abraham. In our modern Christian diction, we may say it means to "remain in the will of God." The implication is that Yahweh is sensing the restlessness and frustration of Abraham as he grows

---

276. M. I. Gruber, "The Many Faces of Hebrew נשׂא פנים 'lift up the face,'" ZAW 95 (1983): 252–60.

277. There are many theories of metaphors. For some brief summaries see Jan G. van der Watt, *The Family of the King: Dynamics of Metaphor in the Gospel According to John* (Leiden: Brill, 2000), 1–24.

old, hence the divine command for Abraham to stay with the divine plans. Interestingly when this command is placed in the context of Genesis 16, we see the full implication of the divine statement here. Hagar is said twice to have run from the "face of Sarai" her mistress in verses 6 and 8. In short, Yahweh is saying that Abraham should stay in the divine presence. He should not leave or run away from it. Surprising enough, though absent in other pericopes, Abraham is said to have fallen twice upon his "faces" in deep reverence to God (vv. 3a and 17a). This implied that Abraham understood literally the demand of Yahweh to walk or live before his face. In the same way, Abraham's speech to Yahweh in verse 18 was that Ishmael should live "before his faces", that is, Ishmael should be given the full right of an heir or a covenant partner rather than the unborn Isaac. In the preceding passage in Genesis 16:12 Ishmael is said to "live in the faces of his brothers." Thus from this perspective, it is not accidental that the narrator will make reference to the "faces of Sarai" in Genesis 16:6 and 8, the "faces of Yahweh" in Genesis 17:1, the "faces of Abraham" in Genesis 17:3 and 17, and also to tell his readers that Yahweh commanded Abraham to live or stay before "his face" in order to be "perfect."

In particular, the metaphor of the "faces of Yahweh", even though common in Old Testament narratives, presupposes a bodily or anthropomorphic metaphor for Yahweh whereby some parts of the body are employed to describe certain divine activity. Thus we see often the "hand of God," "the mouth of God," "the back of God," "the eyes of God," "the face of God" or even the "ears of God." These are metaphoric ways to describe God's activity. For the Old Testament, which abhors physical representations of Yahweh, metaphorically Yahweh was understood to have a "face, ears, hands, back, and eyes."[278] In biblical thought, the "faces of Yahweh" stand broadly for divine presence. However, in the present context, the "faces of Yahweh" connote divine revealed will, which Yahweh wanted

---

278. See Tryggve N. D. Mettinger, "Israelite Aniconism: Developments and Origins," *The Image and the Book: Iconic Cults, Aniconism, and the Rise of Book Religion in Israel and the Ancient Near East*, ed. Karel van der Toorn (Bondgenostenlaan: Uitgeverij Peeters, 1997), 173–204; Ronald S. Hendel, "Aniconism and Anthropomorphism in Ancient Israel," *The Image and the Book: Iconic Cults, Aniconism, and the Rise of Book Religion in Israel and the Ancient Near East*, ed. Karel van der Toorn (Bondgenostenlaan: Uitgeverij Peeters, 1997), 205–228.

Abram to follow. In the preceding divine speeches, Yahweh had revealed to Abraham his will; hence the demand to "walk before my faces" is a reminder to Abraham to stay in this revealed will.

The second metaphor is the metaphor in verses 4b and 5c where Yahweh called Abraham metaphorically the "father of multitude of nations." The metaphor of fatherhood is fairly common also in the Bible.[279] In Genesis for example, Jabal was said to be the "father of tent-dwellers" in Genesis 4:20, and Jubal was the "father of all who handle the harp and organ" in Genesis 4:21. The idea of father in these two texts is that of originator or the source of "something." In almost the same way, Abraham is going to be the "source" of many nations, that is, many nations are going to trace their origin to Abraham. In this perspective, Yahweh is promising Abraham a lofty status beyond the status of a patriarch which is traditionally understood to be the founder of a particular nation to the founder of different nations. Looking backward, the narrator associates Abraham with the nations of his days such as the Arabs, Edomites, Midianites, and some of the nations of the east. For example, look at how the narrator ends the Abrahamic cycle in Genesis 25:6. After mentioning the different sons of Abraham's concubines he said, "But while he was still living, he gave gifts to the sons of his concubines and sent them away from his son Isaac to the land of the east." This in itself points to the quest to connect the seeds of Abraham with the different nations of the east.[280]

Lastly, there is also another metaphor in verse 14. The metaphor lies in the verbal phrase, וְנִכְרְתָה הַנֶּפֶשׁ הַהִוא מֵעַמֶּיהָ which is literally translated, "and he shall be cut off from among his people." The metaphor of "cutting off" is often used in the biblical thought to describe the "execution" or "killing" of a person that does not follow or obey a revealed command.[281]

---

279. For example see the metaphor of God as father in the following verses Exodus 4:22; 19:4; Deuteronomy 32:6, 11; Jeremiah 3:4; 3:19; 31:9; Isaiah 63:16; 64:7; Hosea 11:1; Malachi 1:6; 2:10.

280. Similarly, there is a metaphoric nuance in the phrase, מַלְכֵי עַמִּים מִמֶּנָּה יִהְיוּ translated, "kings of peoples will come from her" in verse 16. The idea in this phrase is that "kings as many as people" will come out of the descendants of Sarah. However, it could also mean "rulers of people," that is, rulers of many people will come out of the descendants of Sarah.

281. See for example Exodus 12:15; Leviticus 7:20; 19:8; 22:3; Numbers 9:13; 15:30; 19:13, 20.

Linguistically, the image of "cutting off" might have come primarily from an agricultural environment where the farmer cuts an unwanted branch of a tree in order to promote the continuous wellbeing of the tree.[282] Here, Abraham's future descendants are depicted as a kind of a "tree" and a person who refuses to practice circumcision is expected to be removed from this covenant community.

3.4.1.4.2. Wordplay

There are three wordplays in the divine speeches of this pericope. The first of these wordplays is on the new name אַבְרָהָם or "Abraham."[283] In our discussion in Genesis 12:1–3 we showed that there is a wordplay or paronomasia in the name of אַבְרָם with the sound of the Hebrew word for blessing (ברך). However, in the case of the "new name", Abraham, the wordplay is not with blessing but with the phrase, אַב־הֲמוֹן גּוֹיִם, that is, "father of multitude of nations." This phrase is repeated twice in order to bring home the relationship between "Abraham" and the rhyming to the sound of the אַב־הֲמוֹן גּוֹיִם in verses 4b and 5c.[284] This wordplay connects the sounds as well as the meaning of the phrase אַב־הֲמוֹן גּוֹיִם to the name of Abraham. By this association, the change of the name Abram to Abraham is seen as a prophecy of the nationalities that will come out from Abraham. Thus the name, instead of looking backward to the table of nations in Genesis 10, looks forward into the future, when Abraham will become the "father of many nations."[285] The change of name by Yahweh here is significant since

---

282. See for Isaiah 9:18; 14:8; 18:5; 37:24; 44:14; Jeremiah 6:6; 10:3; 22:7.

283. The personal names in the Bible have been the object of several studies. For these different studies see Richard S. Hess, "Issues in the Study of Personal Names in the Hebrew Bible," *CR:BS* 6 (1998): 169–192.

284. Sometimes in biblical narratives names and the associated wordplay around them function like rhyme or meter, which controls the thrust of the entire narratives. For the study of biblical wordplay on names based on sound, anagram, association and other forms see Moshe Garsiel, *Biblical Names: A Literary Study of Midrashic Derivations and Puns* (Ramat Gan: Bar-Ilan University press, 1991); William Hallo, "Scurrilous Etymologies," *Pomegranates and Gold Bells: Studies in Biblical, Jewish, and Near Eastern Ritual, Law, and Literature in Honor of Jacob Milgrom*, eds. David P. Wright, David Noel Freedman and Avi Hurvitz (Winona Lake, Indiana: Eisenbrauns, 1995), 767–776.

285. Y. Zakovitch, "Explicit and Implicit Name-Derivations," *HAR* 4 (1980): 167–80; idem, "A Study of Precise and Partial Derivations in Biblical Etymology," *JSOT* 15 (1980): 31–50.

name-change in the Biblical world carries importance. Names are not mere labels or nomenclatures given to people. On the contrary, they are often seen as a "window" into the future of the name bearer. Hence, the divine wordplay that here associates the name Abraham with nations, presupposes in the mind of the narrator that different nations will come from Abraham, but most importantly, many nations will associate or identify themselves as Abraham's descendants.

The second wordplay is also in a name. This time it is in the name יִצְחָק or Isaac in verse 19. Abraham in the preceding verse laughed at the divine proposition that Sarah will give birth to a son. This son, according to God, will be the heir of Abraham. Against this proposition, Abraham laughed and questioned to himself the wisdom of the divine speeches. When he finally spoke in verse 18, he had his own proposition namely that his heir should be Ishmael rather than Isaac. Contrary to this proposition, Yahweh underscores his determination to give him an heir through Sarah rather than through Hagar. And to remind him of his jesting or laughter, God decided to call this future child by the laughter of his father. It is surprising to see how laughter is associated with Isaac within the Abrahamic narratives. In fact, the characters Abraham, Sarah and Ishmael are all at one point or the other associated with the "laughter" as the motivation for the name Isaac.[286] In this present context, Yahweh gave "laughter" as the name of his unborn son because "he had laughed at the thought" of having a child through Sarah.

The next wordplay under consideration is in the name of Ishmael in verse 20. As already seen, Abraham protested in verse 18 that Ishmael should be his heir. In response to this suggestion, Yahweh said in verse 19 that "וּלְיִשְׁמָעֵאל שְׁמַעְתִּיךָ הִנֵּה בֵּרַכְתִּי אֹתוֹ" literally, "and as for Ishmael, I have heard you, behold, I will bless him." The name Ishmael means, "the Lord has heard." Using this, Yahweh said to Abraham that he had "heard" Abraham's request to bless Ishmael, and that he was going to bless Ishmael. Thus Yahweh is using the "heard" inherently in the name "Ishmael" as wordplay in response to Abraham's request to consider Ishmael.

---

286. See Genesis 18: 12–15; 21:6, 9.

Similarly, there is wordplay on the name Sarai in verses 15–16. The name Sarai means "princess" and hence Yahweh promised that "kings of people" would come from her. The wordplay lies in the inherent association between royalty in the name "Sarai" or "Sarah" which is closely connected with the phrase לְגוֹיִם מַלְכֵי עַמִּים מִמֶּנָּה יִהְיוּ. Consequently, the idea of royalty in the name of Sarai or Sarah is re-echoed in the divine promise of royal heirs for Sarah.

From this overview, it seems that Yahweh used wordplay with the names of each of the characters of the present narrative, whether Abraham, Sarah, Ishmael or Isaac. This wordplay is significant particularly in the context of a new name or change of name for Yahweh. In the wordplay on these names, Yahweh changed the destinies of these characters. Consequently, while the characters' changed names point to their destinies, Yahweh's change of a new name points to his ability to bring about the promises behind these names. In this sense, Yahweh's name, "El-Shaddai", reveals his ability to fully realize the destinies of these characters.

3.4.1.4.3. Irony

Ironies are "embedded throughout Genesis."[287] However, for our present study, there are inbuilt ironies in the present pericope that are worth mentioning.[288] Four of these ironies can be highlighted. The first irony lies in the name of Isaac, which means "laughter." In this name, "both the power of God and the limitations of human faith are embodied."[289] There is irony because the action of laughter by Abraham becomes eternally engraved in the naming of the anticipated "seed." The divine speech points to the incongruousness of Abraham's laughter, and the name of the "seed" becomes a true representation of human attitudes of unbelief towards the divine promise. In the same way, the name also indicates the power of God to bring about his purposes against human doubt or unbelief. Thus by giving "Isaac" the name "laughter," Yahweh points to the eternal conflict between human and divine perspectives.

---

287. See Turner, *Genesis*, 15.
288. On the identification and nature of biblical ironies see Edwin M. Good, *Irony in the Old Testament* (Sheffield: The Almond Press, 1981), 14–38.
289. See Sailhamer, *The Pentateuch as Narrative*, 159.

The second irony lies in the "polite rejection" of Ishmael who, despite his circumcision and blessing, was not allowed to be the full heir of Abraham. Ishmael is mentioned as blessed in Genesis 17:20 and circumcised in Genesis 17:23–27, but he was denied the significant status of the heir to Abraham. This begins, in the patriarchal narrative, the reoccurring motif of a rejected firstborn. The irony here is that "Ishmael and his mother Hagar" did no wrong. In fact, they are the "underdogs" of the stories because the different terms for oppression particularly used in the exodus were readily applied to Hagar in Genesis 16. She was in the wilderness looking for water for herself and her child just as the Israelites did in the subsequent narratives of the exodus. The life of Hagar and her son typified, even though not perfectly, the events of the exodus. The roles are changed though, because in the future the Egyptians will oppress the Israelites, however, in the world of the patriarch, it was Sarah that oppressed Hagar. After such oppression and trauma, Hagar and her son were not considered fitting to have a place in the future of Abraham. Where Sarah was mentioned and her name even changed, there is no mention of Hagar. She was omitted from the text and it is only the fruit of her body, namely Ishmael, who appears in the text. If God had changed the name of Hagar like he changed those of Sarah and Abraham, what would he have called her? We have no clue because she was absent in the text and the divine speech did not consider her important enough to address. However, despite such silence in the text, Hagar was present in her son, though not given the accolades and blessings like Sarah.

The third irony lies in the heart of the phrase "father of multitude of nations." Here, we only see Ishmael as the heir of Abraham, but from the divine perspective Abraham is considered the "father of many nations." The image of multitudes coming out of a man who at the moment is unsure of an heir is a great irony. The opening divine speeches presented an image of Abraham basking in the euphoria of his future descendants, but at the end of the divine speeches we see him with his "only" son Ishmael who was rejected by God. It is ironic that the divine speech sees "multitudes" while Abraham's vision, as evidenced in his only speech, was primarily concerned with just a single heir. The divine speech appears to have seen "multitudes" in the same place where Abraham saw old age and barrenness.[290]

Lastly, there is an irony in the patterning of the story itself, which, though talking about the past, is actually about the future, that is, the audience of the narrator. For example, the phrase אַחֲרֶיךָ "after you" appears seven times when one considers the inclusion of the related phrase אַחֲרָיו ("after him") in verse 19. These phrases are futuristic. In fact, they describe the "long time" after Abraham is gone. It is the future from the divine perspective. The irony lies in the framing of the narrative, which, though talking about the past, has its major interests in the concerns of the future. In this understanding, the past is about the future because the past in this sense is the future. The divine speeches even though talking about Abraham, Sarah, and Isaac are clearly not about these people but about the "descendants" who are, ironically, the original readers of this text.

3.4.1.5.4. Euphemism

Tal observed that euphemisms "[b]eing a social *sine qua non* . . . are as old as language itself."[291] On the other hand, as "nice talk" or speech, they are not only found in human language but also within the divine speeches, hence the narrator of the Abrahamic narratives shows the presence of these respectable euphemisms in the divine speeches.[292] One such euphemism is found in the divine speech of verses 9–14. This euphemism is in the term "flesh" (בָּשָׂר) or rather in the phrase "flesh of your foreskins," that is, בְּשַׂר עָרְלַתְכֶם.[293] This term is a euphemism that is sexual in nature. It is used to describe the "penis" or "male" sexual organ of Abraham's seeds. Like most cultures, the "female" or "male" sexual organs are often veiled in great

---

290. On the motif of heroic barrenness in the Hebrew Bible see Rachel Havrelock, "The Myth of Birthing the Hero: Heroic Barrenness in the Hebrew Bible," *BibInt* 16 (2008): 154–178.
291. Tal, "Euphemisms in the Samaritan Targum of the Pentateuch," 110.
292. In rabbinic sources the term use for euphemism is לשׁון נקייה that is "clean tongue or language." See Ibid., 111.
293. The Targum of the Samaritan Pentateuch used the term קלפה for "foreskin" which is a word derived from Arabic. For the use of Arabic as euphemism see Tal, "Euphemisms in the Samaritan Targum of the Pentateuch," 121–129.

euphemism.²⁹⁴ In the Bible, a similar practice can be seen. In particular, several times the Bible uses euphemism for sexual organs or sexual intercourse. For example, within the Old Testament there are the euphemisms such as "to know" (Gen 4:1), "to lie with" (Lev 18:22), "to enter/go into" (2 Sam 16:21), "to approach" (Lev 18:6, 14, 19 cf. Lev 20:16) "to stand before" (Lev 18:23), "come near a woman" (Gen 20:4), "to touch" (Gen 20:6) or even "to eat" (Prov 30:20, cf. Gen 39:6) which stands for sexual intercourse. Similarly, there are also euphemisms for the sex organ such as "feet" (Isa 7:20), "thigh" (Num 5:22, cf. Gen 24:2), "hand" (Isa 57:8), "nakedness" (Exod 28:42, cf. Lev 20:17), and "flesh" (Lev 15:2, cf. Ezek 16:26; 23:10).²⁹⁵ The concern of the Old Testament to speak in euphemistic terms comes from its desire to be less offensive.²⁹⁶ Since within these ancient societies the mentioning of a "sex organ" was a taboo, it is not surprising that in describing the rite of circumcision Yahweh employed euphemism in the term, בְּשַׂר עָרְלַתְכֶם or the "flesh of your foreskins" rather than mentioning the "sexual organ." Yahweh here used an inoffensive term to describe the rite of circumcision. The importance of covenant is hereby drawn particularly by its close association with one of the most "important" and sensitive part of the human anatomy. By such an association, Yahweh has readily underscored the importance of the covenant. It is significant to also note that circumcision of the sex organ here is closely associated with the region

---

294. Shalom M. Paul has given an insightful treatment of the sexual euphemism "plowing the heifer" in Samson stories see Shalom M. Paul, "'Plowing the Heifer' in Judges 14:18: Tracing a Sexual Euphemism," *Sacred History, Sacred Literature: Essays on Ancient Israel, the Bible, and Religion in Honor of R.E. Friedman on His Sixtieth Birthday*, ed. Shawna Dolansky, 163–167 (Winona Lake, Indiana: Eisenbrauns, 2008), 163–167; idem, "Euphemistically 'Speaking' and a Covetous Eye," *HAR* 14 (1994): 193–204.

295. On the comparison of these euphemisms and more euphemistic expressions between the Bible and ancient Near Eastern documents see Paul, "The Shared Legacy of Sexual Metaphors and Euphemisms in Mesopotamian and Biblical Literatures," *Sex and Gender in the Ancient Near East*, eds. Simo Parpola and R.M. Whiting, Part II. Proceedings of the XLVII Roncontre Assyriologique Internationale, Helsinki, 489–498 (Helsinki: The Neo-Assyrian Text Corpus Project, 2002), 489–498.

296. This quest to speak in euphemism could also be seen in the Ugaritic texts particularly the use of "hand" and "staff" for penis see Cyrus H. Gordon, "Poetic Legends and Myths from Ugarit," *Berytus* 25 (1977), 61 and Tal, "Euphemisms in the Samaritan Targum of the Pentateuch," 110.

of "procreation" and consequently points to the sexual undertones particularly in the light of the promise of future descendants.[297]

3.4.1.4.5. Hyperbole

Hyperbole as we have already seen is a kind of exaggerated expression. Within the present pericope we see a hyperbolic statement in the phrase אַב־הֲמוֹן גּוֹיִם or "father of multitude of nations." This term is hyperbolic since from hindsight we now know that Abraham was actually the father of a single nation rather than plenty of nations. The Ishmaelites and the Midianites might be conceived to be nations that stemmed directly from Abraham, however, even with this, the description "multitude of nations" goes beyond these few nations, and thus should be treated as hyperbolic. Like the preceding hyperboles of the Abrahamic narratives such as the divine comparison of Abraham descendants to the "dust of the earth" and the "stars of the heavens" the image of the "multitude of nations" also strikes one with such force as the preceding ones.

Biblical hyperboles are not intended to deceive or even confuse, but to emphasize the importance of the thing or object that is hyperbolized.[298] In this case, the continuous divine hyperbole around the theme of descendants shows the importance of descendants in the context of the patriarchal narratives and the Pentateuch as a whole. Thus divine hyperbole stressed the importance that Yahweh attached to the subject of securing future descendants for Abraham. This theme in the divine speech points to the future orientation of these speeches. Even though they are located in the past, they are primarily concerned about the future. With graphic and

---

297. For use and explanations of some modern euphemisms see H. Rawson, *A Dictionary of Euphemisms and Other Doubletalk* (New York: Crown Publishers, 1995) and J. S. Neaman and C. G. Silver, *A Dictionary of Euphemisms* (London: Hamish Hamilton, 1983).

298. Abraham Mitrie Rihbany speaking of the oriental use of hyperbole and similar language, particularly in Syrian society, observed, "A case may be overstated or understated, not necessarily for the purpose of deceiving, but to impress the hearer with the significance or insignificance of it. If a sleeper who has been expected to rise at sunrise should oversleep and need to be awakened, say half an hour or an hour later than the appointed time, he is then aroused with the call, 'Arise, it is noon already . . . ' Of a strong and brave man it is said, 'He can split the earth.' The Syrians suffer from no misunderstanding in such cases. They discern each other's meaning." See Rihbany, *The Syrian Christ* (London: Houghton Mifflin Company, 1923), 109.

vivid hyperbole, Yahweh underscored the importance of this theme, and by such hyperbolic emphasis, he gave to us a clue about the major concern of these speeches.

In this perspective, the divine hyperboles are extravagant exaggerations, which appear to point the reader to the main concern of the divine speeches. As a literary instrument to show emphasis, the divine hyperboles looked beyond themselves to זֶרַע or "seed" of Abraham. The divine hyperboles are not in themselves important but their importance lies in the emphasis which they give the main concern of these divine speeches. They help in focusing the mind of the reader to stay with the major concern of the patriarchal narrative. This suggests that the issue of land, while also important, is not hyperbolized by Yahweh. On the contrary, all the hyperboles already treated are all focused on the descendants of Abraham. This explicitly suggests the importance of this theme in the divine speeches. In a sense, it is logical to give priority over to the theme of descendants since without descendants the possession of land became useless. Thus from the divine perspective, the land is placed in importance under the subject of descendant and this is glaringly seen by the amount of divine hyperbole devoted to it.

3.4.1.4.6. Repetition

McEvenue has rightly observed, "[i]t is evident at a first reading that Genesis 17 is marked by much repetition of words, phrases, ideas."[299] In particular, the fifth divine speech employs the mechanics of repetition.[300] This kind of repetition is known as an "envelope structure."[301] According to Revell, this is a literary device employing a unique form of repetition for "rhetorical purposes" whereby "[i]n a structure of this sort, the initial words (A) are repeated at the end (A'), enclosing B, material ancillary to the

---

299. McEvenue, *The Narrative Style of the Priestly Writer*, 147.

300. For example the phrase בִּמְאֹד מְאֹד is repeated in verses 2, 6, and 20. Speaking of this same repetition McKeown noted, "[r]epetition of key words in the passage and the gift of a new name for the patriarch heighten the rhetorical impact and deliver the unmistakable message that, in spite of the unexplained delay, God intends to fulfill his promises. Repetition is an important device for producing emphasis in Hebrew, and this device is applied twice in this passage. The words that are repeated are בִּמְאֹד מְאֹד and גּוֹיִם אַב־הֲמוֹן. See See McKeown, *Genesis*, 100.

301. Revell, "The Repetition of Introductions to Speech as s Feature of Biblical Hebrew," 93.

point thus forcefully presented."[302] In the text, we see first the promise of the birth of Isaac repeated in verses 19 and 21. Similarly, Yahweh's covenant with Isaac is also repeated in these two verses. The verse at the center of these repetitions is verse 20 which does not mention Isaac but centers on Ishmael. By this scheme, the divine speeches place Isaac in both the beginning and end of the divine speeches, thus suggesting that it is Isaac that is actually the "center" of the divine promises and not Ishmael. The question of Abraham placed "Ishmael" at the center, however, the divine interest is with Isaac and not Ishmael. Using the literary device of repetition, the last speech of Yahweh could be outlined thus:

    A   Focus on Isaac v. 19
        B   Ishmael v. 20
    A'   Focus on Isaac v. 21[303]

Structurally, even though Ishmael appears to be at the center of this speech as seen in this envelope structure, the attention is on the double repetition of Isaac which brackets this frame. In photographic language, Isaac has two shots while Ishmael is given one. The rhetorical purposes of this repetition become obvious Yahweh has already determined to further his purposes through Isaac against the wishes of Abraham. Ironically, there is a kind of irony or even mockery inherent in these double repetitions of Isaac and the placement of Ishmael in the center. Literally speaking, Ishmael is at the center because Abraham's question is about him, however, theologically speaking, Yahweh has Isaac at the center of the divine promises. Stylishly, Yahweh places emphasis not on Ishmael, but on Isaac. The divine

---

302. Ibid.
303. Jonathan Magonet has structured the entire Abrahamic narratives in an illuminating chiastic structure which centers on Genesis 16 with Hagar and Ishmael occupying the heart of the Abrahamic cycle. However, he treated the centrality of Hagar and Ishmael as a "false climax." See Jonathan Magonet, *Bible Lives* (London: SCM Press, 1992) cf. John Goldingay, "The Place of Ishmael," *The World of Genesis: Persons, Places, Perspectives*, eds. Philip R. Davies and David J. A. Clines. JSOTSup Series 257 (Sheffield: Sheffield Academic Press, 1998), 146–149.

speech here employs the help of repetition to underscore the significance of the Isaac in the divine plan. Furthermore, Revell noted:

> [t]he 'envelope' persuasive language of this type makes use of the basic function of repetition: to draw something to the attention of the addressee, and mark it as significant for the speech. The **B** component, if used, presents material in relation to which the item repeated is particularly significant.[304]

The divine rhetoric here is centered on "Isaac" and it is the focus on "Isaac" that closes the divine speech. Yahweh through the means of "envelope structure" of repetition placed the emphasis on Isaac the conceived heir of Abraham from the divine point of view, but he also politely acknowledged the significance of Ishmael as seen in his promises of blessing to him. The politic of the divine speech is seen by his repeated emphases on his perspectives, while still acknowledging the importance of Abraham's point of view.

3.4.1.4.7. Allusion

The use of the verb פרה in verse 6 appears to be an allusion to the divine mandate to Adam and Eve at creation. There, God said to this first couple, "be fruitful and multiply" (פְּרוּ וּרְבוּ). This verbal connection between the divine speeches to Abraham and the creation account may not be entirely accident. The narrator seems to indicate that Abraham is a kind of a "new Adam" since Abraham is promised almost the same categories as found in the divine command to Adam and Eve at creation. Similarly, the same verbal connection is seen in the divine blessing to Noah in Genesis 9:1, 7. It also appears that the narrator is forging a verbal connection between Abraham and Noah. This last connection is almost complete with the presence of תָמִים in verse 1, which also appears in the description of Noah in Genesis 6:9.[305] Thus the narrator wanted us to see Abraham not only as

---

304. Revell, "The Repetition of Introductions to Speech as a Feature of Biblical Hebrew," 95.
305. There are other verbal connections such as or "I will establish my covenant" which appeared in Genesis 6:18, 9:11 and in Genesis 17:7 and 19.

a "new Adam" but also as a "new Noah" to whom God promised great descendants. The difference between the preceding two verbal connections is that while the preceding ones are commands, פרה in particular in the divine speech to Abraham is in *hifil* perfect, thus showing that the realization of the desired seeds for Abraham will be under divine power rather than the procreative ability of Abraham.

The significance of these verbal connections and links is clear. The narrator wants his reader to know that a new epoch has now begun in Abraham. This new epoch is similar but also different from the preceding divine activities at creation and during the time of Noah. The cosmic and universal perspectives in the creation and flood narratives are within this pericope slanted to embrace the story of a particular family. This cosmic drama of God is now screened through the plot of a family story. This story describes God's quest to bless Abraham and to give him future descendants. From the obscurity of his genealogical tree in Genesis 11, Abraham moved to the limelight as the "father of multitude of nations."

There is another allusion to the divine statement in Genesis 12:1–3 that Yahweh will make great the name of Abraham. As we have seen, the clause in the divine speech namely וַאֲגַדְּלָה שְׁמֶךָ or "and I will make your name great" is a metaphorical speech which underscores the divine quest to make Abraham great and famous. Here, in the present pericope, Yahweh actually moved the motif of Abraham's name further. Thus, rather than just making the name of Abraham a mere metaphor of future greatness or fame, in the present pericope Yahweh actually changed the name of Abraham in order to show such greatness in the phrase "the father of a multitude of nations."

The reference to "kings coming out" from Abraham and Sarah in verses 6 and 16 is an allusion to the motif of making Abraham a great nation in Genesis 12:1–3. The promise of nationhood in that text already looked forward to the "kings" which are said to come out of Abraham. In the same way, the reference to "kings" in the present pericope also looks backward to the divine speeches and their promises of nationhood. Abraham already assumed a kingly role particularly in his battle with the kings of the east and his presence in the "valley of kings" in Genesis 14. This kingly attribute is also reflected in Genesis 23:6 when Abraham is described as a "mighty prince" among us by the Hittite community in the land.

Thus back and forth the present pericope looked forward and backward to the events surrounding the life of Abraham and within the context of the book of Genesis. The narrator identifies Abraham with Adam and Noah in the past, but also with "kingship" and "royalty" in the future. The allusions in these divine speeches allow the reader to move from the horizon of the past to the horizon of the future. The reader is told about the past, but also through allusion pointing him to the future particularly in the institution of kingship and royalty that becomes synonymous with the Davidic dynasty.

3.4.1.5. Significance

The divine speeches in this pericope have four underlying significances for the readers of the Abrahamic narratives. Firstly, the divine speeches underscore an ironic twist as seen in the motif of name changes. Yahweh first called himself "El-Shaddai" here in the same context where he changed the names of Abram and Sarai. Hence, the new names for Abram and Sarai also match the new name of Yahweh as "Almighty." In particular, Yahweh assumed a prophetic name that describes his "Almightiness" in the face of Abram's predicament; thus the new name "Almighty" for Yahweh is significant because Yahweh is saying "I am able to bring to pass the full meaning of your new names." Consequently, while the new names for Abram and Sarai point to Yahweh's desire for a multitude of descendants for them, the new name of Yahweh points to his awesome power and ability to bring to pass the full meaning which is represented by their new names. From this understanding, Yahweh's self-disclosure of a new name is given here because this self-disclosure is intended to help Abram and Sarai realize that Yahweh is able to accomplish the difficult thing in their lives, that is, the birth of a possible heir for Abram and Sarai. In this perspective, the reader of the Abrahamic narratives must realize the close relationship and connection between the new names for Yahweh, Abram and Sarai in the overall understanding of this pericope.

Secondly, the divine speeches also seek to redirect Abram to the revealed will of Yahweh as seen in the previous divine speeches since Abram had clearly deviated from this by Hagar's episode in the preceding chapter. To this end, Yahweh rightly commanded Abram to "walk before me, and be perfect" (v. 1). The "perfection" desired from Abram by Yahweh is not some high-sounding moral obedience, but to walk in the light of the revealed truth which primarily centered on believing Yahweh to give him an heir through Sarai and not through Hagar.

Thirdly, these divine speeches, also like the preceding speeches, eliminate possible heirs to Abram. In this particular pericope, Yahweh disqualified Ishmael as a possible heir to Abram just as he had earlier dismissed Lot and Eliezer as possible heirs for Abram. This disqualification of Ishmael as a possible heir becomes important in the looming shadow of Ishmael cast through the entirety of the Abrahamic narratives. In addition, the divine speeches also characterize Abram by showing the desperateness in the condition of Abram and the temptation to seek other means and alternatives rather than trusting Yahweh to bring to pass the divine promises for his life.

Lastly, the reader of the Abrahamic narratives must realize the importance of these literary-styled divine speeches in this present pericope, especially in their function and quest to move the plot of the Abrahamic narratives forward. In moving the story forward, it also complicates the plot by the elimination of possible heirs to Abram and the mind-blowing promises of Yahweh to make Abram the "father of a multitude of nations."

3.5.1. Genesis 18:1–33

3.5.1.1. Structure

The present pericope is no doubt strange, and the strangeness comes from the depiction of Yahweh in this text. As seen in the preceding pericope, Abraham had at least three divine theophanies (Gen 12:7, 15:1, 17:1); however, in none of these appearances was the physical form of Yahweh given. It seems more priority was given to the divine speeches than the physical form of appearance. Here, we see Abraham "lifting up" his eyes and "seeing" three men, but the narrator has already told us that the Lord "appeared" to Abraham in verse 1. The representation of Yahweh in three persons who came to house of Abraham not only to eat, but actually to "feast" is the closest image of the "physicalness" of Yahweh we can find in the pages of the Old Testament.[306] Accordingly, this theophany has been described as "the high point of divine revelation in the patriarchal narratives allowing divinity to show a human face."[307] Significantly, the privilege of hosting Yahweh physically is a privilege not given to anyone before Abraham and even after Abraham. The greatest of Israel's prophets, Moses, asked Yahweh if he could see his face, but Yahweh showed him his back and refused to give Moses the privilege of gazing on the divine (Exod 33:23). But this is the opportunity given to Abraham, that is, to see the divine person, and for the divine person to also dine in his house. In this particular event, lies the quest of the narrator to characterize Abraham. From the narrator's point of view, Abraham saw Yahweh and even had Yahweh eat at his tent. This characterization elevates Abraham above the level of other saintly individuals before or after him, and hence gives him a special place in the founding of the religion of the Jewish people. The importance of this appearance cannot be overemphasized because it seeks to promote the view that Abraham enjoyed a kind of divine intimacy that nobody in the past or since has.

Ironically, the narrator connects the same story of the divine visit to Abraham to the visit of Sodom and Gomorrah, hence contrasting the hospitality of Abraham with the inhospitable attitudes of the people of Sodom and Gomorrah and the spiritual insensitivity of his nephew.[308] In all these comparisons, Abraham stands tall as the only "covenant partner" and real "friend" of Yahweh, thus Yahweh could "eat and drink" but could not do the same in Sodom and Gomorrah. The narrator moves us scene after scene to tell the unique friendship that exists between Yahweh and Abraham, which is typified by the visit, but most importantly by the beauty of the divine monologue in verses 17–19.[309]

---

306. See D. Goodman, "Do Angels Eat?" *JJS* 37 (1986): 160–75.
307. See McKeown, *Genesis*, 103.
308. See W. C. van Hattem, "Once Again: Sodom and Gomorrah," *BAR* 44 (1981): 87–92; S. P. Jeansonne, "The Characterization of Lot in Genesis," *BTB* 18 (1988): 123–29; S. Lasine, "Guest and Host in Judges 19: Lot's Hospitality in an Inverted World," *JSOT* 29 (1984): 37–59.
309. See M. Goshen-Gottstein, "Abraham-Lover or Beloved of God," *Love and Death in the Ancient near East: Essays in Honor of Marvin H. Pope*, eds. J.H. Marks and R. M. Good (Guilford: Four Quarters, 1987), 101–104.

However, we have to pause here and ask what informed the narrator's physical depiction of Yahweh? Why did he depart from the norm of biblical narration in order to tell us about this physical visit of Yahweh? Why here and not in other places at the beginning of the pericope? Why place the episode adjacent to the destruction of Sodom and Gomorrah? While these questions are valid some of them may not be answered with any certainty. All that can be said at this point is that the narrator, having told us about the covenant in Genesis 17, now gives us a visit from Abraham's covenant partner namely Yahweh, and by so doing, he underscores the close spiritual relationship between these two covenant partners. It was in the context of this close relationship that Yahweh ate at Abraham's tent, and in return, after eating, reemphasized his promise of a son, shared with Abraham a secret, and allowed Abraham to intercede or bargain for the souls of men and women of Sodom and Gomorrah. These activities such as "visiting," "feasting," "chatting after meals," "sharing of secrets" and "debates on important issues" are categories found in an atmosphere of friendship. The social context of this pericope is no doubt the ancient near Eastern "friendship" and the archaic word "covenant" should actually be replaced by Yahweh's "eternal friendship" with Abraham. It appears the setting of this present pericope derived its framing from the social context of friendship of the oriental people. In fact, the people of Sodom and Gomorrah were doomed because they were unfriendly to these divine visitors.

Since this present chapter relates to the next chapter, often the structure of the present pericope is drawn together with chapter 19.[310] Hence, Wenham outlined these two chapters together as thus:

---

310. There is a chiastic structure around Genesis 18 particularly from verse 1 to 15. For the description of this chiastic structure and its relationship to Ugarit story of Aqhat see Yitzhak Avishur, *Studies in Biblical Narrative: Style, Structure, and the Ancient Near Eastern Literary Background* (Tel Aviv-Jaffa, Israel: Archaeological Center Publication, 1999), 57–74.

1. Abraham's visitors look toward Sodom (18:16)
  2. Divine reflections on Abraham and Sodom (18:17–21)
    3. Abraham pleads for Sodom (18:22–33)
      4. Angels arrive in Sodom (19:1–3)
        5. Assault on Lot and his visitors (19:4–11)
          6. Destruction of Sodom announced (19:12–13)
        7. Lot's sons-in-law reject his appeal (19:14)
      8. Departure from Sodom (19:15–16)
    9. Lot pleads for Zoar (19:17–22)
  10. Sodom and Gomorrah destroyed (19:23–26)
11. Abraham looks toward Sodom (19:27–28) Summary (19:29)[311]

This structure shows the stylistic arrangement of the material of this pericope. However, the structure, while showing a palistrophical kind of chiasm whereby the first part of a passage is patterned to mirror the second, removes Genesis 18:1–15 from this palistrophic structure, and the summary in Genesis 19:29 does not fit any of the materials in the first section.[312] This observation makes the structure a little bit questionable. Hence while we could observe some patterning or stylistic arrangement of the material by the narrator, it is however not a clear-cut palistrophic structure particularly when we take the entirety of the two chapters into consideration. To avoid this problem, and in light of our present interest in Genesis 18, we will outline the structure of this chapter based on the occurrences of the dialogues as thus:

---

311. Wenham, *Genesis 16–50*, 41.cf. Wenham, *Genesis 1–15*, 157.
312. Palistrophic structure is defined as "the arrangement of material in a V-shaped pattern so that material in each step moving in toward the center mirrors material on the corresponding step moving out from the center." See Hartley, *Genesis*, 4.

> Introduction vv. 1–2
>> First Dialogue vv. 3–5
>>> Second Dialogue v. 6
>>>> Narrator Description vv. 7–8
>>>>> Third Dialogue vv. 9–10
>>>>>> Narrators' Description v. 11
>>>>>>> Fourth Dialogue vv. 12–15
>>>>>>>> Narrator's Description v. 16
>>>>>>>>> Divine Monologue vv. 17–19
>>>>>>>>>> Fifth Dialogue vv. 20–21
>>>>>>>>>>> Narrator's Description v. 22
>>>>>>>>>>>> Sixth Dialogue vv. 23–32
>>>>>>>>>>>>> Conclusion v. 33

The speeches or dialogues wind from the door of Abraham's tent in verse 1, under the tree in verse 8, and move like a staircase to the dusty road of Sodom. The second, third, fourth and fifth dialogues are followed by the narrator's description. Often this description seeks to describe, explain or try to wind the last dialogue into the next one, thus the placement of them within the dialogue scenes that preceded them. Each of the dialogues shows change of subject, introduction of a new character or the departure of other characters from the discourse.

Following the structure, verses 1–2 introduce the main characters of the pericope, Yahweh ("three men") and Abraham. It also provides the setting of this narrative as the "plain of Mamre."[313] The first dialogue shows Abraham persuading these persons to come to his "tent" and to rest before going forward on their journey. This persuasion worked and these three persons came into the tent of Abraham to eat. The persuasion of these opening verses matches the persuasion of Abraham in the closing verses of 23–32. Just as Abraham persuaded Yahweh to eat at his "house" he also

---

313. See K. A. Deurloo, "Narrative Geography in the Abraham Cycle," *OtSt* 26 (1990): 48–62.

persuades him to be lenient on his judgment of Sodom. This dialogue is primarily an invitation to eat, however, it moves beyond this initial reason to a more prophetic one. The next dialogue in verse 6 introduces the discussion between Abraham and Sarah. Here, Sarah was given commands to bake food for the strangers. Her comments or perspectives are not given until we see her again in verse 12. The narrator follows this dialogue up by giving a summary of the preparation for these strangers. Through the description of the narrators in these verses (vv. 7–8), we see the original invitation in verses 4–5 to "wash" their legs, "rest" and "eat" bread, actually become a feast. After the feast (vv. 9–10), these strangers asked for Sarah, and one of them, who is definitely Yahweh himself, spoke in the first common singular in verse 10 prophetically reiterating the divine promise of a son to Abraham's family. The narrator now, in form of a flashback, breaks the story temporarily here in order to tell us about the plight of Abraham and Sarah in verse 11. The dialogue resumes in verses 12–15 with Sarah laughing and the divine rebuke of her inability to trust him. The next verse (v. 16) closes the four dialogues at the "tent" of Abraham and seeks to move the narrative forward by showing the "strangers" exit from under the tree at Abraham's tent to the road to Sodom.

The narrator moved the reader from the "tent" of Abraham directly into the mind of Yahweh. We also moved from the "thought" of Sarah in the last verse to the "thought" of Yahweh in the present verses (vv. 17–19). The "thought" of Yahweh bridged the change of scene from the "tent" of Abraham to the subsequent discussions on the road to Sodom. The monologue describes how Yahweh holds Abraham in high esteem, and hence answering the possible reason why Yahweh heeded to his plea to be fair to the Sodomites. From this monologue we see Yahweh initiating the subject of the subsequent longest discourse in verses 20–21. But before the response by Abraham, the narrator has quickly described in verse 22 the going to Sodom by the angelic messengers and hence preparing the ground for the intercession between Abraham and Yahweh. This is then followed by the intercession in verses 23–32 and the concluding remarks in verse 33.

3.5.1.2. Literary Context

The present pericope has literary and thematic relationships with the preceding pericopes and the subsequent narratives. We are told that Yahweh appeared to Abraham at the "trees of Mamre." This is a reference to Genesis 13:18 where we are told that Abraham settled down in this region of the Promised Land.[314] It was here also that we are also told that Lot pitched his tents at the gate of Sodom in Genesis 13:12. The story of the present pericope appears to continue from the events of that chapter, particularly in verse 13, which earlier had flash forwarded the events now about to be narrated, that is the destruction of Sodom. To show the continuity between the present pericope and Genesis 17:27, the story moves smoothly from this verse to Genesis 18:1. In fact, contrary to the identification of the subject of the theophany as "Abraham" by the NIV, the Masoretic text only noted the "Lord appeared to him" that is continuing the thought in Genesis 17:22. Thus the name "Abraham" was not mentioned until verse 6. After the ending of this pericope in verse 33, the narrator noted that when Yahweh finished talking to Abraham he went away.[315] This same phraseology was used of Yahweh's departing after the theophany of chapter 17 in verse 22. Thematically, we see once more in the divine monologue of Genesis 18:17–19, the theme of making Abraham a great nation and the families of the earth getting blessed through him. We have already seen this same motif in Genesis 12:1–3.

Similarly, there is an implicit reference to the covenants of the preceding chapters (15 and 17). This is seen in the close and passionate way Yahweh speaks of Abraham in the monologue and the understanding that Abraham will help his children to keep the "word of the Lord" (v. 19). It also assumes the changing of the names of Abraham and Sarah since Yahweh called them using the new names. At the end of the divine monologue of verse 19, the clause reads: "לְמַעַן הָבִיא יְהוָה עַל־אַבְרָהָם אֵת אֲשֶׁר־דִּבֶּר עָלָיו" translated, "so that the Lord may bring upon Abraham that which he had spoken about him." What "Yahweh has spoken about Abraham" consists of

---

314. See W. M. Alston, "Genesis 18:1–11," *Int* 42 (1988): 397–402.
315. See B. Uffenheimer, "Gen 18–19, A New Approach," *Mélanges A. Neher*, ed. E. A. Levy-Valensi. (Paris: Librairie d'Amérique et d'Orient, 1975), 145–53.

the concern for descendants and land in the preceding pericopes, in short, all Yahweh promised to Abraham.

Our present pericope also has relationship with the chapter following it. This is readily seen in the reappearance of the characters of the present pericope, but particularly in that the divine monologue bridges the two chapters together. There is a striking unity between the two chapters as shown by Wenham's structuring of the two chapters above. In particular, there is a literary quest by the narrator to bind the two chapters into a unified whole. This unification is not merely by repetition of words or characters within the two chapters, but the sequential nature of the plot of the two chapters which complement each other. The chapters are bound so well together that the quest to find their possible history of independent existence becomes difficult.

The subsequent destruction of Sodom also draws much not only from our present pericope but also from the flood narratives.[316] For example, the phrase "Yahweh remembered Abraham" in Genesis 19:26 reminds one of the similar phrase when "Yahweh remembered" Noah and his family in the ark.[317] This similar close association of the destruction of Sodom with the flood narrative can be seen in passing references to divine displeasure,[318] the use of the key verb שחת to describe the destruction,[319] the angels putting out their hands to bring Lot into the house correlates with Noah's putting out his hands to bring the dove into the ark,[320] angels' shutting the door compared with Yahweh shutting the door of the ark,[321] and the verb מטר was used to show that Yahweh rained judgment in both the Sodom episode and the flood.[322] Thus, through these observable parallels, the narrator aligned the destruction of Sodom to the motif of "universal destruction" that he had already narrated. In this comparison, the narrator shows the

---

316. See Wenham, *Genesis 16–50*, 42.
317. Gen 8:1.
318. Gen 6:5–8 cf. Gen 18:17–21.
319. Gen 6:13, 17, 9:11, 15 cf. Gen 18:28, 31, 32; 19:13, 14, 29.
320. Gen 19:10 cf. 7:16.
321. Gen 19:10 cf. 8:9.
322. Gen 7:4 cf. 19:24.

enormity of the crime of the Sodomites, and through this means, also characterized Abraham as righteous.

Consequently, our present pericope stands within this motif of contrast whereby Abraham's hospitability and righteousness become indirectly compared with the activities going on in Sodom. Similarly, while Yahweh came to announce to Abraham and his wife the coming of their "son" (vv. 10–15), on the other hand, Lot and his family were told of the destruction of Sodom.[323] The tent-life of Abraham is contrasted with the house of Lot in Sodom.[324] In the same way, the laughter of Sarah in the context of the divine promise (v. 12) is also contrasted with laughter of the "son-in-laws" of Lot about Yahweh's determination to destroy Sodom.[325]

From this correlation to the subsequent and preceding elements of his stories, the present pericope is knitted neatly into the motif and the literary framing of the Abrahamic cycle. The narrator binds his materials together by drawing similarities and contrasts between his present story and the past stories, but most importantly with stories he was yet to tell.[326]

3.5.1.3. Grammatical Analysis

The grammatical analysis will center mainly on the use of quotative frames, the construction of the verbal syntax, the nature of the dialogical speeches and the only divine monologue.

3.5.1.3.1. Quotative Frames

Within this pericope, quotative frames are employed in order to introduce the different dialogues found in the passage. According to our structure, the first dialogue consists of verses 3 to 5. In this dialogue we see two

---

323. Gen 19:12–13.
324. Gen 18:1 cf. 19: 3, 11.
325. Gen 19:14.
326. Nachman Levine has also drawn attention to the synchronic transaction between the present text and the neighboring episode at Sodom. He has rightly observed the movement of dynamic synchrony whereby the same angels that pronounced the birth of a child for Sarah also caused the destruction of Sodom. In the same way, he also shows how the barren Sarah becomes fertile and the fertile Sodom becomes barren since Sodom at end of the story was turned into ash and salt. Thus there is a kind of symmetry, opposition and closure between the two stories. See Nachman Levine, "Sarah/Sodom: Birth, Destruction and Synchronic Transaction," *JSOT* 31, no. 2 (2006): 131–146.

participants, namely Abraham and Yahweh. The discourse marker וַיֹּאמַר in verse 3 introduces the long and persuasive invitation of Abraham. It is interesting to note that the first dialogue shows the persuasiveness of Abraham. He persuaded Yahweh and the other two angelic beings to eat at his tent. This persuasiveness is also seen in his arguments in the verses, which seek to persuade Yahweh to be lenient with the inhabitants of Sodom. Thus this persuasion of Abraham bracketed this pericope and it is found at the beginning and end of the present unit. To the long persuasive speech of Abraham, the divine entourage only replied כֵּן תַּעֲשֶׂה כַּאֲשֶׁר דִּבַּרְתָּ which is translated "so do, as you have said." The two quotative frames introduced the participants and gave us perception into their parts in the building of the story. For example, we are going to see more of Abraham's persuasiveness again, and similarly, we are going to see more of Yahweh's agreement not only to eat at Abraham's tent, but also his agreement to be lenient with the people of Sodom.

The second dialogue is also introduced by the discourse marker וַיֹּאמַר in verse 6. While the preceding dialogue took place outside the tent, the second dialogue took place between Sarah and Abraham in the tent. Similarly, while the preceding discourse took place between Abraham and some unknown strangers, the second dialogue was between Abraham and his wife. This dialogue is centered on preparation for this unexpected guest. Naturally, Abraham turned to his wife in order to see that these men are taken good care of. The speech of Abraham here is mainly commandfirst to Sarah and likely the servant who was given the responsibility to prepare the young cow. Sarah's voice is not heard here, she is silent, and it is only in verses 12–15 that we will hear not only her speech, but also her inward thoughts.

The third dialogue is primarily focused on the divine promise (vv. 9–10). This scene has Yahweh, the two angelic beings and Abraham, with Sarah eavesdropping behind the door. In verse 10, we see the true identity of these strangers particularly in the clear use of first common personal pronoun to speak rather than the third masculine plural that we see in the preceding verse. In verse 9, the speech of these strangers is introduced by the discourse marker וַיֹּאמְרוּ while in verse 10, it is the discourse marker וַיֹּאמַר.

The fourth discourse is concerned with Yahweh's response to the laughter of Sarah (vv. 12–15). Even though speaking to Sarah, initially the speech was directed at Abraham (v. 13a). The discourse marker וַיֹּאמֶר in verse 13 introduces two rhetorical questions by Yahweh which need no answer. However, being afraid, Sarah responded to the first question, and Yahweh also replied by affirming that Sarah did laugh. This dialogue, through the emphasis that Sarah was behind the door and the narrator's allowing us into the thoughts of Sarah, establishes one single thesis—that Yahweh is omniscient and that he knows the thoughts in the heart and thus his prediction that Sarah will give birth in the next year should be taken seriously.[327] Ironically, the omniscience of Yahweh is juxtaposed with his seeming uncertainty about whether there are enough righteous people in Sodom.[328]

Significantly, there is the divine monologue following the fourth discourse (vv. 17–19). This divine monologue is introduced by the discourse marker אָמָר. The divine monologue gave an inward perception of Abraham by Yahweh. In this rare inward perception of Yahweh, we see Yahweh talking about the greatness of Abraham, his descendants and the certainty that they will obey Yahweh in order to "do righteousness and justice", which are the same virtues that are absent in Sodom. We see the only divine

---

327. This omniscient portrayal of Yahweh should be contrasted with the popular reading by process theology that Yahweh did not actually know what was taking place in Sodom as underscored by his statement in verses 20–22. Yahweh's omniscient character here should help in the interpretation of these subsequent verses since it presupposes Yahweh knows the thoughts of Sarah even when he is physically located under the tree. This suggests that Yahweh's decision to go to Sodom is not primarily a verification exercise, that is to know whether the wrongs mentioned are actually committed by the inhabitants of Sodom, but the trip to Sodom is to show the fairness of Yahweh to these sinners because all this while we are told already they are wicked people (Gen 13:13). Yahweh came in order to give them the opportunity to prove the allegation against them to be wrong, but instead these same people went ahead to even mistreat the "judge of the earth." With the legal terminologies such as the "judge of the earth," "justice," "righteous," "wicked," "the way of the Lord," and "doing righteousness and justice," within this pericope, it is likely it is more an issue of divine justice and fairness rather than on the doctrine of "omniscienceness" as presupposed by process theology. See H. F. Peacock, "'Translating 'Mercy,' 'Steadfast Love' in the Book of Genesis," *BT* 31 (1980): 201–7.

328. Against the omniscient character of Yahweh, Michael Carasik has drawn attention to the many instances in the biblical narratives whereby there is description of Yahweh as if he is limited in his attribute of omniscience. Hence, Yahweh needs to "test" or "try" the heart in order to know the thoughts of human characters. See Michael Carasik, "The Limits of Omniscience," *JBL* 119, no. 2 (2000): 221–232.

monologue in the Abrahamic cycle and at the heart of this divine monologue are the key issues of Abraham's greatness, prosperity, future descendants and their fidelity to the "way of the Lord." We see an inward vision of Yahweh, that is, the thoughts of Yahweh about Abraham, which is also contrasted with the fate of the Sodomites. The literary function of this monologue is obviously as a tool of characterization because in these inward divine speeches we see the cherished place that Abraham and his descendants occupied in Yahweh's heart.[329]

The fifth dialogue sets the agenda for the discussion in the sixth dialogue, that is, the wickedness of Sodom (vv. 20–21). The speech of Yahweh is introduced here by וַיֹּאמֶר. The fifth dialogue has Yahweh, Abraham and the two angels; however, the narrator intrudes in verse 22 to exit the two angels for their mission in Sodom, and thus leaves Abraham and Yahweh to continue the dialogue. In this understanding, the sixth dialogue is actually the continuation of the fifth, but now focused on Abraham and Yahweh.

The last dialogue now beams the light on Abraham and Yahweh (vv. 23–32). This last dialogue is introduced by the discourse marker וַיֹּאמַר. It is framed in a kind of question and response form. Even though it is primarily polite, it questions the divine justice in condemning the righteous and the wicked to a similar fate.[330] This same critique comes up again within the wisdom literature and thus it might point to the quest to associate Abraham with the ancient wisdom tradition. Persuasively, Abraham questioned the divine verdict to destroy all the inhabitants of Sodom and through his intercession he was able to secure the safety of ten righteous people from Sodom, even though at the end of the story no righteous persons were found in Sodom because Lot's wife perished outside of Sodom, Lot's daughters were involved in incest, and Lot himself was portrayed as

---

329. See H. Schweizer, "Das seltsame Gespräch von Abraham und Jahwe (Gen 18:22–33)," *TQS* 164 (1984): 121–39.
330. See S. E. Balentine, "Prayers for Justice in the OT: Theodicy and Theology," *CBQ* 51 (1989): 597–616. See E. Ben Zvi, "The Dialogue between Abraham and YHWH in Gen 18:23–32: A Historical–Critical Analysis," *JSOT* 53 (1992) 27–46; J. Blenkinsopp, "Abraham and the Righteous of Sodom," *JJS* 33 (1982): 119–32; idem, "The Judge of All the Earth: Theodicy in the Midrash on Gen 18:22–33," *JJ* 41 (1990): 1–12; C. S. Rodd, "Shall Not the Judge of All the Earth Do What Is Just (Gen 18:25)," *ExpT* 83 (1971/72): 137–39; T. J. Mafico, "The Crucial Question concerning the Justice of God," *JTSA* 42 (1983): 11–16.

the father of the immoral nations of the Moabites and Ammonites.[331] In this way, the narrator seems to suggest that indirectly there were no righteous people in Sodom because the family of Lot, even though temporarily saved by the intercession of Abraham, later destroyed themselves in the cave at Zoar (Gen 19:29–38).

3.5.1.3.2. Syntactical Considerations

Even though our discussion of the verbal syntax is primarily defined around the divine speeches, since the present dialogues are interrelated with the speeches of Abraham and even Sarah, we will make reference to these relationships in appropriate places. Beginning with the first discourse, Abraham grammatically requested that these guests should not "pass over" (תַעֲבֹר) him in verse 3. Then he followed this first request with three verbs focusing on the comforts of these strangers. He asked them to "take water," "wash their legs" and "rest" under the tree. Thus these three verbs (יֻקַּח, וְרַחֲצוּ, וְהִשָּׁעֲנוּ) describe the things that Abraham wanted from the strangers. Looking at these verbs closely shows that the strangers are the ones to benefit and not Abraham; hence the strangers have nothing to lose. Similarly, Abraham followed this request by telling the strangers what he will do to them. Interestingly, he began also with the verb לקח which had initially started the three verbs of verse 4, and then also refocused the action of the verbs on the strangers. Thus he said, "I will take a piece of bread, and they will refresh your hearts, and [then] after you pass over." Significantly, at the end of Abraham's speech in verse 5, he repeated "pass over" twice which might be a possible hint to the strangers that he has no intention to further delay them after the actions of these verbs. The acceptance of this selfless request from Abraham by these strangers ultimately confirms in the words of Abraham, he has "found favor" in their eyes (v. 3).

The second dialogue between Abraham and Sarah has three imperative verbs (מַהֲרִי, לוּשִׁי, וַעֲשִׂי) with the preceding verb מַהֲרִי as the governing verb. The translation of these verbs goes like this: "hurry . . . knead and

---

331. See Z. Weisman, "Ethnology, Etiology, Genealogy, and Historiography in the Tale of Lot and His Daughters (Gen 19:30–38)," "*Sha'arei Talmon*": *Studies in the Bible, Qumran and the Ancient Near East presented to S. Talmon*, ed. M. Fishbane and E. Tov (Winona Lake: Eisenbrauns, 1992), 43–52.

prepare bread." The earnestness and haste to prepare a meal or feast for these strangers is shown by the occurrence of the verb מהר thrice in the space of two verses. This word also occurred in the command of the angels to Lot and his family to make haste in order to escape the destruction at Sodom. The usage here appears to show the total amount of devotion and haste the family of Abraham exercised towards these strangers in contrast to those of Lot who in the midst of danger were reluctant to leave Sodom until commanded to make haste to escape by these angels.[332]

The third dialogue has the domineering verb אָשׁוּב in the divine speech of verse 10. This verb is preceded by its cognate in absolute form שׁוֹב which seeks to intensify and emphasize the action of the main verb אָשׁוּב. In this particular context, the verb denotes certainty of divine action in relationship to Sarah having a child though she has passed the age of child bearing. The divine emphasis is that he has determined to visit Sarah and to give her a child. As our discussion on the metaphor of Yahweh's return will seek to show, Yahweh's return to Abraham's house is another way of saying that Yahweh will provide Abraham with an heir through Sarah. This verb is further repeated in verse 14. Thus the force of these two verbs join together and its further repetition gives the idea of "certainty" that Yahweh will surely give the family of Abraham a son.

In the divine monologue that follows, the verb מְכַסֶּה becomes central to the syntax as well as the semantic of this divine speech especially in the context of Sarah hiding her thoughts from Yahweh. Out of fear Sarah wanted to hide her thoughts from Yahweh, but in contrast, out of deep respect for the future greatness of Abraham, Yahweh is seeking to share with Abraham his inward thoughts. Grammatically, the object of the verb כסה here is the clause "what I am about to do" or rather "what I am doing" (אֲשֶׁר אֲנִי עֹשֶׂה). This is connected to the *vav* and non-verbal clause of verse 18 which seeks to emphasize the future greatness of Abraham. Following from this *vav* and non-verbal כִּי clause, the clause in verse 19 is immediately followed by the

---

332. For the treatment of danger, particularly in relationship to the night, see W. W. Fields, "The Motif 'Night as Danger' associated with Three Biblical Destruction Narratives," "*Sha'arei Talmon*": *Studies in the Bible, Qumran and the Ancient Near East presented to S. Talmon*, ed. M. Fishbane and E. Tov (Winona Lake: Eisenbrauns, 1992), 17–32; M. Stol, "Blindness and Night-Blindness in Akkadian," *JNES* 45 (1986): 295–99.

verb יָדַעְתִּיו which reiterates divine certainty that the children of Abraham will keep the "way of the Lord."

The fourth dialogue has the two key verbs namely אֵרְדָה and אֶרְאֶה. The second verb has its object in the entire verbal clauses which end the verse (v. 21). Yahweh is going down to see or experience the wickedness of Sodom by himself. He wants to give the Sodomites a fair hearing, thus seeing here becomes a metaphor for experience.

The "bargain" for the righteous in the present pericope occupies the attention of the fifth dialogue. At the opening of Abraham's speech is the verb תִּסְפֶּה which is also repeated in verse 24. Using this verb, Abraham observed the unfairness in killing the righteous with the wicked. In the divine speeches that follow there is also the reoccurring verb מצא which appears in the context of these divine speeches six times. Abraham is sure that there are going to be righteous people in Sodom and it is from this motif of "finding" that this verb is continuously employed.

3.5.1.4.3. Dialogical Speeches

The divine speeches in this pericope go beyond the visionary nature of the preceding divine speech in Genesis 17 to the concrete contexts of life. It took place in the "heat" of the day in front of Abraham's tent, under the tree, and on the dusty road to Sodom. It did not take celestial or otherworldly form, but has its context in the daily routines of everyday life.[333] Similarly, the divine speeches do not take merely the form of announcement, but within this pericope each of the divine announcements, whether of the birth of Isaac or the impending destruction of Sodom, were readily engaged or even challenged by the human characters of the story.

These divine dialogues are placed within the matrix of human interactions. They are life-like and graphically presented. Yahweh moved from being God to a human-like character whose divine identity was temporally shelved away. In this particular depiction, the divine speeches attained a humanness that is not present in other divine speeches within the Abrahamic cycle. Here, Yahweh visits, eats, chats, argues with the wife of his host, and

---

333. For some helpful description of the everyday life in the biblical world see Richard E. Averbeck, Mark W. Chavalas and David B. Weisberg, eds. *Life and Culture in the Ancient Near East* (Bethesda, Maryland: CDL press, 2003).

like a human guest, was escorted afterward. At this point in the Abrahamic narratives, the divine speeches are given a relaxed and friendly atmosphere. This relaxed atmosphere, however, did not rule out the seriousness of the divine announcement of the birth of Isaac and the impending destruction of Sodom.[334] Though these events are serious and fundamental, Yahweh's speeches were conveyed in an atmosphere of feasting.

Why the portrayal of the character as well as the speeches of Yahweh in this mood? What is the narrator seeking to accomplish? Why this particular point in the Abrahamic narrative? The answers to these questions lie in the literary context of our present pericope. Genesis 17 has already shown the covenant relationship between Yahweh and Abraham, and as a covenant fellow, who according to the divine monologue will become great in the future and with his descendants walking in "the way of Yahweh," it becomes necessary that Yahweh will also walk toward the tent of this great character. Thus the inevitable aim of this dialogical exchange between Yahweh and Abraham's family is to characterize Abraham. This characterization becomes obvious especially since it is the only place where Yahweh eats and appears in such a disguised physical form.[335] For the narrator writing in a context where such divine visits may be rare or even non-existent, associating Abraham with this highly "physical Yahweh" increases the religious prestige of Abraham. In fact, Yahweh eating food at the tent of Abraham already connotes the respect or trust that Yahweh had for the patriarch. If this is so, it implies that Yahweh approves of Abraham and his descendants, and thus will bring to pass all that he said about them. In this present pericope, the narrator lowered the veil on Yahweh and moved us to

---

334. On the discussion of biblical birth narratives see Simon B. Parker, "The Birth Announcements," *Ascribe to the Lord: Biblical and Other Studies in Memory of Peter C. Craige*, ed. Lyle Eslinger and Glen Tyler. JSOT 67 (Sheffield: Sheffield Academic Press, 1988), 133–149.

335. Concerning the characterization of Yahweh in the Pentateuch, Clines observed, "that the God in the Pentateuch is a character in a novel. God in the Pentateuch is not a 'person'; he is a character in a book. And there are no people in books, no real people, only fictions; for books are made, not procreated. Even when the characters have the same name as real people and they remind us vividly of the real people whose names they bear, they are still made of a paper. Even if I should write my autobiography, the readers of my book will not be encountering me, but only the fictive character I have chosen to create in my writing." See Clines, *Interested Parties*, 190.

see not only the physical appearance of him, but also the hidden thoughts of Yahweh. In fact, Abraham shared his food with Yahweh, and Yahweh shared his secret thoughts with Abraham.

Consequently, these dialogues are primarily designed to characterize Abraham and to show that Abraham has gone to a great level of spiritual or even mystical relationship with Yahweh, which demands Yahweh physically revealing himself to him and to also share with him his secret thoughts. To this end, the narrator moved Abraham from the obscurity of his genealogical tree to the present point of intimate conversation with Yahweh under his own family tree. From this close relationship, Yahweh will become synonymous with the "God of Abraham" and it is from this perspective that later traditions preserved the memory of the character Abraham.

3.5.1.3.4. Divine Monologue

The divine monologue takes the reader into the mind of Yahweh in order to see the perception of Yahweh concerning a matter or a person. It is a rare opportunity to gain insight or see into the mind of Yahweh for whom the narrator tells the story.[336] The importance of these occurrences of divine monologue cannot be overemphasized because it is a departure from the reticent character of the biblical narrator who normally withholds information to now a most generous telling of divine perceptions on given events or persons. As a mode of describing perception, divine monologue helps the narrator to characterize the persons or events described. The description of such perception is reliable because the narrator himself is in mutual agreement with the perception or point of view given within these divine monologues.[337] Thus, in divine monologue we see at work the perception, point of view or ideology that controls the entire attitude of the divine towards the events or persons described.

---

336. For the numerical significance of biblical monologues see Nobel Hans, "gedachten tellen. Numerieke structuuranalyse en de elf gedachten Gods in de Genesis - 2Koningen,"[PhD Dissertation University of Groningen, 1993].

337. Often in prophetic genre the divine monologue and the voice of the prophet are difficult to trace. See Mark E. Biddle, *Polyphony and Symphony in Prophetic Literature: Reading Jeremiah 7–12*. SOTI, vol. 2 (Macon, Georgia: Mercer University Press, 1996), 28.

In our present pericope, the divine monologue is actually a rephrasing and restatement of the prior divine speeches. It is a summary of the different speeches that Yahweh has already made about Abraham and his descendants.[338] The divine speech as reflected in the monologue is framed with great optimism about the future obedience of Abraham's descendants to the "way of Yahweh." It also shows confidence that Abraham will teach his "children" about "justice" and righteousness. Such obedience is a distinguishing mark of the divine speeches in the Abrahamic narrativesthe narrator presents divine speeches that are laden with great promises of prosperity, blessing, growth and progress to Abraham and most importantly to the future descendants of Abraham. Since this narrator is a descendant of Abraham it is possible that his optimism about the future of the nation of Israel impacted his selection, arrangement and presentation of these divine speeches. The narrator saw the future as brighter and glorious for the descendants of Abraham since even the divine monologue captured such optimism. The inner thoughts of Yahweh are framed around the greatness of Abraham and the prosperity of his descendants. These descendants are described as being taught by Abraham himself to keep the "way of the Lord." In a way, this divine monologue likely expresses the hope and expectation of the narrator's generation for a deeper relationship between Yahweh and the descendants of Abraham.

3.5.1.4. *Stylistic Aspects*

We will now turn our attention to the stylistic features of the divine speeches in this pericope. Even though some of these stylistic features appear ordinary and simple, they have profound meaning when placed together with the stylistic features of the previous pericopes. Together, these speeches make a great impression on the reader who is often captivated not only by the theology of these speeches but their simple literary features. Yahweh's speeches were deemed important, hence the literary features are employed in order to underscore the importance of the speeches.[339]

---

338. For example, the motif that Abraham will be a great nation is a restatement of the divine speeches in Gen 12:1–3; 13:14–17; 15:1–21; 17:1–22.

339. As already seen in our previous treatment of the divine speeches, no doubt ancient Israel believed that Yahweh had revealed himself to the patriarch Abraham who is credited

3.5.1.4.1. Metaphor

As the few cases of metaphor and metaphoric utterance in the preceding pericopes have readily shown, it appears that metaphoric utterances are common in the divine speeches of Abrahamic narratives. Metaphors are significant in these speeches because they seek to communicate profound truths which are framed in simple imagery or description. Often metaphoric utterance moves the level of meaning from the domain of the everyday physical category to another level of meaning which clearly transcends the first level of meaning. This new level of meaning is reached by the rearrangement, supplanting, transforming or transcending of the original physical meaning of the categories involved. The power of metaphor lies in its ability to connect two different categories together in mutual relationship.

Some metaphors have lost their metaphoric sense because of overuse or over-familiarity. For example, Yahweh in Jeremiah 6:19 talks about the "fruit of their thoughts" this is a tree imagery which conceives of human thought as a "fruit" on a tree. For the ancient Israelite society to which

---

with the founding of the Old Testament faith. This revelation was not only presented in bland prose, but the speeches of Yahweh were replete with metaphors, simile, euphemism, repetition, wordplay, allusion and other literary devices in order to stress their theological importance. Aesthetics became a vehicle of theology since these literary devices were not conceived as ends in themselves, but as a means to an end, that is, the understanding of the theological foundation or origin of the Abrahamic faith. The narrator artistically crafted his stories and within these stories he preserved a place of great importance to the divine speeches and within these divine speeches are stylistic features that indicate the profound importance the narrator wanted placed on these speeches. In particular, no character in the Abrahamic narratives has the luxury of such decorated speeches, not even the main human character, Abraham, but only Yahweh's speeches. By such consistent presentation of divine speeches with stylistic features that the narrator denied other characters, the narrator already revealed his biased identification with the point of view of Yahweh. One may argue that the concentration of these simply stylistic features in the divine speeches is because the characters in Abrahamic narratives have too little space to speak since ordinary characters in Samuel and Kings have stylistic features in their speeches. Admittedly, this is true, but the refusal to give space to other characters and the concentration of stylistic features in the divine speeches already is significant since it shows that the narrator is primarily concerned with the working out of the issues in the divine speeches. Every other interest in the story becomes secondary or subservient to the issues within the divine speeches. In fact, often in Abrahamic narratives, it is the issues in the divine speeches that set the plot or agenda of the subsequent stories. The story of Abraham would have taken a different turn had Yahweh not spoken in Genesis 12:1–3. It is this speech and the subsequent divine speeches that move the stories forward to a particular end. The present task is to present the literary features in this pericope.

Stylistic Aspects of the Divine Speeches

the original metaphor was addressed, such a metaphor is powerful because of their agricultural background. However, in a technological society like ours, the possibility of misunderstanding or even neglecting this particular metaphor, and others like it, is real. In fact, "fruit" is often used nowadays in normal everyday life outside the reference to a physical fruit, yet without the metaphoric sense. In this regard, the metaphoric sense of its usage is lost.

In the same way, the metaphoric language of the divine speeches within the present pericope appears to have no metaphors because of our over-familiarity with the passage. However, three metaphors are found within this present pericope. The first metaphor or metaphoric language within the divine speech is found in verse 10. The verse reads: אֵלֶיךָ כָּעֵת חַיָּה וְהִנֵּה־בֵן לְשָׂרָה אִשְׁתֶּךָ שׁוֹב אָשׁוּב. This divine statement lacks the usual verbs for pregnancy, conception or giving of birth such as הרה and ילד.[340] On the contrary, the only verb in this sentence שׁוב goes beyond its normal meaning of "return" in order to function metaphorically for conception and giving of birth. As an announcement of birth, one would have expected the occurrence of הרה and ילד here, as usually is the case of the divine announcement of birth; however, the divine speech here has no such verbs, but instead it has the verb שׁוב.[341] At least one of these two verbs, or combination of the two, appears in the divine announcement of childbirth. Thus for example, the two verbs הרה and ילד appeared in the divine announcement of the birth of Ishmael in Genesis 16:11 and the birth of Samson in Judges 13:5. In the present pericope with its vivid picture of divine visitation one would expect the mentioning of these verbs, but instead the divine speech employs metaphoric language that merely says, "I will certainly return to you" and Sarah will have a child. The divine "return" is not to be understood as a literal or physical returning of Yahweh back into the house of Abraham, but here means Abraham and Sarah will

---

340. שׁוב is also repeated in exactly the same phrase in verse 14 as in verse 10. There the text reads: אָשׁוּב אֵלֶיךָ כָּעֵת חַיָּה וּלְשָׂרָה בֵן. In this particular instance in as the preceding one, שׁוב is used in place of the normal verbs of conception, pregnancy and giving of birth. Yahweh's "return" to Abraham's house is understood as a metaphor for childbirth.

341. On birth announcements as type-scene see Alter, "How Convention Helps Us Read: The Case of the Bible's Annunciation Type-Scene," *Prooftexts* 3 (1983): 115–30.

experience divine visitation by the act of childbirth. Unfortunately, in their treatment of this verb, J. A. Thompson and Elmer A. Martens ignore the metaphorical nature of שׁוב and categorize this present text under physical motion even though the context suggests otherwise. Though they identify the possible "non-theological" usage of שׁוב, they do not explore the metaphoric ramifications of this verb.[342] This neglect of the metaphoric dimension of שׁוב is problematic since the general use of שׁוב in the Bible appears to move from this physical nuance of turning or physical motion to the metaphorical plane of repentance or returning to Yahweh.[343] In this particular occurrence, the birth of the promised child at the said time by Yahweh would be a true indication that Yahweh had "returned" or visited again the family of Abraham.[344] In this context, the verb שׁוב stands out as a metaphor for divine visitation particularly the birth of Isaac by Sarah. Like "fruits" that are a metaphor taken from the "tree", the use of שׁוב as a metaphor seems to come from the imagery of a journey whereby somebody who goes on a journey is expected to return. This travelling imagery coincides with the depiction of Yahweh as travelling to Sodom. Even though it is not expressly stated, it appears literally that Yahweh is on a journey to Sodom; thus while his going on a journey to Sodom is to bring about the destruction of this city, his "return" will bring about life to the family of Abraham. In this way, the imagery of a journey contrasts the divine attitude towards the family of Abraham and the inhabitants of Sodom, thus putting these two places in direct opposition.

Also employed metaphorically is the phrase, כָּעֵת חַיָּה which is often translated "as the time of life" or even the smooth translation "next year." Precisely what does this phrase כָּעֵת חַיָּה mean? Even though כָּעֵת is a common word in biblical narratives, the phrase כָּעֵת חַיָּה only occurs in two

---

342. J. A. Thompson and Elmer A. Martens, "שׁוב," *Dictionary of Old Testament Theology and Exegesis*, vol. 4, ed. Willem A. Van Gemeren (Grand Rapids, Michigan: Zondervan, 1997), 55–59.

343. For example, שׁוב is employed in the context of marital relationship (Jer 3:1), description of the emotion of anger (Gen 27:44; 2 Kgs 23:26), reverting ownership of a property (1 Kgs 12:26), changing loyalty (Jer 4:1), and the return of Yahweh to bless his people (Zech 1:3; Jer 42:10).

344. In the same way, *BDB* also ignores the metaphoric nature of שׁוב in the present context and classifies שׁוב as descriptive of physical motion in this text. See *BDB*, 996–1000.

places in the entire Bible, repeated twice in the divine speech here and once in Elisha's speech to the barren Shunamite woman and once in the comment by the narrator on the fulfillment of Elisha's words to this woman.[345] In particular, since the first occurrence of this phrase occurred twice in the divine speech, it should be expected that it has certain significance. According to *BDB*, the phrase is literally "*at the time* (when it is) *reviving*,"[346] that is, a metaphor for "spring", because during spring plants bring forth leaves and flowers. In this particular instance, there appears to be an extended metaphor inherent in the divine use of this phraseology because Sarah, like the season, is now barren, but at spring it is expected that plants will bring forth leaves or flowers, thus in almost the same way, Sarah is expected to also give birth. In this particular correlation, there is an apparent relation between the barren state of Sarah and nature itself since Sarah is associated with the blossoming of the spring season. Thus the phrase כָּעֵת חַיָּה is employed as a metaphor in close relationship to the barren state of Sarah.

The next metaphor is the phrase דֶּרֶךְ יְהוָה which occurs in the divine speech of verse 19. This verse partly reads: וְשָׁמְרוּ דֶּרֶךְ יְהוָה. The nominal phrase דֶּרֶךְ יְהוָה is the metaphor in view here. The phrase is a common metaphor for divine commandments. It occurs several times in Deuteronomy and other passages of the Old Testament.[347] Even though the "way of the Lord" is not a physical path, but a spiritual one, דֶּרֶךְ itself is a normal word for "way"[348] which is now affixed or joined together to "יְהוָה" in construct relationship. Ironically, Yahweh is on his "way" to Sodom, and here Yahweh admonishes Abraham to teach his children "his way." In this particular context, the phrase דֶּרֶךְ יְהוָה should not merely be translated to mean "commandments" but the divine revelation given by Yahweh to Abraham. Yahweh desired that Abraham should teach his children the content of the divine revelation. Reminiscent of the Deuteronomistic re-

---

345. See 2 Kings 4:16–17.
346. See *BDB*, 312.
347. See Deuteronomy 8:6; 10:12; 11:22, 28; 19:9; 26:17; 28:9; 30:16. See also Joshua 22:5; Judges 2:22; 2 Samuel 22:22; 1 Kings 2:3; 3:14; 8:58; 11:33, 38; 2 Kings 21:22; 2 Chronicles 6:31; Job 21:14; 23:11; 34:27; Psalms 25:4, 9; 27:11; 37:34; 51:15; 67:3; 81:14; 86:11; 95:10; 119:3; Isaiah 42:24; 58:2; 63:17; 64:4; Micah 4:2; Zechariah 3:7 and Malachi 2:9.
348. For example see Genesis 3:24; 35:3; 38:16, 21.

dactor, Yahweh employed this metaphor to describe his relationship with Abraham. Yahweh's commandments to Abraham, just like the path to the "tree of Life" in Genesis 3:24, must be kept by Abraham's descendants.

The last metaphor under consideration is found in verses 20–21. The metaphor occurs in the phrase זַעֲקַת סְדֹם וַעֲמֹרָה and its synonym הַכְּצַעֲקָתָהּ. These two synonyms are translated as "the cry of/or against Sodom and Gomorrah" and "like the cry against it." The "cry" of Sodom in this particular context is not merely a physical cry since in Genesis 19 when the two angels reached Sodom there were no people on the streets of Sodom crying. The understanding of these two phrases is that Yahweh employed the metaphor of "crying" to describe the many complaints lodged against Sodom by the victims of its atrocities.[349] Hence, this metaphor carries with it an emotional tone that ultimately justifies the destruction of Sodom. There is also an indirect relationship between the "cry" of Sodom and the "laughter" of Sarah. Interestingly, Yahweh responded to the "laughter" of Sarah with a rebuke, and also a fiery rebuke against the inhabitants of Sodom because of the "cry" of the helpless victims of their wicked deeds. In this perspective, it appears the "laughter" of Sarah is juxtaposed indirectly with the "cry" of Sodom since both of these opposing categories occur within the same pericope.

On the other hand, we could also ask ourselves, "Who are the victims of Sodom's wickedness? Who are the people crying to Yahweh? Are they strangers or passersby? Are these victims within the Sodomite society or outside it?" Unfortunately, the narrator did not tell us the identity of the ones who cried to Yahweh against Sodom. The narrator merely told us that the cry of these people comes before the "faces of Yahweh."[350] We could be doubly sure that they do not live within Sodom itself since there were no righteous people in Sodom apart from Lot's family. However, even though we have no idea who these victims are, particularly their identity and relationship to Yahweh, yet interestingly, Yahweh came in order to give a face to these faceless victims of Sodom's crimes. In the metaphor of "cry" the

---

349. Similarly, the related phrase צַעֲקָתָם was used to describe the "cry" or "pain" of Israelites in Egypt. See Exodus 3:7.

350. Genesis 19:13.

whole force of "complaint and protest" which are directed against Sodom received an appropriate label. This metaphor helps to characterize Sodom because Sodom, like the Egyptian oppressors in the subsequent story of the exodus, brought before Yahweh the "cry" of his helpless people. It is also possible that the "cry" here comes from the "sinful" deeds of the inhabitants of Sodom. In the worldview of the Old Testament, it appears "sinful actions" form a kind of "cry" to God, hence the blood of Abel which cries to Yahweh from the ground for vengeance (Gen 4:10).[351]

3.5.1.4.2. Rhetorical Questions

Rhetorical questions are questions primarily asked not because the speaker wants an answer but for literary effect and for either denying or affirming a particular perception.[352] Rhetorical questions are fairly common in the Bible as well as in other Semitic languages.[353] For example, most of the divine speeches in the last half of the book of Job are rhetorical questions.[354] This literary phenomenon is also fairly common in the poetic sections of the Bible such as the prophetic literature whereby Israel's prophets employed the power of rhetorical questions in order to assert their theological messages.[355] On the other hand, one can also find rhetorical questions scattered within biblical prose and these occurrences often provide insight into the depths of biblical narratives.[356]

In our present pericope, three rhetorical questions are found in the divine speeches. These rhetorical questions are located in verses 13, 14 and 17. The first

---

351. In the thought of the ancient world, it appears that sinful deeds cause a breach in the divine and natural order. It is this breaching of the divine order that possibly calls to Yahweh for redress. The possible connection between the natural/divine order (for example, the Egyptian Maat) in relationship to this text was brought to my notice by my second reader, Ehud Ben Zvi.
352. See J. Frank, "You Call that a Rhetorical Question? Forms and Functions of Rhetorical Questions in Conversation," *JP* 14 (1990): 723–738.
353. M. Held, "Rhetorical Questions in Ugaritic and Biblical Hebrew," *Eretz-Israel: Archaeological, Historical and Geographical Studies* 9 (1969): 71–79.
354. R. Koop, "Rhetorical Questions and Implied Meaning in the Book of Job," *BT* 39 (1988): 415–423.
355. See W.A. Brueggemann, "Jeremiah's Use of Rhetorical Questions," *JBL* 92 (1973): 358–374.
356. See K.M. Craig, Jr., "Rhetorical Aspects of Questions Answered with Silence in 1 Samuel 14:27 and 28:6," *CBQ* 56 (1994): 221–239.

two are directed at Abraham because of the laughter of Sarah, and the last rhetorical question is found within the only divine monologue in the Abrahamic cycle. We will now begin with the first rhetorical question. The text reads: וַיֹּאמֶר יְהוָה אֶל־אַבְרָהָם לָמָּה זֶּה צָחֲקָה שָׂרָה לֵאמֹר הַאַף אֻמְנָם אֵלֵד וַאֲנִי זָקַנְתִּי. The interrogative particle לָמָּה introduces this rhetorical question and there is an element of surprise by the divine use of the demonstrative particle to qualify the laughter of Sarah.[357] The rhetorical question points to the laughter which, as noted earlier, is a reoccurring motif in the Abrahamic cycle. The answer to the "why" of this rhetorical question is actually obvious—that is, there is no reason for Sarah to laugh at the divine promise. Thus the rhetorical question underscores the unnecessary nature of Sarah's laughter and, building on this thought, the next question follows it up by showing the naivety of laughing at Yahweh.

The next question reads: הֲיִפָּלֵא מֵיְהוָה דָּבָר which is translated "Is anything too hard for the Lord . . .?" The obvious answer to this question is "nothing."[358] Hence from the divine viewpoint, everything is possible. This perspective is a sure rebuke against the laughter and inward doubts of Sarah in verse 10 which suggest that her barren condition cannot be changed. However, Yahweh questioned this assumption since nothing is actually difficult for him.[359] The second rhetorical question hence points to the absurdity of laughing at a divine promise since nothing is difficult for him to do, and to underscore this thesis, Yahweh once again repeats for Sarah the same promise of verse 10 in verse 14. It appears that Sarah's thought in verse 12 is cast in question form, thus for this single question by Sarah, Yahweh responded in two rhetorical questions challenging the assumption of this initial question.[360]

---

357. Wenham, *Genesis 16–50*, 37; Gesenius, *Gesenius' Hebrew Grammar*, 136c; Muraoka, *Emphatic Words and Structures in Biblical Hebrew*, 136.

358. Speaking concerning this text, Wenham observed, "'[i]s anything too difficult for the Lord?' is a rhetorical question that demands the answer no. God, this passage teaches, is both omniscient and omnipotent." See Wenham, *Genesis 16–50*, 48.

359. See W. Brueggemann, "'Impossibility' and Epistemology in the Faith Tradition of Abraham and Sarah (Gen 18:1–15)," *ZAW* 94 (1982): 615–34.

360. In verse 15, the Targum of the Samaritan Pentateuch seeking to exonerate Sarah from the charge of lying as reported by the Masoretic text rendered כחש as "she acted like a stranger" instead of the harsh statement that "she lied." See Tal, "Euphemisms in the Samaritan Targum of the Pentateuch," 114.

Away from the debates between Yahweh and Sarah as to whether she laughed or not, the next rhetorical question is actually hidden and occurs within the divine monologue. Yahweh is asking himself rhetorically whether to tell Abraham or not about his intended destruction of Sodom. The rhetorical question is found in verses 17–18 and reads:

הַמְכַסֶּה אֲנִי מֵאַבְרָהָם אֲשֶׁר אֲנִי עֹשֶׂה וְאַבְרָהָם הָיוֹ יִהְיֶה לְגוֹי גָּדוֹל וְעָצוּם וְנִבְרְכוּ בוֹ כֹּל גּוֹיֵי הָאָרֶץ.

The rhetorical question has the answer "no" since Yahweh himself stated the reason why he should tell Abraham about his plan. The reason is primarily because Abraham will be great and nations of the earth will depend on him or be blessed through him, hence, since a nation is about to be wiped out, the divine logic goes that this great man whose destiny is intermingled with the destinies of other nations should know about the fate of Sodom. Thus the divine rhetorical question is not merely to characterize Abraham alone but also to show indirectly that Abraham's descendants will play a leading role in shaping the destinies of the nations. In this way, as the second half of this divine monologue suggests, Abraham's descendants are also part of the characterization of this divine monologue. In particular, the rhetorical question is framed to evoke an affirmative answer, that is, Yahweh should tell Abraham about his plans. It is interesting to note that Yahweh points to Abraham's future destiny as a blessing to other nations and places this reason as the first of other reasons for telling Abraham about the fate of a Gentle nation, namely Sodom.[361]

3.5.1.4.3. Euphemism

As we have already seen in the preceding pericopes, few very important euphemisms are found within the divine speeches. In this particular pericope, it is not euphemism *per se*, but the divine avoidance of a taboo word which occurred in the inner rumbling of Sarah. In verse 12, Sarah said, "וַתִּצְחַק שָׂרָה בְּקִרְבָּהּ לֵאמֹר אַחֲרֵי בְלֹתִי הָיְתָה־לִּי עֶדְנָה וַאדֹנִי זָקֵן".

---

361. Such an opportunity given to Abraham to see the future further characterized Abraham as a prophet. He is here depicted as a prophet who is informed beforehand about the fate of Sodom. His intercession also on behalf of Sodom appears to be harbinger to the prophetic oracles about the fate of nations.

which is literally translated, "and Sarah laughed to herself, saying, 'after I am worn out, shall I have sexual pleasure, and my lord is old?'" However, rephrasing this question, Yahweh put Sarah's question differently, he said, לָמָּה זֶּה צָחֲקָה שָׂרָה לֵאמֹר הַאַף אֻמְנָם אֵלֵד וַאֲנִי זָקַנְתִּי, which is normally translated as "Why did Sarah laugh and say, 'will I really have a child, [now] that I am old?'"³⁶² After the discourse marker לֵאמֹר one expects Yahweh will make a direct quotation of the speech of Sarah which is given in verse 12, however, Yahweh paraphrased Sarah's words, and avoided two sexual terms. The two sexual terms employed in the inner speech of Sarah and avoided by Yahweh are בְלֹתִי and עֶדְנָה. The first of the two terms means primarily to "wear out" and this could be wearing out of the clothes, the body, and even days.³⁶³ However, in the present context, the term has the parlance of wearing out of the body due to old age which in relationship to the other noun עֶדְנָה appears to have certain sexual undertones.³⁶⁴

The second term עֶדְנָה³⁶⁵ primarily denotes sexual pleasure and hence Sarah reasoned that her worn-out or unattractive body and her lost sexual pleasures which come from old age are categories that make Yahweh's promise of a child seem in reality too good to be true. These terms (בְלֹתִי and עֶדְנָה) are deliberately avoided by Yahweh because they appear as "taboo words." Yahweh avoided these words for "sexual pleasure" and "sexually being worn-out" and replaced them with the words, "really will I give birth" (אֻמְנָם אֵלֵד) and "I am old" (וַאֲנִי זָקַנְתִּי). Yahweh replaces these "sexual terms" with "giving birth" and "old age." Yahweh technically avoided these terms or merely paraphrased her thought. However, even when one conceives the restatement of Sarah's thought by Yahweh as a paraphrase of what actually Sarah said, we must also know that an ideology is often at work in

---

362. One may say that the "subtle changes in the wording of Sarah's thoughts reveal that the Lord was not simply restating her thoughts but was interpreting them" [See Sailhamer, *The Pentateuch as Narrative*, 167], however, this interpretation by Yahweh is euphemistically done.

363. See Deuteronomy 8:4; Psalms 32:3; Lamentation 3:4; Job 36:11.cf. *BDB*, 115.

364. Wenham noted, "Sarah describes herself as 'worn out,' a decrepit old woman. She could certainly not expect to enjoy the pleasures of younger women in being a mother or perhaps even of sexual intercourse with her husband, for he too is quite old." This observation by Wenham also infers the possible sexual nature of this term. See Wenham, *Genesis 16–50*, 48.

365. See *BDB*, 726.

paraphrase or indirect quotation since things are now interpreted or translated from the point of view of the person quoting the original speeches of the person quoted. In this perspective, we could say that Yahweh's paraphrase actually tried to avoid these sexual terms which are presented as key elements in the thought of Sarah.

Thus "giving of birth" and "old age" as mentioned in the divine restatement of Sarah's thought are seen from the perspective of euphemism since Yahweh avoided these sexual terms and employed innocent terms such as "birth" and "old age" in order to describe the thoughts of Sarah.

3.5.1.4.4. Irony

One is struck by the ironical description of Yahweh in this present pericope. He is not the "usual Yahweh" we see in other narrative portrayals of him within the Abrahamic stories. Here, we find Yahweh eating, feasting, chatting and even travelling. Yahweh's transcendence, even though emphasized for example in his ability to see through Sarah's thoughts, is dominated by the immanence of Yahweh. He is humanized and brought down to sit metaphorically under the "tree" of our humanity. In particular, concerning the subject of irony, we see about three ironies of the present text in the light of our preceding reading.

Firstly, it is ironic that Yahweh blesses the "tent" of Abraham in this pericope, and then goes down to destroy the city of Sodom.[366] There seems to be a contrast between the fate of Sodom and the blessing and prosperity of Abraham and his descendants. In this regard, the divine monologue in verses 17–19 is at a strategic point in the story because it occurred when Yahweh left Abraham's tent and was on his way to the city of Sodom. It is here that Yahweh, in deep thought, extolled the virtues of Abraham and his descendants. This is contrasted by the repeated mentioning of the sins of the Sodomites (vv. 20–33). At the end, the hospitality of Abraham is also contrasted with the hospitality of Lot (vv. 1–8, cf. 19:1–3).[367]

---

366. See J. L. Ska, "L'arbre et la tente: la fonction du décor en Gen 18:1–15," *Bib* 68 (1987): 383–89.

367. See T. D. Alexander, "Lot's Hospitality: A Clue to His Righteousness," *JBL* 104 (1985): 289–91; V. H. Matthews, "Hospitality and Hostility in Genesis 19 and Judges 19," *BTB* 22 (1992):3–11.

Secondly, the irony in this present pericope is not only in the contrast between the destiny of Abraham and the fate of Sodom, but also a contrast between the "Abraham" of the preceding pericopes and the "New Abraham" of this present passage who successfully persuaded Yahweh to eat at his tent, and also successfully challenged Yahweh to be fair to the wicked inhabitants of Sodom.[368] The Abraham we had met so far in the preceding narratives, even though vocal, did not match the present one because we see him through his invitation speeches in verses 1–5 and his debate with Yahweh in verses in 23–33. Even though the reason for this new, persuasive Abraham is expressly given, the literary context suggests that, after the covenant relationship between Abraham and Yahweh in Genesis 15 and subsequently in Genesis 17, the status of Abraham seems to have been transformed from the silent Abraham of Genesis 12 and 13 and the skeptical Abraham of Genesis 15–17, to the now vocal Abraham in the present pericope who persuasively invites Yahweh to his "tent" and also plays a great role in shaping the destiny of the inhabitants of Sodom.

However, despite the differences between the present portrayal of Abraham and the preceding one, there is an obvious continuity within the characterization of Abraham. One such continuity is the narrator's portrayal of Abraham as a prophet. This ideology runs throughout the entire literary portraits of Abraham in the preceding narratives to this present point because even here, though not expressly stated, Abraham is conceived as a "prophet" who not only chats with God but also plays a very important role in shaping the destinies of nations. In this constant picture of Abraham as a prophet, the narrator gives us a hint to the ideological function of his stories. Though this will preoccupy our attention in the subsequent chapter, at the moment we can only make a passing remark that this present narrative saw Abraham as a prophet and hence his life mirrors the lives of his future descendants.

---

368. Wenham, noting the eloquent nature of Abraham's invitation speech, observed that Abraham's "greeting is eloquent, indeed quite long-winded by biblical standards (cf. 19:2) and very deferential." He employs the use "conventional, polite opening . . . suggesting that Abraham is laying on the charm in his attempt to make them stay." See Wenham, *Genesis 16–50*, 45.

Beyond these portraits, the picture of Abraham becomes actually the picture of all his descendants, and since emphasis is placed on the greatness and prosperity of his descendants, the prophetic role of Abraham moves toward the future of his descendants whereby the story of Abraham becomes actually the story of his descendants. In a sense, the Abrahamic cycle of stories is not about Abraham *per se* but about his descendants. It is interesting to note that since the narrator is also a descendant of Abraham his interest may be primarily concerned about the fate of these descendants rather than Abraham himself, and thus, even when Abraham is presented, the undertones of the text points toward the prosperity and greatness of the descendants. In fact, the prosperity of Abraham is not mentioned for "Abraham's sake" but because it has a relationship with the destinies of the many descendants of Abraham. In this particular perspective, Abraham's story is actually the story of his children and the prophetic role of his life here appears to be a reflection of the cardinal role ancient Israel's prophetic heritage will occupy in the future.[369]

Lastly, there is the ironic twist in the motif of laughter within the Abrahamic narrative. God rebukes the laughter of Sarah but appears to be less dramatic with the same laughter by Abraham in Genesis 17:17. After having a good meal, prepared and cooked by Sarah, it appears impolite for Yahweh to squabble over the laughter of his hostess, however Yahweh, because of the importance of the subject of the Abrahamic heir, ignored this customary decorum and pointed out to his hostess that she laughed. In fact, Yahweh showed her the absurdity of laughing at his promises since nothing is impossible for him to carry out. However, what is amazing is the total silence of Yahweh over the laughter of Abraham in a similar context of Yahweh promising an heir through Sarah in the preceding pericope. Yahweh implied that because Abraham had laughed the child's name would be called "laughter." In a masculine dominated society, is there a different attachment to the laughter of a man and that of woman? Is laughter defined along gender lines? Was it conceived culturally that the laughter of a woman is more embarrassing than that of a man? Why was Abraham's laughter appropriate and that of Sarah inappropriate? How is

---

369. Ibid., 44.

humor interpreted in relationship to gender? The answer to these questions is hard to say because the text does not provide us with substantial evidence. However, judging from the way Yahweh responded to Sarah, it becomes obvious that laughter has some kind of gender-bias. In some primitive societies, it is inappropriate for women to talk in the gathering of men, or even for a woman to eavesdrop on their conversation. If this is the case here, then the divine rebuke over the laughter of Sarah is understandable. Hence it shows Yahweh worked under the cultural parameters of the present text. However, if this is not so, then what caused the unpleasant rebuke by Yahweh at the laughter of Sarah? We can only guess because the present text gives the reader two accounts of laughter by the different genders, and while registering a divine rebuke over one, indirectly ignores the other.

3.5.1.4.5. Allusion

Allusions, as already stated, are powerful tools by which the narrator connects his works in order to carry over and point to the motifs already discussed or to the ones to be discussed in the subsequent narratives. In this sense, allusion forms a literary framework in which either explicitly or implicitly works are bound together. While some allusions could show repetition, continuity, and progress of a given thought or motif, on the other hand, it could show discontinuity and contrast between a particular category in its past and future form.

In the present pericope, we see three explicit allusions in the divine speeches. The first allusion in the divine speech is found in verse 18 which modifies the initial promise made to Abraham by Yahweh in Genesis 12:1–3. The modified form here reads: וְאַבְרָהָם הָיוֹ יִהְיֶה לְגוֹי גָּדוֹל וְעָצוּם וְנִבְרְכוּ בוֹ כֹּל גּוֹיֵי הָאָרֶץ. In this allusion to the original promise, there is the addition of the adjective עָצוּם which means "mighty"[370] and the replacement of מִשְׁפְּחֹת (families) of the earth with גּוֹיֵי (nations). The allusion here intensifies the original promise, and with the location of such allusion in the divine monologue, it partly underscores its significance since it seeks to suggest that the inner thought of Yahweh is centered on these earlier divine promises. The significance of this

---

370. See Numbers 14:12; Deuteronomy 9:14; 26:5.

allusion is that it connects the present pericope with the first divine speech to Abraham. Pointing out to the reader that even though years have passed, the thoughts of Yahweh are preoccupied with the first promises Yahweh made to Abraham. In the occurrence of the allusion in the divine monologue the narrator already gives a hint that Yahweh is going to redeem his promises since they are the preoccupation of his thought.

The second allusion is found in verse 19 which seems to direct the reader to the book of Deuteronomy, and hence, the Law of Moses or subsequent divine revelation. We have already talked about the phrase, "the way of the Lord." This phrase, even though looking backward to the entire revelation or self-disclosure of Yahweh to Abraham, is also an allusion to the Deuteronomistic code particularly as seen in the reoccurring Deuteronomistic phraseology within the context of usage. These Deuteronomistic phraseologies include terms such as וְשָׁמְרוּ, לַעֲשׂוֹת צְדָקָה וּמִשְׁפָּט, and יְצַוֶּה.[371] Even though this is not conclusive, the reference to "the way of the Lord" in these divine speeches is a harbinger to the Mosaic legislation, which appears Deuteronomistic in phrasing. The occurrence of this allusion is significant not merely because it is found in the divine speech or even this divine monologue, but it is the futuristic mood by which the "way of the Lord" is framed. Yahweh is speaking about the future descendants of Abraham and how Abraham will "command" his future children to obey the "way of the Lord." In this particular future orientation of this divine speech lies the power of the allusion to Deuteronomy, because there, as here, Yahweh is telling the future generation of Israelites after the exodus about the necessity of following the "way of the Lord." Thus Yahweh's speech opens for the reader a window into the world of tomorrow. As usually characteristic of the narrator of the Abrahamic narratives, these words are framed with a high degree of optimism. It is this last characteristic that differentiates the divine speech with the Deuteronomistic codewhile the divine speech has a positive and optimistic view of Israel's future, on the contrary, the Deuteronomistic

---

371. These phraseologies in English are "they keep," "to do righteous and justice," and "he commands." See Deuteronomy 5:32; 8:1; 6:24; 4:1, 5, 14; 4:45; 11:32; 12:1, 19;

code is replete with the reoccurring theme of Israelite stubbornness and rebelliousness.[372]

The last allusion is to the flood where also a divine monologue preceded the destruction of the inhabitants of the earth. The divine monologue in Genesis 6:5–13 is comparable with the divine monologue here in Genesis 18:17–21 because each of these divine monologues preceded a catastrophic destruction. The narrator observed that Noah found favor with Yahweh (v. 8) and in almost the same way, Abraham found favor with Yahweh (v. 3, cf. v. 17–21). However, the narrator in the Abrahamic story placed Abraham at the center of the divine monologue rather than at the fringe like we see in the absence of Noah in the divine monologue of Genesis 6:7. This suggests the central role that Abraham and his descendants will occupy in the subsequent biblical narratives. Thus through these allusions by means of association, contrast and analogy the narrator fits his stories to the preceding narratives and even looks ahead to the world beyond the time of Abraham. Like the preceding divine speeches, through allusions, Yahweh's speeches bridge the world of the past and the future.[373]

3.5.1.5. Significance

The divine speeches in the present pericope reveal important motifs in the reading of the entire Abrahamic narratives. Four such important motifs emerge from our preceding studies of the present pericope. Firstly, the literary-styled speeches in this pericope are given within a casual atmosphere of a friendly meal between Yahweh and Abraham. These divine speeches show the progress in the growing friendship between Abraham and Yahweh, and thus reiterate the full significance of the covenant relationship between Yahweh and Abraham in the preceding pericopes. Such an intimate covenant relationship did not stop in adoption of new names by the parties

---

372. Part of the last words of Moses to the Israelites are "For I know your rebellion and your stubbornness; behold, while I am still alive with you today, you have been rebellious against the Lord; how much more, then, after my death?" (Deut 31:32). This negative view of Israelites' future is clearly seen in the entire chapter 31 of Deuteronomy and in the song of Moses of the next chapter.

373. In subsequent biblical narratives such as Judges 19, the image of Sodom here becomes a source of continual allusions. See Alter, "Sodom as Nexus: The Web of Design in Biblical Narrative," *Tikkun* 1.1 (1986): 30–38.

involved, as seen in the preceding pericope (17:1–22), but culminates here in a friendly visit and meal with Yahweh at Abram's tent. It is the first and the last time Yahweh is graphically portrayed as "eating." Consequently, the mood and speeches of Yahweh in this pericope aid in the characterization of Abraham because it appears Abraham is the only person in the entire Bible whom Yahweh eats with in his home. In this particular portrayal, Yahweh honored Abraham and eternally presented him as a "friend of Yahweh."

Secondly, in the present pericope, the divine speeches reveal the doubt of Sarah which complements the doubts of Abraham as readily seen in the preceding pericope whereby Abraham seeks to adopt Ishmael as a possible heir (17:18). In particular, both of them laughed at the divine promise of an heir. In this perspective, Yahweh's speeches focused the searchlight on Sarah and readily show the inability of Sarah, as well as Abraham, to trust in the promises of Yahweh (9–15). Thus the motif of doubt and laughter continue through the present pericope, showing the increasing complication of the plot of the Abrahamic cycle since even the two main characters in these narratives lack full trust in Yahweh to bring to pass his pronounced promises. Similarly, the divine speeches also reiterate divine commitment to give Abraham an heir by Sarah despite the doubts of Abraham and Sarah at critical points in the narrative. Yahweh categorically says that he will visit or return again in order to bring to pass his promises to Abraham. One would have expected Yahweh to grow tired of the inability of Abraham and Sarah to trust him for an heir, but after the mild rebuke of Sarah, Yahweh reiterates his resolve to fulfill his promises in the lives of Abraham and Sarah.

In addition, the divine speeches also show the compassion and love of Yahweh for the wicked inhabitants of Sodom and Gomorrah. In particular, Yahweh walked down the dusty road to Sodom and Gomorrah in order to give the inhabitants of these cities a fair trial. He came down from heaven to verify or confirm the atrocities of these cities rather than just punishing them out rightly without verification from heaven.

Lastly, the divine speeches continued the characterization agenda by the portrayal of Abraham as an intercessor, and mediator, hence a blessing to the nations as wicked as the Sodomites. In this particular act, Abraham fulfills, even though temporally, the motif of the previous divine speeches whereby Abraham and his descendants are expected to become a blessing to the nations of the earth (Gen 12:1–3; 18:18).

3.6.1. Genesis 22:1–19

3.6.1.1. Structure

The story of Abraham has one of its "unforgettable moments" within this present pericope. It is like a "farewell" speech between Yahweh and Abraham since it is the last recorded speech between Abraham and God. The importance of the divine speech here bears on its location within the Abrahamic cycle and its "profound" theological significance in Jewish, Christian and even Islamic thought.[374] In a particular sense, the divine speeches or promises are not new since they are merely the reinstatement of the earlier divine speeches. However, the divine speeches here are in another sense new because they occurred after the birth of Isaac, and hence they are not primarily concerned about the birth of Isaac in particular but the future and destiny of the entire "seeds" of Abraham. This blessing came through the obedience of Abraham to allow his only seed to symbolically die in order to have more.

The structure of the present text begins with the same phrase which occurs in Genesis 15, namely "after these things." This connecting phrase already seeks to link the present story with the immediate story and most importantly with the previous stories in the Abrahamic cycle. It is the "grand finale" between the encounter of Abraham and God and thus its importance is clearly seen in the ways the narrator draws parallels between the first divine speeches in Genesis 12:1–3 and the present pericope. We will talk about this similar framing of the beginning and ending of the encounter between Yahweh and Abraham in the subsequent studies but for the present it suffices to note that the beginning and ending of Abraham's encounter with God is characterized by an attitude of "blind obedience" to follow Yahweh despite the cost. In this portrayal the narrator seeks, no doubt, to arouse his audience to imitate the "way of Abraham" whose

---

374. On the contemporary and political rereading of this story see Yvonne Sherwood, "Abraham in London, Marburg-Istanbul and Israel: Between Theocracy and Democracy, Ancient Text and Modern State," *BibInt* 16 (2008):105–153.

beginning and ending are characterized by a life of obedience to the hard commands of Yahweh to leave first the family ties and secondly to kill his only son. In both of these divine speeches, Yahweh assaults the family bond which in ancient times was one of the cherished and close unit of relationships within the human society.

Based on the scene of dialogues within the present pericope, there are five dialogues between the characters of this pericope namely Yahweh, Abraham, Isaac, and the two servants. The structure is represented in the following way:

Introduction v. 1a
   First dialogue vv. 1b–2
      Description vv. 3–4
         Second Dialogue v. 5
           Description v. 6
               Third Dialogue vv. 7–8b
            Description vv. 8c–10
         Fourth Dialogue vv. 11–12
      Description vv. 13–14
   Fifth Dialogue vv. 15–18
Conclusion v. 19[375]

The structure shows the importance of the divine speeches which are located at the beginning and the end of this pericope. At the center of this pericope is the dialogue between Abraham and his son. It is the only dialogue between a "father and son" in the entire Abrahamic cycle. In fact, it is the first speech between "a father and his son" from the beginning of Genesis to this particular point of the narration. Why is it that by means of structure and at a critical moment the narrator bracketed the speech of the father and the son in the middle of the "farewell" speeches between

---

375. See also Avishur, *Studies in Biblical Narrative*, 75–103.

Yahweh and Abraham? The answer to this question is quite obvious. The narrator wants his readers to know that Yahweh has now realized the first of his promise, and hence the right place to show this realization of the divine promise is in these last recorded speeches between Yahweh and Abraham. In this particular instance, the narrator is seeking, by this structure, to invite the readers to see how Yahweh has fulfilled his promises by the portrayal of the father and his son at the center of this farewell speech.

This point is vividly brought to the reader's mind by the emotional nature of this conversation. Isaac is asking about the sacrifice and Abraham affirming Yahweh's ability to provide himself with a sacrifice. As we are going to see, there is a verbal irony here and even double meaning in Abraham's speech to his servants in verse 5 and the speech to his son in verses 7–8b. He told the servants he and Isaac were going to worship God and come back to them. Is this really true? He also told Isaac that Yahweh would provide himself with a sacrifice. Was he really speaking the truth or was he evading Isaac's question? In both of these incidences, the narrator proved that Abraham was a man of faith who even though he might have tried to cover his true intention, his statement proved prophetic since at the end of the story they really worshipped Yahweh and the two of them actually returned together. And to Isaac's question, the Lord actually provided for himself a sacrifice.

In this narrative portrayal, the narrator once again recourses to the dominant motif of casting Abraham as a prophet who truly saw the events of the future. For the audience of the narrator, such an image of Abraham as a prophet becomes significant since his descendants are promised greatness. Thus, since these descendants are the same readers or audience of the narrator, it is not hard to see them understanding or seeing the life of Abraham through their contemporary prisms. In this way, the story of Abraham ceases to be of "antiquarian" interest for these readers, but becomes the foundation or basis for contemporary reality.

3.6.1.2. Literary Context.

The relationship between the present pericope and its immediate literary environment is significantly obvious. This is particularly seen in the relationship between this passage and the preceding pericope in Genesis 21[376]. In accordance with the divine promise, Sarah conceived and gave birth to a son whom Abraham named Isaac. In her own words, Sarah said, "God has made me laugh (צְחֹק), *and* all who hear (הַשֹּׁמֵעַ) will laugh (יִצְחַק) with me."[377] Ironically, Ishmael whose name is closely associated with the verb שמע also laughed (מְצַחֵק) in a sense with or against Sarah (Gen 21:8).[378] It is this laughter that caused the expulsion of him and his mother from the "house of Abraham" to the wilderness. The narrator juxtaposed the wilderness ordeal of Ishmael and his mother with the ordeal of Isaac and his father in the present pericope. Situating the present pericope in its literary environment, Wenham outlined a paralleled relationship between this pericope and the preceding chapter. This relationship is tabled thus:

God orders Ishmael's expulsion (21:12–13)	God orders Isaac's sacrifice (22:2)
Food and water taken (21:14)	Sacrificial material taken (22:3)
Journey (21:14)	Journey (22:4–8)
Ishmael about to die (21:16)	Isaac about to die (22:10)
Angel of God calls from heaven (21:17)	Angel of the LORD calls from heaven (22:11)
"Do not fear" (21:17)	"Fear God" (22:12)
"God has heard" (21:17)	"You have obeyed (heard) my voice" (22:18)
"I shall make into a great nation" (21:18)	"Your descendants will be like stars, sand," (22:17)

---

376. Zakovitch has shown the literary connection of the events of this chapter to the events of Genesis 21 and even chapter 23 to 24. See Zakovitch, "Juxtaposition in the Abraham Cycle," 519–20; 520–22.

377. Genesis 21:6.

378. There is wordplay between the speech of Sarah, the name of Ishmael and his action of laughing. In a sense, Ishmael whose name means "God has heard" becomes now "the one who hears" and "laughed" against or with Sarah. There is also an extended wordplay in the divine speech of the same chapter, whereby God told Abraham to "hear" (שמע) the voice of Sarah (v.12).

God opens her eyes and she sees well (21:19)	Abraham raises his eyes and sees ram (22:13)
She gives the lad a drink (21:19)	He sacrifices ram instead of son (22:14)[379]

This table reveals the obvious quest by the narrator to contrast the two sons of Abraham. He successfully accomplishes this by placing the destiny of the two sons side by side. In this regard, the different motifs expressed in the present pericope have inter-penetrating relationships with the one preceding it. Thus Genesis 21 looks forward to 22 and similarly 22 looks back to the plight of Ishmael in 21. As also observed by Wenham, the relationships between these two pericopes go beyond the use of the same narrative template to the presence of verbal affinity between the two stories. Thus, for example, the narrator employs the same phrases in the same story such as "the lad" (22:5, 12; 21:12, 17–19), "early in the morning Abraham took" (22:3; 21:14; cf. 18:27), and "shall inherit" (22:17; 21:10; 15:3–4)."[380] There is also the close affinity between the present pericope and the preceding account of Hagar and Ishmael's plight in Genesis 16 and 22. Wenham also noted these relationships in terms of the appearance of the angel of the Lord, the phrasing of the promise as "I will multiply your descendants"(22:11, 15; 16:7, 9–11), and the dominance of the verb ראה which explains the presence of the "well" and the significance of the "place" in these stories.[381]

Significantly, the present narrative is framed in the light of the first divine speech to Abraham in Genesis 12:1–3. Cassuto, Rendsburg and Wenham have noted the similarity in phraseology.[382] This phraseology is seen in the occurrence of almost similar commands, "Go" (וְלֶךְ־לְךָ) to the land which I

---

379. See Wenham, Genesis 16–50, 99. cf. S. Nikaido, "Hagar and Ishmael as Literary Figures: An Intertex*tual Study," VT 51, no. 2 (2001): 219–242.*
380. See Wenham, *Genesis 16–50*, 99.
381. Ibid.
382. U. Cassuto, *From Noah to Abraham* (Jerusalem: Magnes, 1964), 296; Rendsburg, *The Redaction of Genesis* (Winona Lake, Indiana: Eisenbrauns, 1986), 27–52; Wenham, *Genesis 16–50*, 99.

will show you in Genesis 12:1 and to the land of Moriah" in Genesis 22:2.[383] The phrasing of the divine speech here in order to imitate or follow the first divine speech is greatly ideological since it shows that crucial decisions were placed at the beginning and the end of Abraham's encounters with Yahweh, and through these two hard commands, the patriarch came out as a man of faith and obedience to Yahweh. In this particular frame of thought, the narrator also indirectly demands such a way of life from his contemporary readers who happened also to be "seeds" of Abraham.

3.6.1.3. Grammatical Analysis

We will now turn our attention to the concerns in the present pericope that have grammatical nuances. The subject under consideration will revolve around the nature of the quotative frames, the dialogical speeches, and syntactical considerations.

3.6.1.3.1. Quotative Frames

The only discourse marker employed through this pericope is וַיֹּאמֶר. It actually occurs thirteen times in the space of nineteen verses. The concentration of this discourse marker is found in verse 7, which stresses the heightening of the discourse in this verse. According to the structure drawn above, the heightening discourse in this verse corresponds neatly to the center of our structure above in verse 7. The opening of verses 1 and 2, וַיֹּאמֶר was used to introduce the speeches of Yahweh and equally to present those of Abraham. In all, three וַיֹּאמֶר were used to stress the speech and response in this first dialogue. The first was employed to present the address of Yahweh to Abraham, and וַיֹּאמֶר hence said, "Abraham." In response, the second discourse marker presented Abraham's reply which was simply, "הִנֵּנִי" or translated, "Here I am." This divine call was followed by an instruction or command, which was also introduced by the last discourse marker of this first dialogue. The response of Abraham is sandwiched between the calling of Abraham's name and the divine instruction. The short response of Abraham in this first discourse and his silence after the last speech of

---

383. On the relationship between the land of Mount, Mount Moriah and the site of the Solomon's temple see Kalimi, "The Land of Moriah, Mount Moriah, and the Site of Solomon's Temple in Biblical Historiography," 345–362.

Yahweh in this first dialogue points to the obedience of Abraham and his willingness to forfeit his son for the wish or desire of Yahweh.

The second dialogue in verse 5 was between Abraham and his servant. Here only one discourse marker introduces the speeches of Abraham. Like Yahweh's instruction to Abraham which ends in silence, the agreement of these two servants to the wishes of their master also was expressed by their silence. In this regard, the silence of a given character shows agreement to do the course of action or requests suggested by the leading character. Thus the silence of these two servants corresponds well with the silence of Abraham after the divine instructions of the preceding dialogue.

The third dialogue, which according to our structure, forms the heart of the present pericope by its location at the center of the five dialogues, begins in verse 7 and is introduced by וַיֹּאמֶר. If the servants in the preceding verses where silent because they were servants, Isaac as the son and heir of Abraham was given the freedom of speech. The speech of Isaac in verse 7 is primarily concerned with the logic of the journey; that is, carrying all the ingredients of sacrifice without actually taking the expected sacrifice. But first Isaac's speech, just as the divine speech, also has the luxury of "calling" first, in this context, "my father", which is introduced by וַיֹּאמֶר and then another וַיֹּאמֶר introducing his major speech. There is similarity between the speeches of Yahweh and Isaac even though from different points of view. Yahweh called Abraham by his name, "Abraham," but Isaac called "Abraham," "my father." In response to the call, "my father" in verse 7a, Abraham replied, "Here I am my son," with וַיֹּאמֶר introducing the call and the response each of these times. To the question of Isaac, Abraham replied that, "Yahweh will provide himself with a sacrifice", but also added the phrase, "my son" at the end of his answer in verse 8. The phraseology of "his father," "my father," and the repetition twice of "my son" was used in order to heighten the emotional nature of this central dialogue. By such an emotional dialogue between father and son, the narrator paints the inadequate nature of Yahweh's demands for the "sacrifice" of Isaac, hence a possible polemic against child sacrifice. However, since the narrator already told us that this request by Yahweh is actually a "test", our fears are partly dispensed by such an assurance by the narrator.[384]

Just like the initial speech of Yahweh in the first dialogue and the speech of Isaac in the third dialogue, the speech of Yahweh in the first dialogue followed after the same patterning—first a summons or call, and then the saying or stating of the summons or call. In this context, the angel of the Lord, first of all, called the name of "Abraham" twice in order to stop Abraham from striking his son who is already tied down to the altar of sacrifice. The repeated calling of Abraham's name is to stop, and then when Abraham stopped, the angel of the Lord now presents to him the whole intention of this divine test. The two speeches of the angel of the Lord are introduced by וַיֹּאמֶר and the response of Abraham was also introduced by the same. As in the original speech of Yahweh to Abraham, the reply of Abraham back to Yahweh was merely "here I am." This short response by Abraham also conveys the obedient responses of Abraham each time to the divine calling of his name.

The last dialogue is also introduced by וַיֹּאמֶר in verse 16. Here, it seems, Yahweh after the sacrifice continued the dialogue with Abraham. Yahweh actually swore by himself to give Abraham and his descendants a dominant place in the affairs and the destiny of the world. That is seen by Yahweh's predicating the continuous blessing of the nations upon the wellbeing of Abraham's descendants. Significantly, this is the first time in the divine speeches of the Abrahamic narrative for Yahweh to bind himself to the promise to Abraham by means of an oath. It seems this swearing speech of Yahweh should be understood in the light of similar oath-taking speeches between Abraham and Abimelech in Genesis 21:22–31, which underscore the fidelity of each of the parties to show continual kindness to the descendants of each of the participants. Similarly, by such oath-taking Yahweh bound himself forever to preserving and watching over the descendants of Abraham. This point itself seems ideological since it shows the narrator's quest to underscore the thesis that Yahweh's protective presence will continually abide over the descendants of Abraham.

---

384. On the problem of "test" and its usage in reference to the divine being see Carasik, "The Limits of Omniscience," 221–232 (especially page 223).

Within the matrix of these dialogues and the arrangement of the quotative frames that introduce them, the narrator shows powerfully how each dialogue is built on another. The divine speech is placed at the beginning and ending of this pericope, thus preserving in a sense the central subject of the pericope, namely Isaac. It appears through this narrative, that God preserved the life of Isaac, which itself is a foretaste of divine deliverance for the future descendants of Isaac. The future of Abraham lies in Isaac, and since all the descendants of Abraham, including the narrator and his readers, are part of these descendants, the identification with Isaac becomes inevitable. In the survival of Isaac lies the survival of the entire race, and thus becomes a prototype of subsequent deliverances of the "seeds" of Abraham in history.

3.6.1.3.2. Syntactical Considerations

The first dialogue in verses 1–2 is hinged on the verb נִסָּה.[385] In fact, the entire story hinges on this verb because without it we could not discern accurately the divine intention behind the "unusual" request by Yahweh. Even though a common term in the exodus and wilderness narratives,[386] it was the first and the last time this verb was used in the narratives of Genesis. It occurs often in the context of the Israelites' rebellion and the outcome of the testing is normally negative.[387] Using the term itself on Abraham might be the quest of the narrator to draw a comparison between Abraham and his descendants in the wilderness narratives. The object of this verb is "Abraham" and it governs the subsequent verbs by the conjunction *vav* attached to the discourse markers in verse 1 and even 2.

In the second dialogue, Abraham employed the imperative form of the verb יֹשֵׁב to describe the desired activity he wanted these servants to engage in while he and Isaac go to worship. Grammatically, the activities of Abraham and Isaac are described by means of

---

385. It appears that נִסָּה is often used negatively when it has humans as subjects and positively when God is the subject. For other nuances of נִסָּה see Terry L. Brensinger, "נִסָּה," *Dictionary of Old Testament Theology and Exegesis*, vol. 3, ed. Willem A. VanGemeren (Grand Rapids, Michigan: Zondervan, 1997), 111–113.

386. Exodus 15:25; 16:4; 17:2; 20:20; Numbers 14:14; Deuteronomy 4:34; 6:16; 8:2; 16; 13:4; 28:56 and 33:8.

387. Ibid.

three verbs namely וְנֵלְכָה, וְנִשְׁתַּחֲוֶה וְנָשׁוּבָה. The speech of Abraham is divided into two clauses, which are שְׁבוּ־לָכֶם פֹּה עִם־הַחֲמוֹר and וַאֲנִי וְהַנַּעַר נֵלְכָה עַד־כֹּה וְנִשְׁתַּחֲוֶה וְנָשׁוּבָה אֲלֵיכֶם. The first clause describes his command to the servants, however, the second clause describes what he and Isaac intend to do at the designated place. The two clauses are connected by *vav* attached to a non-verb, which here should be translated in contrast relationship to the first clause.

The third dialogue in verses 7 and 8 is focused on Abraham's answer to Isaac's question. The verb, which is literally translated "seeing", is syntactically important; however, here it carries the idea of "divine provision." The question by Isaac and the reply by Abraham are interestingly framed in an inclusio. This inclusio is in the phrase וַיֵּלְכוּ שְׁנֵיהֶם יַחְדָּו translated, "and they walked together." This phrase appears at the end of verse 6 and at the end of verse 8, thus suggesting the importance of this enclosed discussion between Abraham and his son. This inclusio already validates the centrality of this dialogue as the heart of the present pericope.

The fourth dialogue in verses 11–12 shows the prominence of the double כִּי clauses which reads: כִּי עַתָּה יָדַעְתִּי כִּי־יְרֵא אֱלֹהִים אַתָּה. This is translated, "because now, I know that you fear God." In these double כִּי clauses, the second clause actually is the object of the first, that is, the verb ידע has as its object the clause after it. On the other hand, the first כִּי clause is also syntactically connected to the preceding two main clauses namely, אַל־תִּשְׁלַח and אַל־תַּעַשׂ. The relationship between these two clauses and the כִּי clause is to provide the reason why the two actions of the preceding verbs are prohibited.

The last dialogue in verses 16–18 has two כִּי clauses. The first כִּי clause in the company of the particle יַעַן provides reasons for the activity of the second clause in verse 17. In fact, there is no need to translate the כִּי second as "that" or "because" since the force of these two grammatical particles כִּי and יַעַן also seem to apply there. Thus Yahweh wanted to reciprocate the action of the first כִּי clause by the verbal activities in the second כִּי clause. Syntactically, the כִּי clauses represented firstly what Abraham had done and secondly the activities that Yahweh will do for Abraham and his descendants in light of the deed of Abraham in the first כִּי clause.

3.6.1.3.3. Dialogical Speeches

We now turn our attention to the divine speeches in the midst of these dialogues. It is not an accident that Yahweh has the last word in the pericope. The speech of Yahweh literally bracketed the dialogues as a frame at the beginning and at the end of the present pericope. We will concentrate on the significance of these last speeches to Abraham as seen in the fifth dialogue. Here, Abraham returns to being a silent character and only listening to the promises which are made to him and his future descendants. At the tail end of the divine speeches in verse 18 is the clause, עֵקֶב אֲשֶׁר שָׁמַעְתָּ בְּקֹלִי which actually becomes the last words on the divine lips to Abraham. Syntactically, this clause stressed the already mentioned divine blessings on the obedience of Abraham. Why did the narrator frame the divine speeches in such a way in order to emphasize these clauses? This present clause breaks away from the preceding clauses by the intermittent similes and metaphors of verse 18. In fact, it appears the clause is a subordinate clause of the verb ברך, that is, the blessing of the descendants of Abraham to the nations hinges upon the obedience of Abraham to the voice of Yahweh. It then follows that for the subsequent descendants to have this kind of influence or respect in the international community they also need to obey the voice of Yahweh. In this sense, the dialogue also reflects the desire to make Abraham the model for future generations.

The presentation of the divine speeches in relationship to the speeches of human characters, such as the one of Abraham and his son, takes us closely into the world of the text. In this world of the text, Yahweh has the final say because it is Yahweh at the end that pronounced divine blessing on Abraham and his descendants. Talking about descendants, the narrator also moved the story beyond the characters of Abraham and Isaac to their "seeds." It is interesting to note that while the narrator and even Yahweh referred to Isaac by name in the early part of the narrative, at the end, however, the divine speeches move beyond Isaac to the "seeds" of Abraham. This transition is a movement between the characters of Abraham and Isaac to their descendants.

Like the preceding divine speeches of Yahweh, the future of Abraham and his descendants are cast in high optimism. Abraham, from the obscurity of Terah's genealogy, is now given a dominant place in the affairs of the international community. This optimism is clearly framed in the basic denominators of increased descendants, prosperity, conquest, and blessing to the nations of the world. In this constant image lies the narrator's propelling motif. Through the divine speeches we see the soul of the narrator because it appears these divine speeches are the reasons for his telling the story. They seem to provide hope, prosperity and abundance to the members of the Abrahamic descendants. As our subsequent discussion will seek to show, the presence of metaphor, simile, euphemism, repetition and allusion spicing the divine speeches becomes a pointer to the major motif underscoring the present narrative. The narrator, through this highly optimistic picture in Yahweh's speeches, seeks to encourage and provide hope for a nation that is seeking identity and a place within the geography of the ancient near Eastern society. Thus the divine speeches are highly artistic rhetoric which points beyond Abraham and Isaac to the world of the narrator, and it is here the interest of the original readers and the narrator are clearly entwined.

3.6.1.4. *Stylistic Aspects*

As we have seen throughout the preceding pericopes, stylistic features are readily found in divine speeches. Yahweh's speeches are spiced with various forms of stylistic features which point to the theological importance of these narratives since Yahweh is primarily the only character whose speeches are decorated with such literary features. The presence of these literary features such as metaphor, simile, euphemism, wordplay, irony and even repetition points ultimately to the powerful skill of the narrator, but also his quest to point to his readers that in these speeches lie the importance of the entire Abrahamic narratives. In fact, there is no Abraham without them since everything in the story of Abraham hangs on these speeches. It is not surprising then to see a lot of these features in them because they form the core of this cycle and it is around these divine speeches that ancient Israel's claim to historical existence emerged. We will now turn our attention to the simple stylistic features found within the divine speeches in this present pericope, and to partly see the immediate importance of these literary features within the divine speeches.

3.6.1.4.1. Metonymy

We have earlier seen that metaphor, or metaphoric expressions in particular, are often found in the divine speeches. Like the discussion on the use of the "house of your father" in our treatment of Genesis 12:1–3, we have seen how metaphor has some relationship to metonymies. In fact, the relationship between metaphor and metonymy are particularly thin. As already seen in our preceding treatment of Genesis 12, metonymy could be defined as the use of the part of something in order to describe the whole. For example, people speak in metonymy when "crown" or "throne" is used to describe "royalty" or "kingship." In this example, an object of kingship, namely a "crown", is now substituted in describing royalty. In some specific contexts, these pure metonymies could have metaphoric nuances. This occurs when the interrelatedness or association inherent in metonymies is somehow stretched to embrace a new unrelated category. For example, "Napoleon swallowed the crown of France." In this example, even though "crown" maintains its metonymic sense, it is now placed within a metaphoric context whereby the verb "swallowed" connotes "defeat."

In our passage, a metonymy was used in the divine speech in 17c particularly in the nominal construct שַׁעַר אֹיְבָיו. This phrase literally means, "gate of their enemies." The pronominal suffix "their" points back to the "seeds" of Abraham who are the subject of the divine blessing. In particular, this phrase שַׁעַר אֹיְבָיו is the first time it is employed in the Bible. The phrase reoccurred subsequently in the patriarchal narratives in Genesis 24:60 when the family of Rebekah blessed her. But even there, it is not שַׁעַר אֹיְבָיו but שַׁעַר שֹׂנְאָיו whereby שֹׂנְאָיו becomes a synonym for אֹיְבָיו. Literally, Abraham found himself at the "gate" of the city of the Hittite after the death of Sarah in Genesis 23. However, here, the cordial relationship between Abraham and the Hittites fits more the "gate of friendship" rather than the "gate of one's enemy." In the phrase, שַׁעַר אֹיְבָיו the שַׁעַר or "gate" itself is a metonymy for "cities." Closely reading this שַׁעַר as a metonymy, modern translators have translated the phrase as "the cities of their enemies" whereby "gate" which is a part of the city becomes a substitute for the city.

But what is the significance of the use of "gate" as a metonymy for entire cities? To answer this question one must understand the importance attached to the city gate in ancient society. For example we see in biblical narrative that the city gate is the site for commercial activities, legal transactions, marriage, assembling of an army, entertainment and other social activities. However, this metonym שַׁעַר is placed within a metaphoric context particularly in the divine expression, וְיִרַשׁ זַרְעֲךָ אֵת שַׁעַר אֹיְבָיו which is literally translated, "your seeds will possess or inherit the gates of their enemies." Thus, in this divine expression, to possess the "gate" of one's enemies is to "conquer" your enemies. In this particular metaphoric usage, "possessing the gate of your enemies" becomes a metaphor for conquest or victory over enemies. Consequently, the divine speech promised the "seeds" of Abraham victory or the conquest of possible enemies, which is represented by the possession or taking over of the city's gate.

In this reading, the initial metonymy שַׁעַר אֹיְבָיו is employed in this context metaphorically by Yahweh to describe victory over enemies of Abraham and his descendants. Hence the terms "seed" and "gate" in verse 17c are not literal or physical "seeds" and "gate" but metaphors employed by the divine speaker whereby "seed" stands for "Abraham's descendants" and "gate" for the "cities" or in modern terminology, the "power base" of possible enemies.

3.6.1.4.2. Simile

The simile as a means of comparison is obvious in the divine speech. The two similes employed are found in verse 17b. The text partly reads זַרְעֲךָ כְּכוֹכְבֵי הַשָּׁמַיִם וְכַחוֹל אֲשֶׁר עַל־שְׂפַת הַיָּם which is literally translated, "your descendants will be like the stars in the heavens and like the sands which are on the seashore." The first simile already occurred in the divine speeches of Genesis 15:5, however, there is a difference between the occurrence there and the one here. The emphasis of the former is on the impossibility of any man ever counting the descendants of Abraham, however, the emphasis of the latter is not primarily related to counting but the sheer innumerable children of Abraham. Despite this little difference, the two categories similarly refer to the same descendants of Abraham. Most importantly, they ascribe infinite numbers of children to the descendant of Abraham. In the biblical narrative, with its sensitivity towards numbers as particularly seen in head counts and censuses, the image or comparison of one's descendants to the "innumerable" stars is itself a desirable thing. Innumerable children itself is seen as an indicator of divine blessing. The numberless nature of the starry world became, from the divine point of view, a similar template by which to gauge or measure the children of Abraham.

The second simile compares the descendants of Abraham to the "sand of the seashore." This simile looks similar to the other simile in the divine speech "like the dust of the earth" in Genesis 13:16. However, the attention to the "sand" on the seashore particularly brings this simile within the specificity of the seaside. The simile as the preceding one explores the innumerability of the heirs of Abraham. From the human point of view, they are uncountable. Both these two similes employed in this pericope clearly suggested that Abraham's children are going to be numerous just like the tiny specks of sand on the seashore and the sparkling stars in the sky. Interestingly, the divine similes here juxtaposed the two horizons namely "the heavens" and "the seashore." In ancient and modern times, the two domains of these divine similes had normally evoked a sense of mystery and awe. Looking at the sea and sky, human beings had generally wondered at the mysteriousness of these regions.[388] It was such awe that provoked religious feelings as evidenced in the worship of the objects in these domains. Yahweh took his comparison from the spectacular world of the heavens and the seashore, thus to eternally engrave in the minds of the readers the beauty of these divine promises.

What purposes does the narrator seek to achieve by his constant reference to this "ideology of numbers" or in particular the innumerable numbers of descendants for Abraham? Even though it is hard to articulate, to say the least, the narrator saw great numbers as indications of divine blessing. Moreover, the struggle for survival in the ancient world necessitates the philosophy of being "fruitful and multiply" because it is through such fruitfulness that one could "subdue" or conquer the earth. In such ancient economies, numbers are necessary for advancement and development. In particular, there is security in numbers because the continuous existence of a people in those ancient times depended largely on their numbers.

---

388. See J. Edward Wright, "Biblical Versus Israelite Images of the Heavenly Realm," *JSOT* 93 (2001): 59–75.

Hence, the narrator's constant reference to such numbers by way of vivid similes proved that the narrator understood procreation or multiplicity of the Abrahamic race as an indispensable ingredient for the survival of the Abrahamic faith.

3.6.1.4.3. Hyperbole

We have already described the occurrence of divine exaggeration or hyperbole in our previous treatment of the divine speeches. The significance of these divine exaggerations or hyperboles lies in the fact that they serve as pointers to the interest of the divine being within the text of the Bible. Since these interests are also shared by the narrator and the community of his readers, these divine hyperboles or exaggerations help us to see the interests that formed the origin or concerns of the text. The divine exaggerations in this context are found in verse 17b, particularly in the use of the two similes to describe the future descendants of Abraham. Yahweh said that he was going to greatly multiply the descendants of Abraham and he compared their numbers to the "stars" of heaven and the "sands" on the seashore. These two similes should not be taken literally since they are meant to be hyperbole, that is, an exaggeration which is intended to emphasize the fruitfulness of Abraham particularly seen in the large numbers of children. This is the first time that we find in the divine speeches the combination of two similes in order to emphasize the great numbers of Abraham's descendants. The occurrence of these similes here is significant in light of the nature of these divine speeches as "farewell" speeches of Yahweh to Abraham. Even though these two similes are combined to create an obvious literary effect, their importance lies in their theological significance.

The intention of this divine hyperbole here is primarily for emphasis. Yahweh wants to emphasize the significance of the descendants for Abraham. In fact, all the similes in the divine speeches are comparisons made directly with the heirs of Abraham. The motif of land, despite its importance in the Abrahamic narratives, did not receive such similes. In this choice to hyperbolize the children of Abraham above all other interests shows the significant attachment of the narrator to the theme of great numbers of future children for Abraham. Since the narrator and the original readers are all members of Abraham's descendants it is not hard to see the vested interest in this reoccurring theme.

Through these divine hyperboles, the narrator and the original readers saw themselves and rightly understood the significance of their existence. They are here today because Yahweh brought them to be, thus their origin, identity and continuous existence are rooted in the promises of Yahweh to Abraham. In this way, the author and the original readers defined for themselves a divine destiny since they are the outcome of the promises of Yahweh to Abraham. In these hyperboles of innumerable sparkling stars and tiny sands on the seashore, the narrator and the original readers carved an identity for themselves.

3.6.1.4.4. Euphemism

The pericope presents euphemism in the divine speeches. As we have already seen in the previous treatment of euphemism, the use of euphemism or polite speech is not only common in the biblical narration but also within the divine speeches. There are three euphemisms that are clearly seen within this pericope. The first euphemism is seen in the divine use of the word "sacrifice" for the murder or killing of Isaac. In verse 2, Yahweh demanded a horrible thing from a father, that is, the killing of the only son of Abraham; however, Yahweh did not use the terms "killing," "slaughter," or "murder" to describe this act. Instead, Yahweh employed a religious word which here acts as a euphemism for "killing" or "slaughter." This religious term sounds nice and even polite. If Abraham's neighbors had asked, where are you going, he would have responded, "to offer" a "sacrifice." This term עֹלָה or "sacrifice" first used by Yahweh in verse 2 was also used twice in its normal sense of sacrifice in the dialogue between Abraham and Isaac, and once in this same normal sense in the narrator's description of the actual sacrifice of the ram.[389] Why should Yahweh call "slaughter" or "murder" a sacrifice? Even though it is possible that human "sacrifice" may be conceived in the same terms as animal sacrifices in the ancient world,[390]

---

389. See verses 2, 7–8, 13.
390. On the Canaanite background of this passage see Avishur, *Studies in Biblical Narrative*, 95–103.

whatever the socio-religious conceptions behind the present usage, the use by Yahweh is highly euphemistic. Yahweh in the context of the present pericope with its ominous presence of looming death, does not make mention of death, killing or slaughter.[391] The divine speeches refused the usage of these terms. In the same way, these terms are absent in the narrator's description of the scene. Thus, even though the text looms with the vision of death, the word "death" is, ironically, absent. It is the use of "euphemism" in the divine speech and the use of the ordinary connotation of sacrifice by the narrator that helps to bring about this realization. Generally, we see death looming, but it is ironically absent from the lips of the characters as well as the narrator of the present pericope.

There are also two euphemisms that occur in the divine speeches in verse 12. Yahweh told Abraham, "אַל־תִּשְׁלַח יָדְךָ אֶל־הַנַּעַר וְאַל־תַּעַשׂ לוֹ מְאוּמָה". This is literally translated, "Do not stretch your hands against the boy and do not do to him anything." This is the appropriate place to describe the "sacrifice" for what it is, that is, "killing," or "slaughter." However, the divine speeches employ euphemism for these terms. The first verb could mean hurting somebody, but the domain of the verb itself is within euphemism. Yahweh refused to use the terms that had to do with "killing" or "slaughter." In fact, in the next verb, he uses a common verb for "doing." Like the modern context, statements such as "I saw them doing it," "They were doing the thing" or even "just do it" could presuppose sexual undertones because the modern terms "doing it" or "do" have become a euphemism for sex. The divine usage of the innocent verb of "do" here to dissuade Abraham from carrying out the killing of his son and the refusal to use the usual vocabulary for "killing" or "slaughter" to describe the actions of Abraham for what it is, shows the overriding euphemistic orientation of the present narrative. In a story that seeks to describe one of the horrible practices of ancient society, namely human sacrifice, one expects the use of

---

391. On the horrors of human sacrifices in the ancient Near East see Ellen F. Morns, "Sacrifice for the State: First Dynasty Royal Funerals and the Rites at Macramallah's Rectangle," *Performing Death: Social Analyses of Funeral Traditions in the Ancient Near East and Mediterranean*, ed. Nicola Laneri (Chicago: The Oriental Institute of the University of Chicago, 2007).

these terms; however, stylishly the narrator avoided the terms but still made his point clear at the end of the story.[392]

3.6.1.5.5. Repetition

One fundamental phrase repeated in the divine speech was the phrase, אֲשֶׁר־אָהַבְתָּ אֶת־יִצְחָק בִּנְךָ אֶת־יְחִידְךָ which is translated, "your son, your only one, the one you love, Isaac." In particular, the phrase "your son, your only one" appears in verses 12c and 16. The significance of this phrase is to characterize Abraham by underscoring his willingness to do the unthinkable in deep obedience to Yahweh. It also sets the emotional tone of the narrative because such repetition puts before the reader's eyes the possible severing of the intimate bond between a father and his son. The repetition also brings to the fore the silence of Sarah. This repeated phrase, especially in relationship to the love of Abraham for Isaac, also makes one wonder what Sarah would have done in this context? Was she even told? The emphasis on the love of the father that runs through the story is overwhelming. It is not an overemphasis to say that this pericope was written from this perspective. We could see the love of the mother in the story of Hagar and Ishmael in Genesis 21:1–21. However, it seems the present narrative complements such emphasis on the love of the mother. The patriarchal nature of the ancient society normally does not give the female gender a dominant role, however, the story of Hagar a slave and her meeting with the angel of Yahweh and his divine promises to her, is a departure from this norm. The present pericope could have done the same for Sarah; however, the narrator is primarily concerned with Abraham.

In the same way, we also hear in the divine speeches, the repetition of the verb חָשַׂכְתָּ translated, "you did not hold back." This is repeated twice

---

[392]. For the study of human sacrifice in ancient Israel see R. W. Green, *The Role of Human Sacrifice in the Ancient Near East*. ASOR Dissertation Series 1 (Missoula, Massachusetts: Scholars, 1975); J. A. Hackett, "Religious Traditions in Israelite Transjordan," *Ancient Israelite Religion: Essays in Honor of Frank Moore Cross*, eds. P. D. Miller, P. D. Hanson and S. D. McBride (Philadelphia: Fortress, 1987); J. D. Levenson, *The Death and Resurrection of the Beloved Son: The Transformation of Child Sacrifice in Judaism and Christianity* (New Haven: Yale University); Naomi Steinberg, "The Problem of Human Sacrifice in War: An Analysis of Judges 11," *On the Way to Nineveh*, eds. Stephen L. Cook and S. C. Winter, 114–135 (Atlanta, Georgia: Scholars Press, 1999), 114–135.

(vv. 12c, 16c). In the same category as the preceding phrase, the repetition of this verb helps with the characterization of Abraham. In a text that is about to finally bring to an end the story of Abraham, the divine speech helps to see Abraham as a good person who did not "hold back" from Yahweh the most precious gift to him. In short, Abraham loved the giver and not the gift. The repetition also underscores the quest of the narrator to speak by this narrative to his contemporary audience. If Abraham refused to hold back the precious gift of a son from Yahweh, there is the implied need for the descendants of Abraham to practice such selfless giving.

The last repetition in the divine speeches under consideration is the word ברך in verses 17 and 18. This theme of divine blessing has generally interpenetrated the various divine speeches. The last repetition of the verb in the divine speeches to Abraham occurred significantly in relationship to the "nations of the earth." The text synchronized the relationship between future Israel and other nations by the verbal clause, כֹּל גּוֹיֵי הָאָרֶץ וְהִתְבָּרֲכוּ בְזַרְעֶךָ. In the last speeches of Yahweh, the vision of Israel in close relationship to the nations of the earth is significant particularly in light of the narrow, particularistic interests of subsequent Israelite communities. Here, however, Yahweh predicated the nations' blessing on the "seeds" of Abraham. Simply put, the divine speech here put the descendants of Abraham or Israel in continuous relationship to the nations of the earth. From the obscurity of the Shemites' genealogical tree, Abraham is now thrust to the world and blessing of the nations of the earth is dependent or keyed on the wellbeing of his future descendants. This universal vision is in itself optimisticthe narrator and his original audience will have rightly understood the implication of these words of Yahweh. This is a bogus claim in the ancient world particularly in the inconsequential nature of the nation of Israel in ancient near Eastern geography, social maps and politics; however, the narrator presents these visions of the past because it is the only one that could guarantee the future survival of Israel. The ideology of election or selection and its relationship to the destiny of the nations created a profound frame of mind whereby ancient Israel saw herself as indestructible because she has a universal destiny which comes from an exclusive, divine election.

3.6.1.4.6. Suspense

Even though the narrator already told us in verse 1 that Abraham was merely tested, yet the feeling of suspense is seen in the story and this suspense was only resolved when Yahweh called on Abraham in verse 11 from heaven. This feeling of suspense is only perceived when we see through the eyes of the character of the story and temporally ignore the statement of the narrator in verse 1. The suspense is enhanced by the seemingly unnecessary explanation of the narrator about the two servants, which appears to be a ploy to delay the story temporally. We also see the narrator giving us some details about the story such as the saddling of donkeys, arrival, discussion with servants, discussion with the son, preparation of the altar and then the gradual raising of the hands of Abraham to kill his son. Through these delays, the narrator slowed the story and in this slowing of the story, a reader is overcome by the suspense of the narrative. Most importantly, from the point of view of the divine speech, there is inexactness in Yahweh's first speech. He told Abraham to go to "one of the mountains" which lies in a region which is only first mentioned here. Why should the sacrifice be carried out only in this particular place? What is the significance of this place? Why a three days' journey into this region? These questions come to the mind of the reader because the first speeches of Yahweh are somehow vague, particularly the part of the location and the reason for the sacrifice to be done there. From the point of view of Abraham, we only can see a silent Abraham throughout the three days' journey. We do not know what he is thinking about. What was on the mind of Abraham in the period of these three days? However, when Abraham spoke with his son in verse 7, he seems to have overcome the initial shock and doubt any father would have had about the demand of killing his only son.

The suspense in this story creates for this pericope a literary beauty that pushes the reader to read to the end, because even though it is said to be a "test" at the beginning, what constitute a "test" from the divine being is hard to define, especially when this is the first time the term is employed in the Bible. The use of the term itself also plays a literary role, that is, the characterization of Abraham. From the narrator's point of view, Abraham was tested and found faithful and worthy of the covenant Yahweh made with him. Abraham was the first and the last person in Genesis whom the narrator classified his ordeals as a test from Yahweh. This itself shows the significant role that the narrator gives the character of Abraham. In this first use of the term, the narrator places Abraham on high spiritual and literary pedestals. Abraham now stands tall above every other character in Genesis. He was tested and found faithful.

Thus the term נסה or "test", which normally should dispense the reader's suspense since one already knows that the story is a mere test, further creates anxiety for the reader because all the lives or characters seen thus far in Genesis are free from this test. The question, "will Abraham pass this test?" comes over and over again to the mind of the reader. Why should Yahweh give Abraham this kind of test? What is its significance? Why Moriah? Why on the mountain? These questions in themselves create suspense and it is in the framework of this suspense that the narrator cast the plot of the story.[393]

3.6.1.4.7. Irony

As already briefly observed, there is a verbal irony in the entire story because even though the reader understands the divine command to Abraham is merely a test, the characters in the story are ignorant of this knowledge. In this way, the narrator places the readers above the characters because we already know what Abraham and Isaac did not know. This privileged information has great significance because it makes the characters life-like since in the real world we do not always know the divine motivation or reasons for certain actions.

The narrator also framed the stories in other kinds of ironies. The first kind of irony is seen in his excessive divine anthropomorphism. Like Abraham, the deity in this pericope does not "know" but it is at the end of the "test" that he now "knows" that Abraham loves him more than his son. The use of ידע in this pericope and even in Genesis 18–19 is an excessive use of anthropomorphic language for God whereby Yahweh is cast

---

393. The progression of the divine speeches in this pericope also shows suspense. For example, after the preliminary divine speeches in verses 1–2, the divine speeches do not appear until at the critical moment when Abraham has already raised the knife to sacrifice his son. In addition, even at this point, Yahweh began first by calling on Abraham in verse 11, then persuading Abraham not to sacrifice his son in verse 12, and then finally the speeches from verse 15 to 18. The silence of Yahweh from verses 3–10 helps to create an atmosphere of suspense.

into a human form. The anthropomorphism or humanization of Yahweh raises several questions. For example, why such anthropomorphism? Why the humanization of Yahweh in this same place, which also underscores his transcendent nature? There is no doubt that the narrator knows that Yahweh knew everything and could do everything. However, for the main plot of this story to be reached, that is, the characterization of Abraham as a faithful servant of Yahweh, the narrator has to cast the story into a "test" and "knowledge" kind of framework whereby Yahweh now undergoes the process of knowing. It may also presupposes that the term ידע or "knowing" stands here far beyond the normal knowledge of the contingencies of the future to an intimate and deeper kind of knowledge between Yahweh and Abraham since the term is also used as an idiom for intimate sexual relationship. However, even at this, Yahweh still undergoes the process of knowing, which itself is anthropomorphic in nature.

3.6.1.4.8. Allusion

There are allusions in the present pericope particularly within the divine speeches. The reference to multiplication and blessing of the seeds of Abraham in verses 17–18 employed the language and phraseology that resonate with the similar theme in the creation account of Genesis 1:26–28. Seen in this perspective, Yahweh appears to restate the original mandate he gave Adam and Eve. By this allusion to the creation account, as already observed, Abraham is placed on this same theological footing as Adam. In fact, it is possible to see in this continual theme of multiplication in the patriarchal narratives a reinstatement of the original mandate to Adam, and hence an evolving concept of a new creation through the seeds of Abraham. Thus the allusion to creation appears to characterize Abraham. However, beyond such characterization, it also furthers the plot of the story since these same mandates or promises were also rephrased or reinstated to the patriarchs following Abraham.

Similarly, there is also the allusion to the first divine speeches to Abraham in Genesis 12:1–3. The speech of Yahweh to Abraham ends with a major theological theme, that is, the theme of Abraham and his seeds becoming a blessing to other nations. To this end, Yahweh said, בְזַרְעֲךָ כֹּל גּוֹיֵי הָאָרֶץ which is translated, "in your seeds all the nations of the earth will be blessed." In Genesis 12:3, the text reads: וְנִבְרְכוּ בְךָ כֹּל מִשְׁפְּחֹת הָאֲדָמָה. Even though there is a slight difference in phrasing, the semantics of these two divine speeches are the same since they all emphasize the blessing of the nations through Abraham and his seeds. In particular, the mentioning of this theme in the last speech of Yahweh to Abraham is quite significant since, theologically speaking, it brackets the Abrahamic cycle within this dominant motif. Looking back to the divine speeches of Genesis 12:1–3, it ends with the theme of blessing to the "families of the earth," and in almost the same way, these last divine speeches also end with the theme of Abraham and his descendants becoming a blessing to the nations of the earth. Thus like a theological inclusio, the theme of divine blessing to Abraham and his seeds opens as well as closes the divine speeches to Abraham.

This allusion to the first divine speech is significant, not merely in the light of Jewish or Christian postulations or readings, but from the point of view of the author and his original readers. For example, one may ask, for these people what does it mean to them that "the nations of the earth" will become blessed in Abraham? Does this blessing mean the contribution of monotheism to enrich the religious speculation of humanity? Is it in material terms whereby Abraham's seeds become a channel of divine material assistance to the nations of the world? Or is it a political vision of the dominance of the seeds of Abraham over other nations? At present, it is difficult to answer these questions, however, it appears to incorporate all these many ramifications of the word blessing. At the end, it suffices to say that for the narrator as well as his original readers, Abraham and his descendants are placed in a significant role to impact or touch the rest of humanity. The narrator places Israel above all other nations, and defines their continuous blessings in the divine promises made to Abraham and his descendants. This claim already seemed arrogant from a human perspective, however, for the narrator Yahweh had chosen to only bless the nations of the earth through Israel. This is an optimistic picture of the future of ancient Israel because from this divine perspective Israel's role in the community of nations is hereby envisaged. The author takes an optimistic picture of the past because it is needed in order to address the present predicaments of his original readers, thus the optimistic past has a deep relationship to the present and future of the world and the audience of the author of the Abrahamic stories.[394]

In addition, the author also makes allusion to the preceding divine speeches in Genesis 13:14–18 and 15:1–5, particularly in relationship to the many descendants of Abraham who are compared to the stars and the sand on the seashore in verse 17. In the same way, the motif of blessing in verse 18 also alludes to the motif of Abraham becoming a blessing to

---

394. In the present pericope with its looming picture of death, Yahweh presents at the end graphic pictures of abundant children for Abraham in the simile of the stars in the sky and the tiny sands of the seashore. Through the obedience of Abraham, Yahweh brings to a climax the promises already made in the preceding pericopes. The narrator emphasized the importance of this present pericope by framing the divine speeches in light of the first divine speech and also drawing allusion to this first divine speech. The narrator understood the significance of this present passage and thus succeeded in portraying Abraham as tested and tried by Yahweh himself and found faithful. To show the significance of this passage, the divine speeches are spiced with metaphor, similes, hyperbole, euphemism, irony, suspense and allusion. These simple literary devices give the present pericope its present appeal. However, beyond such artistic interests in the present passage, original readers of the present pericope might have seen in this symbolic sacrifice, a metaphor for their continuous survival, because like Isaac, future Israelites will be brought to the "altar" of sacrifice, to the very brink of non-existence, and like this present pericope, Yahweh has intervened to bring about the continuous survival of the children of Abraham. Thus apart from the antiquarian interest in the past, the present story also provides an unconscious or even conscious identification with Isaac because in a literal sense, the descendants of Abraham, in particular the original readers and the narrators, are for the moment in the "loins of Isaac", hence typologically also situated their existence in terms of the brooding death and picture of survival at the end of the present pericope. Significantly, Yahweh promised the descendants of Abraham after the trial of Abraham a dominant role in the political affairs of the nations of the earth. This last picture in the divine speech understood the destiny of the nations of the earth in terms of the divine blessing in the descendants of Abraham. The picture is generally optimistic and the narrator wanted to present to his readers an optimistic picture of the past. While the divine speeches in the primeval narratives are filled with brooding pictures of stubbornness and rebellion, the future of the descendants of Abraham is filled with vivid optimistic pictures of the descendants of Abraham conquering the "gates" of their enemies, "becoming fruitful" and the nations of the earth defining their destinies on the Abrahamic blessing. In this sense, the destiny of the nations is predicated on the divine blessing on the descendants of Abraham. It lifts up the descendants of Abraham from the nomadic tents and places them within the context of the international community. In this sustained and constant optimistic picture of Israel's past by the optimistic narrator lies the ideology of the present narrative. Why is a positive and optimistic past appealing to the narrator? Why is a positive image of the past even necessary since it is possible to see the past either in positive or negative lenses? What do these positive images from the past about the descendants of Abraham mean to the original readers of these divine speeches in concrete terms? What functions did these excessive optimistic pictures of the past play in the context of existence for the readers and narrator of the Abrahamic cycle? It is the answers to these questions that will preoccupy the next chapters of the present study.

the nations in Genesis 17, particularly the portrayal of Abraham as the "father of multitude of nations" in Genesis 17:4b and 5c. Consequently, these divine speeches take over the different motifs of the preceding divine speeches and bring them now to a climax with the graphic description of Abraham as a faithful follower of Yahweh.

3.6.1.5. Significance

The divine speeches in this pericope present important motifs for the reader of the Abrahamic narratives. From the foregoing studies, five important motifs could be underscored in the reading of these divine speeches within the context of these pericopes. Firstly, the divine speeches climax the tension and suspense of the entire Abrahamic narratives through the acknowledgement by Yahweh of the faith and obedience of Abraham. These divine speeches are the last speeches between Yahweh and Abraham and hence underscore their importance to the author of the Abrahamic narratives and the original audience of these stories. As "farewell divine speeches," it is interesting that these divine speeches brought to a climax the characterization agenda of the previous divine speeches because readers, through the artful presentation of the divine speeches, come to see Abraham as a man of "faith and obedience" to Yahweh. Consequently, Abraham exits in the world of the narrative here in the imposing power of this present pericope, which portrays him as a man of unflinching loyalty to Yahweh. In the same way, the divine speeches, through allusion and repetition, reiterated the previous motifs of Abraham and his descendants becoming a blessing to the nations of the earth (22:18). On the other hand, to reiterate divine unflinching commitment to bless Abraham, Yahweh, for the first time in the Genesis narrative, sworn by himself to bring to pass all his promises concerning Abraham (22:16). Yahweh swearing by himself is significant, especially in a speech that is the final divine dialogue between Abraham and Yahweh. The swearing presupposes the eternal commitment of Yahweh to actualize the entirety of his promises to Abraham. In particular, Abraham becomes the first character in Genesis to whom Yahweh swore, thus showing the characterization of Abraham through these divine speeches. In this particular portrayal, Abraham rose above the previous characters of the book of Genesis and hence asserted his importance in the formative story of the Pentateuch. Similarly, the last speeches of Yahweh to Abraham also show the positive disposition of the divine speeches whereby God eternally pursued the good and wellbeing of Abraham and his descendants. This motif of goodness and wellbeing for Abraham and his descendants become an abiding motif throughout the preceding speeches and now finds climax in this pericope. Yahweh had moved Abraham from the obscurity of history towards the limelight by identifying with Abraham and his commitment to forever bless him and his descendants. Interestingly, the progression of the Abrahamic stories is worth noting here because slowly the story of Abraham develops from his call in chapter 12, the covenants of chapter 15 and 17, Yahweh's visit of chapter 18, and now Yahweh's swearing in chapter 22 to forever keep the promises he has made to Abraham and his descendants. In particular, Yahweh's speech ends with the triumph of Abraham over the "gates of his enemies" and the promise of an innumerable multitude of descendants. In this last scene, Abraham and his descendants become important stakeholders in shaping the destinies of the nations of the world. The reader of the Abrahamic narratives must realize that it is this motif, which is rephrased in several different metaphors and idioms, which forms the most significant function of these narratives. Consequently, this last pericope underscores this basic thesis that Abraham and his descendants are destined by Yahweh to influence and shape the destinies of the nations of the world by becoming a blessing to them.

3.7.1. Conclusion

Despite the differences of the six pericopes as to their sources, the commonality of content as well as the stylistic devices binds together these narratives in the Abrahamic traditions. In particular, the study of the stylistic features helps us to underscore the importance of these divine speeches and their place in shaping the Abrahamic traditions. This chapter has explored the presence and artful use of words in the divine speeches. The reason for such study lies in the persuasion that the stylistic features in the divine speeches and the narrative world of the Abraham stories are composed by means of words, and it is through understanding the way words are artistically employed in portraying the events and characters of these stories that we come close to understanding the intent of these stories. To this end, Gunn and Fewell rightly observed:

> The search for narrative significance is the scrutiny of words. The story world—with its setting, its events, its characters—is a verbal construct, a world made of words. In narrative, life is language. Words create the narrative world, and words hold the key to the significance of that world.[395]

The study of the divine speeches and the devices used by the narrator to portray the divine being becomes fundamental in telling us about this "narrative world" and even possibly the issues that impinge on this constructed narrative world from the world of the narrator. It is obvious that the words employed to describe this "narrative world" come from the world of the narrator since he has to use his present language or diction in order to describe or tell his stories. In addition, there are indications that it is not only the words he borrowed in his quest to describe the world that had already gone, but he also uses the existential categories of his own world in order to make sense of the past, thus slanting the divine speeches in order to address the issues of his own world. We have not yet pursued this train of thought; we have merely in this chapter explored the different literary devices employed by the divine speaker in his speeches which point to their significance in the Abrahamic narratives. In the chapter that follows, we hope to show the functions of these divine speeches as reflected in the "interpenetrating" relationship between the constructed narrative world of the Abrahamic cycle and the world of the narrator. The artful use of language in the divine speeches points beyond its aesthetic importance to its possible functions in speaking to the world of the "seeds of Abraham," that is, the world of the author and his original audience. In this way, God speaking to Abraham is actually not speaking to him, but to his descendants in the world of the future. Abraham in this perspective becomes not merely a verbal construct, but a powerful ideological construct in order to speak to the world of the author of these stories. Hence the narrative is not

---

395. Gunn and Fewell, *Narrative in the Hebrew Bible*, 147.

mainly about the past as much as it is about the present situation of the author and his original audience. By speaking to Abraham, God is, in this understanding, speaking again and again to the descendants of Abraham who are, ironically, the original readers of these stories.

CHAPTER FOUR

The Functions of the Divine Speeches

4.1. Introduction

In our quest to define the possible functions of the divine speeches within the Abrahamic narratives, we must acknowledge the underlying presupposition of the present research, namely the assumption that there is an inseparable relationship between style and semantics or between the stylistic features in a narrative and its possible meaning.[1] This underlying assumption presupposes that style or stylistic features of any given text in the Bible are not primary for mere aesthetic reasons, but they are vehicles or bearers of certain theological or ideological functions.[2] The stylistic features within a given text are part of the "furniture of the storyworld" which ultimately directs the mind of the reader towards some conceived design in a particular work.[3] In this sense, literary devices or stylistic features of a given biblical text or pericope are carriers of semantic functions. Underscoring this relationship, Bar-Efrat observed:

---

1. Concerning stylistics relationship to semantics see Stephen Ullmann, "Stylistics and Semantics," *Literary Style: A Symposium*, ed. Seymour Chatman (London: Oxford University Press, 1971), 133–152.

2. Identifying such aesthetic and ideological orientations of the narrative, Chatman rightly observed, "[r]hetoric working to ideological ends persuades us of something outside the text, something about the world at large." See Chatman, *Coming to Terms: The Rhetoric of Narrative in Fiction and Film* (Ithaca, New York: Cornell University Press, 1990), 197.

3. For example, Uri Margolin has noted how the stylistic feature of naming merely a character by the narrator could help create the "belief worlds" of a given work. See Margolin, "Naming and Believing: Practices of the Proper Name in Narrative Fiction," *Narrative* 10, no. 2 (2002): 107–127.

The study of stylistic details reveals these nuances of meaning, which may be compared to the overtones in music which, while not carrying the melody itself, determine the timbre of the sounds and therefore influence the character of the piece to a considerable extent. Style has expressive value, it enriches or emphasizes the main meaning reflected in the sentences, while at the same time, because of the emotional charge often transmitted through it, determining the reader's attitude to what is happening.[4]

This relationship does not merely determine the reader's attitude but points towards the intent of the narrative and even the possible intention of the author.[5] Consequently within the study of the divine speeches, the stylistic features are primarily instruments or tools by which the narrator showcases or points to his ideological or theological purposes. The relationship between style and semantics justifies our present quest to find purpose or underlying functions behind the decorated speeches of Yahweh within the Abrahamic narratives. It also shows that the author of these narratives was not primarily concerned with the aesthetics of these speeches, but with the message which these aesthetic elements carry. Thus the stylistic features in the divine speeches are rhetorically crafted as "mediators" of meaning. They stand as signposts which ultimately point us to something higher than themselves. In this role as mediator or conveyor of meaning, these

---

4. Bar-Efrat, *Narrative Art in the Bible*, 198.
5. The "represented world" of narrative is the product of verbal construct and it is through the understanding of the stylistic features of this world that we understand the purpose or intent of such represented world. Tamari Yakobi has underscored the mediatory role of speech in communication of the intent of the narrative. Speaking of the place of speeches in this mediation, Yakobi noted, "[e]veryone can speak in his own voice, without citing, invoking, or hiding behind anyone else; only the maker of fictions must in principle speak through the voices of others, and these voices all of his own making, from the primary speaker or narrator down. Like the characters, whose monologues and dialogues he in turn introduces, this official speaker must therefore be seen as a mediator relaying the implicit (world, theme, effect) from its authorial point of transmission or origination to its point of reception and decoding by the reader" [See Tamari Yacobi, "Narrative Structure and Fictional Mediation," *Poetics Today* 8, no. 2 (1987), 335]. Certainly, within the Abrahamic cycle, the divine being becomes the "official speaker" because his speeches reveal the main concern of the narrative.

artistic or aesthetic features of the text occupy a secondary role, that is, they derive their significance in relationship to the meaning or possible reasons for their presence in the divine speeches. Seen from this subservient role, the level of semantic becomes a natural transition between the preceding studies in the stylistic features of the text to our present quest to find the possible functions for the stylistic features found within the divine speeches.[6] The presence and consistent use of the literary devices within the divine speeches, despite the possible diversity of sources, shows that these speeches perform certain functions within the canonical location of the Abrahamic cycle.

The path before us becomes a little foggy because of the nature of the divine speeches. The fogginess comes from the tricky nature of the divine speeches especially as depicted in biblical narrative. The complicated nature of the divine speeches comes from their double significance on the level of story and ultimately above the story. In the first level, the divine speeches function on the level of conversation or exchange between the characters of the story. On the second level, also known as the discourse level, the reader looks beyond the story to see the reasons why Yahweh spoke the way he did, particularly in relationship or interaction with categories not expressively stated in the story.[7] Thus the speeches of Yahweh perform functions outside the world of the narrative by its implicit quest to speak to the world of the author. Ellen van Wolde describes the speeches attributed to the

---

6. The primary role of biblical speeches in a purely artistic or aesthetic role should be clearly defined. For example, in his study of 1 Samuel, J. McDonald has noted the closeness of dialogue to poetry rather the narration [MacDonald, "Some Distinctive Characteristics of Israelite Spoken Hebrew," *BO* 32 (1975): 162–75]. In the same way, Sternberg has underscored the primarily aesthetic purpose of biblical narrative in his definition of biblical narrative in term of its aesthetic, historiographical and ideological nature [See Sternberg, *The Poetics of Biblical Narrative*, 1–57].

7. The narrator uses the characters' speeches and actions, while the author employs the narrator in order to fulfill certain goals. Ultimately, in fictional works, the narrator is "a pawn in the author's general scheme." He is the invisible hand which pulls the strings. He is the master puppeteer who though invisible in the text makes the persons, events and speeches of a work to conform to his overall design and purpose [See Nomi Tamir-Ghez, "The Art of Persuasion in Nabokov's Lolita," *Poetics Today* 1, no. 1/2 (1979): 65–83]. However, in biblical narratives, the narrator assumes a divine and omniscient character, which appears to restrict and limit freedom of the human author. See Sternberg, *The Poetics of Biblical Narrative*, 1–57.

characters in biblical narrative as "embedded discourse."[8] Speaking of the significance of this "embeddedness," van Wolde observed:

> . . . the narrator does not tell merely *about* actions by characters or *about* situations but also looks *through* the eyes of the characters and speaks *through* their mouths. The narrator then surrenders the observations or narrative point of view to those characters in the narrative, so that character's texts (*discourses*) that are embedded in the narrative's text (*narrative*) emerge. Through this embedding of texts in texts, the reader is being guided in a certain direction, since the information that the reader obtains is always determined by the textual perspectives or subject-oriented views of the narrator . . .[9]

For van Wolde, embedded discourses of the narrator point ultimately to the perspective of the narrator and guide the reader towards a particular textual interpretation. Hence the narrator uses the character as his mouthpiece since through the character or characters, he speaks to the reader and most importantly his own world. On this higher dimension, we ask in fictional novels, why did the narrator assign these speeches to a particular character? What did the narrator hope to achieve by such attributive speeches? How are such attributive speeches in line with the overall purpose of the entire work?[10] In the study of biblical narrative, we could also ask the same questions even though phrased differently because of its claim as history.[11] For example, we could ask, why did the biblical author as-

---

8. Ellen van Wolde, "Who Guides Whom? Embeddedness and Perspective in Biblical Hebrew and in 1 Kings 3:16–28," *Journal of Biblical Literature* 114, no. 4 (1995), 623.
9. Ibid.
10. On the study of this literary phenomenon see M. Fludernick, *The Fictions of Language and the Languages of Fiction: The Linguistic Representation of Speech and Consciousness* (London: Routledge, 1993); A. Banfield, *Unspeakable Sentences: Narration and Representation in the Language of Fiction* (Boston: Routledge, 1982); D. Cohn, *Transparent Minds: Narrative Modes for Presenting Consciousness in Fiction* (Princeton: Princeton University Press, 1978); M. Jahn, "Contextualizing Represented Speech and Thought," *Journal of Pragmatics* 17 (1992): 347–67.
11. There are intriguing relationships between historical and fictional narratives. For the treatment of this relationship see Gerard Genette, Nitsa Ben-Ari, and Brian McHale,

sign, select, or arranged these divine speeches? We could also ask, are these divine speeches a verbatim transcription of the divine speeches or are they fabricated?[12] Even though we could not dislodge the consistent claims of the author that Yahweh spoke these words which he now reports back to his audience, we all know that the art of transcribing or retelling reported speeches conceals certain artificiality because first the author has to convert the speeches of God that were initially given in an oral form to a written form.[13] However, often this artificiality is concealed in an air of "directness" or "real-life like imitation" of the human conversation.[14] For example, the process of transfer from an oral speech to the present written form already

---

"Fictional Narrative, Factual Narrative," *Poetics Today* 11, no. 4 (1990): 755–774.

12. For the transcription of speeches in ancient narratives, even though there may be a quest at a verbatim transcription, most narrators or historians employ a lot of freedom in the reporting of the direct speech of their characters. A good example of this practice is seen in the historical narratives of Thucydides (*The Peloponnesian War* 1.22). Concerning the speeches of his characters, Thucydides noted, "[t]he speeches are given in the language in which, as it seemed to me, the several speakers would express, on the subjects under consideration, the sentiments most befitting the occasion, though at the same time I have adhered as closely as possible to the general sense of what was actually said." [*Thucydides*, trans. C.F. Smith (New York: Putnam, 1928), 41]. It is possible that the narrator of Abrahamic narrative exercised a certain degree of freedom in the transcription of the divine speeches.

13. Concerning this artificiality, Rimon-Kenan observed, "no text of narrative fiction can show or imitate the action it conveys, since all such texts are made of language, and language signifies without imitating. Language can only imitate language, which is why the representation of speech comes closest to pure mimesis, but even here I believe ... there is a narrator who 'quotes' the characters' speech, thus reducing the directness of 'showing.' All that a narrative can do is create an illusion, an effect, a semblance of mimesis ..." [Rimon-Kenan, *Narrative Fiction*, 108]. Similarly, noting this artificiality, John Frow observed, "[f]rom this structural fact flows another: that every piece of speaking may embed another piece of speaking. I can cite myself or you or another as speaking, at another time and place (whether real or fictive), in the first person: 'He said to me 'I don't understand.' A *secondary* speech situation is thus embedded in the *primary* speech situation, and in principle this embedding could go on forever. The embedded speech may be directly reported, or it may be fully subsumed within the speaker's voice ('he said he didn't understand'), or it may be present only as a tonal inflection in that voice ('He didn't understand!')." See John Frow, *Genre: the New Critical Idiom* (London: Routledge, 2005), 41.

14. On the contrary, the artificiality of a direct speech is evidently clear. Speaking of this Meir noted, "[f]rom a linguistic perspective, conversation in real human discourse is to be differentiated from dialogue in a literary context. Genuine conversation rambles with the inclusion of non-essential material, varying in trajectory and generality characterized by frequent changes of subject orientation. Arguments are often left unresolved, and key statements are always readily identifiable ..." however, "dialogue in literature is often artfully constructed" [Meir, *Speaking of Speaking*, 6]. For detailed treatment of the

impinges the necessity of compromising these initial oral speeches to fit the written form. There are many studies that have shown that oral conversations are different from written forms, hence the divine speeches would have undergone certain adjustments in order to fit the writing medium employed by the author.

Secondly, the speeches of Yahweh might have been originally given in Aramaic since Abraham initially might have spoken Aramaic and not Hebrew; however, the story itself has comes to us in Hebrew rather than Aramaic, thus suggesting the possibility that the author has translated or retold a story in Hebrew which was originally given in Aramaic. In this particular understanding, the divine speeches which were given originally by Abraham in Aramaic, are now forced into a new language namely Hebrew.[15] In the process of this translation, or retelling, the story or the divine speeches in particular has to be adapted to the grammar, syntax and even semantics of another language.[16] No doubt, in these processes of either translation or retelling in a new language, the speeches of God are expected to be rephrased or even readapted in conformity to the dictates of the Hebrew language, hence preserving the stylistic features that are originally in Aramaic to a new language would have been really difficult or even impossible. Underscoring the complexity of this problem, Samuel D. Luzzatto noted:

> The various dialogues reported by the sacred Scriptures, since spoken in times prior to its recording, must not make us believe that they were uttered by their different interlocutors precisely as they are written; and that therefore the language of Moses was the very same one as that of Jacob, of Abraham, of Noah, of Lamech, and even of Adam. Such reasoning would also make us deem that the same was the language of

---

differences between spoken and written discourses see Brian Paltridge, *Discourse Analysis: An Introduction* (London: Continuum, 2006), 13–19.

15. On the use of the Hebrew language in the Second Temple period see Jehoshua M. Grintz, "Hebrew As the Spoken and Written Language in the Last Days of the Second Temple," *JBL* 79 (1960): 32–47.

16. Concerning the treatment of translation as mimesis see Sternberg, "Polylingualism as Reality and Translation as Mimesis," *Poetics Today* 2, no. 4 (1981): 221–239.

the Pharaohs, and that of Laban, who, on the contrary, as we know, spoke Egyptian and Aramaic, respectively. It is necessary to recognize then that the divine writer conveyed the other people's speech in his own language, and that therefore the Hebrew discussions of [Abraham and his sons] could have been uttered in a Hebrew somewhat different from that of Moses, and closer than it to Aramaic.[17]

Lastly, the story of Abraham appears to have been a story that had possibly lived in oral traditions before the final decision to commit this oral story to written form. This oral story might have been written, adapted or even modified significantly in order to meet with the new challenges in the historical context of the author and his possible audiences. In this process of adaption, the author might have retold a story for which he himself was not an eyewitness in light of his own contemporary context but while also being loyal to the basic tenets of the traditions he had inherited.[18]

Even though all these processes are hypothetical to say the least, the contention of the present work is that the author or redactor has a major influence in redirecting, rephrasing or even retelling an old story of father Abraham in order to meet the immediate challenges of his audiences. Since we cannot reconstruct the possible historical context in which the author lived with certainty, we can only note his powerful artistic skills in the translation, retelling or most importantly, the re-presentation of the speeches of his characters.[19] In this difficulty, though not an airtight per-

---

17. Samuel D. Luzzatto, *Prolegomena to a Grammar of the Hebrew Language*, trans. Aaron D. Rubin (New Jersey: Gorgias Press, 2005), 78.

18. Concerning this adaption, Goldingay noted, "[o]ne of the ways in which Old Testament writers formulate and express their message for their particular hearers is by considering the significance for their day of archetypal events or motifs such as exodus or God's covenant with David, which belong to their people's history and are continually reinterpreted and reappropriated in the context of Israel" Goldingay, *Theological Diversity and the Authority of the Old Testament*, 8.

19. The historical context of the Abrahamic cycle is hard to locate, however, there are clues within the text such as the divine speeches which show a particular way of thinking. On this concern, Norman Habel observed, "[w]e may not know the precise historical audience to whom the Abrahamic narratives were addressed, but we can discern specific schemas of thought within these narratives that represent Abraham . . . in a particular way and that promote a particular ideology." See Norman C. Habel, *The Land is Mine:*

spective, we would note the general characteristics of these divine speeches in the interpenetrating relationship between the worlds of the story and the world of the author and his audience.

4.2. General Characteristics

Looking at each of the divine speeches in our study, they appear to reveal common characteristics that demonstrate, ultimately, that in their present usage they underscore a similar ideological template despite their possible origins in different sources. The following are some basic characteristics of the divine speeches that directly come from our study in the preceding chapter. Firstly, the divine speeches in the Abrahamic cycle express a high degree of optimism. This unmistakable optimism is clearly reflected in the repetitive themes of prosperity, blessing, great name, royalty, nationhood, phenomenal expansion and international glory for the "seeds of Abraham."[20] Concerning this optimistic vision of the good life particularly in Genesis, Whybray noted that Genesis "serves as an introduction to the OT in more than one way. One of its most important features is its depiction of the life of Abraham and his family as a model for the living of the good life."[21] Underscoring the importance of this optimistic vision for later generations, Whybray further observed:

> For later generationsperhaps particularly those that had experienced the loss of the good life both nationally and individually . . . Security, possession of the land, material prosperity, wealth, a long life, justice, power, wisdom and happiness were all blessings that they longed to possess or to possess in greater

---

Six Biblical Land Ideologies. Overtures to Biblical Theology (Minneapolis: Fortress Press, 1995), 9.

20. The "seeds of Abraham" becomes a label for the anonymous sons and daughters of Abraham in the future. For the study of anonymity in biblical narrative particularly in its association to the issues of identity see Adele Reinhartz, *"Why Ask My Name?" Anonymity and Identity in Biblical Narrative* (New York: Oxford University Press, 1998), 3–15; 187–192.

21. Whybray, *The Good Life in the Old Testament* (London: T & T Clark, 2002), 7.

measure. The picture presented by Genesis is fundamentally a positive and optimistic one."[22]

The centrality of this optimism lies not in the entirety of the narrative, but in the divine speeches. The basis for this moving optimism in the divine speeches might provide clues to the context of the author because it is natural to talk of such optimism in a historical context where these categories are absent. Thus the author draws for his contemporary situation a tradition of optimistic divine speeches rather than the judgmental or negative perception of the Deuteronomistic school.[23] In this sense, the author works directly opposite to the Deuteronomistic school even though there are chances that they both wrote from similar or almost similar historical contexts, which critical scholarship has located, in the exilic or post-exilic world.[24] In this context of exile, the overwhelming optimism becomes relevant because of the absence of these forms. The absence of these forms creates a nostalgic feeling in the past and hence the usage of the Abrahamic stories in order to positively create a counter-picture from the present realities on ground. In this world, there are no blessings, no prosperity, no great name, no royalty, and no nationhood, thus the potency of this positive vision of the past given by the author. On the relationship of the present in telling the story of the past, Harold Scheub has rightly observed, "[s]tory has always been used to provide connections between the present and the past, to study and explain the past within the context of the present."[25] Thus "[s]tory is an artful mixing of images by means of pattern, drawing on

---

22. Ibid., 27.

23. Kari Latvus described this negative aspect of the Deuteronomistic school as the "darker side of God," see Kari Latvus, *God, Anger and Ideology: The Anger of God in Joshua and Judges in Relation to Deuteronomy and the Priestly Writings*. JSOTSupplement Series 279, eds. David J. A. Clines *et al* (Sheffield: Sheffield Academic Press, 1998), 11.

24. On the other hand, a pre-exilic dating is also possible since every human society had continually in every generation pursued an ideal dream of security, prosperity and blessing for all even though rarely attained, thus it is possible that the author wrote from this strong sense of idealistic conviction particularly of a future society whereby the children of Abraham will cease to play the second fiddle in history. In pre-exilic Israelite society, the failure of the monarchy will naturally have fanned such idealism that sought fulfillment in the cherished memories of Abraham.

25. Harold Scheub, *Story* (Madison, Wisconsin: The University of Wisconsin Press, 1998), 13.

the working within two contexts, the past and the present."[26] To this end, Scheub further observed:

> The past has never been frozen in time; it has always been a restless repository of images, the snippets and parings of human existence, brought to life in contemporary times by storytellers who have agendas of their own, and so it is that history is also revisionist history. Does story provide an index to the past in the sense that the past can be perfectly reconstructed as it happened?[27]

The answer is definitely "no" because "[i]t is the function of the storyteller to weave . . . the ancient images" which "encapsulate the deepest dreams, hopes, fears, and nightmares of a society, and the contemporary images that record the evanescent world of experience into a single strand."[28] In this understanding, the possibility of transforming the Abrahamic traditions of the past in order to meet the needs of the world of the author becomes not only necessary, but a patriotic, thing to do. However, despite the popularity of this popular position of critical scholarship, the Abrahamic narrative situated itself in a pre-exilic or even a pre-monarchical world of the Bible. The situation of the Abrahamic cycle in this world did not rule out the possible relevance or retelling of a story which might have taken its final form in an exilic or post-exilic environment.[29] The author of the Abrahamic narrative did not disclose to us his historical location. It is obvious, however, that he is not an eyewitness to the story he was narrating. It appears he was drawing and transforming an inherited Abrahamic tradition which he represented, modified or even influenced in the light of the dysfunctional nature of his world. In this world, while the Abrahamic stories might have had pre-monarchical roots, the author who is possibly situated in the chaotic world of the exile, fashioned the story in order to

---

26. Ibid., 14.
27. Ibid.
28. Ibid.
29. See McKeown, *Genesis*, 10.

address the realities of his world. In this consideration, optimism becomes a remedy for the negativism of his own world.

On the other hand, the canonical situation of this story in a pre-monarchical world could be defended on this similar theme of optimism because, in the absence of royalty, nationhood and prosperity of the pre-monarchical world, the Abrahamic tradition might have developed its positive outlook from this historical context. Ultimately, it is in this historical context that the author at the end situated his story. In this sense, he told us the story of Abraham and not the story of himself. However, in talking about Abraham he also helps us to see his optimistic vision of the past which, no doubt, was relevant to his own world. In the final analysis, whatever the undisclosed historical location of the author, whether in a pre-monarchical world or a post-exilic one, the fact remains that the high optimism of the divine speeches could be situated in any of these worlds and even beyond.[30] It is in this consistent optimism that even the contemporary Jews and Christians after more than two thousand years could still identify themselves with the optimism of these divine speeches. Hence it is possible that by dislocating himself from a historical context, the author aimed possibly at situating the relevance of his story beyond his own time, and thus making his story continually relevant by refusing to situate himself in a given context so that every historical context could draw from the spring of these optimistic divine speeches.

A second characteristic of the divine speeches is their particularistic outlook. It is primarily centered on the "seeds of Abraham." The prosperity, success, blessing and happiness underscored within these divine speeches are largely for the "children of Abraham." In this particularistic outlook, the nations of the world are merely footnotes in the divine speeches, which basically seek, promote and protect the interests of the seeds of Abraham. As was already highlighted in passing, the particularistic interest of the divine speeches is obvious by the fact that it is a "seed of Abraham" (namely the author) that is writing a story for "the seeds of Abraham" and talking about the divine blessing on the "seeds of Abraham." In this way, the

---

30. On the difficulty of dating biblical texts based on linguistic indicators see Martin Ehrensvärd, "Why Biblical Texts Cannot Be Dated Linguistically," *Hebrew Studies* 47 (2006): 177–189.

story of Abraham was written primarily to pursue the interest of the "seeds of Abraham," and it is not surprising that the "seeds of Abraham" were given the central stage in the divine speeches. The nations were held in suspect and their prosperity is readily keyed on their positive relationship or treatment of the "seeds of Abraham." Consequently, the Moabites, Ammonites, Arameans, Egyptians, Canaanites, the formidable civilizations of the Babylonians and the Assyrians, and a host of other inhabitants of the Promised Land are glossed over and ignored, while the central light is beamed on the "seeds of Abraham." The centrality given to the "seeds of Abraham" already shows the sentiments of the divine speeches. To this particular outlook, Clines further observed:

> Fundamental to the ideology of the Pentateuch is the idea that God has chosen the people of Israel from among all the nations on earth. The idea first becomes apparent in Genesis 12, though the language of choosing is not yet used. When Yahweh tells Abram that he will make of him a great nation and that he will bless him and make his name great (12:2), he does not say in so many words that he will *not* bless them or make their name greatbut he implies it. The blessing to Abram has to be preferential and competitive or otherwise Abram's significance for the 'families of the earth' (12:3) is unintelligible.[31]

Interestingly, the author did not create a spurious reason for the election of Abraham and his seedsrather he was silent as to why Yahweh chose only Abraham among the "families of the earth", hence showing further that the treatment of the "seed of Abraham" or Abram as special did not come out of any discerned divine reasons, but a pure attachment of Yahweh to Abraham and his descendants, which borders on divine prerogatives. Such favoritism in the divine speeches already points to the ideological bias of the divine speeches. This particularistic interest is also revealed in the designation of Canaan as the Promised Land for the "seeds of Abraham" even

---

31. David J. A. Clines, *Interested Parties*, 199.

though repeatedly the author pointed out that the land of Canaan was already populated by the Canaanites (Genesis 12:6; 13:7).[32] The repeated divine emphases to give the land to the "seeds of Abraham" at all costs show the particular interest of the divine speeches.[33] This consistent emphasis on the motif of land by the divine speeches while the story level continues the development of the story, however, on the discourse level, might have a relationship to the interests of the author and may have been the possible reason for his writing.[34] In this sense, God's continuous emphasis on the land becomes an answer to the questions on the minds of the contemporary or original readers of his stories.[35] Thus the things on the minds of the author become exactly the same things addressed by the divine speeches. In this particular instance, the author uses the divine speeches not merely to continue the plot but also to address the "landlessness" of his readers or other issues pertaining to land, which comes from the world outside the text, that is, his own world.[36] It will be surprising that Yahweh's emphasis on land will be drawn and told by generations after the events described if these emphases do not have immediate importance or relevance to the audience of the original story.[37] In this way, the divine speeches perform

---

32. On the subject of Canaanites in biblical scholarship and issues surrounding their presence in the Pentateuch see N. P. Lemche, *The Canaanites and their Land*. JSOTSupplement Series 110, eds. David J. A. Clines and Philip R. Davies (Sheffield: Sheffield Academic Press, 1991), 13–24; 63–71; 73–121.

33. On the treatment of land as promise and as problem and its relationship to the Abrahamic cycle see Walter Brueggemann, *The Land: Place as Gift, Promise, and Challenge in Biblical Faith*, 2ed. (Minneapolis: Fortress Press, 2002), 1–26.

34. Even in modern conversation and arguments repetition is a poetic device by which we enhance our argument as we aim at persuading an opponent. See Charles Rains, "'You Die for Life': On the Use of Poetic Devices in Argumentation," *Language in Society* 21, no. 2 (1992): 253–276.

35. In fact, the divine speeches are primarily concerned with "the highest values of this society" that is "land, sons and honor." See Carolyn S. Leeb, *Away from the Father's House: The Social Location of Na'ar and Na'arah in Ancient Israel*. JSOTSupplement 301 (Sheffield: Sheffield Academic Press, 2000), 31.

36. Using the different linguistic and philosophical theories of Derrida, Bakhtin, Jauss and Gadamer, Richard Aczel has also reinterated the dominant role of the narrator as well as the reader in understanding or mapping out the voice in a given literary work. See Richard Aczel, "Understanding as Over-hearing: Towards a Dialogics of Voice," *New Literary History* 32, no. 3 (2001): 597–617.

37. Even though the narrator seeks to efface his presence from the narrative, there are several clues to his presence in the narrative. For example, Karol Berger has rightly

the ideological function, which reassures the original audience of the divine vow to give them the land forever (Gen 13:15). The word "forever" already points to the subsequent generations who also are embraced within this temporal frame.

The third characteristic of the divine speeches is their universal emphasis. Having pointed out the particularistic interest of the divine speeches in the preceding and immediate environment it seems contradictory to also talk about the universalistic interest of the divine speeches. However, even though we have pointed out the primary particular interest of the divine speeches in the preceding discussion, these particular interests are defined or configured in the frame of a universal drama. The universal agenda of the divine speeches is expressed at the beginning and end of the occurrence of the divine speeches in the Abrahamic cycle (Gen 12:3 and 22:18), hence pointing to the symbolic nature of these emphases, and the bracketing of Abraham's prosperity within this design. Abraham is reminded at the beginning and end of his recorded dialogue with Yahweh about the universalistic perspective of the divine speeches. This universal agenda draws heavily from the framing of Genesis since Genesis opens with the picture of God and the entire universe. Significantly, Abraham's story is introduced in the literary context of the table of nations in chapter 10. In this context, the divine speeches no doubt are framed with certain universalistic assumptions. Blenkinsopp rightly observed, "When we step back and take in the" Abrahamic narrative "as a whole, we cannot help being impressed by its remarkably irenic and Universalist character."[38] One particular universalistic assumption is that the destiny of all nations or the human race is hyphenated to the blessing of the seeds of Abraham. In the matrix of the story of Genesis, particularly in the narrative of Abrahamic cycle, Yahweh's speeches reject possible heirs to the divine blessing, but only channel the

---

observed that "[t]he very choice of the topic, the arrangement of the material, the judgment passed on the actors and events of the narrated history allow us to catch a glimpse, however fleeting, of narrator, implying what kind of a person he is, what his priorities and values are." In biblical narrative, the "priorities and values" of the narrator are clearly seen in the issues that preoccupied the concerns of the divine speeches. See Karol Berger, "Diegesis and Mimesis: The Poetic Modes and the Matter of Artistic Presentation," *The Journal of Musicology* 12, no. 4 (1994), 414.

38. See Blenkinsopp, "Abraham as Paradigm in the Priestly History," 240.

blessing through Abraham and his seeds. The interrelationship between the nations such as Egypt, Canaan, Aram and Mesopotamia within the matrix of the Abrahamic stories revealed the general universal intent of this personal or national story. In this national story, which began with Abraham, lies a story that is also universal and even cosmic in its consequences as understood by subsequent readings by Judeo-Christian traditions.

Another general characteristic of the divine speeches is the elevated language used.[39] This elevated language is seen in the presence of rare words, wordplay, alliteration, repetition, paronomasia, euphemism, hyperbole and irony. The presence of these literary devices is further strengthened with the additional use of metaphor or metaphorical language, simile and rhetorical questions. This use of elevated language naturally reveals the persuasive nature of these divine speeches since the embroidered language is usually an indicator of the rhetorical inclination of a given text. The biblical text often looks innocent at face value. Beyond the innocent face on the surface, however, lies the masked presence of rhetoric which clearly aims at persuasion.[40] This elevated language in the speeches of Yahweh is often absent or lacking in the speeches of other characters of the same pericope, hence signaling or indicating the rhetorical nature of these divine speeches. The elevated language embosses the content of Yahweh's speeches and makes them the high points of the Abrahamic narratives. Similarly, the elevated language also forcefully draws the attention of the reader to the contents of the divine speeches because the presence of the stylistic devices magnifies them. On this plane, the divine speeches are apparently endowed with an active presence and significance within the text. In a sense, they become the colorful part of the Abrahamic cycle since these artistic features brilliantly bring the text vividly to the attention of the reader. As an instrument of persuasion, it appears that the divine speeches present colorfully the divine

---

39. On the use of language as a tool of ideology in contemporary discourses see Bambi B. Schieffelin, Kathryn A. Woolard and Paul V. Kroskrity, eds. *Language Ideologies: Practice and Theory* (New York: Oxford University Press, 1998), 3–331.

40. On the relationship between rhetoric and style see Marie H. Nichols, "Rhetoric and Style," *Patterns of Literary Style*, vol. 3, ed. Joseph Strelka (London: The Pennsylvania State University Press, 1971), 130–143.

views on issues by consistently promoting or furthering a particular interest or even sanction through the artful use of words.[41]

Similarly, a characteristic of the divine speeches is a futuristic orientation of these speeches. Ironically, while the Abrahamic narrative is about the past, the divine speeches are focused on the future. They are the only edifice that addresses the future clearly. In these divine speeches, we see clearly the destiny of the "seeds of Abraham." They are pointers to the world of tomorrow in the midst of persons and events of the past. In this defining futuristic role, the divine speeches are actually the future from where the author is writing. It is pointing to a world that is future in the story, but which already is the reality of the author. The issues of the divine speeches are cast in a future that, from the point of view of the author, has already begun. As the only discourse directly focused on the future, the divine speeches fulfill certain ideological purposes since they are the only part of the story that is, technically speaking, not past but future, that is in temporal direction to the world of the author and his original readers. By defining the speeches of Yahweh to deal with "future descendants, future land, future nationhood and future imperial power" the divine speeches become a voice of the future, which is speaking ironically in the world of the past. The past in this particular instance is actually no longer the past, but the future is already leaning towards the world of the author and his audience.[42] It is part of the world that is already experienced by the author and his readers or a world he clearly envisaged that is rightly theirs. Thus the divine speeches become a window to the world of tomorrow. They help us to see the major things that are important from this world of tomorrow. The author speaks partly from this future world because he is not an eyewitness to the events he is describing and, hence, he gives us certain

---

41. Margaret D. Zulick has observed that despite the "absence of rational abstraction" in Hebrew method of rhetoric, "there is present in the Hebrew Bible a consistent attitude toward the power of speech, of eloquence and debate, and of persuasion." See Zulick, "The Active Force of Hearing: The Ancient Hebrew Language of Persuasion," *Rhetorica* 10, no. 4 (1992), 369.

42. Talking in particular of the land promises, Brueggemann noted the use of the land promises by a later generation, hence he observed, "even though the land promises in the tradition are in purportedly old traditions, they are now to be completely understood in terms of subsequent ideological claims of important use to a later interpretive community," [Brueggemann, *The Land*, xiv].

clues to the most important things in his own world, namely the issues of land, royal splendor, nationhood, self-rule and other possible political and religious interests.[43] In this particular sense, the divine speeches are actually the future in microcosm. In this place, the interest of the divine and human author converged since both of them have shared interest in this world of the future. The shared interests in this same world are clearly expressed in the interests of the divine being and the author on these highlighted categories. Concerning this shared interest, Berger noted:

> [b]oth the personage and the narrator belong to the world presented in the literary work, but while the world presented dramatically may be a single world, the world presented diegetically [at the discourse level] must consist of at least two distinct and hierarchically related ontological levels, the world to which the narrator belongs and the different, subordinated, world which he presents.[44]

These shared interests point to a higher intersubjective relationship between the narrator and this world of tomorrow as reflected in the divine speeches. Thus the narrator, even though reticent in the most part of biblical narration, dropped down for the moment such a curtain of reticence in his attributive divine speeches, because his interests in the past are particularly presented in the divine speeches since it is the only part of the narration that directly addresses his own world. It is possible that the reason he took the pains to narrate the past, or the Abrahamic traditions in particular, is because of these divine speeches and their relevance to his own world. In these shared interests in the future, we see the envisioned conception of the world of tomorrow by the author, which may not necessarily be the experienced world but could be a reflection or projection of a desired world. In either case, the author's interest in the world of the future coincides with

---

43. These many shades of expectations could be summed up in the word, "greatness." The narrator underscores that Yahweh had promised the "descendants of Abraham" greatness. On the "politics" in literary and non-literary forms see Marjorie Garber, "'Greatness': Philology and the Politics of Mimesis," *Boundary 2*, 19, no. 2 (1992): 233–259.

44. Berger, "Diegesis and Mimesis," 414.

Yahweh's interest in the same world and hence points to the interpenetrating relationship between the past where Abraham had lived and the future where the author is currently living or had already began to live.

Finally, a general characteristic of the divine speeches is their obvious emphasis on Yahweh's covenant or distinct relationship with Abraham and his descendants. The divine speeches, though primarily addressing mundane or ordinary realities such as land, state or politics, also underscore an overwhelming interest in the spiritual relationship between Yahweh and the patriarch. The highest expression of this spiritual relationship is in the making of the covenant between Yahweh and the patriarch. It is no wonder that the covenant was repeated several times and references to this category were made in several other places because the spiritual outlook of the divine speeches present this category or issue as a matter of urgency and priority. The spiritual relationship that began between Yahweh and Abraham is expected to further continue in the lives of the future descendants. In this particular outlook, the cordial spirituality between Yahweh and Abraham is expected to characterize the lives of these future descendants. Consequently, the divine speeches work in the mind of the reader to see the emphases, concerns and interests of Yahweh on this subject of spirituality for the descendants of Abraham.

4.3. The Ideological Functions

From the preceding characteristics of the divine speeches, it becomes obvious that the divine speeches are not merely purposed for decorative or stylistic intents rather they appear to underscore certain functions within the "intersubjective" world of the author and the world of Abraham.[45] In

---

45. The "narrator" himself functions as part of the "rhetoric" of the narrative. He is a "persona" or a "creature" of the author. In this perspective, he functions as a "character" whose existence in a text by his way of telling the story is a creation of the author in order to satisfy some ideological purposes in telling the story. In this regard, Richard Walsh had questioned fairly the treatment of the "narrator" as a "distinct and inherent agent of fictional narrative." Walsh has largely argued that since he is a creation of the author, the "narrator" as other characters in a narrative, function as part of the rhetoric of the narrative. See Walsh, "Who is the Narrator?" *Poetics Today* 18, no. 4 (1997): 495–513.

this sense, the traditions of Abraham are repeatedly told because they fulfill certain functions in the world of the author. This point is significant because stories, especially biblical stories, are not told for the sake of telling storiesrather they are told because they fulfill certain functions in the world of the storyteller and his audience. Often the functions of these stories are basically defined in some subjective ideological categories. Despite the problem of the term, we decided to treat these possible functions in the definition of ideology because of several reasons.[46] In particular, three of these reasons are hereby underscored.

Firstly, the functions of the divine speeches are not expressively stated particularly in its relationship to the world of the author. Instead, the reasons for these divine speeches in the Abrahamic narrative in tandem to the world of the author are clearly hidden, masked or even out-rightly denied. In this clandestine or concealed nature of the divine speeches in their relationship to the world of the author, the divine speeches exhibit a significant characteristic of ideology because often ideology is hidden or unexpressed. Consequently, the best term that clearly embraces the hidden undertones of the divine speeches in their relationship to the world of the author is ideology.[47] In this *hidden-ness* of the relationship of the divine speeches to the world of the author, the author wanted to be at least objective. However, such objectivity does not rule out the certainty that the present piece of narrative seeks to appease or satisfy some ideological functions in the world of the author. In fact, the need for telling this story again, especially in a world different from the world of Abraham by the author, comes from the conviction that this story in its present form fulfills certain functions in his own world. If not, there is no need to tell the story when it has no function to fulfill in the world of the author.

---

46. Concerning the problem of ideology, Jorge Larrain noted, "[i]deology is perhaps one of the most equivocal and elusive concepts one can find in the social science; not only because of the variety of theoretical approaches which assign different meanings and functions to it, but also because it is a concept heavily charged with political connotations and widely used in everyday life the most diverse signification." See Jorge Larrain, *The Concept of Ideology* (London: Hutchinson & Co., 1984), 13.
47. On the defining place of ideology in the writings of biblical writers and the reading of contemporary Bible readers see Clines, *Interested Parties*, 9–25; 26–275.

Secondly, at the discourse level, the direct speeches, even though they appear to be a direct quote of the divine being, still show the interpenetrating presence of the world of Abraham and the concerns and issues in the world of the author. The author employed the divine voice not only to speak to Abraham but also to speak to the issues of land (for example its boundary), state, prosperity, nationhood, foreign policies, and even a possible imperialistic agenda.

Thirdly, the divine speeches aim at the persuasion of its readers. The persuasion of the divine speeches comes from the general habit of the biblical writers in their artful skill at "covert persuasion" while appearing ordinarily to tell a story. For most readers, the concealed persuasiveness of the Hebrew Bible is largely unnoticed because it seeks to win over its reader towards the adoption of its worldview as the only norm. Underscoring the quest of the Hebrew Bible to persuade, Habel noted:

> The narratives of the Hebrew Scriptures are more than chronicles of events; the law codes are more than records from legal archives; the oracles and songs are more than aesthetic expressions of poets caught up in personal rapture. Most biblical texts push a point. They seek to win over the minds of the implied audience and persuade those who hear the message that the beliefs announced in the text are authoritative and true.[48]

Lastly, "ideology" seems neutral rather than using the word "theology" because theology is often associated with God and issues of spirituality. Often the spiritual connotations of this term ignore the everyday realities or existential issues addressed by the author such as land, state, prosperity, nationhood and international blessings. Even when these issues are highlighted the interest is purely their spiritual nuances. The neglect that often occurs when the term "theology" is used to define the speeches of God, make the use of "ideology" more appropriate because of its "secular" or

---

48. See Habel, *The Land is Mine*, 9.

"not too religious" connotations.⁴⁹ While there are different understandings of the term "ideology," we define the term simply, "as the implicit or explicit expression of the self-interest" of the author or narrator within a text.⁵⁰ Such self-interest might not be necessarily negative, but it shows the quest to preserve, promote, and protect the interests of a particular group, groups or an individual. The author of the Abrahamic cycle told his story from a particular ideological angle that promotes or protects the self-interests of Abraham and his descendants.⁵¹ It is in the context of such self-interest or conflicting agendas that Alter has described our age as an "ideological age."⁵² However, our age is no more ideological than the age of the biblical author since, as rightly noted by Patrick Corbett, "there is nothing new about ideological conflict; it is old as religion itself."⁵³ We now turn to describe or define the possible ideological functions of these divine speeches particularly on the discourse level.

---

49. Stephen E. Fowl has rejected the general treatment of the Abrahamic narratives as ideological. He noted the different interpretations of the Abrahamic cycle by Philo, Paul and Justin Martyr. For Fowl, the different interpretations show no ideologies by the imposition of the ideology of the interpreter on the Abrahamic narratives [See Fowl, "Texts Don't Have Ideologies," *BibInt* 3, no. 1 (1995): 15–34; idem, *Engaging Scriptures: A Model for Theological Interpretation* (Oxford: Blackwell Publishing, 1998), 62–96; see especially chapter five which is titled "Who Can Read Abraham's Story?" in pages 128–160]. However, the different interpretations of a particular text do not rule out its ideological nature. On the contrary, it establishes the ideological nature of the text from the point of view of the narrator and his world, and the interpreter and his own world.

50. According to Habel, "ideology" is a "pattern of beliefs" which "functions to promote the social and political cause of a particular group in society, to justify its vision, and to promote its interpretation of reality as truth." See Ibid., 12.

51. Every "story is presented in the text through the mediator of some 'prism,' 'perspective,' 'angle of vision,' verbalized by the narrator through not necessarily his" [Rimon-Kenan, *Narrative Fiction*, 72]. In such particular literary angle, the ideological facet in a novel or literary work is often conceived as "the norms of the text," and "consist of a general system of viewing the world conceptually; in accordance with which the events and characters of the story are evaluated." Often, "the 'norms' are presented through a single dominant perspective, that of the narrator-focalizer. If ideologies emerge in such text, they become subordinate to the dominant focalizer, thus transforming the other evaluating subjects into objects of evaluation . . . Put differently, the ideology of the narrator-focalizer is usually taken as authoritative, and all other ideologies in the text are evaluated from 'higher' position" [Ibid., 81]. For most of the biblical narrative, the ideology of the narrator is often hidden in the divine speeches since the narrator never contradicts or opposes the speeches of the divine being or his representatives.

52. Alter, *The Pleasures of Reading in an Ideological Age*, 206–38.

53. Patrick Corbett, *Ideologies* (London: Hutchinson & Co, 1970), 9.

The first ideological function of the divine speeches is to provide hope or consolation to the original readers who have no land, no nationhood, and not even the expected political structure.[54] Brueggemann talks about "the ideological force of land texts" which serves "the *hopes of those who anticipate receiving land*."[55] He also speaks of the "hopelessness," "rootlessness" and "expulsion"[56] that goes through the Abrahamic narrative. Contrary to this, however, "the power of anticipation" is found "rooted in the speech of God."[57] Historically, the assumption of the Abrahamic narrative is that the context of the divine speeches is situated within the pre-monarchical world; however, the monarchical and the post-monarchical world have also the need of the comforting reassurance of the divine voice which, even though located canonically in the times of Abraham, echoes also the hope and aspirations of the exilic or post-exilic world.[58] The author wanted to provide his original readers with a word of hope from Yahweh who eternally promised the land to the descendants of Abraham. Since the author and his audience were "descendants of Abraham" it becomes natural to tell them once again the vision of the past, which consists of elements and concerns that are missing in his own world. Such a vision of the past becomes a remedy for the ills of the present world from the vantage point

---

54. Drawing from the excessive optimistic vision in Genesis, Whybray noted that this vision is an "encouragement for the future" generation. See Whybray, *The Good Life in the Old Testament*, 27.

55. Brueggemann, *The Land*, xxi.

56. Ibid., 17–22.

57. Ibid., 16.

58. Even though the quest of Joel S. Kaminsky to read the entirety of the Isaac stories in the Abrahamic narratives (for example the expelling of Hagar and the Akedah) as "humor" is unconvincing, his thesis that there is an underlying theology of hope within these stories is no doubt right. Making this connection, Kaminsky said, "[o]ne of the major themes in Genesis is God's promises to the patriarchs. There are times when humans are expected to trust God's promises even when they seem unrealistic or even impossible. Inasmuch as God's promises require the patriarch to develop a hope that rejects a common-sense worldview, one should not be surprised to find humor in these narratives. There is a structural affinity, as well as direct connection, between humor and hope. Each proclaims that the reality of everyday life does not necessarily have the final word" [See Joel S. Kaminsky, "Humor and the Theology of Hope: *Isaac as a Humorous Figure*," *Interpretation* (2000), 373]. This hope is not only for Abraham but also for his descendants.

of the author.⁵⁹ The lofty vision of prosperity and blessing for Abraham and his descendants in terms of royalty, state, nationhood, and blessing among the nations of the world is a vision that, even though necessary in the pre-monarchical world, has its fullest relevance in the political and social chaos of the post-monarchical world of the exile. It is in this world that the "descendants of Abraham" needed a hope in an overwhelming world seeking to render them extinct. In this world where the structures of power are gone, the author provided a vision from their past where the divine speeches clearly address the issues of their day. The author holds out for his readers a ray of hope in a world that is filled with the complications that ultimately become a threat to their existence.⁶⁰ The positive picture in these divine speeches provides an alternative reality or picture to the ills of his world. It becomes an alternative consciousness or a substitute reality that goes contrary to the existential realities of his own world. It is an opposite picture imbued with great ideology that has its root in the traditions of Abraham.⁶¹ In this picture, everything wrong with his own world was clearly corrected in this alternative reality. Using the concept of "third-consciousness" by White, the divine speeches present words from another world where the negativism of the present world is turned around in favor

---

59. In fact, the entire Pentateuch is framed in order to explore the ingredients of these divine speeches, especially as expressed in the promise of God to the ancestors which the narrator might have understood to find now fulfilled in his own time. In this perspective, Walter Zimmerli underscored that God's promise to the ancestors "constitutes the . . . subject matter of the patriarchal history," [Zimmerli, *Old Testament in Outline*, trans. David E. Green (Edinburgh: T & T Clark, 1978), 109] and Clines had opined that the Pentateuch is built around the motif of threefold promise to the ancestors in times of descendants or progeny, land and a divine-human relationship. For Clines, Genesis develops the promise of descendants, Exodus and Leviticus centered on the divine-human relationship and Numbers-Deuteronomy finally focused on the promise of the land [Clines, *The Theme of the Pentateuch*, 29].

60. To this end, Westermann had rightly observed, "[i]t was supremely important for the later period that the promises to the patriarchs were unconditional. Later generations, under imminent threat, could reawaken the promises adapted to their situation and dealing with the preservation of the people and the retention of the land, so as to cling to God's assurance when both were in jeopardy." See Westermann, *Genesis 12–36*, 230.

61. This is primarily the deconstructive position. According to Kim I. Parker, "[D]econstruction is the name given to the critical operation which opposes the opposites which the text tries to hide, and reinstates the opposites as equally significant" [See Parker, "Speech, Writing and Power: Deconstructing the Biblical Canon," *Journal for the Study of the Old Testament* 69 (1996), 95]. In this understanding, the positive emphases by the narrator implied possibly the absence of these positive realties in his own world.

for the "seeds of Abraham." It is the combination of such ideological interests and aesthetic skills that had led Sternberg to describe the biblical author as an "artful ideologist" rather than "an incompetent didacticist."[62]

Secondly, a possible function of the divine speeches is the quest to provide the original readers or audience with a robust identity in a world that consistently challenged their distinctive personality.[63] It is always certain that the loss of political institutions or religious structures strikes a blow to the identity of a people like the Jews especially in the midst of an overwhelming pluralist society which characterized the exilic period. For many Jews, the loss of the state and the temple clearly affected their self-understanding.[64] The "descendants of Abraham" needed a new and an enduring identity that was deeply rooted in a solid tradition and not based on any temporal or disappearing identifiers of clan or tribe. It is a new identity that is not based on ethnic or cultural solidarities but on the firm foundation of tradition which is also defined in a universal context. Significantly, this new identity is framed in recognition of the neighboring nations. F. V. Greifenhagen noted the place of Egypt in the ideological map of Genesis and its role in shaping Israel's identity.[65] Concerning the ideological role of Egypt in carving an identity for ancient Israel, Greifenhagen observed:

> [r]ather than functioning primarily as a specific geographical or ethnographic reference, the 'Egypt' of Genesis seems to be over determined as an ideological marker of difference in the construction of a narrative of Israel's origin.[66]

---

62. Sternberg, *The Poetics of Biblical Narrative*, 38.
63. On the inherent politics of identity within the Abrahamic narratives see Mark G. Brett, *Genesis: Procreation and the Politics of Identity* (London: Routledge, 2000), 49–85.
64. The world of exile was a world where structures of powers were redefined. In this world there is need for a new self-understanding. See Jacob Neusner, "Exile and Return as the History of Judaism," *Exile: Old Testament, Jewish, and Christian Conceptions*, ed. James M. Scott, Supplement to the Journal for the Study of Judaism (New York: Brill, 1997), 221–38. cf. Edward W. Said, *Reflections on Exile and Other Essays* (Cambridge: Harvard University Press, 2000); Brueggemann, *Cadence of Home: Preaching Among Exiles* (Louisville: Westminster John Knox, 1997).
65. F. V. Greifenhagen, *Egypt on the Pentateuch's Ideological Map: Constructing Biblical Israel's Identity*. JSOTSupplement Series 361, eds. David J. A. Clines *et al* (Sheffield: Sheffield Academic Press, 2002), 24–45.
66. Ibid., 45.

In particular, the author makes this new identity a product of long history that is not connected to the temple or state but only based on a mere ritual of circumcision which, though taken from the ancient Near Eastern context, is now redefined in order to assert new meaning and identity for the children of Abraham. It is identification to this rite of circumcision and one's fidelity to the covenant Yahweh made to Abraham which now is conceived to be the basis for one's identity.[67] For the author of the Abrahamic cycle, one's identity is forged by his identification with the covenant, and not by other religious or priestly sacrifices. The sacrifice of Isaac, in particular, points out the futility of sacrifices and the emphasis on faith in Yahweh as the only necessity for the descendants of Abraham. Identity in this sense does not come from fidelity to any social or religious forms but to Yahweh. Such fidelity to Yahweh is expressed by the sign of the covenant namely circumcision. It is not surprising that the author forged for "future Israel" or "his own contemporaries" a new identity that is primarily defined along the lines of obedience and trust in the covenant made with Yahweh. This new identity created for these children of Abraham is a new identity in order to survive the onslaught of a hostile world that seeks to swallow them.[68] The new identity redefines and reasserts their importance on the socio-political landscape of this world. In a new world that is different from the world of their fathers, the author created a new identity for these children of Abraham by transforming an old tradition in order to serve this new context.

Thirdly, the divine speeches function as a tool of polemics. In more recent times, works have recognized the "sublime rhetorics" of biblical narratives. For example, J. Daniel Hays has shown the underlying criticisms of Solomon by the Deuteronomistic narrator of 1 Kings 1–11 which on the surface seems to praise Solomon, but turns out to be a scathing critique of

---

67. Blenkinsopp treats "circumcision" in Genesis 17 as a mere sign in the same category as the Noah's rainbow. However, his treatment of circumcision in this perspective fails to note the significance of circumcision in the forging of identity as suggested in the rhetoric of Genesis 17. See Blenkinsopp, "Abraham as Paradigm in the Priestly History," 237.

68. Concerning the role of creative imagination in the narrative construction of identity see Theodore R. Sarbin, "The Role of Imagination in Narrative Construction," *Narrative Analysis: Studying the Development of Individuals in Society*, eds. Colette Daiutte and Cynthia Lightfoot (California: Sage Publications, 2004), 5–20.

the regime of Solomon.[69] In addition, Menakhem Perry has talked about "counter-stories," "counterplots," and "conflict of ideologies" which lie "behind every biblical story."[70] For Perry, biblical narrative "is an arena of ideological dialogism, a polyphony of human perspectives that reflects a hierarchy of clashing agendas, whose conflict ultimately serves a divine agenda that is not identical to any of them."[71] On a large scale, Amit similarly has underscored "hidden polemics" within the biblical narratives particularly the contentions between the northern narrators and the narrators from Judah.[72] Concerning such hidden polemics, she observed:

> Hidden literary polemic refers to a conceptual confrontation that found its expression in written materials, but which due to practical circumstances or rhetorical consideration there was a tendency to conceal. Encounter with the subject of the polemics reveals another side of the ideological aspects reflected in biblical literature, revealing directions and positions concerning controversial issues; recognition of the techniques of concealment, which lends the polemic its hidden character, shows the reader some of the poetical sophistication of the ancient biblical authors.[73]

Furthermore, Amit also recognized explicit or direct polemics within biblical narratives which seek to critique directly northern or southern institutions, persons and events.[74] In the same sense, even though there are possible hidden polemics within the divine speeches, the God of the Abrahamic cycle explicitly took sides with the ancient Israelites in con-

---

69. J. Daniel Hays, "Has the Narrator Come to Praise Solomon or to Bury Him? Narrative Subtlety in 1 Kings 1–11," *Journal for the Study of the Old Testament* 28, no. 2 (2003): 149–174.
70. Menakhem Perry, "Counter-Stories in the Bible: Rebekah and her Bridegroom, Abraham's Servant," *Prooftexts* 27 (2007), 276.
71. Ibid.
72. Amit, *Hidden Polemics in Biblical Narrative*, trans. Jonathan Chipman (Leiden: Brill, 2000), 99–168.
73. Ibid., vii.
74. Ibid., 189–220.

text of history. Thus the divine speeches provide not only the justification for the rejection of the Arameans, Ishmaelites, Egyptians, Moabites, and Ammonites in the narration of sacred history but also reiterate the defining role of ancient Israel among these nations which are treated as footnotes and thus on the margin of sacred history. In fact, the divine speeches present a slanted view, namely that Yahweh shows absolute favoritism towards Abraham and his seeds. In particular, the polemics in the divine speeches lie in the way by which the divine speeches eliminate possible heirs to the Abrahamic covenant and place the divine choice on Isaac and him alone. Often the potential heirs such as Ishmael, Eliezer, and Lot are thrown off the list by an unknown divine gauge or parameters of choice and not necessarily their flawed moral characters. However, in some cases, the divine characterization of these individuals already signals their rejection such as, for example, Yahweh's reference to Ishmael as a "donkey of a man" or the association of Lot with the wicked Sodomites.[75] It is a powerful polemics or rhetorics which direct the attention of the reader to the "otherness" of the neighboring nations and the "appropriateness" of the "seeds of Abraham" for their role in history.[76] The "otherness" of the other nations is clearly defined in the divine speeches—the welfare of the "children of Abraham" is stressed and the incompatibility of the other nations is tacitly underscored.[77]

---

75. Ze'ev Weisman has pointed to the use of animal epithets or appellations as a form of political satire against opponents, see Weisman, *Political Satire in the Bible*. Society of Biblical Literature 32 (Atlanta, Georgia: Scholars Press, 1998), 10–13.

76. R. Christopher Heard treated the Moabites, the Ammonites, the Ishmaelites and the Egyptians as part of the "diselection" agenda of the narrator especially in the context of identity definition of the post-exilic Yehud community, see Heard, *Dynamics of Diselection: Ambiguity in Genesis 12–36 and Ethnic Boundaries in Post-exilic Judah*. Society of Biblical Literature (Atlanta, Georgia: Scholar Press, 2001), 172–184.

77. The "otherness" of the other nations already presupposes an ideological posture of the Abrahamic narratives and the divine speeches. To this end, Habel observed, "[A]n ideology . . . incorporates the factor of contestation, the text being the literary product of the struggle. The purpose of the text is to persuade the thinking of that audience or, alternatively, to condemn the thinking of that audience as alien to the true ideology of the speaker in the text. Although it may not be possible within the limits of each text to identify precisely the 'other' whose ideas are being opposed, the dominant images and aspirations of the extended literary complexes usually provide sufficient images, beliefs, and aspirations to formulate the basic elements of the ideology being espoused. In some cases the 'other' may be constructed by the text as an evil opponent rather than faithfully reflecting the ambiguities of an actual historical situation. The rhetoric of some texts is blatant and aggressive, whereas others are made more subtle and aesthetic in tone. Some

Fourthly, another function of the divine speeches lies in the quest of the divine speech to legitimize certain religious or social forms in the world of the author.[78] The divine speech, for example, legitimizes circumcision, the invalidity of human sacrifice, monotheism, and the right of ancient Israelites to the land of Canaan. It also clearly defines and possibly legitimizes social relationships. It is possible that the author expected that the way Abraham deals with the people of other nations would be a model for the social relationships between his contemporaries and the Gentile world. In this sense, the social relationships have become defined and structured along the lines of these traditions; hence the treatment of Hagar and Ishmael, Lot and his Moabites and Ammonites descendants, and the Canaanites, become a model for social relationships. It appears that the different aspects of Abraham's life, particularly his relationships with the ancestors or eponyms for these tribes, embody the expected relationship, which ought to characterize the "seeds of Abraham" and these other nations. Most importantly, Yahweh endorses the supremacy of Israel over men of other nationalities because it is only in the seeds of Abraham that the nations of the earth could be blessed.

Lastly, the divine speeches are cast as prophecy; hence they fulfill the role of prophetic speeches. Abraham was explicitly named by Yahweh as a prophet (Gen 20:7), the narrative in Genesis 15:1 was cast in a prophetic fashion with the frame "the word of the Yahweh came to Abram," and there the divine speeches focused on the future of the "children of Abraham", particularly the exodus. Similarly, Yahweh saw through the heart of Sarah even though she stood behind the door away from him. He also prophetically told of the birth of Isaac within a year. The futuristic orientation of the divine speeches ultimately suggests that the author cast the divine speeches as prophecy. In addition, the prophetic nature of the divine speeches is

---

ideologies present a frontal attack; others stand without comment like silent parables." See Habel, *The Land is Mine*, 12.

78. Legitimizing function is one of the basic functions according to Andrew D. H. Mayes who opined that there are three basic functions of ideology namely it functions as an integrating system, a framework to justify or legitimize the authority or interest of a particular group and lastly, it functions as a distorting prism which blurs reality in order to satisfy the interest of a dominant group. See Mayes, "Deuteronomistic Ideology and the Theology of the Old Testament," *Journal for the Study of the Old Testament* 82 (1999), 61.

seen in the repeated emphasis that Abraham will become the father of a multitude of nations. Thus the divine speeches are conceived as a window on the world of tomorrow. This prophetic casting of the divine speeches helped to fulfill certain functions in the lives of the original readers. One of these functions in particular is that Yahweh was faithful to his promises, and since the descendants of Abraham are almost in the same context as Abraham without land, they also see the possibility of realization the promises made to Abraham in their time.

Significantly, it is within the treatment of the divine speeches as prophetic speeches that the early Christians understood Abraham and his significance for their theology. Paul, especially, saw the divine speeches to Abraham as an appropriate foundation for the early church. In particular, he even went ahead to underscore the prophecy in the mere words of the author as also prophetic, hence his treatment of Genesis 15:6 as a prophecy which ultimately has relevance and fulfillment in the life of the early church (see Gal 3:6–29; Rom 4:9–25). For Paul and the early church, the divine speeches as well as the narratives surrounding these divine speeches are deemed prophetic, hence transforming the entire story into a prophecy that has its fulfillment in the salvific work of Jesus Christ.

4.4. Conclusion

The conscious presence of stylistic features in the divine speeches is indicative of a carefully discerned purpose since a distinctive style in a piece of a literary work is often an indication of intent.[79] In this sense, there is a correlation between stylistic devices and purpose. Thus, Eugene H. Falk described the style in a work in terms of "force" which provides a literary

---

79. Describing the connection between the artistry of Genesis and its artistry, M. H. Segal observed, "[t]he rich material of the book, with all its variety of style and vocabulary, is arranged methodologically and skillfully in a logical and chronological sequence, all forming a distinct and complete unity. The book is clearly the work of a . . .literary artist who composed it with a definite and preconceived plan and with fixed purpose . . ." [Segal, *The Pentateuch: Its Composition and its Authorship and other Biblical Studies* (Jerusalem: Magnes Press, 1967), 30]. Nothing shows this conceived purpose more fully than the concentration of stylistic features in the divine speeches.

work with a "thematic coherence." Speaking of this "force" of style in its relationship to purpose, Falk observed:

> If we recognize that style governs the cohesion of individual works, we may conclude that what may be called 'force' is the counterpart in literature of natural law in the sciences. Obviously, natural law is operative regardless of whether the emergence of a phenomenon is seen to be the result of chance occurrences, or of coincidental conditions, or of human experimentation. A work of literature *is* a creation, and therefore its cohesive wholeness is the result of a formative intention, of an application of stylistic means and patterns by which the parts are linked together and unified. As in the world of natural phenomena, this is true regardless of the degree of consciousness with which that intention is carried out.[80]

Even though his definition of the "stylistic forces" in the category of sequential, causal and generic forms is broadly conceived, his conclusion that style is a true indication of thematic coherence or higher purpose in a literary piece is quite helpful. In particular this conclusion suggests a possible function for the divine speeches. In this regard, this chapter presents the general characteristics and the possible ideological functions of these divine speeches to the original audiences of the author. These ideological functions include its purpose as speeches of hope, a vehicle of forging new identity, tools for polemics, instruments of legitimization, and it significance as prophetic oracles. Concerning the last function, the early church draws from the understanding that the divine speeches to Abraham were not merely speeches only meant for Abraham, but that these speeches had relevance which transcends the world of Abraham and the author to the world of the early church. For members of the early church, it was not the stylistic features of the text that was their primary concern but the prophetic nature of the divine speeches. They saw in Yahweh's speeches to Abraham

---

80. Eugene H. Falk, "Stylist Forces in the Narrative," *Patterns of Literary Style*, vol. 3, ed. Joseph Strelka (London: The Pennsylvania State University Press, 1971), 42.

a shared interest that, even though not originally envisaged by the author, no doubt lies within the border of his intent by the characterization of the divine speeches as prophecy.

CHAPTER FIVE

Conclusion

"Speech", observed Helmut Bonheim, "is a universal ingredient of narrative" which in most stories occupies a dominant place.[1] Significantly, the biblical narratives also describe characters whose speeches are clearly important to the understanding of the intent of the narratives. In particular, God in biblical narrative is also depicted as a speaker who by the medium of speech expresses his point of view, which most often conforms or verbalizes the unexpressed views of the author. If "God is the principal speaker in the Pentateuch," as argued by Clines,[2] then it is necessary to study his speeches in light of the possible connection which exists between his speeches and the intention of the author. On the other hand, even when we cannot ascertain fully the possible functions of the divine speeches in the entirety of the Pentateuch it remains true that "[n]o matter what the precise significance is, speech is a prominent element in the characterization of God in the Pentateuch."[3] This characterization is often achieved not merely by the vehicle of content but also by the means of stylistic form. The warning of Meier in respect to structural studies is also in place here. Meier observed:

> Because there is no means of separating random noise within a text from the necessary (or even optional) structural phenomena, one may easily attribute macro-structural significance to

---

1. Helmut Bonheim, *The Narrative Modes: Techniques of the Short Story* (Woodbridge, Suffolk: D. S. Brewer, 1982), 110.
2. Clines, *Interested Parties*, 203.
3. Ibid., 204; see also Dale Patrick, *The Rendering of God in the Old Testament*. Overtures to Biblical Theology, vol. 10 (Philadelphia: Fortress, 1981), 13–27.

insignificant features. This tendency is evident in structural studies of biblical literature that have proliferated in the past two decades, discerning great artistry and subtlety in nearly every biblical text analyzed. Chiasms and palindromes of even the most mundane linguistic features have become popular devices (in all biblical genres) whose discovery is sufficient to identify high art. Both discourse analysis and such structural studies suffer from the same lack of control, for it has long been a truism that the human mind can discover order even in the most chaotic field.[4]

As we come to the close of the present study we must ask ourselves whether we have really seen stylistic features in the divine speeches or are we under the kind of the delusion of the human mind as suggested by Meier? The various studies on the divine speeches by Labuschagne, Meier himself, White and Warning have shown generally the presence and use of stylistic devices in biblical narratives. Within the Abrahamic narratives in particular, the speeches of God are framed stylistically in order to underscore certain ideological functions. Consequently, the stylistic features in the divine speeches are not just a mere "shell of thought" which primarily serves an aesthetic function, but also helps to emboss the ideological functions of the six divine speeches within the Abrahamic cycle (Gen 12:1–9; 13:14–17; 15:1–21; 17:1–27; 18:1–33; 22:12–18).[5] To this end, the Abrahamic narrative was crafted in a specific way, with specific interests, specific characters and specific expectations. It is ideological in this sense because it is a story told in the narrow confinement of these specifics.

Coming to the last chapter, we will briefly review the findings of the preceding chapters. The first chapter presents the problem, the significance of the study, the pericopes of study, the delimitation and the defining research questions underpinning the present work.

Underscoring the stylistic character of biblical speeches, the second chapter engages the different studies that have been carried out on the

---

4. Meier, *Speaking of Speaking*, 16.
5. Nichols, "Rhetoric and Style," 141.

artistic nature of the divine speeches in biblical narratives. It first describes major works already done in the quest to understand various forms of literary devices used in direct discourses of biblical narrative. It also analyses specific literary works carried out primarily in divine speeches. In the general works on biblical speeches, we evaluated the works of Conroy, Revell, Longacre, Niccacci, Savran, and Miller, while on the specific works, we appraised the works of Labuschagne, White, Warning, and Meier. The review of these works reveals that there is a conscious literary artistry at work in biblical speeches, and most importantly, in the divine speeches. Secondly, it justifies the present quest to study the divine speeches. Lastly, the preceding works, despite the quest to understand the mechanics of biblical speeches, have generally ignored or glossed over the stylistic features and significance of the divine speeches particularly as seen in Abrahamic cycle.

The third chapter identifies the presence and use of stylistic devices within the divine speeches of the Abrahamic narratives. It studies each of the six pericopes in terms of its literary context, structure, textual analysis, quotative frames, syntactical considerations, possible dialogue, and then the different stylistic features of the six pericopes. We noted the presence and use of metaphor or metaphoric language, simile, irony, paronomasia, alliteration, euphemism, suspense, wordplay, gradation, repetition, and allusion. The overall summary of this chapter is that there is the presence of stylistic features in the speeches of the divine being which often are not found in the speeches of other characters of the Abrahamic cycle. The concentration of these stylistic features in the speeches of Yahweh ultimately reveals the importance that the author or redactor attaches to the divine speeches.

The fourth chapter draws a close relationship between stylistics and semantics. It underscores the thesis that divine speeches were not in the Abrahamic narratives for mere aesthetic or decorative purposes but that they rather, beyond their aesthetic quality, fulfill a semantic function. It is such semantic purposes that formed ultimately the basis for the original reason, which prompted the telling or writing of the story by the author. This chapter makes a general survey of the characteristics of the divine speeches, that is, their common features despite their possible origin in diverse sources. Why the author or redactor brought these sources together and what common features went through the speeches of Yahweh in these discourses. The general characteristics of the divine speeches are namely its excessive optimism, elevated language, futuristic orientation, spiritual relationship, particularistic worldview, and universal dimension. This chapter stresses the presence of these common denominators in the divine speeches and also underscores their possible functions. Looking at the divine speeches in the light of the study, the possible functions of these divine speeches are namely its usage as speeches of encouragement, a tool to legitimize social and religious categories, its role for the construction of identity, and its function as prophetic oracles. It is in the last function that the New Testament understands the stories of Abraham. In particular, it treats both the narration as well as the divine speeches as prophecies which find fulfillment in the person of Jesus Christ. Thus, whether in Pauline epistles or even in the Gospels, Abraham's seeds, for example, are not merely Jews, but encompass the people of every nationality who have welcomed or accepted the gospel of Jesus Christ. In this redefinition of the ideology of "seeds of Abraham" as found in the divine speeches of the Abrahamic stories, Abraham ceases to be the father of the Jews only but now the "father of the nations," hence the divine blessing is expected to reach the nations through Jesus Christ who is now conceived to be his "promised seed." In this understanding, he is typologically understood in the category of the new Isaac. Thus the New Testament explored the universalistic dimensions of the divine speeches in order to construct for these early church believers a new identity that transcends the original identity, which is primarily rooted in their physical ancestry to Abraham. This new identity moves the figure of Abraham from being a mere Jewish patriarch to now an international figure who is conceived to be the father of all people that are now united by their common exercise of faith as the children of Abraham. Significantly, this new identity is not based on promises of land, royalty, state, international expansion, or material prosperity or even the rite of circumcision, but on the identification of such a person to the ministry and death of Jesus Christ. Consequently the early church was not interested in the mere aesthetics of the Abrahamic text, but its prophetic character. This prophetic nature of the divine speeches, even though clearly envisaged by the author of the Abrahamic cycle, is now enhanced and redefined beyond the original intention which readily aided the construction of a new identity for a new people who are not "seeds of Abraham" in the original understanding but who now are "sons and daughters" of Abraham because of their faith in Jesus Christ. For the early church, Abraham is a prophet and the Abrahamic narratives are prophetic oracles that find their fulfillment in their own time. The futuristic elements or characteristics of the divine speeches and the construction of Abraham as a prophet already validate this prophetic connotation or reading of the Abrahamic narratives by the early church as prophecies.

The prophetic ideology of the divine speeches becomes not merely defined and limited around the original physical seeds of Abraham but now extends to all men and women in Jesus Christ. In this particular instance, the ideology moves beyond the restricted racial boundaries in order to speak to a new community of faith that is increasingly or predominantly Hellenistic in nature, hence embracing the ancient environment of the Greco-Roman world. It is within this ideological reference that the early church creates for herself a new identity as children of Abraham. Thus, after the passage of time, the speeches of Yahweh became a prophetic instrument in the founding of a new community of believers, hence suggesting the "intersubjective" identification of the early church with the divine speeches of the Abrahamic cycle.

If these ideologies become powerful tools to redefine or bring into being a new community by the exploration of its prophetic nature and power to create a new identity, is it also possible to read or understand these ideological functions of the divine speeches as universal or inter-cultural forms which function or redefine the identity of a people, providing them with the needed encouragement, enhancing their spirituality and providing them with a future far beyond their current existential realities? Could these divine speeches transcend their historical roots or attachment to a particular people in order to speak hope to a new world that the text itself never clearly envisaged? If the same text provided a new identity and hope for the New Testament church can this same text have relevance or importance for African, Asian, or Latin American churches which struggle daily with issues of identity, landlessness, hopelessness, insecurity, and dysfunctional states? Even though this line of thought is not immediately followed in this work, the Christocentric understanding of these divine speeches as purely prophetic text for the construction of their identity in purely spiritual forms could possibly be embraced in order to engage the physical and socio-political undertones behind these divine speeches in the Abrahamic narratives. Thus, while the pure spiritual reading and Christocentric interest should be maintained it should be enhanced in order to address the problem of landlessness, dysfunctional states, and possible ills of the African, Asian and Latin American societies. We could identify with the rhetoric and ideology of the text as we bring comfort and hope, a new identity, spiritual edification and prophetic insight to a world, which in many ways still looks like the world of the author that crafted this timeless tale.

From the preceding observations, the following conclusions become inevitable in the present study. Firstly, the study of the divine speeches underscores an interpenetrating relationship between the rhetoric and the possible existential concerns in the world of author. Since the author told his stories from the point of view of his present world, it is no doubt that divine speeches seek not merely to address the bygone times but also the world of the author. Secondly, one primary concern of the author is to provide hope, comfort and wellbeing for his world. He offers this hope and comfort by transforming or retelling the old stories of father Abraham for his original audience. Thirdly, the author provides the original readers with a new identity in a world that challenged or seemed to swallow the old identity of Israel. Lastly, the present study shows that the author spoke prophetically to the ills of his world by pointing his readers to a future whereby Yahweh will give them the land, international glory, nationhood, wealth and prosperity. This optimistic picture has continued to sound a familiar chord in the life of modern Israel, thus showing the overwhelming hope offered by the author in this portrait.

From the foregoing, the following recommendations could be made for the Christian church. Firstly, the leadership of the contemporary church, like the author of the Abrahamic cycle, must seek by all means to provide hope in the midst of landlessness, hopelessness and the identity crisis of the modern age. Secondly, the church, like the author, must take or treat seriously the existential realities of the present world and its relationship to the survival of its members. Thirdly, the Christian church must reiterate or invigorate a new identity which is not derived from the rituals of the church but on the true meaning of what it means to be a Christian and a child of Abraham. Similarly, the church must, like the author, speak prophetically to the ills of the present world as it particularly affects its parishioners. Lastly, like the author, despite his particular local interest, the church must create a universal or global vision whereby through its ministration, it will become a blessing to the nations of the earth. In this particular way, the church becomes a true replacement or continuance of the role of ancient Israel as the one who is positioned through the divine speeches to be a blessing to the nations of the earth.

Despite the different aspects covered in the present work, there are other areas that need further research since these areas were either deliberately ignored or not pursued. Four of these areas need further study. One of the areas is the need to make an independent study of the sources (J, E, D, P) and see the distinctive stylistic features of each of the sources especially in reference to the stylistic features of the divine speeches. Such diachronic methodology will throw light on the unique way by which each of the sources describes the divine speeches. This study will also highlight the possible functions which each of the sources uses as a particular aspect of the Abrahamic cycle. Even though the present work treats synchronically the functions of the divine speeches, the possibility of treating diachronically the functions of these divine speeches could also be pursued whereby instead of treating the functions of these sources as complementary, it may be possible to highlight the "tension" or even conflict between these functions. Secondly, further detailed or independent study needs to be done on the nature of the secondary speeches of other characters of the Abrahamic cycle and how these speeches define, develop or even conflict with the point of view of the divine speeches. The speeches of Abraham, Lot, Sarah, Pharaoh, his servants, king of Sodom, inhabitants of Sodom, Melchizedek, and other characters could show interesting uses of these speeches in order to enrich the plot of the Abrahamic narratives. It is even possible to show how these "secondary voices" within the text complement or even conflict with the "primary voice" or the "official character" of the Abrahamic narrative, namely God. Significantly, further study will need to be undertaken in order to show the harmony between these primary voices in order to truly understand the complexity of the divine voice in the Abrahamic cycle especially the intriguing relationship between the divine voice and the implied audience or the needs of the original readers. In what manner did the present existential context of the author influence his adapting, rephrasing and representing of the inherited Abrahamic tradition? In addition, further study needs to be undertaken in order to closely relate the ideological functions of these divine speeches in light of New Testament theology. This relationship is not merely a prophecy-fulfillment framework but to show how the New Testament redefined, reinterpreted or re-appropriated the ideologies of the divine speeches in order to confront the challenges of the Greco-Roman world. Lastly, the appropriation of the divine speeches should also engage the existential realities in our modern world, whether in Africa, Asia, the Americas or Europe, especially in the midst of the hopelessness, landlessness, identity crises, ethnic-psychological displacements, poverty, and political and religious unrest. In this engagement of the existential context, we move from the mere study of the stylistic features of the divine speeches towards understanding the true intention of the author who, though invisible, spoke to the concrete needs of his own world, and by following his footsteps, "all the families of the earth" will become once again blessed, or in the original words of the author, "וְנִבְרְכוּ בְךָ כֹּל מִשְׁפְּחֹת הָאֲדָמָה."

Bibliography

Aaron, David H. *Biblical Ambiguity: Metaphor, Semantics, and Divine Imagery.* Leiden: Brill, 2001.

Aczel, Richard. "Understanding as Over-hearing: Towards a Dialogics of Voice." *New Literary History* 32, no. 3 (2001): 597–617.

Ahlström, G. W. *The History of Ancient Palestine.* Minneapolis: Fortress, 1993.

Albright, W. F. *Archeology of Palestine and the Bible.* New York: Revell, 1935.

_____. *The Biblical Period from Abraham to Ezra.* Pittsburgh: The Biblical Colloquium, 1950.

_____. *From the Stone Age to Christianity,* 2d ed. Baltimore: John Hopkins Press, 1946.

_____. *Yahweh and the Gods of Canaan.* London: School of Oriental and African Studies, University of London, 1968.

Alexander, T. D. "A Literary Analysis of the Abraham Narrative in Genesis." [PhD Dissertation Queen's University of Belfast, 1982].

_____. "Lot's Hospitality: A Clue to His Righteousness." *JBL* 104 (1985): 289–91.

Allan, Keith and Kate Burridge, *Euphemism and Dysphemism: Language as Shield and Weapon.* New York: Oxford University Press, 1991.

Alston, W. M. "Genesis 18:1–11," *Int* 42 (1988): 397–402.

Alter, Robert. *The Art of Biblical Narrative.* New York: Basic Books, 1981.

_____. "Biblical Imperatives and Literary Play." *"Not in Heaven": Coherence and Complexity in Biblical Narrative,* eds. Jason P. Rosenblatt & Joseph C. Sitterson, Jr., 13–27. Bloomington: Indiana University Press, 1991.

_____. *Genesis: Translation and Commentary.* New York: W. W. Norton & Company, 1996.

_____. "How Convention Helps Us Read: The Case of the Bible's Annunciation Type-Scene." *Prooftexts* 3 (1983): 115–30.

_____. *The Pleasures of Reading in an Ideological Age.* New York: A Touchstone Book, 1989.

———. "Sodom as Nexus: The Web of Design in Biblical Narrative." *Tikkun* 1.1 (1986): 30–38.

Amit, Yairah. *Hidden Polemics in Biblical Narrative*, trans. Jonathan Chipman. Leiden: Brill, 2000.

———. "Progression as a Rhetorical Device in Biblical Literature." *JSOT* 28, no. 1 (2003): 3–32.

Andersen, Francis. *The Sentence in Biblical Hebrew*. Janua Linguarum, Series Practica 231. The Hague: Mouton, 1974.

Andrew D. H. Mayes, "Deuteronomistic Ideology and the Theology of the Old Testament." *JSOT* 82 (1999): 57–82.

Averbeck, Richard E., Mark W. Chavalas and David B. Weisberg, eds. *Life and Culture in the Ancient Near East*. Bethesda, Maryland: CDL press, 2003.

Avishur, Yitzhak. *Studies in Biblical Narrative: Style, Structure, and the Ancient Near Eastern Literary Background*. Tel Aviv-Jaffa, Israel: Archaeological Center Publication, 1999.

Axskjöld, Carl-Johan. *Aram as the Enemy Friend: The Ideological Role of Aram in the Composition of Genesis–2 Kings*. ConBOT 45. Stockholm: Almqvist & Wiksell, 1998.

Baden, Joel S. "The Tower of Babel: A Case Study in the Competing Methods of Historical and Modern Criticism." *JBL* 128, no. 2 (2009): 209–224.

Bailey, Nicholas A. "Some Literary and Grammatical Aspects of Genealogies in Genesis." *Biblical Hebrew and Discourse Linguistics*, ed. Robert D. Bergen, 267–282. np: Summer Institute of Linguistics, 1994.

Baker, D. W. "Diversity and Unity in the Literary Structure of Genesis." A.R. Millard and D.J. Wiseman, eds. *Essays on the Patriarchal Narratives*, 189–205. Leicester: IVP, 1980.

Bal, M. *Murder and Difference: Gender, Genre, and Scholarship on Sister's Death*, trans. M. Gumpert. Bloomington: Indiana University Press, 1988.

Balentine, S. E. "Prayers for Justice in the OT: Theodicy and Theology." *CBQ* 51 (1989): 597–616.

Banfield, A. *Unspeakable Sentences: Narration and Representation in the Language of Fiction*. Boston: Routledge, 1982.

Barnes, W. Emery. "Ancient Corrections in the Text of the Old Testament (*Tiqqun Sopherim*)." *The Canon and Masorah of the Hebrew Bible*, 379–414. New York: Ktav, 1974.

Barrick, William D. "The Integration of OT Theology with Bible Translation." *MSJ* 12, no. 1(2001): 15–31.

Barthes, Roland. "Style and Its Image." *Literary Style: A Symposium*, ed. Seymour Chatman, 3–15. London: Oxford University Press, 1971.

Bartor, Asnat. "The 'Juridical Dialogue: A Literary-Judicial Pattern." *VT* 53, no. 4 (2003): 445–464.

Beitzel, B. J. "Exodus 3:14 and the Divine Name: A Case of Biblical Paronomasia." *TJ* 1 (1980): 5–20.

Ben-Porat, Ziva. "The Poetics of Allusion: A Text-Linking Device." *A Semiotic Landscape: Proceedings of the First Congress of the International Association for Semiotic Studies*, ed. S. Chatman. The Hague: Mouton, 1979.

———. "The Poetics of Literary Allusion." *Journal for Descriptive Poetics and Theory of Literature* 1 (1976): 105–28.

Ben Zvi, E. "The Dialogue between Abraham and YHWH in Gen 18:23–32: A Historical–Critical Analysis." *JSOT* 53 (1992): 27–46.

Berger, Karol. "Diegesis and Mimesis: The Poetic Modes and the Matter of Artistic Presentation." *The Journal of Musicology* 12, no. 4 (1994): 407–433.

Berlin, Adele. *Poetics and Interpretation of Biblical Narrative*. Sheffield: Almond Press, 1983.

Bethlehem, Louise Shabat "Simile and Figurative Language." *Poetics Today*, vol. 17, no. 2 (1996): 203–240.

Biale, D. *Eros and the Jews: From Biblical Israel to Contemporary America*. New York: Basic Books, 1992.

Biddle, Mark E. *Polyphony and Symphony in Prophetic Literature: Reading Jeremiah 7–12*. Studies in Old Testament Interpretation, vol. 2. Macon, Georgia: Mercer University Press, 1996.

Bimson, J. J. "Archaelogical Data and the Dating of the Patriarch." A. R. Millard and D. J. Wiseman, eds. *Essays on the Patriarchal Narratives*, 59–92. Leicester: IVP, 1980.

Blenkinsopp, Joseph. "Abraham as Paradigm in the Priestly History of Genesis." *JBL* 128, no. 2 (2009): 225–241.

———. "Abraham and the Righteous of Sodom." *JJS* 33 (1982): 119–32.

———. "The Judge of All the Earth: Theodicy in the Midrash on Gen 18:22–33." *JJS* 41 (1990): 1–12.

———. *The Pentateuch: An Introduction to the First Five Books of the Bible*. The Anchor Bible Reference Library. New York: Doubleday, 1999.

———. *The Pentateuch*. New York: Doubleday, 1992.

Bloom, H. trans. D. Rosenberg, *The Book of J*. London: Faber & Faber, 1991.

Blum, E. *Die Komposition der Vätergeschichte*. Neukirchen: Neukirchener Verlag, 1984.

Blum-kulka, Shoshana, ed. *Politeness*. Amsterdam: North-Holland, 1990.
Bonheim, Helmut. *The Narrative Modes: Techniques of the Short Story*. Woodbridge, Suffolk: D. S. Brewer, 1982.
Bonneau, Normand. "The Illusion of Immediacy: A Narrative-Critical Exploration of the Bible's Predilection for Direct Discourse." *Theoforum* 31 (2000): 131–151.
Bradford, Susan. *Genesis*. Septuagint Commentary Series. Leiden: Brill, 2007.
Brenner, A. and Fokkelien van Dijk-Hemmes, *On Gendering Texts: Female and Male Voices in the Hebrew Bible*. Leiden: Brill, 1993.
Brensinger, L. "נָסָה." *Dictionary of Old Testament Theology and Exegesis*, vol. 3, ed. Willem A. VanGemeren, 111–113. Grand Rapids, Michigan: Zondervan, 1997.
Brett, Mark G. *Genesis: Procreation and the Politics of Identity*. London: Routledge, 2000.
Brettler, Marc Zvi. *The Creation of History in Ancient Israel*. London: Routledge, 1995.
Brewer, William F. "The Nature of Narrative Suspense and the Problem of Rereading." *Suspense: Conceptualizations, Theoretical Analyses, and Empirical Explorations*, eds. Peter Vorderer, Hans Jürgen Wulff and Mike Friedrichsen, 107–128. Mahwah, New Jersey: Erlbaum, 1996.
Brichto, Herbert C. *Toward a Grammar of Biblical Poetics: Tales of the Prophets*. New York: Oxford University Press, 1992.
Bright, John. *A History of Israel*, 3d ed. Philadelphia: Westminster, 1981.
Brodie, Thomas L. *Genesis as Dialogue: A Literary, Historical and Theological Commentary*. London: Oxford University, 2001.
Brown, Penelope and Stephen C. Levinson. *Politeness: Some Universals in Language Usage*. Cambridge: Cambridge University Press, 1999.
Brown, William P. *Seeing the Psalms: A Theology of Metaphor*. Louisville, Kentucky: Westminster John Knox Press, 2002.
Brueggemann, Walter. *Cadence of Home: Preaching Among Exiles*. Louisville: Westminster John Knox, 1997.
_____. *Genesis*. Interpretation. Atlanta: John Knox, 1982.
_____. "'Impossibility' and Epistemology in the Faith Tradition of Abraham and Sarah (Gen 18:1–15)." *ZAW* 94 (1982): 615–34.
_____. "Jeremiah's Use of Rhetorical Questions." *JBL* 92 (1973): 358–374.
_____. *The Land: Place as Gift, Promise, and Challenge in Biblical Faith*, 2ed. Minneapolis: Fortress Press, 2002.

Bullinger, E. W. *Figures of Speech Used in the Bible*. Grand Rapids, MI: Baker, 1968.

Caird, G. B. *The Language and Imagery of the Bible*. Philadelphia: The Westminster Press, 1980.

Carasik, Michael. "The Limits of Omniscience." *JBL* 119, no. 2 (2000): 221–232.

Carr, D. M. *Reading the Fractures of Genesis: Historical and Literary Approaches*. Louisville, Kentucky: Westminster Press, 1996.

Casanowicz, Immanuel M. *Paronomasia in the Old Testament*. Boston: Norwood Press, 1894.

Cassuto, Umberto. *A Commentary on the Book of Exodus*, trans. Israel Abrahams, reprint. Jerusalem: Magnes and The Hebrew University, 1983.

_____. *A Commentary on the Book of Genesis: From Noah to Abraham*, vo. 2. Jerusalem: Magnes, 1964.

_____. *From Noah to Abraham*. Jerusalem: Magnes, 1964.

Chatman, Seymour. *Coming to Terms: The Rhetoric of Narrative in Fiction and Film*. Ithaca, New York: Cornell University Press, 1990.

Chisholm, Jr., Robert B. "Wordplay in the Eighth-Century Prophets." *BSac* 144, no. 573 (1987): 44–52.

Christensen, Duane L. "Anticipatory Paronomasia in Jonah 3:7–8 and Genesis 37:2." *RB* 90, no. 1 (1983): 261–263.

Clements, Ronald. *Abraham and David: Genesis XV and its Meaning for Israelite Tradition*. London: SCM, 1967.

Clines, D. J. A, ed. *The Dictionary of Classical Hebrew*, vol. II, Sheffield: Sheffield Academic Press, 1995.

_____. *The Dictionary of Classical Hebrew*, vol. III. Sheffield: Sheffield Academic Press, 1996.

_____. *The Dictionary of Classical Hebrew*, vol. V. Sheffield: Sheffield Academic Press, 2001.

_____. *The Dictionary of Classical Hebrew*, vol. VI. Sheffield: Sheffield Academic Press, 2007.

_____. *Interested Parties: The Ideology of Writers and Readers of the Hebrew Bible*. JSOTSup Series 205. Sheffield: Sheffield Academic Press, 1995.

_____. *The Theme of Pentateuch*. JSOTSup 10. Sheffield: JSOT, 1978.

Coats, G. W. "Lot: A Foil in the Abraham Saga." *Understanding the Word: FS B. W. Anderson*, ed. J. T. Butler, E. W. Conrad, and B. C. Ollenburger. JSOTSup 371, 13–32. Sheffield: JSOT Press, 1985.

Coats, George W. *Genesis: With an Introduction to Narrative Literature*. Grand Rapids, MI: William B. Eerdmans Publishing Co, 1983.

Cohen, Mordechai Z. *Three Approaches to Biblical Metaphor: from Abraham Ibn Ezra and Maimonides to David Kimhi*. Leiden, The Netherlands: Koninklijke Brill, 2003.

Cohn, D. *Transparent Minds: Narrative Modes for Presenting Consciousness in Fiction*. Princeton: Princeton University Press, 1978.

Cohn, Robert L. "Narrative Structure and Canonical Perspective in Genesis," *JSOT* 25 (1983): 3–16.

Conroy, Charles. *Absalom!: Narrative and Language in 2 Sam 13–20*. Rome: Biblical Institute Press, 1978.

Coombs, James H. "Allusion Defined and Explained." *Poetics* 13 (1984): 475–88.

Corbett, Patrick. *Ideologies*. London: Hutchinson & Co, 1970.

Cotter, David W. *Berit Olam: Studies in Hebrew Narrative and Poetry-Genesis*. Collegeville, Minnesota: The Liturgical Press, 2003.

Craig Jr., Kenneth M. *A Poetic of Jonah: Art in the Service of Ideology*. Columbia, South Carolina: University of South Carolina Press, 1991.

_____. "Rhetorical Aspects of Questions Answered with Silence in 1 Samuel 14:27 and 28:6." *CBQ* 56 (1994): 221–239.

Crenshaw, James. *Prophet Conflict*. BZAW 123. New York: Walter de Gruyter, 1971.

Cross, Jr., Frank M. "Yahweh and the God of the Patriarchs." *HTR* 55 (1962): 225–59.

Damrosch, David. *The Narrative Covenant: Transformations of Genre in the Growth of Biblical Literature*. San Francisco: Harper & Row, 1987.

Davies, E. W. *The Dissenting Reader: Feminist Approaches to the Hebrew Bible*. Aldershot: Ashgate, 2003.

Davies, Philips R. and David M. Gunn, "Pentateuchal Patterns: An Examination of C. J. Labuschagne's Theory." *VT* 34, no. 4 (1984): 399–406.

Dawson, David Allan. *Textlinguistics and Biblical Hebrew*. JSOTSup 177. Sheffield: Sheffield Academic Press, 1994.

Delaney, C. "Abraham and the Seeds of Patriarchy." *Genesis: A Feminist Companion to the Bible*, ed. Athalya Brenner. Sheffield: Sheffield Academic Press, 1998.

de Regt, L. "Devices of Participant Reference in Some Biblical Hebrew Texts: Their Importance in Translation." *Jaarbericht "Ex Oriente Lux,"* 32 (1991–92): 150–71.

———. *Participants in Old Testament Texts and the Translator: Reference Devices and their Rhetorical Impact.* Assen, The Netherlands: Van Gorcum, 1999.

de Vaux, R. *The Early History of Israel*, trans. D. Smith. Philadelphia: Westminster, 1978.

Deurloo, K. A. "Narrative Geography in the Abraham Cycle." *OtSt* 26 (1990): 48–62.

Diamond, A. R. Pete. "Interlocutions: The Poetics of Voice in the Figuration of YHWH and His Oracular Agent, Jeremiah." *Int* (2008): 48–65.

Dorson, R. M. "Oral Styles of American Folk Narrators." *Style in Language.* Cambridge, Massachusetts: Cambridge University Press, 1960.

Dreifuss, Gustav and Judith Reimer, *Abraham: The Man and the Symbol. A Jungian Interpretation of the Biblical Story.* Wilmette, Illinois: Chiron, 1995.

Ehrensvärd, Martin. "Why Biblical Texts Cannot Be Dated Linguistically." *Hebrew Studies* 47 (2006): 177–189.

Ekkehart Malotki, *Hopi Time.* Berlin: Mouton, 1983.

Ellingworth, Paul and Aloo Mojola, "Translating Euphemisms in the Bible." *BT* 37, no. 1 (1986): 139–143.

Emerton, John A. "Abraham and Damascus in Some Greek and Latin Texts of the Hellenistic Period," *Sacred History, Sacred Literature: Essays on Ancient Israel, the Bible, and Religion in Honor of R.E. Friedman on His Sixtieth Birthday*, ed. Shawna Dolansky, 179–193. Winona Lake, Indiana: Eisenbrauns, 2008.

Enright, D. J. ed. *Fair of Speech: The Uses of Euphemism.* Oxford: Oxford University Press, 1986.

Eskhult, Mats. *Studies in Verbal and Narrative Technique in Biblical Hebrew Prose.* Acta Universitatis Upsaliensis, Studia Semitica Upsaliensia 12. Uppsala: Almqvist, 1990.

Exum, J. Cheryl. "Of Broken Pots, Fluttering Birds and Visions in the Night: Extended Simile and Poetic Technique in Isaiah." *CBQ* 43 (1981): 331–352.

Falk, Eugene H. "Stylist Forces in the Narrative." *Patterns of Literary Style*, vol. 3, ed. Joseph Strelka, 42–50. London: The Pennsylvania State University Press, 1971.

Fields, W. W. "The Motif 'Night as Danger' associated with Three Biblical Destruction Narratives." "Sha'arei Talmon": *Studies in the Bible, Qumran and the Ancient Near East presented to S. Talmon, ed.* M. Fishbane and E. Tov, 17–32. Winona Lake: Eisenbrauns, 1992.

Fludernick, M. *The Fictions of Language and the Languages of Fiction: The Linguistic Representation of Speech and Consciousness.* London: Routledge, 1993.

Fokkelman, Jan P. *Narrative Art and Poetry in the Books of Samuel: A Full Interpretation Based on Stylistic and Structural Analyses*, vol. 1–4. Assen, The Netherlands: Van Gorcum, 1993.

———. *Narrative Art in Genesis: Specimens of Stylistic and Structural Analysis.* Eugene, Oregon: Wipf and Stock Publishers, 1991.

Fowl, Stephen E. *Engaging Scriptures: A Model for Theological Interpretation.* Oxford: Blackwell Publishing, 1998.

———. "Texts Don't Have Ideologies." *BibInt* 3, no. 1 (1995): 15–34.

Fox, Michael V. *Character and Ideology in the Book of Esther.* Columbia, South Carolina: University of South Carolina Press, 1991.

Frank, J. "You Call that a Rhetorical Question? Forms and Functions of Rhetorical Questions in Conversation." *JP* 14 (1990): 723–738.

Frow, John. *Genre: the New Critical Idiom.* London: Routledge, 2005.

Fuchs, Esther. *Sexual Politics in the Biblical Narrative: Reading the Hebrew Bible as a Woman*, JSOTSup 310. Sheffield: Sheffield Academic Press, 2000.

Garber, Marjorie. "'Greatness': Philology and the Politics of Mimesis." *Boundary 2*, 19, no. 2 (1992): 233–259.

Garsiel, Moshe. *Biblical Names: A Literary Study of Midrashic Deriviations and Puns.* Ramat Gan: Bar-llan University press, 1991.

Genette, Gerard. Nitsa Ben-Ari, and Brian McHale, "Fictional Narrative, Factual Narrative." *Poetics Today* 11, no. 4 (1990): 755–774.

Gesenius, *Gesenius' Hebrew Grammar* ed. E. Kautsch, trans. A. E. Cowley. London: OUP, 1910; repr. 1966.

Gibson, J. C. L. *Language and Imagery in the Old Testament.* Peabody, MA: Hendrickson Publishers, nd.

Gillmayr-Bucher, Susanne. "The Woman of Their Dreams: The Image of Rebekah in Genesis 24." *The World of Genesis: Person, Places and Perspectives*, eds. P. R. Davies and D. J. A. Clines. JSOTSup 257. Sheffield: Sheffield Academic Press, 1998.

Gilmour, Rachelle. "Suspense and Anticipation in 1 Samuel 9:1–14." *JJSC* 9, no. 10 (2009): 2–16.

Ginsburg, Christian D. *Introduction to the Massoretico-Critical Edition of the Hebrew.* New York: Ktav, 1966.

Goddard, Harold. *The Meaning of Shakespeare*, vol. 2. Chicago: Chicago University Press, 1965.

Goldenberg, Gideon. "On Direct Speech and the Hebrew Bible." *Studies in Hebrew and Aramaic Syntax Presented to Professor J. Hoftijzer on the Occasion of his Sixty-fifth Birthday*, eds. K. Jongeling, H.L. Murre-Van Den Berg and I. Van Rompay, 79–96. Leiden: Brill, 1991.

Goldingay, John. "The Patriarchs in Scripture and History." A. R. Millard and D. J. Wiseman, eds. *Essays on the Patriarchal Narratives*, 11–42. Leicester: IVP, 1980.

———. "The Place of Ishmael." *The World of Genesis: Persons, Places, Perspectives*, eds. Philip R. Davies and David J. A. Clines. JSOTSup Series 257, 146–149. Sheffield: Sheffield Academic Press, 1998.

———. *Theological Diversity and the Authority of the Old Testament*. Grand Rapids, Michigan: Eerdmans, 1987.

Good, Edwin M. *Irony in the Old Testament*. Sheffield: The Almond Press, 1981.

Goodman, D. "Do Angels Eat?" *Journal of Jewish Studies* 37 (1986): 160–75.

Goshen-Gottstein, M. "Abraham-Lover or Beloved of God." *Love and Death in the Ancient near East: Essays in Honor of Marvin H. Pope*, eds. J. H. Marks and R. M. Good, 101–104. Guilford: Four Quarters, 1987.

Green, R. W. *The Role of Human Sacrifice in the Ancient Near East*. ASOR Dissertation Series 1. Missoula, Massachusetts: Scholars, 1975.

Greenstein, Edward L. "Jethro's Wit: An Interpretation of Wordplay in Exodus 18." *On the Way to Nineveh*, eds. Stephen L. Cook and S. C. Winter, 155–171. Atlanta, Georgia: Scholars Press, 1999.

Greifenhagen, F. V. *Egypt on the Pentateuch's Ideological Map: Constructing Biblical Israel's Identity*. JSOTSup Series 361, eds. David J. A. Clines et al. Sheffield: Sheffield Academic Press, 2002.

Grintz, Jehoshua M. "Hebrew As the Spoken and Written Language in the Last Days of the Second Temple." *JBL* 79 (1960): 32–47.

Grisanti, Michael A. "The Missing Mandate: Missions in the Old Testament," *Missions in a New Millennium: Change and Challenges in World Missions*, ed. by W. Edward Glenny and William H. Smallman. Grand Rapids: Kregel, 2000.

Gruber, M. I. "The Many Faces of Hebrew נשא פנים 'lift up the face.'" *ZAW* 95 (1983): 252–60.

Grüneberg, K. N. *Abraham, Blessing and the Nations: A Philological and Exegetical Study of Genesis 12:3 in its Narrative*. Berlin: Walter de Gruyter, 2003.

Guiraud, Pierre. "Immanence and Transitivity of Stylistic Criteria." *Literary Style: A Symposium*, ed. Seymour Chatman, 16–23. London: Oxford University Press, 1971.

Gunkel, Hermann. *Genesis: übersetzt und erklärt.* 6th ed. Göttingen: Vandenhoeck, 1964.

———. *Genesis.* Macon, Georgia: Mercer University Press, 1997.

———. *The Legends of Genesis: The Biblical Saga and History,* trans. W. H. Carruth. New York: Schocken, 1966.

———. *The Stories of Genesis,* trans. John Scullion, ed. William Scott. Vallejo, California: Bibal Press, 1994.

Gunn, D. M. and D. N. Fewell, *Narrative in the Hebrew Bible.* OBS. London: Oxford University Press, 1993.

Gutmann, J. "Abraham in the Fire of the Chaldeans: A Jewish Legend in Jewish, Christian and Islamic Art." Frühmittelalterliche Studien: Jahrbuch des Instituts fur Frühmittelalterforschung der Universität Münster 7 (1973): 342–52.

Habel, Norman C. *The Land is Mine: Six Biblical Land Ideologies.* Overtures to Biblical Theology. Minneapolis: Fortress Press, 1995.

Habel, Udo J. *Intertextuality, Allusion, and Quotation: An International Bibliography of Critical Studies.* Westport, CT: Greenwood, 1989.

Hackett, J. A. "Religious Traditions in Israelite Transjordan." *Ancient Israelite Religion: Essays in Honor of Frank Moore Cross,* eds. P. D. Miller, P. D. Hanson and S. D. McBride. Philadelphia: Fortress, 1987.

Hallo, William. "Scurrilous Etymologies." *Pomegranates and Gold Bells: Studies in Biblical, Jewish, and Near Eastern Ritual, Law, and Literature in Honor of Jacob Milgrom,* eds. David P. Wright, David Noel Freedman and Avi Hurvitz, 767–776. Winona Lake, Indiana: Eisenbraus, 1995.

Hamilton, Victor P. *The Book of Genesis: Chapters 1–17.* Grand Rapids, MI: William B. Eerdmans Publishing Co, 1990.

Hans, Nobel. "gedachten tellen. Numerieke structuuranalyse en de elf gedachten Gods in de Genesis - 2Koningen."[PhD Dissertation University of Groningen, 1993].

Hartley, John E. *Genesis: New International Biblical Commentary.* OTS. Peabody, Massachusetts: Hendrickson Publishers, 2000.

Hatav, G. "(Free) Direct Discourse in Biblical Hebrew." *Hebrew Studies* 41 (2000): 7–30.

Havrelock, Rachel. "The Myth of Birthing the Hero: Heroic Barrenness in the Hebrew Bible." *BibInt* 16 (2008): 154–178.

Hays, J. Daniel. "Has the Narrator Come to Praise Solomon or to Bury Him? Narrative Subtlety in 1 Kings 1–11." *JSOT* 28, no. 2 (2003): 149–174.

Heard, R. C. *Dynamics of Diselection: Ambiguity in Genesis 12–36 and Ethnic Boundaries in Post-Exilic Judah*. Atlanta, Georgia: Society of Biblical Literature, 2001.

Held, M. "Rhetorical Questions in Ugaritic and Biblical Hebrew." *Eretz-Israel: Archaeological, Historical and Geographical Studies* 9 (1969): 71–79.

Hendel, Ronald S. "Aniconism and Anthropomorphism in Ancient Israel." *The Image and the Book: Iconic Cults, Aniconism, and the Rise of Book Religion in Israel and the Ancient Near East*, ed. Karel van der Toorn, 205–228. Bondgenostenlaan: Uitgeverij Peeters, 1997.

_____. "Leitwort Style and Literary Structure in the J Primeval Narrative." *Sacred History, Sacred Literature: Essays on Ancient Israel, the Bible, and Religion in Honor of R. E. Friedman on His Sixtieth Birthday*, ed. Shawna Dolansky, 93–109. Winona Lake, Indiana: Eisenbraus, 2008.

Herzberg, Walter. *Polysemy in the Bible*. University Microfilms International, 1981.

Hess, Richard S. "Issues in the Study of Personal Names in the Hebrew Bible." *CR:BS* 6 (1998): 169–192.

Hiebert, Theodore. "The Tower of Babel and the Origin of World's Cultures." *JBL* 126, no. 1 (2007): 29–58.

Holter, Knut. "The Wordplay on ('God') in Isaiah 45:20–21." *SJOT* 7, no. 1 (1993): 88–98.

Honeyman, A. M. "Merismus in Biblical Hebrew." *JBL* 17, no. 1 (1952): 11–18.

Horwitz, W. J. "Audience Reaction to Jeremiah." *CBQ* 32 (1970): 555–64.

Hough, Graham G. *Style and Stylistics*. London: Routledge, 1969.

Houtman, Alberdina. "The Role of Abraham in Targum Isaiah." *AS* 3, no. 1 (2005): 3–14.

Howard, Jr., D. M. and M. Grisanti, eds., *Giving the Sense: Understanding and Using Old Testament Historical Text*. Grand Rapids: Kregel, 2003.

Jacobsen, Thorkild. *The Treasure of Darkness: A History of Mesopotamian Religion*. New Haven: Yale University Press, 1976.

Jahn, M. "Contextualizing Represented Speech and Thought." *JP* 17 (1992): 347–67.

Jeansonne, S. P. "The Characterization of Lot in Genesis." *BTB* 18 (1988): 123–29.

Johnstone, Barbara. *Repetition in Arabic Discourse: Paradigms, Syntagms, and the Ecology of the Language*. Amsterdam: Benjamin Publishers, 1991.

Joseph A. Fitzmyer, "The Interpretation of Genesis 15:6: Abraham's Faith and Righteousness in a Qumran Text." *Emanuel: Studies in Hebrew Bible*

Septuagint and Dead Sea Scrolls in Honor of Emanuel Tov, eds. Shalom M. Paul, Robert A. Kraft, Lawrence H. Schiffman and Weston W. Fields, 257–268. Leiden: Brill, 2003.

Joüon, Paul and T. Muraoka, *A Grammar of Biblical Hebrew*. SB 27. Rome: Pontifical Biblical Institute, 2008.

Kaddari, Menaḥem Zevi. "The Syntax of כִּי clause in the Language of Ben Sira." *The Hebrew of the Dead Sea Scrolls and Ben Sira: Proceedings of a Symposium Held at Leiden University* 11–14 December 1995, eds. T. Muraoka and J. F. Elwolde, 87–91. Leiden: Brill, 1997.

Kalimi, Isaac. "The Land of Moraih, Mount Moriah, and the Site of Solomon's Temple in Biblical Historiography." *HTR* 83, no. 4 (1990): 345–362.

———. "Paronomasia in the Book of Chronicles." *JSOT* 67 (1995): 27–41.

Kaminsky, Joel S. "Humor and the Theology of Hope: *Isaac as a Humorous Figure*." *Int* (2000): 363–375.

Kawashima, Robert S. *Biblical Narrative and the Death of the Rhapsode*. Bloomington: Indiana University Press, 2004.

Keel, Othmar. *The Symbolism of the Biblical World: Ancient Near Eastern Iconography and the Book of Psalms*, trans. Timothy J. Hallett. Winona Lake, Indiana: Eisenbraus, 1997.

Kitchen, K. A. "Genesis 12–50 in the Near Eastern World." *He Swore an Oath: Biblical Themes from Genesis 12–50, Studies for D. J. Wiseman*, 67–92. Cambridge: Tyndale House, 1993.

———. *On the Reliability of the Old Testament*. Grand Rapids: Eerdmans, 2003.

———. "The Patriarchal Age: Myth or History?" *BAR* 21 (1995): 48–57.

Kittay, Eva. *Metaphor: Its Cognitive Force and Linguistic Structure*. Oxford: Clarendon Press, 1987.

Kogut, S. "On the Meaning and Syntactic Status of הִנֵּה Biblical Hebrew." *Studies in Bible*, ed. S. Japhet, 132–54. Jerusalem: Magnes Press, 1986.

Konkel, A. H. "צעקה." *Dictionary of Old Testament Theology and Exegesis*, vol. 3, ed. Willem A. VanGemeren, 827–30. Grand Rapids, Michigan: Zondervan, 1997.

———. "זעקה." *Dictionary of Old Testament Theology and Exegesis*, vol. 1, ed. Willem A. VanGemeren. Grand Rapids, Michigan: Zondervan, 1997.

Koop, R. "Rhetorical Questions and Implied Meaning in the Book of Job." *BT* 39 (1988): 415–423.

Kövecses, Zoltán. *Metaphor: A Practical Introduction*. Oxford: Oxford University Press, 2002.

Kugel, James L. *Traditions of the Bible: A Guide to the Bible As it was at the Start of the Common Era*. Cambridge, Massachusetts: Harvard University Press, 1998.

Labuschagne, Casper J. "Additional Remarks on the Pattern of the Divine Speech Formulas in the Pentateuch." *VT* 34, no. 1 (1984): 91–95.

_____. "The Pattern of the Divine Speech Formulas in the Pentateuch." *VT* 3 (1982): 268–96.

_____. "Pentateuchal Patterns: A Reply to P.R. Davies and D.M. Gunn." *VT* 34, no. 4 (1984): 407–413.

_____. "Some Significant Composition Techniques in Deuteronomy." *Scripta Signa Vocis: Studies about Scripts, Scriptures, Scribes and Languages in the Near East Presented to J. H. Hospers*, ed. H. L. J. Vanstiphout et al, 121–31 Groningen: Egbert Forsten, 1986.

_____. "Significant Compositional Techniques in the Psalms: Evidence for the Use of Number as an Organizing Principle." *VT* 59 (2009): 583–605.

Lakoff, George. "The Contemporary Theory of Metaphor." *Metaphor and Thought*, ed. Andrew Ortony, 202–251. 2ed. Cambridge: Cambridge University Press, 1993.

_____ and Mark Johnson, *Metaphors We Live By*. Chicago: The University of Chicago Press, 1980.

Larrain, Jorge. *The Concept of Ideology*. London: Hutchinson & Co., 1984.

Lasine, S. "Guest and Host in Judges 19: Lot's Hospitality in an Inverted World." *JSOT* 29 (1984): 37–59.

Latvus, Kari. *God, Anger and Ideology: The Anger of God in Joshua and Judges in Relation to Deuteronomy and the Priestly Writings*. JSOTSup Series 279, eds. David J. A. Clines et al. Sheffield: Sheffield Academic Press, 1998.

Leeb, Carolyn S. *Away from the Father's House: The Social Location of Na'ar and Na'arah in Ancient Israel*. JSOTSup 301. Sheffield: Sheffield Academic Press, 2000.

Leenzenberg, Marten Michiel. *Context of Metaphor: Semantic and Conceptual Aspects of Figurative Language Interpretation*. Plantage Muidergracht: Universiteit van Amsterdam, 1995.

Lemche, N. P. *Ancient Israel: A New History of Israelite Society*, trans. F. Cryer. Sheffield: JSOT Press, 1988.

_____. *The Canaanites and their Land*. JSOTSup Series 110, eds. David J. A. Clines and Philip R. Davies. Sheffield: Sheffield Academic Press, 1991.

_____. *The Israelite in History and Tradition*. London: SPCK, 1998.

Leonard, Jeffrey M., "Identifying Inner Biblical Allusions: Psalm 78 as a Test Case," *JBL* 127, no. 2 (2008): 241–265.

Levenson, J. D. *The Death and Resurrection of the Beloved Son: The Transformation of Child Sacrifice in Judaism and Christianity.* New Haven: Yale University.

Levine, Baruch A. "'Seed' Versus 'Womb': Expressions of Male Dominance in Biblical Israel." *Sex and Gender in the Ancient Near East,* eds. Simo Parpola and R.M. Whiting, Part II. Proceedings of the XLVII Roncontre Assyriologique Internationale, Helsinki, 337–343. Helsinki: The Neo-Assyrian Text Corpus Project, 2002.

Levine, Nachman. "Twice As Much of Your Spirit: Pattern, Parallel and Paronomasia in the Miracle of Elijah and Elisha." *JSOT* 85 (1999): 25–46.

———. "Sarah/Sodom: Birth, Destruction and Synchronic Transaction." *JSOT* 31, no. 2 (2006): 131–146.

Long, V. P. ed., *Israel's Past in the Present Research: Essays on Ancient Israelite Historiography.* Winona Lake, Indiana: Eisenbraus, 1999.

Longacre, Robert E. *An Anatomy of Speech Notions.* Lisse: Peter de Ridder, 1976.

———. "Discourse." *Tagmemics,* vol. 1, Aspects of the Field, eds. R. M. Brend and K. L. Pike. The Hague: Mouton, 1976.

———. "Discourse Peak As Zone of Turbulence." *Beyond the Sentence: Discourse and Sentential Form,* ed. Jessica R. Wirth. Ann Arbor: Karoma Publishers, 1985.

———. *The Grammar of Discourse.* TLL. New York: Plenium, 1983.

———. *Joseph: A Story of Divine Providence—A Text Theoretical and Textlinguistic Analysis of Genesis 37 and 39–48.* Winona Lake, Indiana: Eisenbraus, 1989.

Luzzatto, Samuel D. *Prolegomena to a Grammar of the Hebrew Language,* trans. Aaron D. Rubin. New Jersey: Gorgias Press, 2005.

Mafico, T. J. "The Crucial Question concerning the Justice of God." *JTSA* 42 (1983): 11–16.

Magonet, Jonathan. *Bible Lives.* London: SCM Press, 1992.

Mann, Thomas W. *The Book of the Torah: The Narrative Integrity of the Pentateuch.* Louisville, Kentucky: John Knox Press, 1988.

Margolin, Uri. "Naming and Believing: Practices of the Proper Name in Narrative Fiction." *Narrative* 10, no. 2 (2002): 107–127.

Martens, E. *Plot and Purpose in the Old Testament.* Leicester, InterVarsity Press, 1981.

Martin, Gary D. *Multiple Originals: New Approaches to Hebrew Bible Textual Criticism.* SBL. Atlanta, Georgia: Scholars Press, 2010.

Matthews, Kenneth A. *Genesis 11:27–50:26*. The New American Commentary, vol. 1B. Nashville, Tennessee: Broadman & Holman Publishers, 2005.

Matthews, V. H. "Hospitality and Hostility in Genesis 19 and Judges 19." *BTB* 22 (1992): 3–11.

McDonald, J. "Some Distinctive Characteristics of Israelite Spoken Hebrew." *BO* 32 (1975): 162–75.

McEvenue, S. E. *The Narrative Style of the Priestly Writer*. Analecta biblica. Rome: Biblical Institute Press, 1971.

McFall, Leslie. *The Enigma of the Hebrew Verbal System: Solutions from Ewald to the Present Day*. Historic Texts and Interpreters in Biblical Scholarship. Sheffield: Almond, 1982.

Mckane, William. "Observations on the Tiḳḳûnê Sôpe'rim." *On Language, Culture, and Religion: In Honour of Eugene A. Nida*, eds. M. Black and W. Smalley. Approaches to Semiotics 56, 53–77. The Hague: Mouton, 1974.

McKeown, James. *Genesis*. The Two Horizons Old Testament Commentary. Grand Rapids, Michigan: William B. Eerdmans Publishing Co., 2008.

Meier, Samuel A. *Speaking of Speaking: Marking Direct Discourse in the Hebrew Bible*. Leiden: Brill, 1992.

Melamed, E. Z. "Euphemisms and Textual Alterations of Expressions in Talmudic Literature." *Benjamin De Vries Volume*, ed., E. Z. Melamed, 119–48. Jerusalem: Tel Aviv University Research Authority, 1968.

———. "Euphemisms and Textual Alterations in the Mishnaic and Midrashic Texts." *Leš* 47 (1983): 3–17.

Meltzer, Tova. "Stylistics For the Study of Ancient Texts: Wanderings in the Borderlands." *Discourse Analysis of Biblical Literature: What it is and What it offers*. Semeia Studies. SBL, 131–141. Atlanta, Georgia: Scholars Press, 1995.

Miner, Earl. "Allusion." *Princeton Encyclopedia of Poetry and Poetics*, ed. Alex Preminger et al. Princeton, NJ: Princeton University Press, 1974.

Mettinger, Tryggve N. D. "Israelite Aniconism: Developments and Origins." *The Image and the Book: Iconic Cults, Aniconism, and the Rise of Book Religion in Israel and the Ancient Near East*, ed. Karel van der Toorn, 173–204. Bondgenostenlaan: Uitgeverij Peeters, 1997.

Mikos, Lothar. "The Experience of Suspense: Between Fear and Pleasure." *Suspense: Conceptualizations, Theoretical Analyses, and Empirical Explorations*, eds. Peter Vorderer, Hans Jürgen Wulff and Mike Friedrichsen, 37–49. Mahwah, New Jersey: Erlbaum, 1996.

Miles, Josephine. "Style as Style." *Literary Style: A Symposium*, ed. Seymour Chatman, 24–28. London: Oxford University Press, 1971.

Millard, A. R. "Methods of Studying the Patriarchal Narratives as Ancient Texts." A. R. Millard and D. J. Wiseman, eds. *Essays on the Patriarchal Narratives*, 43–58. Leicester: IVP, 1980.

Miller, Cynthia L. "Introducing Direct Discourse in Biblical Hebrew Narrative." *Biblical Hebrew and Discourse Linguistics*, ed. Robert D. Bergen, 199–241. np: Summer Institute of Linguistics, 1994.

———. *The Representation of Speech in Biblical Hebrew Narrative: A Linguistic Approach*. HSM 55. Winona Lake, Indiana: Eisenbrauns, 2003.

Miller, James E. "Sexual Offences in Genesis." *JSOT* 90 (2000): 41–53.

Millic, Louis T. "Rhetorical Choice and Stylistic Option: The Conscious and Unconscious Poles." *Literary Style A Symposium*, ed. Seymour Chatman, 77–94. London: Oxford University Press, 1971.

Mitchell, Christopher W. *The Meaning of brk 'to bless' in the Old Testament*. SBL Dissertation Series 95. Atlanta: Scholar, 1987.

Moberly, R. W. L. *The Old Testament of the Old Testament: Patriarchal Narratives and Mosaic Yahwism*. Minneapolis: Fortress Press, 1992.

Morns, Ellen F. "Sacrifice for the State: First Dynasty Royal Funerals and the Rites at Macramallah's Rectangle." *Performing Death: Social Analyses of Funeral Traditions in the Ancient Near East and Mediterranean*, ed. Nicola Laneri. Chicago: The Oriental Institute of the University of Chicago, 2007.

Muilenburg, James. "Abraham and the Nations: Blessing and World History." *Interpretation* 19 (1965): 387–398.

———. "Form Criticism and Beyond." *JBL* 88 (1969): 1–18.

Muraoka, T. *Emphatic Words and Structures in Biblical Hebrew*. Jerusalem: The Magnes Press, 1985.

———. "On the So-called Dativus Ethicus in Hebrew." *JTS* 29 (1978): 495–98.

Murray, Donald F. "An Unremarked Rhetorical Marker in Biblical Hebrew Prose." *Hebrew Studies* 40 (1999): 33–56.

Naudé, J. A. "The Syntactical Status of the Ethical Dative in Biblical Hebrew." *JSem* 9 (1997): 129–65.

Neaman, J. S. and C. G. Silver, *A Dictionary of Euphemisms*. London: Hamish Hamilton, 1983.

Neusner, Jacob. "Exile and Return as the History of Judaism." *Exile: Old Testament, Jewish, and Christian Conceptions*, ed. James M. Scott, 221–38. New York: Brill, 1997.

Niccacci, Alviero. "Analysis of Biblical Narrative." *Biblical Hebrew and Discourse Linguistics*, ed. Robert D. Bergen, 175–197. np: Summer Institute of Linguistics, 1994.

———. "On the Hebrew Verbal System." *Biblical Hebrew and Discourse Linguistics*, ed. Robert D. Bergen, 117–137. np: Summer Institute of Linguistics, 1994.

Nichols, Marie H. "Rhetoric and Style." *Patterns of Literary Style*, vol. 3, ed. Joseph Strelka, 130–143. London: The Pennsylvania State University Press, 1971.

Niditch, Sussan. "The 'Sodomite' Theme in Judges 19–20: Family, Community, and Social Disintegration." *CBQ* 44 (1982): 365–78.

Nikaido, S. "Hagar and Ishmael as Literary Figures: An Intertextual Study." *VT* 51, no. 2 (2001): 219–242.

Noegel, Scott. "A Crux and a Taunt: Night-Time Then Sunset in Genesis 15." *The World of Genesis: Persons, Places, Perspectives*, eds. Philip R. Davies and David J. A. Clines. JSOTSup Series 257, 128–135. Sheffield: Sheffield Academic Press, 1998.

Olúránkinṣé, Ọlánipèkun. "Euphemism as a Yoruba Folkway." *African Languages and Cultures* 5, no. 2 (1992): 189–202.

Orlov, Andrei A. "'The Gods of My Father Terah': Abraham and the Iconoclast and the Polemics with the Divine Body Traditions in the *Apocalyse of Abraham*." *Journal for the Study of the Pseudepigrapha* 18, no. 1 (2008): 33–53.

Paltridge, Brian. *Discourse Analysis: An Introduction*. London: Continuum, 2006.

Pardes, I. *Contertradictions in the Bible: A Feminist Approach*. Cambridge, MA: Harvard University Press, 1992.

Parker, Kim I. "Speech, Writing and Power: Deconstructing the Biblical Canon." *JSOT* 69 (1996): 91–103.

Parker, Simon B. "The Birth Announcements." *Ascribe to the Lord: Biblical and Other Studies in Memory of Peter C. Craige*, ed. Lyle Eslinger and Glen Tyler. JSOT 67, 133–149. Sheffield: Sheffield Academic Press, 1988.

Parrot, A. *Abraham and His Times*, trans. J. Farley. Philadelphia: Fortress, 1968.

Parry, Donald W. "The 'Word' or the 'Enemies' of the Lord?: Revisiting the Euphemism in 2 Sam 12:14." *Emanuel: Studies in Hebrew Bible Septuagint and Dead Sea Scrolls in Honor of Emanuel Tov*, eds. Shalom M. Paul, Robert A. Kraft, Lawrence H. Schiffman and Weston W. Fields, 367–378. Leiden: Brill, 2003.

Patrick, Dale. *The Rendering of God in the Old Testament*. Overtures to Biblical Theology, vol. 10. Philadelphia: Fortress, 1981.

Paul, Shalom M. "Exodus 1:21: 'To Found a Family'—A Biblical and Akkadian Idiom." *Maarav* 8. Let Your Colleagues Praise You: Studies in Memory of Stanley Gevirtz (1992): 139–42.

_____. "Euphemistically 'Speaking' and a Covetous Eye." *Hebrew Annual Review* 14 (1994): 193–204.

_____. "'Plowing the Heifer' in Judges 14:18: Tracing a Sexual Euphemism." *Sacred History, Sacred Literature: Essays on Ancient Israel, the Bible, and Religion in Honor of R. E. Friedman on His Sixtieth Birthday*, ed. Shawna Dolansky, 163–167. Winona Lake, Indiana: Eisenbraus, 2008.

_____. "The Shared Legacy of Sexual Metaphors and Euphemisms in Mesopotamian and Biblical Literatures." *Sex and Gender in the Ancient Near East*, eds. Simo Parpola and R.M. Whiting, Part II. Proceedings of the XLVII Roncontre Assyriologique Internationale, Helsinki, 489–498. Helsinki: The Neo-Assyrian Text Corpus Project, 2002.

Peacock, H. F. "'Translating 'Mercy,' 'Steadfast Love' in the Book of Genesis." *The Bible Translator* 31 (1980): 201–7.

Perri, Carmela. "Allusion Studies: An International Annotated Bibliography, 1921–1977." *Style* 13 (1979): 178–225.

_____. "Knowing and Playing: The Literary Text and the Trope Allusion." *American Imago* 41 (1984): 117–28.

_____. "On Alluding." *Poetics* 7 (1978): 289–307.

Perry, Menakhem "Counter-Stories in the Bible: Rebekah and her Bridegroom, Abraham's Servant." *Prooftexts* 27 (2007): 275–323.

Philip, Tarja. "Woman in Travail as a Simile to Men in Distress in the Hebrew Bible." *Sex and Gender in the Ancient Near East*, eds. Simo Parpola and R.M. Whiting, Part II. Proceedings of the XLVII Roncontre Assyriologique Internationale, Helsinki, 499–505. Helsinki: The Neo-Assyrian Text Corpus Project, 2002.

Polak, Frank. "Sociolinguistics: A Key to the Typology and the Background of Biblical Hebrew." *Hebrew Studies* 47(2006): 115–162.

Powell, Mark Allan. "What is 'Literary' about Literary Aspect?" *Seminar Papers SBL Annual Meeting* (1992): 40–48.

Pyper, Hugh S. *David as Reader: 2Samuel 12:1–15 and the Poetics of Fatherhood*. Biblical Interpretation Series, vol. 23. Leiden: Brill, 1996.

Rabinowitz, I. L. "Euphemism and Dysphemism: In the Talmud." *The Encylopedia Judica*, vol. 6, 961–62. Jerusalem: Keter, 1996.

Radday, Yehuda and Haim Shore. *Genesis: An Authorship Study in Computer-Assisted Statistical Linguistic*. Rome: Biblical Institute, 1985.

Rains, Charles. "'You Die for Life': On the Use of Poetic Devices in Argumentation." *Language in Society* 21, no. 2 (1992): 253–276.

Rashi, *Bereshith: Chumash With Targum Onkelos, Haphtaroth and Rashi's Commentary*, trans. ed. A. M. Silbermann. Jerusalem: Feldheim Publishers, 1934.

Rawson, H. *A Dictionary of Euphemisms and Other Doubletalk*. New York: Crown Publishers, 1995.

Reinhartz, Adele. *"Why Ask My Name?" Anonymity and Identity in Biblical Narrative*. New York: Oxford University Press, 1998.

Rendsburg, Gary A. "Alliteration in the Exodus Narrative." *Birkat Shalom: Studies Presented to Shalom M. Paul on the Occasion of His Seventieth Birthday*. Winona Lake, Indiana: Eisenbrauns, 2008.

———. "Bilingual Wordplay in the Bible." *VT* 38, no. 3 (1988): 354–357.

———. "Notes on Genesis XV." *VT* 62, no. 2 (1992): 266–272.

———. *The Redaction of Genesis*. Winona Lake, Indiana: Eisenbrauns, 1989.

———. "Word Play in Biblical Hebrew: An Eclectic Collection." *Puns and Pundits: Word Play in the Hebrew and Ancient Near Eastern Literature*, ed. Scott B. Noegel, 137–162. Bethesda, Maryland: CDL press, 2000.

Rendtorff, Rolf. *Canon and Theology: Overtures to an Old Testament Theology*. Edinburgh: T. & T. Clark, 1993.

———. "The Paradigm Is Changing: Hopes—and Fears," *BibInt* 1 (1993): 34–53.

———. *The Problem of the Process of Transmission in the Pentateuch*, trans. John J. Scullion. JSOTSup 89. Sheffield: Sheffield Academic Press, 1990.

———. "The 'Yahwist' as Theologian? The Dilemma of Pentateuchal Criticism." *The Pentateuch*. The Biblical Seminar 39, ed. John W. Rogerson, 15–23. Sheffield: Sheffield Academic Press, 1996.

Revell, E. J. *The Designation of the Individual: Expressive Usage in Biblical Narrative*. Kampen, The Netherlands: Kok Pharos Publishing House, 1996.

———. "The Repetition of Introductions to Speech as Feature of Biblical Hebrew." *VT* 47 (1997): 92–110.

Richard Walsh, "Who is the Narrator?" *Poetics Today* 18, no. 4 (1997): 495–513.

Rihbany, Mitrie. *The Syrian Christ*. London: Houghton Mifflin Company, 1923.

Rimon-Kenan, Shlomith. *Narrative Fiction: Contemporary Poetics*. London: Methuen, 1983.

Rodd, C. S. "Shall Not the Judge of All the Earth Do What Is Just (Gen 18:25)." *Expository Times* 83 (1971/72): 137–39.

Rudin-O'Brasky, T. *The Patriarchs in Hebron and Sodom (Gen 18–19): A Study of the Structure and Composition of a Biblical Story*. Jerusalem: Simor, 1982.

Said, Edward W. *Reflections on Exile and Other Essays*. Cambridge: Harvard University Press, 2000.

Sailhamer, John. *The Pentateuch as Narrative: A Biblical-Theological Commentary*. Library of Biblical Interpretation. Grand Rapids, Michigan: Zondervan Publishing House, 1992.

Sarbin, Theodore R. "The Role of Imagination in Narrative Construction." *Narrative Analysis: Studying the Development of Individuals in Society*, eds. Colette Daiutte and Cynthia Lightfoot, 5–20. California: Sage Publications, 2004.

Sarna, Nahum. "The Anticipatory Use of Information as a Literary Feature of the Genesis Narratives." *The Creation of Sacred Literature*, ed. R. E. Friedman. Berkeley: University of California Press, 1981.

_____. בראשית *Genesis*. JPST. Philadelphia: Jewish Publication Society, 1989.

Savran, George W. "Beastly Speech: Intertextuality, Balaam's Ass and the Garden of Eden." *JSOT* 64 (1994): 33–55.

_____. *Encountering the Divine: Theophany in Biblical Narrative*. London: T & T Clark, 2005.

_____. "Seeing is Believing: On the Relative Priority of Visual and Verbal Perception of the Divine." *Biblical Interpretation* 17 (2009): 320–361.

_____. *Telling and Retelling: Quotation in Biblical Narrative*. Bloomington: Indiana University Press, 1988.

Scheub, Harold. *Story*. Madison, Wisconsin: The University of Wisconsin Press, 1998.

Schieffelin, Bambi B., Kathryn A. Woolard, and Paul V. Kroskrity, eds. *Language Ideologies: Practice and Theory*. New York: Oxford University Press, 1998.

Schlueter, Carol J. *Filling up the Measure: Polemical Hyperbole in 1 Thessalonians 2:14–16*. Sheffield: Sheffield Academic Press, 1994.

Schökel, Alonso. *A Manual of Hebrew Poetics*, trans. Adrian Graffy. SB 11. Rome: Editrice Pontificio Istituto Biblico, 1988.

Schweizer, H. "Das seltsame Gespräch von Abraham und Jahwe (Gen 18:22–33)." *TQS* 164 (1984): 121–39.

Segal, M. H. *The Pentateuch: Its Composition and its Authorship and other Biblical Studies*. Jerusalem: Magnes Press, 1967.

Selman, M. J. "Comparative Customs and the Patriarchal Age." A. R. Millard and D. J. Wiseman, eds. *Essays on the Patriarchal Narratives*, 93–138. Leicester: IVP, 1980.

Sherwood, Yvonne. "Abraham in London, Marburg-Istanbul and Israel: Between Theocracy and Democracy, Ancient Text and Modern State." *Biblical Interpretation* 16 (2008): 105–153.

Shulman, Ahouva. "The Particle נָא in Biblical Prose." *Hebrew Studies* 40 (1999): 57–82.

Simpson, Paul. *Stylistics: A Resource for Students*. London: Routledge, 2006.

Ska, J. L. "L'arbre et la tente: la fonction du décor en Gen 18:1–15." *Biblica* 68 (1987): 383–89.

Slager, D. "The Use of 'Behold' in the Old Testament." *Occasional Papers in Translation and Textlinguistics* 3 (1987): 50–79.

Smith, Gary V. "The Structure of Genesis 1–11." *JETS* 20, no. 4 (1977): 307–319.

_____. "The Use of Quotations in Jeremiah XV 11–14." *VT* 29 (1979): 229–31.

Smith, Mark S. *The Origins and Development of the Waw-Consecutive: Northwest Semitic Evidence from Ugarit to Qumran*. HSS39. Atlanta: Scholars Press, 1991.

Soggin, J. A. "Abraham and the Eastern Kings: On Genesis 14." *Solving Riddles and Untying Knots: Biblical Epigraphic, and Semitic Studies in Honor of Jones C. Greenfield*, ed. Ziony Zevit, Seymour and Michael Sokoloff, 283–291. Winona Lake, Indiana: Einsenbraus, 1995.

_____. *An Introduction to the History of Israel and Judah*, trans. J. Bowden, 2d rev. ed. Valley Forge: Trinity Press International, 1993.

Soskice, Janet M. *Metaphor and Religious Language*. Oxford: Clarendon Press, 1985.

Speiser, E. *Genesis*. ABC. New York: Doubleday, 1964.

_____. *Oriental and Biblical Studies: Collected Essays of E.A. Speiser*. Philadelphia: University of Pennsylvania Press, 1967.

_____. "Wife-Sister Motif in the Patriarchal Narratives." *Biblical and Other Studies*, 15–28. Brandeis: Brandeis University, 1962.

Stadelmann, Luis I. J. *The Hebrew Conception of the World: A Philological And Literary Study*. Rome: Pontifical Biblical Institute, 1970.

Stein, Robert H. *Difficult Sayings in the Gospel: Jesus' Use of Overstatement and Hyperbole*. Grand Rapids, Michigan: Baker Book House, 1985.

Steinberg, Naomi. "The Problem of Human Sacrifice in War: An Analysis of Judges 11." *On the Way to Nineveh*, eds. Stephen L. Cook and S. C. Winter, 114–135. Atlanta, Georgia: Scholars Press, 1999.

Sternberg, Meir. "Double Cave, Double Talk: The Indirection of Biblical Dialogue." *"Not in Heaven": Coherence and Complexity in Biblical Narrative*, eds. Jason P. Rosenblatt and Joseph C. Sitterson, Jr., 28–57. Bloomington: Indiana: University Press, 1991.

_____. *The Poetics of Biblical Narrative: Ideological Literature and the Drama of Reading*. Bloomington: Indiana University Press, 1987.

_____. "Polylingualism as Reality and Translation as Mimesis." *Poetics Today* 2, no. 4 (1981): 221–239.

_____. "Proteus in Quotation Land: Mimesis and the Forms of Reported Discourse." *Poetic Today* 4 (1982): 107–56.

Stol, M. "Blindness and Night-Blindness in Akkadian." *JNES* 45 (1986): 295–99.

Strong, John T. "Shattering the Image of God: A Response to Theodore Hiebert's Interpretation of the Story of the Tower of Babel." *JBL* 127, no. 4 (2008): 625–634.

Syrén, Roger. *The Forsaken First-born: A Study of a Recurrent Motif in the Patriarchal Narratives*. JSOTSup Series 133. Sheffield: Sheffield Academic Press, 1993.

Tal, Abraham. "Euphemisms in the Samaritan Targum of the Pentateuch." *AS* 1 (2003): 112–120.

Tamir-Ghez, Nomi. "The Art of Persuasion in Nabokov's Lolita." *Poetics Today* 1, no. 1/2 (1979): 65–83.

Tannen, Deborah. "Introducing Constructed Dialogue in Greek and American Conversational and Literary Activity." *Direct Speech and Indirect Speech*, ed. Florian Coulmas. Berlin: Walter de Gruyter, 1986.

Thomas, Benjamin. "The Language of Politeness in Ancient Hebrew Letters." *Hebrew Studies* 50 (2009): 17–39.

Thompson, J. A. and Elmer A. Martens, "שוב." *Dictionary of Old Testament Theology and Exegesis*, vol. 4, ed. Willem A. VanGemeren, 55–5. Grand Rapids, Michigan: Zondervan, 1997.

Thompson, T. L. *The Historicity of* the *Patriarchal Narratives*. Berlin: Walter de Gruyter, 1974.

_____. *The Origin of Ancient Israel: The Literary Formation of Genesis and Exodus 1–23*. JSOTSup 55. Sheffield: Sheffield Academic Press, 1987.

Throntveit, Mark A. *The Significance of the Royal Speeches and Prayers for the Structure and Theology of the Chronicler*. Ann Arbor, Michigan: University Microfilms International, 1988.

Thucydides, *Thucydides*, trans. C.F. Smith. New York: Putnam, 1928.

Todorov, Tzvetan. "The Place of Style in the Structure of the Text." *Literary Style: A Symposium*, ed. Seymour Chatman, 29–44. London: Oxford University Press, 1971.

Tollington, J. E. "Abraham and his Wives." *The Old Testament in its World*, eds. R. P. Gordon and J.C. Moor. Leiden: Brill, 2005.

Trebilco, Paul. *The Early Christians in Ephesus from Paul to Ignatius*. Tübingen, Germany: Mohr Siebeck, 2004.

Trible, Phyllis. *Texts of Terror: Feminist Readings of Biblical Narratives*. Augsburg Fortress 1984.

Tryggve Kronholm, "Abraham, the Physician: The Image of the Abraham the Patriarch in the Genuine Hymns of Ephraem Syrus." *Solving Riddles and Untying Knots: Biblical Epigraphic, and Semitic Studies in Honor of Jones C. Greenfield*, ed. Ziony Zevit, Seymour and Michael Sokoloff, 107–115. Winona Lake, Indiana: Einsenbraus, 1995.

Turner, Laurence A. *Announcements of Plots in Genesis*. JSOT 96. Sheffield: Sheffield Academic Press, 1990.

_____. *Genesis*. Sheffield: Sheffield Academic Press, 2000.

_____. "Lot as Jekyll and Hyde." *The Bible in Three Dimensions*, ed. D. J. A. Clines, S. E. Fowl, and S. E. Porter. JSOTSup 87, 85–10. Sheffield: Sheffield Academic Press, 1990.

Uffenheimer, B. "Gen 18–19, A New Approach." *Mélanges A. Neher*, ed. E. A. Levy-Valensi, 145–53. Paris: Librairie d'Amérique et d'Orient, 1975.

Ullmann, Stephen. "Stylistics and Semantics." *Literary Style: A Symposium*, ed. Seymour Chatman, 133–152. London: Oxford University Press, 1971.

van der Merwe, Christo H. J. et al, *A Biblical Hebrew Reference Grammar*. Biblical Language: Hebrew 3. Sheffield: Sheffield Academic Press, 1999.

_____. "Discourse Linguistics and Biblical Hebrew Grammar." *Biblical Hebrew and Discourse Linguistics*, ed. Robert D. Bergen, 13–49. np: Summer Institute of Linguistics, 1994.

van der Watt, Jan G. *The Family of the King: Dynamics of Metaphor in the Gospel According to John*. Leiden: Brill, 2000.

van der Woude, A. S. "Micah in Dispute with the False Prophets." *VT* 19 (1969): 244–60.

van Hattem, W. C. "Once Again: Sodom and Gomorrah." *Biblical Aramaic* 44 (1981): 87–92.

van Hecke, Pierre, ed. *Metaphor in the Hebrew Bible*. Belgium: Leuven University Press, 2005.

van Leeuwen, Raymond C. "What Comes Out of God's Mouth: Theological Wordplay in Deuteronomy 8." *CBQ* 47, no. 1 (1985): 55–57.

van Seters, John. *Abraham in History and Tradition*. New Haven: Yale University Press, 1975.

_____. *The Life of Moses: Yahwist as Historian in Exodus Numbers*. Louisville, Kentucky: Westminster Press, 1994.

_____. *Prologue to History: The Yahwist as Historian in Genesis*. Louisville, Kentucky: Westminster Press, 1992.

van Wolde, Ellen. "Who Guides Whom? Embeddedness and Perspective in Biblical Hebrew and in 1 Kings 3:16–28." *JBL* 114, no. 4 (1995): 623–642.

Vanhove, Martine, ed. *From Polysemy to Semantic Change: Towards a Typology of Lexical Semantic Associations*. Amsterdam: Benjamins, 2008.

Vawter, B. *On Genesis: A New Reading*. London: Geoffrey Chapman, 1977.

Verdonk, Peter. *Stylistics*. London: Oxford University Press, 2003.

Vermes, G. *Scripture and Tradition in Judaism*. SPB 4. Leiden: Brill, 1961.

von Rad, Gerhard. *Genesis*, trans. J. H. Marks. Philadelphia: Westminster, 1972.

_____. *Genesis: A Commentary*, rev. ed. London: SCM, 1972.

_____. *Old Testament Theology*, vol. II. New York: Harper & Row, 1965.

Walsh, Jerome T. *Style and Structure in Biblical Hebrew Narrative*. Collegeville, Minnesota: The Liturgical Press, 2001.

Waltke, B. K. "The Samaritan Pentateuch and the Text of the Old Testament." *New Perspectives on the Old Testament*, ed. J. B. Payne, 212–39. Waco, TX: Word, 1970.

_____. and Cathi J. Fredricks, *Genesis*. Grand Rapids, Michigan: Zondervan, 2001.

Warning, Wilfried. *Literary Artistry in Leviticus*. Leiden: Brill, 1999.

Watson, Wilfred G. E. "Allusion, Irony and Wordplay." *Bib* 65, no. 1 (1984): 103–105.

_____. *Classical Hebrew Poetry: A Guide to Its Techniques*. JSOTSup Series 26. Sheffield: JSOT Press, 1984.

Watts, Richard J. *Politeness*. Cambridge: Cambridge University Press, 2003.

Wehmeier, Gerhard. "The Theme 'Blessing for the Nations' in the Promises to the Patriarchs and in Prophetical Literature." *BTF* 6 (1974): 1–13.

Weisman, Ze'ev. "Ethnology, Etiology, Genealogy, and Historiography in the Tale of Lot and His Daughters (Gen 19:30–38)." "*Sha'arei Talmon*": *Studies in the Bible, Qumran and the Ancient Near East presented to S. Talmon*, ed. M. Fishbane and E. Tov, 43–52. Winona Lake: Eisenbrauns, 1992.

_____. *Political Satire in the Bible*. SBL 32. Atlanta, Georgia: Scholars Press, 1998.

Weiss, R. "Paronomasia in the Bible." *Mishut Ba-Mikra*. Jerusalem: A. Rubinstein, 1976.

Weiss, Andrea L. *Figurative Language in Biblical Prose Narrative: Metaphor in the Book of Samuel*. Leiden: Brill, 2006.

Wellhausen, J. *Prolegomena to the History of Israel*. Atlanta: Scholar Press 1994.

Wenham, Gordon. J. *Genesis 1–15*, vol. 1. WBC. Dallas: Word, 1987.

_____. *Genesis 16–50*, vol. 2. Word Biblical Commentary. Dallas: Word, 1994.

_____. "Pentateuchal Studies Today." *Themelios* 22, no. 1 (1996): 3–13.

_____. "Pondering the Pentateuch: The Search for a New Paradigm." *The Face of Old Testament Studies: A Survey of Contemporary Approaches*, eds. D. W. Baker and B. T. Arnold, 116–144. Grand Rapids, Michigan: Baker Academic, 1999.

_____. "The Religion of the Patriarchs." A. R. Millard and D. J. Wiseman, eds. *Essays on the Patriarchal Narratives*, 157–188. Leicester: IVP, 1980.

Westermann, *Genesis 12–36: A Commentary*, trans. John J. Scullion. Minneapolis: Augsburg, 1985.

_____. *Genesis 12–36: A Commentary*, trans. John J. Scullion. London: SPCK, 1986.

_____. *The Promises to the Fathers: Studies on the Patriarchal Narratives*, trans. D. E. Green. Philadelphia: Fortress, 1980.

White, Hugh C. *Narration and Discourse in the Book of Genesis*. New York: Cambridge University Press, 1991.

White, Roger. *The Structure of Metaphor*. Cambridge, MA: Blackwell Publishers Inc., 1996.

Whybray, R. N. *The Good Life in the Old Testament*. London: T & T Clark, 2002.

_____. *Introduction to the Pentateuch*. Grand Rapids, Michigan: William B. Eerdmans Publishing Co., 1995.

_____. *The Making of the Pentateuch: A Methodological Study*. JSOTSup Series 53. Sheffield: Sheffield Academic Press, 1987.

Wiig, Arne. *Promise, Protection and Prosperity: Aspects of the "Shield" as a Religious Metaphor in an Ancient Eastern Perspective*. Lund: University of Lund, 1999.

Williamson, P. R. *Abraham, Israel and the Nations: The Patriarchal Promise and Its Covenantal Development in Genesis*. JSOT 315. Sheffield: Sheffield Academic Press, 2000.

Wiseman, D. J. "Abraham Reassessed." A. R. Millard and D. J. Wiseman, eds. *Essays on the Patriarchal Narratives*, 139–156. Leicester: IVP, 1980.

Wolff, Hans Walter. "Das Zitat im Prophetenspruch." *Gesammelte Studien zum Alten Testament*, 36–129. Munich: Chr. Kaiser Verlag, 1964.

Wolterstorff, Nicholas. *Divine Discourse: Philosophical Reflections on the Claim that God Speaks*. Cambridge: Cambridge University Press, 1995.

Wright, J. Edward. "Biblical Versus Israelite Images of the Heavenly Realm." *JSOT* 93 (2001): 59–75.

Wright, T. R. *The Genesis of Fiction: Modern Novelists as Biblical Interpreters*. England: Ashgate, 2007.

Yacobi, Tamari. "Narrative Structure and Fictional Mediation." *Poetics Today* 8, no. 2 (1987): 335–372.

Yarchin, William. "Imperative and Promise in Genesis 12:1–3." *Studia Biblica et Theologica* 10 (1980): 164–78.

Zakovitch, Yael. "A Study of Precise and Partial Derivations in Biblical Etymology." *JSOT* 15 (1980): 31–50.

_____. "Explicit and Implicit Name-Derivations." *Hebrew Annual Review* 4 (1980): 167–80.

_____. "Juxtaposition in the Abraham Cycle." *Pomegranates and Gold Bells: Studies in Biblical, Jewish, and Near Eastern Ritual, Law, and Literature in Honor of Jacob Milgrom*, eds. David P. Wright, David Noel Freedman and Avi Hurvitz, 509–24. Winona Lake, Indiana: Eisenbrauns, 1995.

Ze'ev Weisman, *Political Satire in the Bible*. Society of Biblical Literature 32. Atlanta, Georgia: Scholars Press, 1998.

Ziegler, Yael. *Promise to Keep: The Oath in Biblical Narrative*. Leiden: Brill, 2008.

Zulick, Margaret D. "The Active Force of Hearing: The Ancient Hebrew Language of Persuasion." *Rhetorica* 10, no. 4 (1992): 367–380.

Langham Literature and its imprints are a ministry of Langham Partnership.

Langham Partnership is a global fellowship working in pursuit of the vision God entrusted to its founder John Stott –

> ***to facilitate the growth of the church in maturity and Christ-likeness through raising the standards of biblical preaching and teaching.***

Our vision is to see churches equipped for mission and growing to maturity in Christ through the ministry of pastors and leaders who believe, teach and live by the Word of God.

Our mission is to strengthen the ministry of the Word of God through:
- nurturing national movements for training in biblical preaching
- multiplying the creation and distribution of evangelical literature
- strengthening the theological training of pastors and leaders by qualified evangelical teachers

Our ministry

Langham Preaching partners with national leaders to nurture indigenous biblical preaching movements for pastors and lay preachers all around the world. With the support of a team of trainers from many countries, a multi-level programme of seminars provides practical training, and is followed by a programme for training local facilitators. Local preachers' groups and national and regional networks ensure continuity and ongoing development, seeking to build vigorous movements committed to Bible exposition.

Langham Literature provides majority world pastors, scholars and seminary libraries with evangelical books and electronic resources through grants, discounts and distribution. The programme also fosters the creation of indigenous evangelical books for pastors in many languages, through training workshops for writers and editors, sponsored writing, translation, strengthening local evangelical publishing houses, and investment in major regional literature projects, such as one volume Bible commentaries like *The Africa Bible Commentary*.

Langham Scholars provides financial support for evangelical doctoral students from the majority world so that, when they return home, they may train pastors and other Christian leaders with sound, biblical and theological teaching. This programme equips those who equip others. Langham Scholars also works in partnership with majority world seminaries in strengthening evangelical theological education. A growing number of Langham Scholars study in high quality doctoral programmes in the majority world itself. As well as teaching the next generation of pastors, graduated Langham Scholars exercise significant influence through their writing and leadership.

To learn more about Langham Partnership and the work we do visit **langham.org**

www.ingramcontent.com/pod-product-compliance
Lightning Source LLC
Chambersburg PA
CBHW070233240426
43673CB00044B/1779